NEW DIRECTIONS IN FARM, LAND AND FOOD POLICIES

A TIME FOR STATE AND LOCAL ACTION

Editors:

Joe Belden
Gibby Edwards
Cynthia Guyer
Lee Webb

Agriculture Project
Conference on Alternative State and Local Policies
2000 Florida Avenue, N.W.,
Washington, D.C. 20009
(202) 387-6030

Library of Congress Catalog Card Number: 80-66226
ISBN Number: 0-89788-011-0

First Printing: January, 1979
Second Printing: January, 1981

PRINTED BY UNION PRINTERS

The **Conference on Alternative State and Local Policies** is a national clearinghouse and policy research center for state and local public officials and community leaders. In addition to providing research, analysis and technical assistance, the Conference organizes frequent national and regional conferences and operates a nationally recognized publications program featuring innovative policy studies and legislative proposals.

The Agriculture Project was established in 1978 for the purpose of assisting widespread efforts to change farm, land and food policy at the state and local level.

The Project maintains a clearinghouse on alternative legislation, organizes regional and state conferences, and issues numerous policy studies and briefing books in an attempt to bridge the gap between policy-makers and community activists and to help foster the development of effective coalitions around farm, land and food issues.

Henry Hyde · Coordinator
Maggie Kennedy · Assistant Coordinator

Table of Contents

Special Thanks. . .

This reader would have been an impossible task without the ideas, energy and encouragement of many people. Special thanks to Joe Belden, Gibby Edwards and Lee Webb for writing and editing the chapters; to Wendy Gelertner for information and advice on the Research and the Extension/Training chapters, and to Ann Beaudry for her help with the chapter on Preventing Tax Discrimination Against Farm Women.

To John Rowland for the hours spent researching state legislation; to Joel Haggard for organizing the chapter bibliographies, and to Barbara Brundage who literally kept all of the pieces together and the Co-Editors on schedule—with incredible patience and perseverance. Thanks also to Gail Prostrollo for the endless typing of chapters and bibliographies.

To Gibby Edwards for her extraordinary energy and creativity in coordinating the entire design, layout and production of the reader from start to finish. Finally, thanks to the Steering Committee of the Agriculture Project; Cathy Lerza, Jim Rosapepe, Henry Hyde, Peggy Borgers, Joe Belden, Bob Mullins, Dan McCurry, Tom Fox, Tessa Huxley, Elizabeth Ryan and Don Reeves—all of whom helped enormously with information, ideas, contacts and support.

Cynthia Guyer, Coordinator
Agriculture Project
January 1978— June 1980

Production/Graphic Design Editor
Gibby Edwards

Research/Editing Assistant
Barbara Brundage

Graphic/Layout Editors
Cindy Fowler, Patrice Gallagher, Pat Konopka

Typing
Gail Prostrollo, Maggie Kennedy

Typesetting
Art for People, Cheryl Werner, Terry Grimwood

Printers
The Daily Record, Baltimore

Photography and Research Materials
Agricultural Marketing Project (AMP) • California Agrarian Action Project • California Office of Appropriate Technology • Chicago Urbs in Horto • Community Self-Reliance, Inc. • Gardens for All • Greenmarket • Hartford Farmers' Market • Institute for Local Self-Reliance • Pike Place Market • Rural America • Seattle Department of Community Development • Second Harvest Food Banks • Marilyn Schrut • Suffolk County Extension Office • Trust for Public Land • Tuskegee Institute • USDA • and countless other individuals and organizations.

New Directions in Farm, Land and Food Policies

Introduction

Concern and activism around farm, land and food related issues is growing. Soaring food prices and the 1978 farmers' strike reaffirm the fundamental inadequacies of American agricultural policy.

The potential for building broad based coalitions around food and land related issues is enormous. Unlike some of the activism of the 1960s and 1970s, the people working on these issues come from the widest of backgrounds, perspectives and occupations. Family farmers and progressive farm organizations are in the forefront, as are consumer, environmental and religious groups, and, increasingly, neighborhood and community based organizations. Concerned public officials at the state and local levels are also playing an important role. These diverse individuals and constituencies realize that they must work together to effect significant change in America's agricultural and food policy.

People are challenging public policies which have followed corporate priorities and ignored the needs of average citizens and their communities. American agricultural policies have supported a highly energy- and capital-intensive system of food production and distribution. A growing number of individuals, organizations and progressive public officials are raising serious questions about the social and environmental consequences of this system.

These new coalitions and alliances are advocating policies which support a more decentralized and democratic family farm-based agricultural system which will encourage local community and economic development. At the same time they are demanding accountability from public officials and institutions through increased citizen participation in the making of agricultural and food policies at federal, state and local levels.

THE CRISIS OF THE FAMILY FARM IN AMERICA

There are a number of serious problems which have aroused the concern of consumers, farmers and public officials. One of the most important is the rapid and accelerating decline in the number of farmers in this country. In the last 25 years America has lost over 3 million farms. Fewer than 2.7 million farmers remain working the land today.

This disastrous trend has been intensified by a dramatic increase in the cost of production, inflationary land values and a decline in the prices farmers receive for production. In the 1970s, farm operating expenses increased by 61% and at the same time total farm debt jumped from $59 billion up to $94 billion. Inflation, due to increased commercial development and land speculation combined with widespread corporate, foreign and absentee investment in farm land, has doubled the price of agricultural land since 1972.

Together, the rising cost of production and spiralling farm land prices make it next to impossible for new or young farmers to begin farming. The average age of the American farmer is fast approaching sixty. If an individual is not fortunate enough to have inherited a farm, the initial investment for land and operating costs can be close to $400,000.

This rising level of capital required to farm today and the severe financial pressures facing farmers continue to force out of business all but the largest and most prosperous of farmers. As more and more farm families leave the land, farm related services and industries are forced out of business and once stable rural communities begin to disintegrate. The vitality of small town rural life has undergone enormous stress and change over the past forty years.

CORPORATE CONTROL

While the number of farmers working the land decreases each year, corporations are becoming increasingly involved in every phase of food production and distribution. Leaving the actual farm work to the farmer, agribusiness firms have gained enormous control over all major agricultural interests including farm supplies such as equipment, feed, fertilizer and seeds.

At the same time, agribusiness corporations are steadily moving in on the transportation, processing, packaging, marketing and retailing of farm products. The American Agricultural Marketing Association estimates that 50% of the American food supply will be produced under contract with corporations by 1980. (In 1970 only 17% of the food supply was produced under corporate contract.) The production of many commodities is already under a high level of corporate control; 100% of sugar beets; 92% of broilers and 47% of all citrus fruits.

THE CRISIS OF AGRICULTURAL LAND LOSS

Over 2 million acres of farm land are lost each year to land speculation and development pressures. Prime agricultural land near growing cities is increasingly threatened by suburban developments, shopping centers and industrial parks as they expand into rural communities. The increased demand for land forces land prices up, creating higher property taxes that working farmers are unable to pay.

Thousands of additional acres of farm land are irretrievably lost each year to power-line sitings and to the building of dams. Other farm and ranch lands are permanently destroyed as corporations strip-mine for coal. These energy-related developments destroy forever the potential of the land to produce food for future generations.

THE CRISIS OF FOOD PRICES AND QUALITY

Food prices are rising faster than most Americans can afford. Low- and moderate-income families and citizens on fixed incomes find that food is taking up a larger and larger percentage of their annual budgets. Farmers, however, are not benefitting from rising food prices. According to the U.S. Department of Agriculture, only 6% of the rise in food prices between 1954 and 1974 went to the farmer. The food industry which processes, packages, transports and markets food accounted for 94% of the price increases consumers paid for food.

As with agricultural marketing, the food industry is becoming increasingly monopolistic. In 1966 the Federal Trade Commission (FTC) revealed that the 100 largest food manufacturers—representing only .03% of the entire industry—accounted for 71% of the food industry's profits and 60%

of its total assets. In 1972 the FTC reported that over-pricing in 13 "monopolized" food lines cost consumers over $2 billion that year.

As food prices continue to rise, the nutritional quality of available food is declining. The dramatic increase in the use of chemical fertilizers and pesticides and the genetic manipulation of crop varieties have made food less nutritious. Instead of getting back to a more wholesome food production system, the response of the corporate food industry has been to add more chemicals, preservatives and additives to both improve the nutritional quality and to extend the "shelf-life" of food products. The inevitable consequence is higher prices because of increased processing costs.

THE CASE FOR STATE AND LOCAL ACTION

The federal government—to which most Americans have looked for solutions to these problems—seems unable to act. Despite the progressive rhetoric of the Carter Administration and Secretary of Agriculture Bergland, there has been little significant change in the direction of national agricultural policy. Powerful agricultural interests and agribusiness seem to have a hammerlock on agricultural policies in Washington.

Using an exciting combination of innovative ideas, proposed bills, and existing legislation, citizen activists have turned to state and local governments for action. These activists include farmers, environmentalists, religious leaders, consumer and community leaders, and state and local public officals. They see state and local governments as vehicles for positive accomplishments and victories. This development is the beginning of a more responsible and imaginative agricultural and food policy for the United States.

Some farm and national leaders have criticized those who have turned to state and local governments as vehicles for implementing new policies. They argue that states, counties, and cities are largely irrelevant to impacting U.S. agricultural policy and that the only arena to fight for progressive change is the federal level—in Congress and within the U.S. Department of Agriculture.

However, state and local governments have been extremely responsive and innovative in facing many of the existing problems. One reason is that they are more accessible to farmers and citizen activists. Being closer to the problems they are also more receptive to new ideas and approaches. In addition, powerful agribusiness and special interests are unprepared for serious challenges at the local level and are not as organized as they are on the national level.

The new initiatives pouring into state legislatures, county commissions, and city councils are extremely diverse. There is no single national political platform or agenda being pushed throughout the country. Each state, county, and city has its own unique problems, history, economy and geography. These varied factors offer a wide and exciting range of new proposals and approaches. What does unite these diverse proposals and strategies, however, is the common theme of a more decentralized, environmentally and socially responsible, family farm-based agricultural system.

As vital as the new activism is at the state and local level, national agricultural policy remains extremely important. The federal government has the enormous financial resources needed for any real lasting solutions. State and local governments can accelerate the process, however, of changing national policy by creating the exciting programs and working alternatives which will develop the political momentum needed to force changes in national policy.

Equally important, citizen activism is the heart of any change at the state and local level. The real instrument for changing public policy is the energy and commitment of organized citizens. State and local governments have taken the lead precisely because of strong pressure from farmers, consumers, religious leaders, community organizations, and progressive state and local public officials.

New Directions in Farm, Land and Food Policies has been written and edited to assist and encourage this new movement of citizen activists. Responding to the numerous calls for help and assistance over the past year, we have concentrated in this book on presenting the specifics of what amounts to the progressive agenda on farm, land, and food issues for state and local action.

Each of the seventeen chapters includes a narrative outlining the innovative approaches and policy alternatives being proposed and implemented in states, counties, and cities across the country. Following the narratives are several articles and reprints which describe the most exciting of these new proposals. Each chapter includes a reference bibliography and a listing of key organizations to contact on that specific issue. Finally, a Resource and Contact Section at the end of the book contains additional references; newsletters; a listing of relevant federal, state and local agencies; and organizations to contact for further information, publications and technical assistance.

Cynthia Guyer, Coordinator, Agriculture Project
January 1978— June 1980

Lee Webb, Executive Director
Conference on Alternative State and Local Policies

Section I

Section I

Strengthening the Family Farm

Family farms, which have traditionally been the backbone of America's agricultural economy, are in crisis. The most dramatic evidence of that crisis is the steady decline in the number of family farms. In 1978, less than 2.7 million farmers remain working the land; barely over 1% of the total population. This steady decline in the number of family farms since the 1940s has created many ripple effects. As increasing numbers of farmers leave the land, once stable farm communities begin to disintegrate. Feed stores, equipment dealers and other services needed by remaining farmers can no longer make reasonable profits and are forced to close down. The economic and social fabric of rural and small town life has undergone enormous stress over the past 40 years.

Federal agricultural policy is one of the major factors contributing to the decline of the family farm and the life of rural communities across the country. The major programs of federal farm policy benefit larger farmers and the food industry while bypassing—and even discriminating against—family farmers. Price support programs, for instance, primarily reward the largest commercial producers. Acreage limitation (set-aside programs) and soil conservation programs have similar effects in benefitting already successful farmers.

Federal agricultural research and extension programs are also primarily focused on increasing the production and profits of large farmers. Many federal policy makers publicly declare that their goal is to force the small, "inefficient" farmers out of farming. They continue to support policies and programs which benefit large, commercial producers and agribusiness firms.

Efforts to change federal agricultural policy by concentrating resources on strengthening the family farm have repeatedly failed in recent years. This is largely attributable to the influence which agribusiness and corporate farming interests have in Washington. These special interests have successfully been able to frame the debate and set the terms of discussion on the direction of agricultural policy. Supporters of the family farm have won too few victories in Congress and in moving the U.S. Department of Agriculture in the direction of becoming more responsive and accountable to family farmers.

On the other hand, state legislatures have responded to many of the legislative proposals and innovative public policies that Congress has ignored. Working with their state legislators and other progressive public officials, farm organizations and rural-based organizations have successfully voiced the need for policies which encourage a more decentralized and democratic agricultural economy. Important legislative victories on a number of issues have been won in many states across the country.

Chapter 1 of this section, entitled *Access to Land and Capital*, details innovative, new programs underway in a number of states—and proposed in still others—which provide family farmers with increased access to capital and to the low interest credit rates needed to purchase farmland and operate economically viable farms.

Chapter 2, *Opening Up New Markets*, describes initiatives taken by state and local governments to increase local and regional marketing outlets. These "direct marketing" efforts also attempt to give farmers a greater share of the consumer's food dollar by eliminating the middlemen who currently stand between producer and consumer. In addition to bringing farmers and consumers closer together, these new marketing opportunities also lower the cost of food to the consumer by eliminating the added costs incurred by long distance transportation, processing, packaging and retailing mark-up.

Chapter 3, *Stopping Corporate and Absentee Control of Farmland*, details what state legislatures have done to identify and then control—or in some cases prohibit—corporate ownership of farmland. The chapter also details the recent flurry of state initiatives which attempt to prevent foreign investment in farmland.

Chapter 4, *Redirecting Research Priorities*, outlines efforts to redirect the focus of agricultural research away from encouraging the "industrialization" of agriculture and towards the needs of family farmers and rural communities.

Finally, Chapter 5, *New Models For Extension and Training*, outlines the experimental and successful programs initiated to work with the production and management problems of small and family farmers.

Clearly, it is at the state and local level where organized farmers and concerned citizens will continue to be able to make an impact in the overall movement to change agricultural and food policy in America.

Rate of Return to Farm Equity Capital, U.S. and Ten Regions, 1970

Item	Sales class (thousand dollars)							
	100 and over	40 to 100	20 to 40	10 to 20	5 to 10	2.5 to 5	Less than 2.5	All farms
U.S.								
Net returns to equity (%)	6.9	5.9	4.4	2.9	−.1	−6.5	−6.1	2.1
Capital gains	3.9	3.7	3.5	3.4	3.3	3.2	3.3	3.5
Total	**10.8**	**9.6**	**7.9**	**6.3**	**3.2**	**−3.3**	**−3.2**	**5.6**
Region[1]								
Northeast	7.6	6.4	4.5	.9	−2.3	−14.7	−10.8	.2
Lake States	9.1	8.4	8.1	5.7	−2.6	−11.2	−13.3	2.3
Corn Belt	6.3	6.1	4.8	3.0	−.2	−3.9	−10.0	2.6
Northern Plains	5.6	5.1	3.9	2.4	1.9	−7.3	−7.0	2.6
Appalachian	8.0	6.4	3.6	2.5	−2.0	−5.3	−2.0	.4
Southeast	10.7	7.1	2.1	−.3	−1.2	−9.4	−4.8	1.8
Delta States	11.9	9.7	5.7	2.3	1.5	−3.3	−2.7	4.5
Southern Plains	6.2	5.4	4.1	3.7	1.6	−4.8	−4.4	1.9
Mountain	8.6	5.4	4.2	3.3	1.9	−3.9	−5.1	3.2
Pacific	4.2	2.0	1.2	.2	−1.7	−10.9	−5.5	.8

Source: Bruce Hottel and Robert Reinsel. **Returns to Equity Capital by Economic Class of Farm.** Agricultural Economic Report No. 347. Washington, D.C.: Economic Research Service, U.S. Department of Agriculture. 1976.

[1] Does not include capital gains.

AVERAGE PRICE PER ACRE
U.S. FARM LAND BY REGION—1978

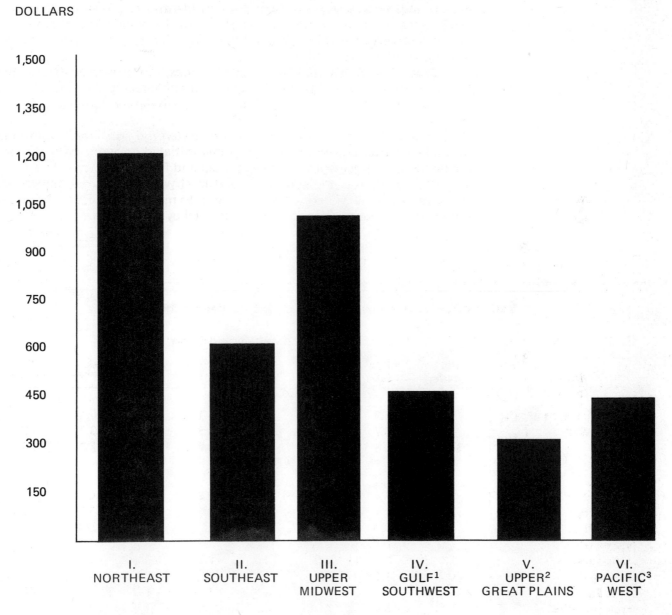

DOLLARS

1,500

1,350

1,200

1,050

900

750

600

450

300

150

| I. NORTHEAST | II. SOUTHEAST | III. UPPER MIDWEST | IV. GULF[1] SOUTHWEST | V. UPPER[2] GREAT PLAINS | VI. PACIFIC[3] WEST |

[1]Excluding New Mexico ($93)
[2]Excluding Wyoming ($101)
[3]Excluding Arizona ($121) and Nevada ($96)

Source: National Farmers Union

Chapter 1

Access to Land and Capital

Farmers need ready sources of capital and credit. Money is needed to purchase land, machinery, seed, livestock, feed, and other inputs. The usual sources are commercial banks and savings institutions, farm product manufacturers, life insurance companies, state and local governments, the Farmers Home Administration (FmHA), and the quasi-federal Production Credit Associations (PCA) and Federal Land Banks.

Getting into farming in the 1970s is a very expensive proposition. As the cost of land and other inputs has soared, the initial capital investment required for beginning a moderate-sized, modern operation in a good farming area has risen to levels of $200,000 to $500,000. This is an enormous sum for any individual. A stark contrast may be seen in the fact that in 1972 the total of capital expenditures, fixed assets, rent, and labor for all U.S. retail trade establishments averaged about $44,000 per store.

The statistics are startling. The price of prime farmland has reached $2,000, and in some cases even $3,000 an acre. Total farm real estate debt in 1977 was more than $56.4 billion. Non-real estate farm debt for that year reached $45.7 billion, up from $3.4 billion in 1940 and $23.8 billion in 1970. Total farm production expenses amounted to $6.7 billion in 1940, $44.0 billion in 1970, and $81.6 billion in 1976. Even farmers with less than $20,500 in gross sales had physical and financial assets of nearly $60,000 in 1976. Moderate-sized farms (gross sales of $20,000 to $39,999) in 1976 had assets averaging $269,636.

This level of capital requirement means that it is now extremely difficult for a young person to begin farming without an inheritance, a huge mortgage, or mostly rented land. The average age of the American farmer is now over 50. And inflated land values for these veterans means that, wanting to retire, they have difficulty finding purchasers of such expensive property.

The Land Banks can provide real estate assistance, as does the Farmers Home Administration (FmHA) which is supposed to be a loan source of last resort for those otherwise unable to find funds, and for low-income producers. But both agencies, part of the U.S. Department of Agriculture, have never had the funds to satisfy fully the demand for their services. Non-real estate, operating loans are made by FmHA and by the Production Credit Associations (PCA).

STATES INCREASE ACCESS TO CAPITAL

To help both the younger and older farmers several states have passed or are considering new legislation which increases the availability of capital and credit. The *Minnesota Family Farm Security Act of 1976* set up that state's Farm Security Program. The Program guarantees, out of a $10,000,000 fund, up to 90% of a bank loan for the purchase of farmland. Applicants for loan guarantees must be capable farmers with a family net worth of less than $50,000. But young and old alike may apply and there are no limits on acreage purchased or money spent on a purchase. The Program also offers

4% interest subsidies or "adjustment payments" on outstanding loan balances, if the applicant's net worth is less than $100,000 and the loan matures within 20 years. **Example 1, A Summary of the Family Farm Security Act** from *The Young Farmers Homestead Act* appears at the end of this chapter.

The Minnesota law has served as a model for bills in several other states. An Iowa bill introduced in April 1978 called for a Family Farm Security Program that is almost identical to the Minnesota act. The Iowa bill would be funded out of existing monies in the state's Rural Rehabilitation Fund.

Modeled on the Minnesota act, the North Dakota Farmers Union drafted and backed legislation entitled the *North Dakota Family Farm Security Act of 1977*. Although the Farm Security Act did not pass the North Dakota legislature in 1977, the state-owned Bank of North Dakota acted on its own initiative. The Bank's Board of Directors undertook an innovative new loan program aimed at reducing the cost of borrowing start-up money for new farmers. The Bank will, on certain loans to new farmers, extend the maximum term of a farm loan from 20 to 40 years, and will provide drastically lower interest rates for the first 2 to 5 years of these loans.

The *Pennsylvania Agricultural Development Authority Act of 1977* would also have provided 90% loan guarantees for a maximum real estate purchase of up to $150,000. A state interest subsidy of one-half the annual interest, or 5% of the unpaid balance (whichever is less) would be made available under the proposed legislation. The Authority would also have the power to make loans of up to $50,000 for non-real estate farm operating expenses.

Minnesota's law and the other states' proposals all call for operation of these programs by a board of bankers, farmers, a production credit association (PCA) representative, and other state officials and representatives.

PROVIDING ACCESS TO LAND

The impetus for the original Minnesota and North Dakota proposals came in part from the *Saskatchewan Land Bank Act of 1972*, a very progressive and a more comprehensive program. Under the Land Bank Act, the provincial government purchases available farmland and then leases it to new or expanding farmers at bargain interest rates. By 1976 the Land Bank had acquired 700,000 acres at a cost of under $60,000,000. Prospective buyers of the Bank's land holdings must have a net annual income of no more than $10,000 and a net worth of no more than $60,000. The terms of transfer include a lifetime lease with an option to buy after five years. The Bank purchases only real estate and buys at market prices. Those who sell to the Land Bank can take payment in cash or can receive an annuity with a bond interest rate. An article describing the success of the Land Bank is: **Example 2, Land Bank Lease Becomes Family's Farm.** Another source of credit assistance for new farmers in Saskatchewan is *Farm Start*, a program of special credits and grants for new livestock producers.

Canada provides other model legislation and programs for states which are searching for ways to make land available to new and young farmers. The Prince Edward Island Development Corporation between 1970 and 1974 bought about 80,000 acres, more than 10% of the farmland in the province, and also put 9,000 idle acres back into production. The *British Columbia Land Commission Act of 1973* instituted a similar program of purchasing farmland on long term lease and payback arrangements.

The Canadian land bank concept has caught the attention of several states. In Montana, State Senator Tom Towe proposed that a purchase and lease program be linked to an attempt to curb foreign investment in Montana farmland. Funds from existing coal taxes would be used to give the Department of State Lands an opportunity to match any offer by an "alien" individual or corporation to buy large tracts of Montana farm or ranchland. If purchased, such land would be leased out to young farmers in family-sized plots.

Other introductions of the Saskatchewan model have been made in California, North Dakota, and South Dakota. The *California Homestead Act of 1976* would have authorized $10,000,000 annually for a New Farm Assistance Corporation to buy up farms and lease or sell them to new operators. In South Dakota the *Homestead Land Act of 1976* would have set up a State Homestead Lands Commission to purchase farmland and sell or lease it back at low price rates. A total of $50,000,000 and a maximum of $200,000 for any one farm could be spent by the Commission for land purchases. A Farmers Union-sponsored bill in North Dakota would have formed in the state's Department of Agriculture a Trust Lands Division with purchase-and-lease powers. At the end of five years a lessee would have the option of securing a perpetual (and thus inheritable) lease or of buying the land. The bill called for funding of the Lands Division by a Bank of North Dakota $20,000,000 bond issue.

OTHER CAPITAL AND CREDIT ISSUES

The entrance of new and young farmers is the agricultural credit issue that has in recent years attracted the most attention at the state policy level. But it is not the only problem. A more complex threat to the family farm is the decline of independent rural banking. The Center for Rural Affairs, a Midwestern public interest organization, has studied this decline in Nebraska. Portions of the Center's report are excerpted in **Example 3, Where Have All the Bankers Gone?**

A comprehensive look at the finance and credit problems of small family producers in one state is provided by the report: **Example 4, Finance Task Force: Final Report** in *The Family Farm in California: Report of the Small Farm Viability Project.*

Resources

ORGANIZATIONS

Farm Credit Administration

490 L'Enfant Plaza East, S.W.
Washington, D.C. 20578
(202) 755-2195

Farmers' Home Administration

U.S. Department of Agriculture
Washington, D.C. 20250
(202) 447-4323

Minnesota Farm Security Program

510 B State Office Building
St. Paul, Minnesota 55155
(612) 296-8435

National Family Farm Coalition

918 F Street, N.W.
Washington, D.C. 20004
(612) 638-6848
Catherine Lerza and Robin Rosenbluth

**National Rural Development
and Finance Corporation**

1300 19th Street, N.W.
Washington, D.C. 20036
(202) 466-6950
Alfredo Navarro, Director

North Dakota Department of Agriculture

Capitol Building
Bismarck, North Dakota 58505
(701) 224-2232
Jim Fuglie

Rural America

1346 Connecticut Avenue, N.W.
Washington, D.C. 20036
(202) 659-2800
Peggy Borgers, Food and Agriculture Policy

Saskatchewan Land Bank Commission

Administration Building
3055 Albert Street
Regina, Saskatchewan,
CANADA S4S 0B1
(306) 565-5321
David Miner, Vice-Chairman

Small Farm Advocacy Program

Center for Rural Affairs
P.O. Box 405
Walthill, Nebraska 68067
(402) 846-5428
Gene Severns, Program Director

BIBLIOGRAPHY

Agriculture Project, Conference on Alternative State and Local Policies, **Assisting Beginning Farmers: New Programs and Responses**. CASLP, 2000 Florida Avenue, N.W., Washington, D.C. 20009. October 1980. $4.95.

Center for Rural Affairs, **Where Have All the Bankers Gone?** Center for Rural Affairs, P.O. Box 405, Walthill, Nebraska 68067. March 1977. $4.00.

Farm Credit Administration (FCA), **Federal Land Banks— How They Operate**. FCA, Information Division, Washington, D.C. 20578.

Farm Credit Administration (FCA), **The Cooperative Farm Credit System**. FCA, Information Division, Washington, D.C. 20578.

Fifty-First Legislative Assembly, 1976, House Bill 770, **South Dakota Homestead Land Act**. Legislative Reference Bureau, State Capitol, Pierre, South Dakota 57501.

Jones, Lawrence, **What Young Farm Families Should Know About Credit**. Economics Research Service, USDA, Washington, D.C. Revised Edition, 1971.

National Rural Development and Finance Corporation (NRDFC), **Introduction to the National Rural Development and Finance Corporation: A Working Paper on Rural Development Policy**, NRDFC, 1300 19th Street, N.W., Washington, D.C. 20036.

North Dakota Department of Agriculture, **The Beginning Farmer: An Exploration of Solutions to Problems Associated with Entry Into Agriculture**. North Dakota Department of Agriculture, Capitol Building, Bismarck, North Dakota 58505. 1979.

Rural America, "Freedom of Entry into Farming," A **Strategies for Rural Action** Paper, Prepared for Third National Conference on Rural America, December 1977, Washington, D.C. Review of legislation at the Federal and state level designed to ease access into agriculture.

"Saskatchewan Land Bank Keeps Land in the Hands of Many," **North Dakota Union Farmer**. North Dakota Farmers Union, 1415 12th Avenue, S.E., Jamestown, North Dakota 58401. January 10, 1974.

Small Farm Viability Project, **Finance Task Force Report**. State CETA office, Rural Affairs Department of Employment Development, 800 Capitol Mall, Sacramento, California 95814. November 1977.

Swackhamer, Gene L., and Raymond J. Doll, **Financing Modern Agriculture**. Research Department, Federal Reserve Bank of Kansas City, Kansas City, Missouri 64198. May 1969. Extensive treatment of how agriculture is financed.

U.S. Senate, Committee on Agriculture and Forestry, Hearings on **Young Farmers' Homestead Act**. U.S. Government Printing Office, Washington, D.C. 20402. June 10 and 11, 1976.

Summary of Family Farm Security Act

EXAMPLE 1

[The following material was submitted by Mr. Eken:]

SUMMARY OF FAMILY FARM SECURITY ACT, H.F. 1984 (S.F. 1895)

The Family Farm Security Act is designed to enable qualifying farmers to obtain loans for the acquisition of farm land. The state will guarantee 90% of the outstanding balance due on a real estate mortgage and will provide state funds for deferral of a portion of the annual payment. A section-by-section summary of the bill follows:

Section 1: States the purpose of the bill: to aid young farmers in obtaining credit for the acquisition of farm real estate by providing state money in guarantee of loans.

Section 2: Defines terms. The bill defines "Lender" to include national or state banks, savings and loans, trust companies, insurance companies, Farm Credit Administration institutions, and, in some cases, individuals who are selling a farm. Also defined is "family farm loan guarantee": an agreement that in the event of default the state shall pay the lender 90% of the sums due and payable under the mortgage. Another important definition is "payment adjustment," meaning an amount of money equal to 4% interest on the principal balance of a family farm security loan.

Section 3: Concerns administration of the law. The family farm security program is to be administered by the Commissioner of Agriculture, who is given rule-making authority.

Section 4: Establishes a family farm advisory council to make recommendations to the commissioner regarding loan applications; to review and appraise the program; and to make general policy recommendations. The council is to consist of seven members: two officers of commercial lending institutions, three farmers, one director of a farm credit association, and an agricultural economist.

Section 5: Describes eligibility requirements for the family farm security program. Loan approval may be granted if:

(1) the applicant is a state resident, or intends to become one;

(2) the applicant has sufficient education, training, or experience in the type of farming for which he wishes the loan, and agrees to participate in a farm management program for the duration of the loan;

(3) the applicant, his dependents and spouse have total net worth valued at less than $50,000 and have demonstrated a need for the loan;

(4) the applicant intends to purchase farm land to be used by the applicant for agricultural purposes;

(5) the applicant is credit worthy according to standards developed by the commissioner.

Section 6: Describes the procedure to be followed in the family farm security program. The applicant first goes to a lender and makes application for a loan. The applicant and lender then complete and forward the application to the commissioner for approval. The commissioner is to develop a screening process to determine eligibility. If the commissioner approves the application, he retains a copy and returns the original to the lender, and the lender and the applicant then complete the transaction for the loan. If the commissioner does not approve the loan, then the application is returned with a statement of reasons for denial.

Approval means that 90% of a loan may be guaranteed by the state; thus, a successful applicant could get a loan from the lender with a reduced down payment. In addition, the commissioner may make a payment adjustment of 4% of the outstanding balance of the loan (see Section 7).

In the event of default on a guaranteed loan, the buyer has 180 days to cure the default. After that time the lender may file a claim with the commissioner. If the commissioner determines that default has indeed taken place, he shall pay the lender the balance due in exchange for the lender's security and interest in the loan. At this point the commissioner may commence foreclosure proceedings. If the state acquires title to the property, taxes shall be levied and paid on the land as though the owner were a natural person.

If foreclosure takes place and title to the property is acquired by the state, the commissioner must take certain steps to sell the property. Advertisement must begin within 15 days of the expiration of the redemption period allowed by law, which is usually one year from the date of foreclosure in the case of farm property. The sale must be advertised for four successive weeks and then, within 15 days of the last advertisement, the property must be sold to the highest bidder.

The loan guarantee shall be void only if the guarantee was obtained by fraud or material misrepresentation of which the lender had actual knowledge.

Section 7: Discusses the terms of the loans. Loans must be transacted on forms approved by the commissioner. The commissioner is to establish an appraisal procedure and must determine the value and income potential of the property before guaranteeing a loan. No guarantee can be issued if the purchase price exceeds the appraised value.

Subdivision 2 of this section authorizes the "payment adjustment". This is a method of reducing the applicant's cash flow burden in the early years of his farm acquisition. During the first ten years of a family farm security loan, the commissioner shall pay to the lender on the applicant's behalf an amount of money equal to 4% of the outstanding principal balance due. Thus, if a loan carries an interest rate of 9%, the applicant pays 5% interest and the state pays 4%. The payment adjustment can be renewed for a second ten-year period. The payment adjustment must be repaid to the state in year eleven, unless the adjustment was renewed for a second ten-year period, in which case the money must be repaid in year twenty-one. The obligation to repay is a lien against the property. To qualify for a payment adjustment the loans must have a maximum term of twenty years.

The applicant, his dependents and spouse must annually submit a net worth statement. In any year in which their net worth exceeds $100,000, the applicant is ineligible for a payment adjustment in that year.

Section 8: Provides authority for inclusion in the program of a special type of loan, called a "seller-sponsored" loan, if the buyer meets the eligibility criteria. Similar to a contract-for-deed, this type of loan is financed in part or whole by the seller of the property. A conventional lender finances the remainder of the loan, if any. Seller-sponsored loans are to be secured by a purchase money first real estate mortgage, evidenced by negotiable notes. The seller's note and the conventional lender's note may carry different interest rates.

Section 9: Governs the sale of property covered by a family farm security loan. If an applicant sells the property, he must immediately liquidate all debt on the property owed to the lender and commissioner. Family farm security loans are not transferable or assumable.

If an applicant fails to maintain the land covered by a family farm security loan in active agricultural production for a period of time longer than one year, the loan is considered to be in default, unless the applicant becomes disabled or other extenuating circumstances occur.

This section also contains an increased tax on capital gains realized on property financed by a family farm security loan and sold before the passage of ten years. The rate of the tax penalty varies according to how long the property was held.

Time elapsed from issuance of loan (years)		
At least—	But less than—	Percent of gain subject to income tax
1	1	100
3	3	90
5	5	80
7	7	70
9	9	60
	10	50

After 10 years, the normal capital gains tax imposed by Chapter 290 shall apply. The above tax shall be waived by the Commissioner of Revenue if the applicant has died or suffered a total disability.

Section 10: Prohibits discrimination against applicants on the basis of race, color, creed, religion, national origin, sex, marital status, disability, political or ideological persuasion.

Section 11: Provides that the guaranteed loan shall not apply to the lending limits placed on State-chartered banks.

Section 12: Amends the income tax law to provide for proper imposition of the capital gains penalty tax discussed above (Section 9).

Section 13: Appropriates money:

For a loan guarantee fund	$10,000,000
For payment adjustment	800,000
For administration	74,300

The sum of all outstanding loans guaranteed at any given time shall not exceed ten times the amount in the loan guarantee fund.

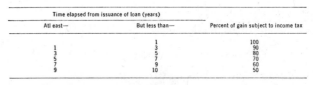

This article is reprinted from "Summary of Family Farm Security Act," Senate Agriculture Hearings on: Young Farmers Homestead Act (S. 2589), pp. 93-95, June 10-11, 1976, U.S. Senate Agriculture Committee.

EXAMPLE 2 Land Bank Lease Becomes Family's Farm

Brian and Linda McKnight with Misty and Chad: buying the land that feeds them.

It was smiles all the way May 25 for Brian and Linda McKnight. They became the owners of the 380 acres of land they had been leasing from the provincial government since 1973 – the first family to buy land from the Saskatchewan Land Bank Commission.

Provincial Agriculture Minister Edgar Kaeding was smiling too. He felt this first sale, with more to follow, would "lay to rest for good those unfounded criticisms (of the plan)." Criticisms that had maintained the province would never sell any of the land to the tenants.

The McKnights paid $47,000 ($125 per acre) for the land, compared to the $22,000 the land bank paid for the land in 1973. Despite the price increase, the young couple is convinced they got a good deal.

Brian McKnight pointed out land values in the area had more than doubled since the land bank was formed.

Brian was enthusiastic about the land bank program. Without it he said he could not have begun farming when he did.

"I'd still be working in the city if not for the land bank," he said. "It's a real good program."

The father of two children, aged three and four years, said he decided to buy the land because of the amount of work he has put into upgrading the buildings.

There was no power, sewer or water connected when he moved in. He said he bought the house for $100 and has remodelled it extensively. He has also added steel grain bins, a shed and a workshop.

"there was nothing here when I started," he said.

And with a young son and daughter he wanted something to pass on to them. He said he plans to take advantage of a $5,000 discount the land bank offers on the home quarter.

Brian leases another half section of land from the land bank which he has no intention of buying.

The land bank has spent $70 million since 1973 to purchase 800,000 acres of farm land across the province.

Gib Wesson, chairman of the land bank commission, explained money paid as rent for the last five years will not go towards the purchase of the land.

He said the rent, which was five per cent of $22,000 for the first three years and five per cent on a moving three-year average on the last two, does not even cover interest on money the land bank had to borrow to buy the land originally.

The land bank is offering a 20-per-cent discount, or $5,000, spread over five years for the home quarter. The rest is sold at market value.

Of the 2,400 lessees in the province, 350 became eligible to buy their land when the five-year waiting period ended Jan. 1, 1978.

Farmers then have the option of buying the land or continuing to rent. Many farmers prefer the rental arrangement since the rent is lower than mortgage payments and there is a provision in the contract to pass the lease on to their children.

This article is reprinted from "Land Bank Lease Becomes Family's Farm," **The Commonwealth**, June 14, 1978.

Where Have All the Bankers Gone?

EXAMPLE 3

Banking in the United States has traditionally been regulated at both the state and federal levels. In the past, the fear of the potentially excessive economic power which would result if control of the banking system were to fall into the hands of a few big banks, has acted to encourage policies at both of these levels which favor individual banking operations over large, multi-unit banking empires. Therefore, many state governments have outlawed branch banking (one bank with branch operations in several locations) and multi-bank holding companies (several subsidiary banks owned by one parent company). Even where they are permitted, branch banking and multi-bank holding companies are closely regulated by the federal government.

Nonetheless, some states have allowed branching and multi-bank holding companies for years, and the trend recently has been away from policies which protect independent banking and in favor of "concentrated banking." (We will group branch banking and MBHCs together under the term "concentrated banking" for convenience).

California was the first state to permit its banks to open branches anywhere in the state (1909).[1] Many states have subsequently passed laws which allow branching to some extent; many limit branching to a certain number of branch offices located in or near the city of the main bank's operation. In the 1930s, federal laws were passed which permitted national banks to branch in a state to the same extent that the state allows state banks to branch.

Today, about two-thirds of the states permit some degree of branch banking. Nebraska, which outlawed branch banking in 1927, has passed a series of laws which loosen the restrictions on branching. As of this writing, Nebraska banks may have no more than two detached offices within the corporate limits of the city.

Bank holding companies were first formed in the early 1900s largely as a means of circumventing the prohibitions against branching which most states still had at that time. Since banks could not open branches in many states, they simply bought existing banks, continuing to operate them as separate subsidiaries. In such cases, all the banks in the group were owned by the same holding company. (This development, incidentally, was largely inspired by the economic squeeze on rural banks in the South, Midwest, and West after World War I to avoid absorption by the big banks on the east and west coasts).

Although several states and the federal government enacted laws to restrict multi-bank holding company formation, the trend continued. Each new wave of bank mergers under holding companies caused a surge in public concern over bank ownership and control being concentrated in a few hands, and resulted in more restrictive legislation.

Nebraska passed a law in 1963 which forbids any corporation from acquiring ownership or control of 25% or more of two or more banks (multi-bank holding companies which existed prior to the passage of the law were allowed to continue but not add more banks). One-bank holding companies (corporations which own 25% or more of only one bank) can own other businesses, such as insurance companies, real estate firms and farm management concerns.

Recently, however, while the trend has been toward more careful regulation of bank holding companies at the federal level, the states have lifted some of their restrictions. Today, about half of the states have no limitations on bank holding companies, and only nineteen of the states, mostly ones with strong agricultural economies, place substantial restrictions on them.[2]

In those states which have liberalized their policies toward MBHCs the effect has been to concentrate control over the state's financial resources. In Minnesota, for instance, which does not restrict holding companies, six corporations own 132 banks which have over half of the states total commercial bank deposits.[3]

Overall, as of 1973, bank holding companies owned 42% of the banking offices in the nation, and held 61.5% of the deposits. The comparable figures are undoubtedly higher today.

The political arguments made for or against branch banking and multi-bank holding companies run, in essence, like this:

For:

1. They are required in order to raise the capital necessary to finance increasingly expensive business operations, especially farming. They therefore encourage more economic growth.

2. They will provide better consumer services, such as longer hours, credit card and electronic banking, and more modern facilities.

3. They have access, because of their size, to more highly trained personnel and technical services.

4. They can operate more efficiently because of a bigger volume of business.

5. They operate more professionally and impartially, administering credit without regard for local personality conflicts.

Against:

1. They are riskier because they concentrate bank assets among fewer bankers, creating increased potential for major bank failures.

2. They will drain bank resources from rural areas in favor of making loans to higher paying industries in urban areas.

3. They will be insensitive to many local concerns, and unsupportive of community needs.

4. They operate less efficiently because of the delay of bureaucracy between the "home office" and the branch or subsidiary bank.

5. They tend to create a monopoly over the financial resources of the state and nation.

A number of studies have attempted to investigate the validity of these claims. These studies have sometimes contradicted each other, and have failed to yield a consensus on many key points of contention. However, some are worthy of mention.

In June, 1975, the Federal Reserve System published a series of studies on rural credit in certain states which had recently changed their laws regarding banking.[4] They found that in Virginia, the changes in bank ownership which resulted from more permissive laws did not adversely affect farm credit. The same conclusion was reached in an Ohio study. However, in Wisconsin, which adopted partial branching in 1968, the study showed that farm lending tended to improve in the branch banks. On the other hand, in Florida, where holding companies had been permitted to purchase rural banks, "farm loans tended to decrease soon after banks became affiliated with holding companies, while at the same time farm loans at other banks were continuing their upward trend."

Two studies were conducted as a part of the same Federal Reserve System project and were reported in preliminary findings but not included in the final published report.[5] One indicated that in Virginia, merged branches did not expand local lending relative to local deposits, as rapidly as a comparable group of independent banks. This implied that the systems were taking deposits from rural branches to increase lending at their urban branches. The other unpublished study found that in a group of North Central states, the impact of holding companies on farm lending was unfavorable.

In addition to these Federal Reserve Studies, a Michigan study indicates that larger banks operating in rural areas tend to disfavor smaller farm operations in favor of large farms.

The study, published in the Journal of the American Society of Farm Managers and Rural Appraisers, found that branch banks tended to place more emphasis on financial statements as an impartial basis for making credit decisions, making it more difficult for small farmers to get credit. Furthermore, these banks often imposed minimum loan sizes which were larger than that which small farmers could effectively use. Moreover, the professional services of the bank and the larger loan limits tended to cater to the large farmers.[6]

Finally, another Michigan study by the same author indicated that farmers who borrowed operating capital were often charged lower interest rates at independent banks, while commercial-industrial loans were lower at the branch banks.[7]

In more general terms, a paper prepared by L. Wayne Dobson, Professor of Banking at the University of Nebraska, surveyed various bank ownership studies and concluded that only two conditions are "reasonably certain" to follow if multi-bank holding companies are permitted:

- a larger percentage of the state's financial wealth will be held or controlled by fewer individuals.

- there will be a larger number of banks owned and controlled by those from outside the trade area served by the banks.[8]

In sum, while there is a considerable amount of disagreement among research findings on the impact of concentrated banking on rural credit, these studies seem to challenge the claims of those who favor changing the law. For the most part, however, the "jury is still out" among the researchers with regard to the question.

SUMMARY/CONCLUSIONS

Using conservative definitions of the terms "independent bank" (one with no ownership connection to another bank) and "bank chain" (a group of four or more banks operating under common management in more than one trade area), we conclude that a larger number of Nebraska banks than is generally believed fall into the grey area between these two concepts of banking. Only 37% of the state's banks are independent, and they control only 26% of the commercial bank deposits in the state. On the other hand, 23% of Nebraska's banks are parts of identifiable chains, and they hold 48% of the state's deposits.

Our preliminary analysis of the performance of these classes of banks indicated that there is little difference between them with respect to making credit available to farmers. Although the chain banks tend to lend a higher percentage of their deposits, these loans are less likely to go to farmers than are loans made by independent banks. Therefore, the independents lend about the same percentage of their deposits to farmers as do the chains.

One significant difference does exist: rural banks which are parts of chains dominated by one of the big five city banks tend to deposit a larger share of their funds in other banks than do other rural banks which operate in the same counties. This indicates that the city bank chains may tend to drain funds from the rural areas in which they operate.

Finally, this introductory report shows that a startling number of rural state-chartered banks (20% of the 328 state banks) have over half of their stock pledged as collateral for a loan made to the stockholder by another bank. This indicates that Nebraska's prohibition against branch banking and multi-bank holding companies is being circumvented by larger banks who are financing the acquisition of rural banks and taking a mortgage on the acquired bank's stock.

These findings reflect a drift toward greater concentration in the financial resources of the state in spite of public laws outlawing branch banking and multi-bank holding companies. We are concerned about the consequences which greater concentration would have on access to credit for small farmers, and on general farm credit stability in drought sensitive regions of the state, and in times of depressed farm prices.

FOOTNOTES

[1] Much of the background material for this section is based on the **Bank Holding Company: Its History and Significance in Modern America**, Association of Registered Bank Holding Companies, Washington, D.C. 1973.

[2] **Compilation of State Laws Affecting Bank Holding Companies**, Association of Bank Holding Companies, January 1977, Washington, D.C.

[3] **Banking and Rural Credit and Other Rural Life Issues**, Joint Religious Legislative Coalition, 1975-76 Official Position Paper, Minneapolis, Minnesota.

[4] **Improved Fund Availability of Rural Banks**, Board of Governors of the Federal Reserve System, Washington, D.C., June 1975.

[5] "An Overview of the Research Program and Results," Ad Hoc Committee to Study Improvements in Marketability of Bank Agricultural Paper, Board of Governors of the Federal Reserve System, unpublished document, 1971.

[6] Hayenga, Wayne A., "Rural Bank Ownership Changes: Effects on Rural Communities and Implications for Agriculture," **Journal of the American Society of Farm Managers and Rural Appraisers**, Vol. 39, No. 1, April 1975, pp. 6-11.

[7] Hayenga, Wayne A., "The Effects of Bank Mergers on Financial Services Available to Rural Michigan Residents," unpublished Ph.D. dissertation, Michigan State University, 1973.

[8] Dobson, L. Wayne, "An Analysis of the Most Frequently Used Arguments in Support of Multibank Holding Companies," unpublished paper, 1976.

This article is reprinted from **Where Have All The Bankers Gone?**, The Center for Rural Affairs, pp. 4-7, 26-30, March 1977.

Finance Task Force: Final Report

EXAMPLE 4

In surveying the financing needs of small farmers, the Finance Task Force found that the gaps in availability of funds are more a function of the experience and financial equity of a farmer than of the size of his farm. Adequate financing is generally available for the well established small farmer with years of experience; a shortage of funds exists for the low-equity farmer and for the beginning farmer who has (or contracts for) the requisite skills to run a successful farm but lacks sufficient collateral. The Task Force therefore concentrated its efforts on exploring alternative means of providing financing to the potentially successful low-equity or beginning farmer and low-resource cooperative.

Only a few lending agencies currently have the ability and the mandate to serve low-equity or beginning farmers. The principal organization in this category historically has been the Farmers Home Administration (FmHA). The Small Business Administration (SBA) recently has joined the FmHA in providing low-equity loans in the rural sector. Other current providers for these farmers include (1) community-based, nonprofit community development corporations, which obtain a portion of their capital from public funding sources, and (2) Business Investment Development Corporations (BIDCOs), also nonprofit corporations, funded by member institutions and designed to promote economic development by spreading loan risk among lenders.

The joint financing capacity of all the sources cited above are inadequate to meet the current and future needs of low-equity and beginning farmers. FmHA alone has a 2.6-year backlog of loan applications, and it is not able to serve cooperatives, which can be a major vehicle for increasing family-farm viability. Neither the FmHA nor the SBA has sufficient personnel to provide technical assistance through supervised credit.

In order to improve and expand the services offered by the existing small-farm finance system, the Finance Task Force recommends that the FmHA and SBA establish complementary programs whereby the FmHA issues guarantees to cover the purchase of farm land and the SBA guarantees loans for operating capital. Both agencies should recognize all kinds of cooperatives and their members as eligible borrowers, and they should institute technical assistance and supervised credit programs. The FmHA could augment its present financing capacity greatly by reducing the reserve it holds against default, retaining only the expected loss from bad debts. It would further increase its effectiveness by adopting a licensee arrangement with Local Development Corporations, Small Business Investment Corporations, and the like. The federal government also should consider increased direct funding of the FmHA.

The Task Force further recommends that the State undertake measures to improve the access of family farmers to land. Such measures should (1) ensure that land be sold at prices consonant with earning capacity, (2) establish means of keeping prime agricultural land in farming, (3) consider controls to limit corporate and foreign ownership of land, (4) support implementation of existing Reclamation Act provisions, and (5) facilitate the long-term lease of public lands to small farmers.

The Task Force also believes that the use of the federal tax preference rate on capital gains as applied to agricultural lands should be restricted, either by eliminating it altogether or by increasing the mandatory holding period beyond one year. The tax preference on income derived from capital gains induces investors to purchase land in the expectation of capital appreciation. This bids up the price of agricultural land and effectively keeps many potential small farmers out of farming, since the land's productive capacity is frequently insufficient to cover the indebtedness incurred to purchase it.

Even if the above recommendations were implemented, however, the financing available to low-equity and beginning farmers would be inadequate to meet present or future needs. Therefore, the Task Force recommends that the State take positive action toward the encouragement of the family farm by instituting the following measures: (1) creation of a Rural Development Office to serve as a public advocate for family farmers, to disseminate information about programs designed to aid them, and to conduct studies, write legislation, and coordinate small-farmer programs when they are enacted, and (2) creation of a financial and technical assistance institution to serve the needs of small farmers. This institution would be able to make grants and subsidize loans to farmers who lacked access to existing lending resources. It could also leverage outside capital and provide technical assistance, either directly or by contracting with local agencies.

This article is reprinted from "Finance Task Force: Final Report," The Family Farm in California: The Small Farm Viability Project, pp. 61-62.

Chapter 2

Opening Up New Markets

At opposite ends of the food distribution system stand farmers and consumers. The growing distance between them is a problem for both—a dilemma of income for the farmer and rising retail food prices for the consumer. Occupying that gap are the food system's marketeers—processors, packagers, wholesalers and retailers. This gap in 1977 amounted to $78 billion; 62% of the nation's retail food bill. This level has remained relatively constant for some time; farmers get about 40 cents or less of the consumer's food dollar.

The consumer/urban side of this issue is presented in Section V, *Building Urban Food Programs*. This chapter deals with farmer/producer issues. Farmers need better markets for their crops and livestock and more control over existing markets. Particularly insecure are small to mid-sized family farmers who are without the market clout of large producers and agribusiness firms. Many family-sized producers are being forced by the economics of their particular commodities into integrated marketing arrangements or "contract farming." This is a rapidly accelerating trend in which both farm markets and prices are controlled by professional brokers and corporate firms. Another difficulty for the family farmer is the rising cost of production. As taxes and the costs of land, fuel, fertilizer, machinery, and other inputs rise, the farmer's return in the marketplace is progressively lowered. At times the return in negative; the farmer's annual income being less than the cost of production.

A partial solution to the farmers' rising input costs are new marketing channels and "direct" marketing systems which help to close the gap between farmer and consumer.

A number of states and localities have begun to institute marketing alternatives for the farmer. Some of these steps are revivals of old methods, such as farmers' markets where producers sell directly to consumers. Other steps are newer and potentially more far-reaching; such as the idea of state or multi-state investigation of and alternatives to commercial grain marketing corporations. Another is for states to encourage purchasing of state-grown farm products by public institutions such as schools, hospitals and governmental agencies.

DIRECT MARKETING INITIATIVES

To date the encouragement of direct farmer-to-consumer sales is the alternative chosen most frequently by states and cities in the area of agricultural marketing. An example is West Virginia's program. Begun in the late 1940s with state and matching federal funds, this effort today consists of state-owned and operated markets in six cities and towns. During 1976 the markets generated sales of farm produce totaling $1.8 million.

Farmers pay a 5 to 8% commission on products consigned to the markets. Commissions help to defray the program's $150,000 cost. Each market has a manager—a state employee—who communicates with his colleagues to help balance out supply and demand for different items in various parts of the state. The West Virginia markets are in buildings open five days a week.

The Montgomery County, Maryland government recently initiated an effort similar to West Virginia's. The Montgomery County Program is described in the section following this narrative: **Example 5, County Goes Into Vegetable Business.** One similar market is soon to be restored in inner-city Washington, D.C. In Dallas, Texas, a cluster of three city block-sized sheds has been providing direct farm marketing space for 30 years. Another open space program, held on city-owned parking lots, is in Honolulu. Such market sheds or buildings exist in cities and towns throughout the United States, although many are now unused. They once were sites of exactly the sort of direct marketing outlets being revived today.

Perhaps the best known and the broadest program of marketing alternatives is in Pennsylvania. Under the innovative direction of state Secretary of Agriculture Jim McHale, Pennsylvania has sponsored "tailgate" markets; linked up farmers and consumer food co-ops; started a state canning facility for use by consumers; and published directories of farmer-to-consumer outlets and opportunities. Examples of the state Agriculture Department's direct marketing newsletter and of a fruits and vegetables information sheet for consumers are included in this chapter: **Example 6, Direct Marketing** and **Example 7, When You Can Buy Fresh Pennsylvania Fruits and Vegetables.** Over the period from 1975 to 1977, producers in Pennsylvania sold more than $114 million worth of commodities in the state's farmers' markets.

Consumers in California can dial a toll-free number for information on farms within the state with excess fruits or vegetables to sell. This effort was initiated by the State Department of Consumer Affairs. Another example of information for consumers is the series of maps put out by a private Washington state producer group, the Puget Sound Farm Markets Association. The Puget Sound maps could be an excellent model for state and local governments. Sections of one of the maps appear at the end of this chapter in **Example 8, Map of King and Pierce County.**

Another private effort worthy of public emulation is the Agricultural Marketing Project. AMP during 1977 organized direct markets, called "food fairs," in 26 cities in Tennessee, Alabama and Mississippi.

Direct marketing generally provides farmers with similar or better returns than conventional outlets. On their side, consumers benefit from lower retail prices. An example is found in the case of milk. In 1976, 344 million pounds of milk in California and 302 million pounds in Pennsylvania were sold directly to consumers. Nationally 1,525 million pounds were marketed directly. The overall average retail price for milk in 1976 was 42.4 cents per quart. But the consumer price for milk marketed directly that year was 36.4 cents nationally, 35 cents in California, and 32 cents in Pennsylvania.*

ENCOURAGING PURCHASE OF LOCALLY GROWN FOODS

Direct farmer-to-consumer selling is the most widespread marketing alternative for agriculture, but it is not the only new avenue under exploration. "Buy local" campaigns and public purchase of locally-grown food are examples of other alternatives. The "Grown in New York" program, undertaken in 1976, included "grown," "processed," or "produced in New York state" labeling, publicity efforts, and promotional campaigns aimed at such specific products as cheese, apples, and wine. Vermont and Massachusetts have also started "buy local" campaigns.

Purchase of domestically-grown commodities by state agencies has become an issue in such states as New York and Massachusetts. In those and certain other states the great majority of food needs are met by imports. The New England states estimate that they import at least 85% of their food. At least some, and perhaps much of that requirement could be met through a rejuvenation of local and regional agricultural economies. To encourage such a trend legislators in New York and Massachusetts have introduced bills directing state purchase of locally-grown food. Under the legislation public institutions such as schools, colleges and universities, cafeterias in government buildings, hospitals, and correctional facilities would give preference to the state's farmers in food purchasing. Massachusetts Representative Mel King proposed this change in *House Bills 699, 700,* and *701 of 1978.* The *New York bill (A. 9079), 1978,* introduced by Assemblyman Maurice Hinchey, would encourage the state's school districts to buy directly from in-state farm producers.

ANTI-TRUST ACTION IN AGRICULTURAL MARKETING

In Kansas, legislation has been proposed to initiate multi-state investigation of commercial grain marketing practices. The original bill (*House Bill 2794*) called for the formation of a state-wide committee which would draft a model multi-state organization. The organization would examine the feasibility of anti-trust action against the grain industry.

The cause of this bill is the near-total control over grain marketing held by a handful of secretive multi-national corporations. In 1972, for example, the big grain trading companies made huge profits on sales of grain to the Soviet Union. Many producers, lacking the grain firms' inside knowledge of Soviet needs, contracted with the firms earlier in the year for delivery of grain at prices much below subsequent levels. When news of the very large Soviet purchases emerged, prices rose.

In summary, farmers lacked and still lack control over markets. Roadside stands, direct marketing systems and incentives to purchase locally-grown products are the first steps toward gaining more control. The Kansas bill suggests much more for the future: ultimate public regulation or control of the marketing of major agricultural commodities. These new marketing alternatives will benefit both farmers and consumers.

*Statistical sources: U.S. Department of Agriculture and U.S. Department of Labor, Bureau of Labor Statistics.

Resources

ORGANIZATIONS

Agricultural Marketing Project

2606 Westwood Drive
Nashville, Tennessee 37204
(615) 297-4088
Lindsay Jones, John Vlcek, Laurie Heise

Agricultural Teams

Farm to Market Project
312 N. Walnut Street (#106)
Youngstown, Ohio 44505
(216) 746-8551
Ron Daniels, Project Coordinator

Department of Agriculture, State of Pennsylvania

2301 North Cameron Street
Harrisburg, Pennsylvania 17120
(717) 787-4737
Penrose Hallowell, Secretary

Department of Agriculture, State of West Virginia

State Capitol
Charleston, West Virginia 25305
(304) 348-2201
Gus R. Douglas, Commissioner

Hartford Food Systems, Inc.

c/o ConnPIRG
30 High Street (#108)
Hartford, Connecticut 06103
(203) 525-8312
Sally Taylor, Farm Market Director

$3.00; free to state officials. Overview of programs to stimulate demand for state grown produce, and to provide fresher and more nutritious produce to consumers.

Killefer, Gail, "The Direct Marketing Alternative," **Nutrition Action**. June 1977. Description of state and local efforts to encourage direct marketing in the U.S.

Lerza, Catherine, "Alternative Marketing Systems," **Strategies For Rural Action**. Prepared for Third annual Conference on Rural America. Rural America, 1346 Connecticut Avenue, N.W., Washington, D.C. 20036. December 1977. Description of buy local campaigns, farmers' markets, cooperatives, buying clubs, marketing orders and marketing boards.

National Commission on Food Marketing (NCFM), **Organization and Competition in Food Retailing**. Technical Study No. 7. Federal Trade Commission, NCFM, Washington, D.C. June 1966. Comprehensive discussion of vertical integration, conglomeration, and concentration in the food retailing sector.

National Commission on Food Marketing (NCFM), **Structure of Food Marketing**. Federal Trade Commission, NCFM, Washington, D.C. June 1966. Similar to above; discusses corporate concentration in food retailing in detail.

Ronco, William, **Food Co-ops**. Beacon, Boston.

Small Farm Viability Project, **Marketing Task Force Report**. State CETA Office, Department of Employment Development, 800 Capitol Mall, Sacramento, California 95814. September 1977. Article describing small farmers' problem of finding a reliable market, and ways in which the small volume producers may bypass the traditional marketing system.

Toothman, James, and Harold Ricker, **An Analysis of Small Food Store Supply Systems**. Pennsylvania State University, College of Agriculture, University Park, Pennsylvania. May 1976. Good article outlining inefficiencies in present food distribution practices, and ways in which wholesalers could lower distribution costs through minor warehouse reorganization.

BIBLIOGRAPHY

Agricultural Marketing Project (AMP), **Marketing Report: Food Fairs**. AMP, Center for Health Services, Vanderbilt Medical Center, Nashville, Tennessee 37232. 1976. $5.00.

Cotterill, Ronald, David Freshwater and David Houseman, **More Effective Direct Marketing: A Proposal to Establish An Inner-City Farmer-Consumer Warehouse in Detroit, Michigan**. Agricultural Economic Department, Staff Paper #77-101, Michigan State University, East Lansing, Michigan. December 1977.

Council of State Governments (CSG), **Merging Producer and Consumer Interests: Domestic Agricultural Marketing in New York and Pennsylvania**. CSG, P.O. Box 11910, Iron Works Pike, Lexington, Kentucky 40511. 1977.

County Goes Into Vegetable Business

EXAMPLE
5

The Montgomery County government is going into the vegetable business. It all starts on Saturday, July 16, when a farmer's market sponsored by county government will open in downtown Silver Spring with County Executive James Gleason officiating.

Located on the parking lot of the Silver Spring Armory at Pershing Drive and Fenton Street, the market will be open Saturdays from 7 a.m. to 1 p.m. and on Thursdays from 4 to 7 p.m. If there is demand, more days may be added.

Under the aegis of county's Agriculture Advisory Committee assisted by the Office of Economic and Agricultural Development (OEAD), the market will serve two purposes, according to Jim Giegerich, director of the office: "It will bring fresh, quality produce directly from the farm to the consumer and at the same time stimulate more business for the county's agricultural industry and for downtown Silver Spring," he said.

The market will be located in the open black-topped area east of the Armory with sellers providing what they need themselves.

A nonprofit corporation is being formed under the guidance of the Agricultural Advisory Committee to handle the management of the market. The committee was appointed by County Executive James P. Gleason several years ago to serve as a liaison between the agricultural and rural community and the County government.

The committee will handle licensing, provide liability insurance, assure product quality, and set a fee schedule for sellers that will make the operation self-sustaining.

Mini-contracts with sellers will assure that the market operations conform with County park and health regulations. A contracted supervisor will provide on-site management and supervision.

The Maryland-National Capital Park and Planning Commission unanimously approved use of its Armory site for the market. Planning Board Chairman Royce Hanson, said "that the board was delighted to provide a place in Silver Spring for this kind of activity. Not only will it be a service to local producers and consumers, but it will help give downtown Silver Spring a lively, exciting atmosphere."

Montgomery and Prince George's county farmers and gardeners who would like to sell their tomatoes, sweet corn, egg plant, cut flowers and other produce at the new farmers market, can apply for a stand with, and obtain further information from Mr. Rene Johnson, county office building, 279-1462.

4-H and Future Farmers of America will have demonstrations at the market.

Anyone with questions about the market should call Rene Johnson at 279-1462.

This article is reprinted from "County Goes Into Vegetable Business," **Montgomery Journal**, Montgomery, Alabama, July 7, 1977.

EXAMPLE 6

Direct Marketing

Can an unsophisticated farm roadside market fabricated from snow fence, steel pipe and a roll of canvas prosper in our sophisticated world?

You betcha.

For proof, travel to Stroudsburg, countyseat of Monroe County, and then meander in a northeasterly direction up Route 209, past 20 miles of signs extolling the amenities of the Poconos, until you are in the Dingman's Ferry section of Pike County.

You'll know when you arrive at the Joshua Heller Farm Market because it is the apotheosis of what you don't expect a prosperous roadside farm market to resemble.

It has a dirt floor. It has no coolers, no fancy bins, no bake-off center for pies and bread, no fluorescent lighting. But it does have air conditioning, the kind that allows breezes to sift through snow fence walls to make hot and sticky August afternoons bearable.

This unassuming little market does a brisk business for many reasons including these: it's located along a well-traveled highway; the area is getting built up; the produce is always fresh and top quality at this genuine farm market.

"We believe our fresh sweet corn is our chief drawing card and we do our utmost to furnish the best sweet corn possible," said Mrs. Joshua Heller who manages the market located on the Heller farm.

Here's an example of Heller Market fastidiousness: when September arrives and corn begins to get wormy, every ear is checked before it is offered for sale. If it has a wormy end, the end is sliced off. "People never complain about this," Mrs. Heller said. "I guess they realize we're fussy people who know a worm can be very repugnant."

Customers can be capricious, Mrs. Heller said. She tells the story of a customer who pulled the husk on an ear of corn and then proceeded to test the corn by taking a bite. "He even had the nerve to put the ear back in the pile of corn," Mrs. Heller said laughingly.

She's a believer in educating customers about the taste and quality of produce. She advocates informing people that tomatoes can't be good tasting and still be firm as a bullet.

The Hellers embarked in the selling-at-roadside business when they had an abundance of sweet corn. They put the corn in a wagon along the highway and persuaded their children to sell it.

The venture went so well that the Hellers decided to plant a lot more corn the next year along with a variety of vegetables. They sold from the wagon for three years before building their present market.

They have also ventured into pick-your-own with strawberries, tomatoes, beans and early peas. Lima beans have been a good P-Y-O crop because so few home gardeners grow this bean. Potatoes have also done well. The Hellers dig potatoes which are picked up by customers as fast as they can be dug.

Everything except such items as cucumbers and zucchini are sold by the quart, basket, bushel etc. However, the Hellers are considering selling P-Y-O strawberries by the pound rather than the quart to avoid the hostility that is sometimes created when a customer with an overfilled container is reminded she has two quarts of berries in a one-quart box.

As for pricing, the Hellers keep theirs in line with prices charged by other markets. When corn first comes in, they charge $1.45 a dozen. Their rock bottom corn price is $1.25.

"We can ask more because our corn is the best," Mrs. Heller said. "It's picked fresh each day. What's left at day's end is fed to our feeder steers."

This article is reprinted from **Direct Marketing**, Department of Agriculture, Marketing Services Division, 2301 N. Cameron Street, Harrisburg, Pennsylvania 17120, December 1977.

Heller's Farm Roadside Market

When You can Buy Fresh Pennsylvania Fruits and Vegetables

EXAMPLE

7

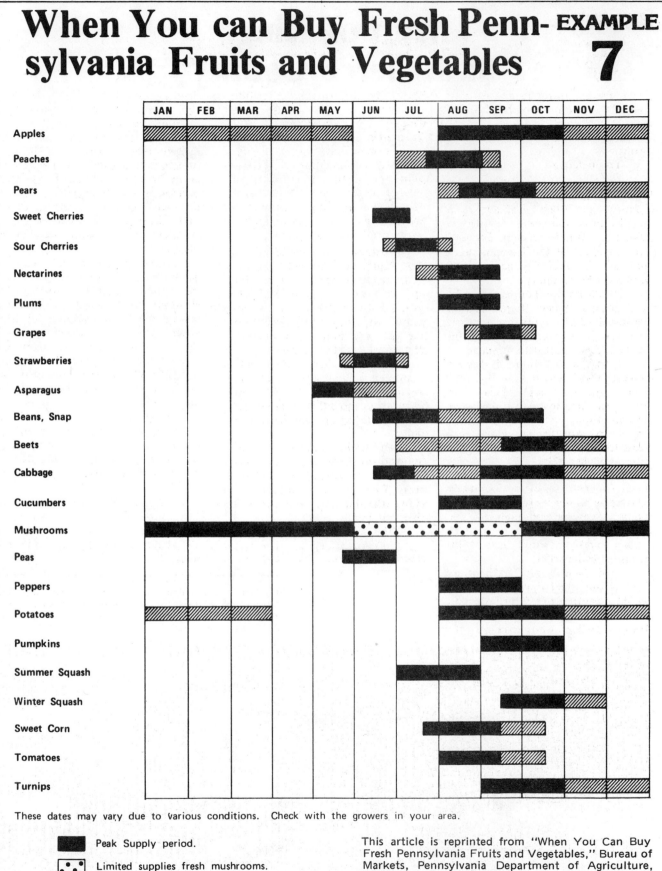

	JAN	FEB	MAR	APR	MAY	JUN	JUL	AUG	SEP	OCT	NOV	DEC
Apples												
Peaches												
Pears												
Sweet Cherries												
Sour Cherries												
Nectarines												
Plums												
Grapes												
Strawberries												
Asparagus												
Beans, Snap												
Beets												
Cabbage												
Cucumbers												
Mushrooms												
Peas												
Peppers												
Potatoes												
Pumpkins												
Summer Squash												
Winter Squash												
Sweet Corn												
Tomatoes												
Turnips												

These dates may vary due to various conditions. Check with the growers in your area.

▰ Peak Supply period.

⁛ Limited supplies fresh mushrooms.

▨ Early harvest or available from storage.

This article is reprinted from "When You Can Buy Fresh Pennsylvania Fruits and Vegetables," Bureau of Markets, Pennsylvania Department of Agriculture, 2301 Cameron Street, Harrisburg, Pennsylvania 17120, November 16, 1976.

EXAMPLE 8

Map of King and Pierce County

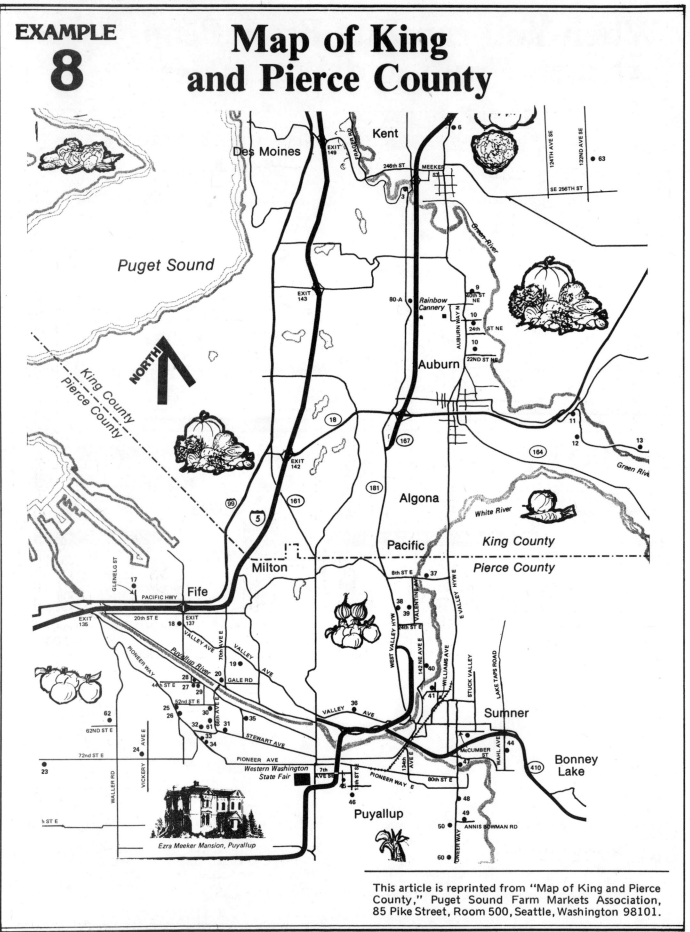

Ezra Meeker Mansion, Puyallup

This article is reprinted from "Map of King and Pierce County," Puget Sound Farm Markets Association, 85 Pike Street, Room 500, Seattle, Washington 98101.

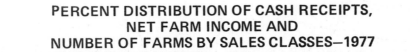

PERCENT DISTRIBUTION OF CASH RECEIPTS, NET FARM INCOME AND NUMBER OF FARMS BY SALES CLASSES—1977

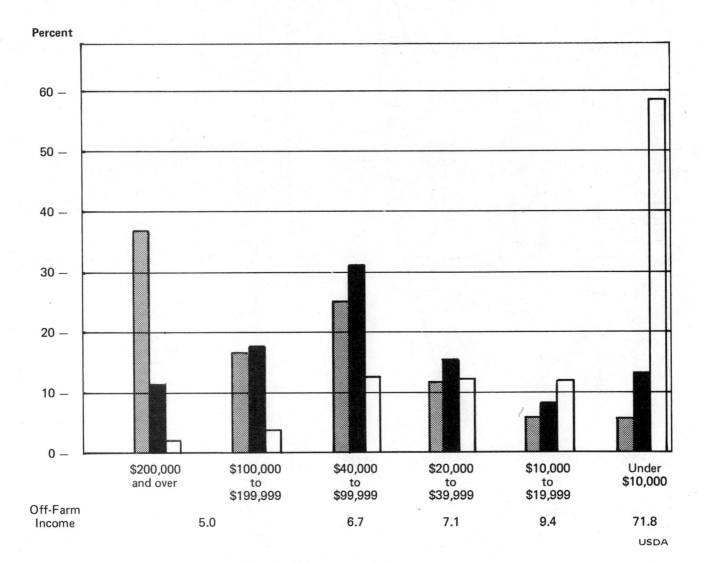

	$200,000 and over	$100,000 to $199,999	$40,000 to $99,999	$20,000 to $39,999	$10,000 to $19,999	Under $10,000
Off-Farm Income		5.0	6.7	7.1	9.4	71.8

USDA

KEY

Cash Receipts

Net Farm Income[1]

Number of Farms

[1]Before adjustment for changes in commodity inventories. Data from Farm Income Statistics, July 1978 (ESCS).

Chapter 3

Stopping Corporate and Absentee Control of Farm Land

The continuing decline in the number of farms nationally and the rising number of corporations, absentee and foreign interests involved in agriculture has alarmed farm organizations and farm communities. Farmers in the Great Plains and Midwest have been particulary worried about this problem. These farmers fear that the California agricultural economy—in which corporations grow, process, transport and market most farm produce—will sweep relentlessly eastward.

The farmers' anxiety has made them politically active. They understand the substantial advantages that corporate farms enjoy. The corporation's legal status allows it to pool capital, enjoy legal liability, have an unlimited life, avoid inheritance taxes, make use of unlimited financial flexibility, take advantage of economies of scale, and perhaps most importantly, reap the financial benefits of favorable treatment by federal tax policies. In addition, the substantial financial resources of most corporations will permit them to accept a long pay back period on their investment or a very low rate return. The family farm would go bankrupt under the same conditions.

Corporate farming may be more profitable, but farmers, concerned citizens and public officials know that they have a disastrous effect on farm communities and rural economies. A classic study of two California communities—one dominated by large corporate farms and the other by small family-owned farms, demonstrated that the family farm community had a higher educational level, a higher standard of living, stronger social organization and stability, and a more varied and heterogeneous community. Farm organizations also point out that agribusiness leads to monopolistic control of both agricultural supplies (inputs) and markets, and thus increases food prices for consumers.

STATE ANTI-CORPORATE FARM ACTS

The growing trend of corporations moving into both agricultural production and distribution has caused many state legislatures to act. Eight states in the Upper Midwest or the Great Plains have enacted or strengthened anti-corporate farming laws in the years since 1971. The states whose legislatures have acted are Iowa, Kansas, Minnesota, Missouri, North Dakota, Oklahoma, South Dakota, and Wisconsin. Four other states (Texas, Nebraska, West Virginia and New York) have mild restrictions on corporate farming through general corporate reporting laws. In addition, farmers in the state of Oregon decided to take the citizens' initiative route to prohibit corporations from farming or owning farmland. The initiative, first proposed in 1975, did not get sufficient signatures to get on the ballot last year, but an active campaign is underway to put it on the ballot in 1978.

State anti-corporate farming statutes vary widely in scope and purpose. The range extends from laws requiring only disclosure of corporate ownership to outright prohibitions including stiff fines of $50,000 for each violation. An example of a weak bill is that of Nebraska. Nebraska farmers and their allies were unable to muster all the support they needed for strong legislation, and had to settle for the *Nebraska Farm Corporation Reporting Act of 1975*. The statute requires only that corporations report their land holdings to the Secretary of State.

Even the weak disclosure laws have been somewhat helpful in the movement to stop corporate farming. The Nebraska statute, for instance, revealed that corporate farming was much more extensive than had been believed. Under the Nebraska Reporting Act, 2,209 corporations filed reports on their land holdings, far more than the 659 that the U.S. Bureau of Census said owned land in Nebraska. The Iowa reporting law pointed out the same pattern. The U.S. Census indicated that there were only 621 corporate farms in that state, but the Iowa law unearthed 2,923. The revelation that corporate farms are more widespread than had been previously assumed is providing ammunition for farm organizations attempting to prohibit corporate farming by statute. An excellent summary of the important revelations of corporate farm ownership caused by reporting laws such as Nebraska's is found in **Example 9, Corporate Farm Invasion Far Exceeds Official Statistics**, by Roger Blobaum, from the January 1977 *NFO Reporter*.

A number of states have laws considerably stronger than Nebraska's. Farm organizations in Kansas for instance won passage of the *Kansas Corporate Farming Law of 1973*. It prohibits corporations with more than 10 stockholders from owning farmland, but allows farmland ownership by certain types of small family owned corporations. The strongest anti-corporate farming law is the *North Dakota Corporate Farming Law* which was originally passed by a state-wide citizen initiative in 1932. It categorically prohibits any corporation from owning agricultural land or operating farms. The law does allow cooperatives, however, to own and operate farms. State anti-corporate farming laws are well described and analyzed in *Corporate Farming and the Family Farm* published by the Council of State Governments. A section of that report: **Example 10, Brief Digest of State Laws on Corporate Farms**, follows at the end of this narrative.

STATES ACT TO CONTROL FOREIGN INVESTMENT IN FARMLAND

The decline of the dollar's value internationally, the sudden wealth of the Arab oil nations, and the rapidly rising value of U.S. farmland have all contributed to increasing foreign investment in American farms. As could be expected, farm organizations are extremely concerned about this trend and are moving to put a stop to foreign ownership of agricultural land. The growing foreign interest in U.S. farmland is described briefly in **Example 11, Foreign Speculation on American Farms**, by Jack Anderson, and in more detail in a March 27, 1978 article in *Business Week:* **Example 12, Foreign Investors Flock to U.S. Farmlands.**

State legislatures have been the primary vehicle used to control growing foreign investment in American farmland. The Minnesota Legislature received in 1977 the proposed *Alien Ownership Act* to prohibit both foreign individual and corporate ownership of Minnesota farmland. A similar *Kansas Alien Ownership Act of 1978* was introduced into that state's legislature. When the state's Attorney General raised questions about the bills' constitutionality, its sponsors immediately introduced another bill to hold a popular referendum amending the Kansas Constitution to make clear the state legislature's ability to take action on foreign ownership of land.

One of the biggest problems facing farm organizations is the difficulty of getting accurate statistics on the extent of foreign ownership of U.S. farmland. The U.S. Comptroller General in *Foreign Ownership of U.S. Farmland: Much Concern, Little Data* has described the state's lack of accurate and current information on foreign ownership, with recommendations for new means to get accurate information. Selections from this report are included as **Example 13, Limited Impact of State Laws on Foreign Investment in U.S. Farmland.**

THE PROGRESSIVE PROPERTY TAX

Farmers and their organizations are also looking at the concept of "progressive" or "graduated" property taxes as a means to control increasing concentration of farmland ownership. Minnesota and North Dakota are the states most actively considering that alternative. In *The Progressive Land Tax: A Tax Incentive for the Family Farm*, Byron Dorgan, the North Dakota State Tax Commissioner, outlines how a progressive property tax penalizes large landowners and corporate farmers. Under the North Dakota and Minnesota proposals, landowners which own over a certain acreage of land must pay a higher property tax rate than smaller landholders and family farmers.

The Washington State Grange is going after corporate and large scale agriculture in a different manner. They have sponsored a state-wide popular initiative called the *Washington Family Farm Water Act* which would give family farmers of a certain size the first right to publicly subsidized irrigation. Since irrigation is so important in certain sections of Washington, this initiative, if passed, would curb the growth of corporate agriculture in major areas of Washington.

CANADA: MODEL LEGISLATION

Several of the American farm organizations have used the legislation and proposals developed by the New Democratic Party in Canada's Western provinces as models for the legislation they have introduced. The Canadian provinces have taken dramatic steps to prohibit corporate and foreign ownership of their land. In some cases they have even tried to stop land ownership by Canadians who don't live in that particular province.

In 1977, for instance, the province of Manitoba passed the *Manitoba Farm Lands Protection Act*. This Act prohibits corporations and foreigners from owning more than 160 acres of land in Manitoba. It further prohibits Canadians who are not farmers from owning more than 640 acres of agricultural land. The Manitoba Provincial Assembly was responding to the fact that more than 1.5 million acres of its land—about 8% of the total—was owned and controlled by absentee owners.

The Manitoba bill was based in part on *The Saskatchewan Farm Ownership Act of 1974*. This law prohibits non-residents from owning land assessed at more than $15,000 by the local municipality. Saskatchewan also hit the corporate farmers hard by requiring that corporations must, within 20 years, dispose of any land over 160 acres that they own.

The Province of Alberta has proposed the *Agricultural and Recreational Land Ownership Act* which would prohibit non-Canadians from buying more than 20 acres of agricultural land in the province, but at the same time the Alberta Provincial government would be allowed to grant broad exemptions to foreign individuals and corporations. The Province of Ontario has taken a different slant. *The Ontario Land Transfer Tax Act of 1978* creates a progressive land transfer tax on sales to non-residents of commercial, industrial, and residential land. On agricultural land, the tax rate is 20% of the total amount of the purchase.

Resources

ORGANIZATIONS

Agribusiness Accountability Publications

c/o Earthworks
3410 19th Street
San Francisco, California 94110
(415) 626-1266

Interfaith Center on Corporate Responsibility

475 Riverside Drive, Room 566
New York, New York 10027
(212) 870-2316

Iowa Department of Justice

Farm Division
Hoover State Office Building
Des Moines, Iowa 50319
(515) 281-6634
Neil Hamilton

National Farmers Organization

475 L'Enfant Plaza, S.W.
Washington, D.C. 20024
(202) 484-7075
Ann Bornstein, Legislative Assistant

National Farmers Union

1012 14th Street, N.W.
Washington, D.C. 20005
(202) 628-9774
Robert J. Mullins

National Land for People

2348 North Cornelia
Fresno, California 93711
(209) 233-4727
George Ballis, Director

BIBLIOGRAPHY

The Agbiz Tiller. A.V. Krebs, Editor, Agribusiness Accountability Publications, 3410 19th Street, San Francisco, California 94110. Newsletter. $12/year for individuals and public interest groups; $30/year for institutions.

Barnes, Peter, editor, **The Peoples Land: A Reader on Land Reform in the United States.** Rodale Press, Emmaus, Pennsylvania 18049. 1975.

Barnes, Peter and Larry Casalino, **Who Owns the Land.** National Land for People, 2348 North Cornelia, Fresno, California 93711. $.75.

Catholic Rural Life. Vol. 26, National Catholic Rural Life Conference, 4625 N.W. Beaver Drive, Des Moines, Iowa 50322. July/August 1977. $.50. Entire issue on concentrating land ownership and the Ag-Land Fund Hearings in Congress.

Center for Rural Affairs (CRA), **Land Tenure Research Guide.** CRA, P.O. Box 405, Walthill, Nebraska 68067. Outline of techniques necessary to determine land tenure patterns.

Comptroller General of the United States, **Foreign Ownership of United States Farmland- Much Concern, Little Data.** #CED-78-132, General Accounting Office, Room 1518, 441 G Street, N.W., Washington, D.C. 20548. June 12, 1978.

Cook, Virginia, **Corporate Farming and the Family Farm.** Council of State Governments, P.O. Box 11910, Iron Works Pike, Lexington, Kentucky 40511. 1976. $1.50.

Interfaith Center on Corporate Responsibility (ICCR), **Manual on Agribusiness Corporations.** ICCR, 475 Riverside Drive, Room 566, New York, New York 10027. 1978. $5.00.

Krebs, Al, **Directory of Major Food Corporations.** Earthwork, 3410 19th Street, San Francisco, California 94110. $3.50.

Morrison, Fred, "State Corporate Farm Legislation," **Toledo Law Review.** Spring 1976.

Morrison, Fred and Kenneth Krause, "The Myth of the All-American Farm," **The Farm Index.** Vol. XIV, No. 5, USDA, Washington, D.C. 20250. May 1975. Review of trends in foreign purchases of U.S. farmland, and recent Federal and state efforts to restrict such ownership.

Perelman, Michael, **Farming for Profit in a Hungry World.** Allanheld, Oseum & Company, 19 Brunswick Road, Montclair, New York 07042. 1978.

Raup, Philip, **Corporate Farming in the United States.** An Unpublished Paper, Department of Agricultural Economics, University of Minnesota. December 1972.

Ray, Victor, **The Corporate Invasion of American Agriculture.** National Farmers Union, 12125 East 45th Avenue, Denver, Colorado 80239. 1968.

Rodefeld, Richard and Kevin Goss, **Corporate Farming in the United States: A Guide to Current Literature.** Department of Agricultural Economics and Rural Sociology, Pennsylvania State University, University Park, Pennsylvania 16802. 1977.

United Presbyterian Church of the United States, **Who Will Farm.** 1244 Interchurch Center, 475 Riverside Drive, New York, New York 10027.

U.S. House of Representatives, Subcommittee on Family Farms and Rural Development, Special Study of the Committee on Agriculture, Hearings on **Obstacles to Strengthening Family Farm System.** 95th Congress, first session. Chairman, Committee on Agriculture, U.S. House of Representatives, Washington, D.C. 20515. September October 1977.

Corporate Farm Invasion Far Exceeds 'Official' Statistics

EXAMPLE 9

The number of farming corporations filing reports to comply with requirements of recently-enacted statutes in six agricultural states far exceeds the estimates quoted by opponents when the controversial laws were debated and passed.

This would appear to strengthen the political position of lawmakers who will be trying again this year to pass similar bills in states like Colorado and Montana where corporation farming is considered a serious and growing problem.

Annual reports filed and open to inspection at the six Midwest capitals now exceed 9,000 and there is strong evidence that a substantial number of corporations, including some big ones, are still ignoring state filing requirements.

States now requiring reports are South Dakota, Nebraska, Kansas, Missouri, Iowa and Minnesota. Several others, including Wisconsin and Oklahoma, recently enacted laws regulating corporate farming activity but do not require annual reports.

The large number of reports filed is more than three times the number of corporations reported for all six states in either the 1969 Census of Agriculture or the much-publicized study issued by the Department of Agriculture. This shows that either these reports were inadequate, as many critics contend, or that there has been tremendous growth in corporate farming activity in the 1970's.

Probably the greatest difference between the Census and USDA estimates and the actual number of corporations filing was in Iowa. It led the states with a first year total of 2,923 corporations, far more than the 621 counted by the Census Bureau, and slightly more than half are categorized as family farms that have incorporated.

Neil E. Harl, an Iowa State University economist, had told Iowa legislators in 1975 that he saw no evidence that non-farm corporations were moving into agricultural production in Iowa. A memorandum he submitted quoting the Census Bureau's count of 621 as a realistic corporation farming figure for Iowa was instrumental in getting a reporting bill substitued for a strong House-passed measure that would

have outlawed non-farm corporations in that state.

The 2,209 reports filed in Nebraska also disclosed much more corporate farming activity than federal reports had shown previously. The Census report for that state, widely quoted by opponents who helped get a reporting bill substituted for a measure containing corporate restrictions, showed only 659 corporations farming in Nebraska.

The Cedar-Knox Rural Action Group, a citizens group advocating tough restrictions on non-farm corporations, said the number of farming cor-

> *"Iowa led the states with a first year total of 2,923 corporation, far more than the 621 counted by the Census Bureau . . ."*

porations in the state appears to have increased by 335% in the last six years. This percentage was calculated by comparing the number of reports now on file at the Capitol in Lincoln with the number reported in the 1969 Census of Agriculture.

Reports on file in Nebraska show about 68% of those filing are family farmers and ranchers, about 31% are investor-owned operations controlled by Nebraskans, and about 2% are farming setups controlled by out-of-state interests.

A recent review of the names of corporations leasing state school lands for agricultural purposes turned up 39 corporations that had failed to file the required state reports.

"This only scratches the surface of non-reporting farm corporations within the state of Nebraska," Francis Wormann of Hartington, chairman of the Cedar-Knox citizens group, declared.

He obviously was right because at least 12 other companies that failed to file were identified in a Center for Rural Affairs survey of land ownership and control in nine Sandhill counties. Courthouse records showed that Omaha industrialist Peter Kiewit's investment

firm, the Kiewit Co., was among them. The records show the company has 43,000 acres in the nine Sandhill counties plus another 38,000 in neighboring Lincoln County.

(Editor's Note: After receiving wide press coverage on his failure to do so, Kiewit's lawyer filed a report showing the company owned over 83,000 acres of land in Lincoln, Logan, McPherson and Thomas counties, Nebraska. Peter Kiewit is is the principal owner and he lists himself as being involved in the day-to-day management of the farmland.)

In Missouri, preliminary reports show 1,382 corporations have filed, including 912 that apparently are family farms that have incorporated. The reports show several companies significantly expanded their holdings when it became apparent that the corporate farm bill would make it through the Legislature.

A total of 135 corporations acknowledge in their reports that they would be prohibited from starting up farming operations under the new Missouri law. These include financial institutions, land developers, drug companies, vending machine firms, florists, and medical groups.

Warren Woolever of the Missouri Department of Agriculture said that it is not known whether all the state's corporations have complied with the law. He also raised the possibility in a news interview that corporations could buy farmland in the future and simply not tell the state about it.

In Kansas, where state law since 1931 has attempted to slow corporate farming activity, a total of 1,037 reports were filed under the reporting law enacted in 1973. This compares with only 328 corporate farms counted in the 1969 Census of Agriculture.

A report prepared for the Kansas Legislative Research Department concluded that approximately 60% of the filings were made by family farmers and ranchers who had incorporated their operations.

This article is reprinted from Roger Blobaum, "Corporate Farm Invasion Far Exceeds 'Official' Statistics," NFO Reporter, January 1977.

EXAMPLE 10

Brief Digest of Salient Points of State Corporate Farm Laws

IOWA FARM REPORTING ACT, Section 3.7 of Iowa Code, Approved July 11, 1975.

Coverage: Family corporate farms, authorized corporate farms, limited partnerships, nonresident aliens owning or leasing agricultural land or engaged in farming, every person acting in a fiduciary capacity on behalf of any corporation, limited partnership or nonresident alien individual who holds farmland in State, any corporation identified as a beneficiary in a report filed with Secretary of State, any limited partnership and any nonresident alien identified as a beneficiary with the Secretary of State, any processor of beef or pork having certain specified interests or buying practices.

Definitions: Family farm corporation means one in which the majority of the voting stock is held by and the majority of stockholders are related to each other as spouse, parent, grandparent, lineal ascendants of grandparents or their spouses and other lineal descendants of the grandparent or their spouses, or persons acting in a fiduciary capacity for persons so related; all stockholders are natural persons or persons acting in a fiduciary capacity for the benefit of natural persons and 60 percent of the gross revenues of the corporation over the last consecutive three-year period came from farming. Authorized farm corporation means one other than a family farm corporation in which the stockholders do not exceed 25 in number and are natural persons or persons acting in a fiduciary capacity for the benefit of natural persons or nonprofit corporations. Processor means a person, firm, corporation, or limited partnership, which alone or with others, directly or indirectly controls the manufacturing, processing, or preparation for sale of beef or pork products having a total annual wholesale value of $10 million or more; any person, firm, corporation, or limited partnership with a 10 percent or greater interest in another person, firm, corporation, or limited partnership involved in the manufacturing, processing, or preparation for sale of beef or pork products having a total annual wholesale value of $10 million or more shall also be considered a processor. Farming means the cultivation of land for the production of agricultural crops; the raising of poultry; the production of eggs, milk, fruit, or other horticultural crops; and the grazing or production of livestock.

Exemptions: Eight kinds of land or corporate entities are exempt from the law.

Substantive provisions: No processor of beef or pork or limited partnership in which a processor holds partnership shares as a general partner or partnership shares as a limited partner shall own, control, or operate a feedlot in' Iowa in which hogs or cattle are fed for slaughter.

Administration: Secretary of State.

Reporting requirements: Extensive annual reporting on forms supplied by the Secretary of State is required of all corporations owning or leasing farmland in Iowa, limited partnerships, nonresident aliens, fiduciaries, and beneficiaries. Since Iowa is the only State applying its law to limited partnership, the reporting requirements for this type of agricultural structure may be worth noting.

For the most part the information required of limited partnership is quite similar to that required of other agricultural structures except for items given below: (a) the term for which partnership is to exist; (b) the approximate number and kind of poultry or livestock owned, contracted for, fed, or kept during the preceding year; (c) if a livestock or crop-share lease, the limited partnership shall disclose the share of the livestock or the crop to which the limited partnership is entitled under the lease; (d) the amount of cash and a description of and the agreed value of the other property contributed by each limited partner; (e) the share of the profits or the other income which each limited partner shall receive by reason of his contribution; (f) the amount of cash and a description of and the agreed value of the other property contributed by each limited partner during the preceding year.

Processors of beef or pork must file a report with the Secretary of State showing, for the preceding year, the number of hogs and cattle owned and fed more than 30 days, the total number of hogs and the total number of cattle slaughtered in Iowa by the processor, and the total number of hogs and the total number of cattle slaughtered by the processor.

Moratorium for extension of holdings: For one year no corporation other than a family farm corporation or an authorized farm corporation shall acquire or lease any additional land in the State. Certain farmlands and a municipal corporation are exempt from the moratorium.

Divestiture: Processor or limited partnership which owns, controls, or operates a feedlot on effective date of act shall have until July 1, 1985, to dispose of the property.

Injunction permitted: Attorney General or county attorney may institute suits to prevent or restrain violations.

Penalties: Conviction of violation of substantive provisions by processors of beef or pork subject to act may be fined not more than $50,000; willful failure to file a required report or willful filing of false information is a public offense punishable upon conviction by a fine of not more than $1,000.

Special provisions: The county assessor is required to file with the Secretary of State, annually, the name and address of every corporation, nonresident alien, trust, or other business entity owning agricultural land in county as shown by the county assessment rolls; the county recorder shall forward to the Secretary of State annually the name and address of each limited partnership owning agricultural land or engaged in farming as shown by county records. The Secretary of State shall request additional information from those covered by act if needed to administer the act.

KANSAS CORPORATE FARMING LAW, Chapter 99, 1973 Session Laws of Kansas.

Coverage: No corporation shall directly or indirectly engage in the agricultural or horticultural business of producing, planting, raising, harvesting, or gathering of wheat, corn, grain, sorghums, barley, oats, rye, or potatoes, or the milking of cows for dairy purposes unless it has 10 or fewer stockholders who are natural persons or corporate trustees, or are guardians, conservators, executors, or administrators of individuals.

Definitions: Incorporators shall live in Kansas and be natural persons and own no stock in another farm corporation.

Exemptions: A tract of land less than 10 acres, contiguous tracts of land which in the aggregate are less than 10 acres, and state-assessed railroad operating property are not deemed land used or usable for farming or agricultural or horticultural purposes and are exempt from reporting requirements of the law.

Administrator: Secretary of State.

Reporting requirements: Name and location of the principal office of the corporation; the name, post office, and residence address of the corporation's officers and board of directors; the amount and par value of each class of authorized stock; the amount of capital stock issued and paid up; a complete and detailed statement of the assets, liabilities, and net worth of the corporation; the names and addresses of stockholders owning at least 5 percent of the stock and the number of shares held by each; the value of the nonagricultural and agricultural assets, stated separately, owned and controlled by the corporation within and outside of Kansas and where located; total number of stockholders. Every foreign corporation organized for profit or under the cooperative type statutes of the State, territory or foreign country of incorporation must file an annual report similar to that required of domestic farm corporations. Nonprofit corporations shall report as well as foreign corporations organized for profit or organized under the cooperative type statutes of the State.

Divestiture: No provisions.

Injunction: No provisions.

Penalties: Any person who fails to file required reports or who files false or misleading information shall be guilty of a class A misdemeanor. The law does not provide penalties for domestic farm corporations which own more than 5,000 acres or for farming any of the restricted crops.

Special provisions: A domestic farm corporation shall pay an annual franchise tax equal to $1 for each $1,000 of the corporation's equity attributable to Kansas; the tax shall not be less than $20 or more than $2,500.

MINNESOTA FAMILY FARM ACT, S.F. No. 1026, Chapter No. 324, 1975.

Coverage: Family farm corporation and authorized farm corporation.

Definitions: Family farm corporation means one in which the majority of the voting stock is held by, and the majority of stockholders are persons or the spouses of persons related to each other within the third degree of kindred; none of the stockholders are corporations; at least one of the related persons resides on or actively operates the farm. Any devise or bequest of shares of voting stock does not disqualify the organization as a family farm corporation. An authorized farm corporation means one with no more than five shareholders all of whom are natural persons; it has only one class of shares; its revenues from rent, royalties, dividends, interest, and annuities must not exceed 20 percent of its gross receipts; a majority of shareholders must reside on the farm or actively engage in farming.

Exemptions: Fourteen categories of agricultural lands or corporate entities are exempt from the law.

Administrator: Commissioner of Agriculture.

Reporting requirements: Extensive and detailed information is required to be filed annually showing use of land; corporate information concerning board of directors, officers, and shareholders; statement of percentage of gross receipts of the corporation derived from rent, royalties, dividends, interest, and annuities. No corporation shall commence farming in the State until the Commissioner of Agriculture has inspected the report and certified that the corporation's proposed operations comply with the law.

Grandfather clause: A corporation owning or leasing farmland on the effective date of the act can in any five-year period expand at a rate not to exceed 20 percent of the acreage owned on May 20, 1973.

Divestiture: If the Attorney General believes that a corporation is engaged in farming in violation of this act, he shall commence an action and shall file notice of pendency of such action with the register of deeds or the register of titles of the appropriate county. If the court finds that lands are held in violation of law, it shall enter an order to this effect. The corporation owning such land shall have five years to divest itself of such land; should land not be divested by required date, the court shall order the land sold at public sale in the manner prescribed for mortgage foreclosure.

Injunction permitted: Any prospective or threatened violation may be enjoined at the initiative of the Attorney General.

Penalties: Failure to file a required report or willful filing of false information shall constitute a gross misdemeanor.

MISSOURI CORPORATE FARM ACT, House Bill 655, Approved July 30, 1975.

Coverage: Family farm corporation, authorized farm corporation, and farm cooperatives (latter subject to reporting requirements).

Definitions: Family farm corporation means one in which at least one half of the voting stock is held by and at least one half of the stockholders are members of a family related within the third degree of kinship including the spouses, sons-in-law, and daughters-in-law; at least one of

the stockholders is a person residing on or actively operating the farm. None of the stockholders shall be a corporation. Authorized farm corporation means that all shareholders, other than any estate or revokable and irrevokable trust, are natural persons; two thirds or more of its total net income must be received from farming.

Exemptions: The law exempts a broad category of farmlands used for various purposes; it exempts land acquired for potential nonfarming purposes and other land controlled through ownership, options, leaseholds, or other agreements entered into with the federal government pursuant to the New Community Act of 1968.

Administrator: Director of the State Department of Agriculture.

Reporting requirements: The usual information is required to be filed annually by family farm corporations and authorized farm corporations.

Grandfather clause: The law permits corporate farms already in existence to expand at a rate of not more than 20 percent in any five years.

Divestiture: The Attorney General must institute an action in the Circuit Court of Cole County, if a foreign corporation, and if a domestic corporation in the circuit court of the appropriate county or counties and shall file a notice of pendency of the action with the county recorder of deeds. The corporation shall comply with the court's order or have two years from the date of the order to divest itself of the land. Lands not divested within the specified time shall be ordered sold by the court in the manner prescribed for mortgage foreclosure.

Penalties: Failure to file or to file falsely is punishable by a fine of not less than $500 or more than $1,000.

NEBRASKA FARM CORPORATION REPORTING ACT, Section Numbers 76-1501-76-1506, 1975 Supplement to the Statutes.

Coverage: Each corporation which has acquired title to agricultural land or which has obtained any leasehold interest or any other greater interest less than fee in any agricultural land in the State.

Definitions: Agricultural land means land used for the production of agricultural crops or fruit or other horticultural products; or for the raising or feeding of animals for the production of livestock or livestock products, poultry or poultry products, or milk or dairy products.

Exemptions: Land owned or leased for farming or capable of being used for farming when such land is within the boundaries of any railroad or utility operating right-of-way.

Administrator: Secretary of State.

Reporting requirements: Name and address of registered office of corporation and its registered agent in the State, and if foreign corporation, address of its principal office in its place of incorporation; total acreage and location listed by county of all lots and parcels of land owned or leased by corporation in growing of crops or keeping and feeding of poultry or livestock; names and addresses of officers and members of board of directors and of all shareholders owning 10 percent or more of corporation's stock; percentage of members of board of directors who are alien; name and address of each alien owning 10 percent or more of its stock; names and addresses of executive officers and managers who are aliens; name and address of each person living on a farm or actively engaged in farming and owning 10 percent or more of its voting stock; any other information which the Secretary of State reasonably determines necessary to enforce provisions regulating aliens who own real property in State.

Grandfather clause: No.

Divestiture: No.

Injunction permitted: No.

Penalties: Each corporation which fails to submit a report required by act or which willfully submits false, fraudulent, or misleading information on any report shall be guilty of a misdemeanor and upon conviction thereof be punished by a fine of not more than $1,000.

NORTH DAKOTA CORPORATE FARMING LAW, Initiative, 1932, Chapter 10-06.

Coverage: Farming by domestic and foreign corporations is prohibited; land held by domestic and foreign corporations in 1932 must be disposed of by July 29, 1942. Any domestic or foreign corporation acquiring rural real estate used or usable for farming after July 29, 1932, shall dispose of such real estate, except such as is reasonably necessary in the conduct of its business, within 10 years after acquisition.

Definition: No definition of family farm corporation or authorized farm corporation.

Exemptions: Cooperative corporations, 75 percent of whose members or stockholders are farmers residing on farms or depending principally on farming for their livelihood; any domestic or foreign corporation may take and acquire title to real estate by deed or other conveyance which is taken or given in exchange for lands acquired prior to March 7, 1935, or in partial or full satisfaction of any mortgage, lien, or other encumbrance.

Administrator: Secretary of State.

Reporting requirements: None.

Grandfather clause: Possession of land held prior to law or acquired after adoption of law must be disposed of within 10 years after acquisition.

Divestiture: Title to real estate held by domestic or foreign corporation in violation of law shall escheat to the county in which real estate is located upon an action instituted by the State's attorney in the county; county shall dispose of such land within one year at public auction to highest bidder. After payment of expenses for escheat and sale, any proceeds shall be paid to corporation formerly owning the real estate.

OKLAHOMA CORPORATE FARM ACT, Article 22, Oklahoma Constitution as amended in 1954 and Oklahoma Session Laws, Chapter 310, Title 18, Section 951, Laws of 1971.

Coverage: Article 22, Section 1, of the Oklahoma constitution of 1907 provided that no alien or person who is not a citizen of the United States shall acquire title to or own land in this State, and the Legislature shall enact laws whereby all persons not citizens of the U.S., and their heirs, who may hereafter acquire real estate in this State by devise, descent, or otherwise, shall dispose of the same within five years upon condition of escheat or forfeiture to the State; the section does not apply to aliens or persons not citizens of the U.S. who may become bona fide residents of the state nor to lands now owned by aliens in this State. A 1954 amendment to Article 22 provided that no corporation shall be created or licensed in the State for the purpose of buying, acquiring, trading, or dealing in real estate other than real estate located in incorporated cities and towns and as additions thereto (see discussion under Constitutionality of Corporate Farm Laws in this *Research Brief*). The Oklahoma Business Corporation Act of 1971 permits foreign and domestic corporations to engage in farming or ranching provided: there shall be no shareholders other than natural persons, estates, trustees of trusts for the benefit of natural persons, if such trustees are either natural persons, banks, or trust companies; not more than 20 percent of the corporation's annual gross receipts shall be from any source other than farming or ranching or both, or allowing others to extract from the corporate lands any minerals underlying the same; there shall not be more than 10 shareholders unless those in excess of 10 are related to lineal descendants or are or have been related by marriage to lineal descendants or persons related to lineal descendants by adoption or any combination of same.

Definitions: See above.

Exemptions: See above. Licenses—licenses issued to foreign or domestic corporations to engage in farming or ranching under Business Corporation Act shall be revoked within five years unless licensee meets specified requirements; licenses issued to foreign corporations under the same act after July 1, 1971, shall be revoked within five years.

Administrator: Secretary of State.

Reporting requirements: Not specified for farm or ranch corporations.

Grandfather clause: Land held legally on or before July 1, 1971, or meeting specified standards under Business Corporation Act is exempt.

Divestiture: Not provided for except in an escheat action provided for in an authorizing statute.

Injunction: No provision.

Penalties: No provision.

SOUTH DAKOTA FAMILY FARM ACT OF 1974, Chapter 47-9, A of SL 1974.

Coverage: Family farm corporations and authorized farm corporations.

Definitions: Family farm corporation is one in which the majority of the voting stock is held by the majority of the stockholders who are members of a family related to each other within the third degree of kindred and at least one of whose stockholders is a person residing on or actively operating the farm and none of whose stockholders are corporations; any devise or bequest of shares of voting stock will not disqualify a family farm corporation. Authorized farm corporation is one with not more than 10 shareholders, whose shareholders are natural persons; whose shares are all of one class; and whose revenues from rent, royalties, dividends, interest, and annuities do not exceed 20 percent of its gross receipts.

Exemptions: Similar to those in the Minnesota Act.

Administrator: Secretary of State.

Reporting requirements: Every corporation engaged in farming or proposing to commence farming shall file annually with the Secretary of State the name, address, and place of incorporation; address of registered office of corporation; its registered agent and, in case of a foreign corporation, the address of its principal place of incorporation; acreage, location by section, township and county of each lot or parcel of land in State owned or leased by the corporation for growing of crops or keeping or feeding of poultry or livestock; names and addresses of officers and members of board of directors; additional information concerning number of shares, names of shareholders and number of shares held, and percentage of gross receipts of corporation derived from rent, royalties, dividends, interest, and annuities are required of a family farm corporation or authorized farm corporation.

Grandfather clause: Similar to that in Minnesota Act except as of July 1, 1974.

Divestiture: Attorney General shall file any order or divestiture with county register of deeds; corporation shall have five years for divestiture; land not divested within prescribed time shall be sold at public sale.

Penalties: Failure to file or willfully filing of false information is a misdemeanor punishable by a fine not in excess of $1,000. Attorney General may bring suit in circuit court of county where agricultural lands are situated if he has reason to believe that a corporation is violating the law.

WISCONSIN CORPORATE FARM LAW, Chapter 238, Laws of 1973; published June 4, 1974.

Coverage: Specified farm corporations.

Definitions: Corporation owning land or carrying on farming operations exempt from law if it has no more than 15 shareholders; lineal ancestors and descendants and aunts, uncles, and first cousins thereof, count collectively as one shareholder, but this collective authorization shall not be used for more than one family in a single corporation; corporation does not have more than two classes of shares; and all of its shareholders, other than any estate, are natural persons.

Exemptions: A corporation may own farmland if the land is acquired by bequest or devise or is acquired in regular course of business in partial or full satisfaction of any mortgage, lien, or other encumbrance held or owned by such corporation, provided the land is sold or otherwise transferred within five years after acquisition and provided such sale or transfer can be made at fair market value; a small investment corporation, or a corporation acting as personal representative or trustee or in any similar fiduciary capacity where the settlor and all beneficiaries are natural persons or charities; land acquired by a corporation to meet pollution control standards; farms engaged in research or breeding operations or production of crop for seed; several other exemptions are permitted.

Reporting requirements: None.

Grandfather clause: Land owned by corporation on effective date of act is exempt.

Prohibited activities: Production of dairy products not including the processing of such dairy products; production of cattle, hogs, and sheep; production of wheat, field corn, barley, oats, rye, hay, pasture, soy beans, millet, and sorghum.

Divestiture: No.

Injunction: Yes.

Penalties: Any corporation violating law or any injunction or order issued thereunder shall forfeit not more than $1,000 for each violation and each day of violation shall constitute a separate offense; district attorney of county in which it appears that a violation has occurred shall bring action for injunction. The court may permit normal farming operations when necessary to prevent loss or damage. An action seeking to require corporation to divest itself of such land within a reasonable time may also be sought.

This article is reprinted from "Brief Digest of Salient Points of State Corporate Farm Laws," *Corporate Farming and the Family Farm*, CSG Research Brief, pp. 16-19.

EXAMPLE 11

Foreign Speculation on American Farms

In past weeks, militant farmers have been swarming like agitated hornets. They have stopped traffic with their tractors, turned goats loose on Capitol Hill, besieged the Agriculture Department and pelted Secretary Bob Bergland with rotten eggs.

Their main gripe is that they aren't getting high enough prices for their crops to make a living. But they have also complained to us of another threat to their livelihood, which has gone largely unnoticed.

Foreign profiteers, the farmers have told us, are buying up American farmland with devalued dollars. Arab, Dutch, German and Italian millionaires have already acquired vast domains all across America and are actively searching for more acreage.

Our own investigation of the farmers' charges indicates a sharp increase in foreign farm purchases. Many acquisitions have been made, we discovered, by dummy corporations set up in the Netherlands Antilles, which are known throughout Europe as a tax haven for siphoning off business profits and unreported income. Dummy corporations are easily set up there. Operating from these palmy, Caribbean outposts, foreign investors are buying land from economically beset American farmers—land their forebears tilled for generations.

In Utah, for example, a combine of Dutch clients has purchased 6,000 acres of prime farmland. This deal was made, however, through California rather than the Caribbean. Local realtors told our reporter Hal Bernton that many Utah farmers are forced to sell because they are unable to keep up their loan payments and are hard up for operating capital.

A spokesman at Mountain Valley Realty of Logan, Utah, told us the same Dutch investors are shopping for another 4,000 acres in the state. They plan to lease the land back to its original owners for another 15 years. In other words, they are more interested in land speculation than farming.

Four corporations, operating out of the Dutch Antilles, have purchased 25,000 acres of cropland in President Carter's home state of Georgia. Foreign investors own at least 150,000 acres in **Missouri. And our sources say two Italian tycoons, with a Curacao corporate front, now own 1,920 acres near Dalhart, Texas.**

One of Oregon's largest agricultural holdings, Green Villa Farms, has been sold to Dutch interests for $5.7 million. The farm had to be sold, the manager reported, because it was almost impossible to make a decent profit growing cabbage, cauliflower, beans, peas and wheat.

The foreign land grabbers like to keep their operations secret. Missouri's agriculture director, Jack Runyon, told us that a group of Arabs visited a small town in his state last summer. Shortly thereafter, some 1500 acres of lush farmland changed hands. Runyon said other purchases were made by 13 companies in the Dutch Antilles. The true owners are hard to trace, he said.

Prestigious U.S. investment firms also purchase land for foreign investors. Among them is the Doane Agriculture Service, Inc., of St. Louis. The board chairman, Forest Goetsch, told us that five percent of Doane's land investment clientele are now foreigners. Until two years ago, Goetsch said, Germans with Deutschmarks to squander were investing heavily in farms in Argentina and Brazil. Now they are focusing on the United States, he said.

No one knows percisely how much U.S. farmland is owned by foreign interests, we discovered. An Agriculture Department official confessed that there is "no reliable data" on the subject. "We need more information," confided another official, "if we are to avoid making decisions in the dark."

There has been no massive turnover of farm property. According to the Agriculture Department, only three percent of the nation's farmland changed hands last year. But of this, up to 21 percent may have involved foreign investors.

Those involved in the land speculation, furthermore, seldom advertise. As one real-estate attorney put it: "This is a very hugh-hush affair. It is a very lucrative market, and lawyers don't talk about it too much."

But occasionally, a discreet advertisement will appear on the financial pages. One intriguing ad invited foreign investors to a Zurich, Switzerland, hotel on March 21 and 22 for a "confidential" discussion of U.S. land bargains. Stated the ad: "It's no secret international investors are eager and able to buy prime U.S. real estate but often do not have the proper contacts to begin negotiations. Zurich Market Day will bring you together and help establish on-going personal contacts."

It is ironic that the farmers should be the victims of the decline of the dollar, for they exported as estimated $23 billion worth of farm produce in 1977, which bolstered the dollar. Nor are they at all responsible for the skyrocketing price of land, which has attracted foreign investors. The cost of land has been driven up mainly by the rapid spread of residential suburbs into the countryside. In the new communities, property taxes have shot up, making it more difficult for the farmers to survive. Federal taxes also make farms good write-offs for the wealthy, who buy up farmland.

©1978, United Feature Syndicate

This article is reprinted from Jack Anderson, "Foreign Speculation on American Farms," **United Feature Syndicate**, 1978.

Foreign Investors Flock to U.S. Farmlands

EXAMPLE
12

Other investment markets have waned, but a cheap dollar, political instability overseas, and a long record of rising prices have made U.S. farmland the single hottest area for foreign investors. Although much of the foreign money is hard to trace, European Investment Research Center, a private consulting firm based in Brussels, estimates that foreigners invested some $800 million in farmland last year. That would come to a startling 30% of all foreign direct investment in the U.S., according to the Commerce Dept. "What we are witnessing," says Kenneth R. Krause, a senior economist for the Agriculture Dept., "is the biggest, continuing wave of investment in American farmland since the turn of the century."

Nor does it look as if the trend is slowing down. Real estate advisers and brokers report that the buying interest, mostly from Western Europe but also from Latin America and Japan, is on the increase. The Arab oil states have apparently not yet been big investors. And marketing activity aimed at the potential investors is heating up. For example, Amrex Inc., a San Francisco-based real estate firm, is holding a meeting in Zurich next week to introduce buyers to sellers who represent as much as $750 million worth of U.S. farmland. Some observers warn that the industry is attracting its share of hucksterism as well. West German newspapers are being flooded with real estate advertisements, apparently from small U.S. brokers, that often offer only an anonymous post office box number for an address.

Predictably enough, U.S. farmers are irate, and the Agriculture Dept. and, most recently, Congress are growing increasingly concerned as well. Despite some recent softening, farmland prices are dramatically higher than they were a few years ago, and critics blame foreigners for much of the speculation. Also, many foreigners can take special tax breaks at home or through Caribbean subsidiaries that give them a significant advantage over domestic investors. Since last year's $24 billion in agricultural exports represented a major component of U.S. trade, Washington is especially worried about increasing foreign control of U.S. farmland.

What also concerns the Agriculture Dept., as well as local farmers, is that the identity of the foreign purchasers is seldom known. Brokers and bankers steadfastly refuse to divulge names, although they claim that most investors

Investment figures of the week

Long-term interest rates fell somewhat, and short rates were stable, as the money supply dropped and the dollar strengthened. Stock prices were generally higher, with broader-based averages doing particularly well.

Money market rates	Latest week	Previous week	Year ago
Federal funds	6.75%	6.72%	4.61%
New three-month Treasury bills	6.30%	6.32%	4.55%
Three-month commercial paper	6.75%	6.75%	4.80%
Stocks			
Average price/earnings ratio* (1,500 stocks)	8.90	8.63	10.42
Average dividend yield* (1,500 stocks)	4.72%	4.79%	3.98%
Dow Jones industrial average	762.56	746.79	965.01
Standard & Poor's 500 stock index	89.35	87.36	101.98
Value Line composite index	92.89	90.51	92.85
Lipper growth mutual fund index	80.69	78.82	83.05
Average daily NYSE volume (millions)	23.9	19.7	20.0
NYSE blocks (10,000 shares and over)	295	227	219
Bonds			
New Aaa utility bonds*	8.60%	8.70%	8.30%
New Baa utility bonds*	9.25%	9.35%	9.00%
New Aa industrial bonds*	8.50%	8.60%	8.10%
U.S. government bonds (8½% issue of 1994-99)	8.14%	8.18%	7.73%
Bond Buyer municipal bond index (20 bonds)	5.58%	5.63%	5.92%

All figures are as of Tuesday, Mar. 14—except those marked*, which are from Friday, Mar. 10 and the Bond Buyer index from Thursday, Mar. 9, 1978.

Data: Salomon Bros., Standard & Poor's Compustat Services, Inc., Lipper Analytical Services Inc.

are wealthy individuals rather than corporations or investment groups. "We simply cannot get a handle on farmland," says a Commerce Dept. official, "since ownership is disguised through the extensive use of trusts, partnerships, and corporations headquartered offshore."

Safe investment. Angry farmers and their allies in state capitals are trying to crack down on foreign investors by seeking registration of ultimate ownership and outright restrictions on foreign purchases. Kansas and Missouri have recently undertaken investigations of foreign investments. And the General Accounting Office is just beginning what will be the most sweeping probe. At the request of the Senate Agriculture Committee, the GAO will try to determine the extent and locations of foreign investment in farmland. "Once we get answers to these questions," says one committee aide, "we will decide what, if anything, we shall do about the trend."

The weakening dollar is only the latest of a number of reasons that foreigners are so attracted to farmland. Political instability in their home countries is pushing foreigners into U.S. investments. With stock and bond prices both down, real estate in general, and farmland in particular, is drawing foreign

money. Many Europeans also believe that agricultural land is guaranteed to retain its value because they anticipate worldwide food shortages in the future. "American agriculture is nothing less than the safest investment around," says Ernst-Ludwig von Bülow, who specializes in U.S. real estate for a Hamburg-based investment fund, Lehndorff Vermögensverwaltung.

Present economic trends in U.S. agriculture have further whetted the foreigners' appetites. Land prices in recent months have fallen or softened just about everywhere, including the corn belt, but more noticeably in the Great Plains. As a result, the current annual rate of growth in farmland values has slowed to 5% or less from 17% a year ago. The slippage is due primarily to the continuing cost-price squeeze on American farmers, which is being worsened by depressed farm prices.

Sunbelt purchases. But if land prices begin soaring again, it still makes sense for the Europeans to buy in, say real estate advisers. Farmland prices in Western Europe are roughly double the price of the same quality land in the U.S.—$3,000 an acre for prime farmland in West Germany and France vs. $1,500 an acre in the U.S. last year, according to Chicago's Northern Trust

Co., which manages about 400 farms in 35 states.

While it is difficult to pinpoint where foreigners are buying most heavily, Jules A. Horn, director of the European Investment Research Center, says the so-called Sunbelt, which runs across the bottom third of the U.S., is attracting most of the money. He considers prices ranging between $600 to $1,000 an acre to be particularly attractive to Europeans. Until the present sag in the land price boom, Horn says, Europeans were far more interested in investing in California and the upper Midwest states such as Illinois and Wisconsin.

Hamburg-based Lehndorff has kept its investors out of the nation's richest farmland states, such as Iowa and Indiana, preferring to concentrate investments in Wisconsin, Missouri, and Arkansas. Singled out by von Bülow: farmland near the resort area of Lake Geneva, Wis., 60 miles from Chicago. "Lake Geneva is gradually expanding," he says, "which means that we may eventually be able to sell the land for construction." Jeffery White, head of Iowa Agronomics Inc., a farm management firm, adds that prices for Southern farmland are down drastically this year, and bargain hunters could come up with good buys in such states as Arkansas and Texas.

Meantime, real estate firms report that the growth in foreign business is providing a major fillip to their sales. Oppenheimer Industries Inc., a Kansas City (Mo.)-based farm brokerage and management firm that operates a rural land portfolio comprising roughly 1 million acres of farm and ranch land, for example, reports that sales to foreign investors more than doubled in the past few years and now account for one-third of its annual volume. A typical Oppenheimer deal recently involved the purchase of a 1,215-acre soybean and corn farm for nearly $1 million by a Western European. Two weeks ago, the company helped an Italian investor buy a 315-acre

citrus grove for $1.4 million. San Francisco's Amrex says that of the approximately $100 million in agricultural deals that it arranged last year, half were with foreigners.

Unfair competition. What especially worries U.S. officials is the possible widespread use of foreign tax havens by farmland investors. Lionel S. Steinberg, director and former president of the California State Board of Food & Agriculture, finds it "totally objectionable" for foreign investors to buy California land through corporations headquartered in the Dutch Antilles, for example, which require payment of little or no income taxes. "This is unfair competition and a threat to bona fide family farming in the U.S.," says Steinberg, noting that tax-privileged foreign investments make it difficult for prospective local buyers to compete.

Nothing sinister. Understandably, brokerage firms, banks, and other intermediaries for foreigners are defensive about their activities. "Much of the paranoia concerning absentee ownership is due to poor communications," declares Reed J. Oppenheimer, vice-president for Oppenheimer's international activities. "These people are not the suspicious cloak-and-dagger people they are made out to be," he says.

Nevertheless, Oppenheimer concedes that foreigners "often purchase through a foreign corporate entity," which he adds, is designed "to facilitate tax considerations in their own countries and here." But he argues vehemently that they are not driving up land prices, except possibly in what he describes as "a few isolated cases." "The well-heeled American farmers who can afford it are the ones who are driving up land prices," he maintains. And, Oppenheimer adds, only 3% of all farmland turns over each year.

What bothers dealers and managers of U.S. farmland is the new breed of promoters. "They are difficult to identify, but they are all over Europe huck-

stering farmland. We assume most of them are American brokers trying to cash in on what they perceive to be a booming market in Europe," says the vice-president of a large Midwestern bank, who prefers not to be identified. "We worry about them because they claim buyers can make 10%, 15%, or more in net returns on their farm investments, and that is just ridiculous."

'Something solid.' The bank official's point explains why large, U.S. institutional investors and corporations have generally shied away from investing in farmland on anything but a very modest scale. Bankers and agricultural economists generally agree that, depending on crops, productivity, and location, net cash returns on professionally managed farms rarely exceed 4% and are usually closer to 2%, without taking into account debt servicing and taxes. "Investors seeking fast or high gains should definitely not be in agriculture," cautions a vice-president for one of the big Chicago banks.

The European investors and their American intermediaries would be far happier if all the fuss died-down. "The trend toward land investments by Europeans stems from the need for a safety factor, like gold," argues Horn of the European Investment Research Center. "These investments are not made for speculation, but forever." However, the controversy seems destined to continue simmering for the foreseeable future. Warns a staffer on the Senate Agriculture Committee, which will review the GAO's probe: "We have no intention of dropping this issue until all the facts are in." ∎

This article is reprinted from "Foreign Investors Flock to U.S. Farmlands," Business Week, p. 79, March 27, 1978.

Limited Impact of State Laws on Foreign Investment in U.S. Farmland EXAMPLE 13

In the aggregate, State laws do not significantly inhibit foreign ownership of land. The laws range from general prohibitions on such ownership to a total absence of provisions dealing with this subject. There are so many different provisions, exceptions, and stipulations that even classifying the laws into general categories is difficult. These differences seem to mirror the diversity of State perceptions as to whether foreign ownership of land constitutes a present or potential problem in the State.

Classification of State Laws

As of May 1978, 25 States had laws that placed some constraints on aliens acquiring or holding farmland. As summarized below and discussed in more detail in Appendix II, some of these laws had more than one type of restriction or requirement. Also, 13 States had laws that placed restrictions on corporate ownership of U.S. farmland.

	Number of States
Restriction on alien ownership of U.S. farmland	25
General prohibition or major restrictions on nonresident alien ownership of land	9
Restrictions on size of landholdings or duration of ownership	11
Restrictions on inherited land	9
Restrictions on acquisition of State property	4
Other minor restrictions on ownership	6
No restrictions on alien ownership of U.S. farmland	25
Restrictions on corporate ownership of U.S. farmland	13

Some of the restrictions were major, while others were minor and seemed to be of little practical importance in deterring alien investment in U.S. land.

The nine States that have laws that generally prohibit, or restrict in a major way, individual alien investors residing outside the United States from owning real estate in their names are Connecticut, Indiana, Kentucky, Minnesota, Mississippi, Missouri, Nebraska, New Hampshire, and Oklahoma. Most of these States have some exceptions to the general provisions on nonresident aliens, and some have limitations on ownership of land by resident aliens.

Five States have laws that limit the total acreage that aliens can acquire or hold. These are Iowa, Missouri, Pennsylvania, South Carolina, and Wisconsin. The limits range from 5 acres to 500,000 acres. Six States (Illinois, Indiana, Kentucky, Mississippi, Nebraska, and Oklahoma) have laws that restrict aliens from owning land for more than a specified time. Illinois permits aliens to acquire land, either by purchase or inheritance, but requires them to dispose of it within 6 years. The other five States require aliens to dispose of all or part of their landholdings within specified times if they do not become U.S. citizens or, in the case of Oklahoma, U.S. citizens or residents of the State.

The laws of the 13 States that restrict corporate ownership of real estate vary in complexity and degree of severity— some apply to all corporations (regardless of whether aliens are involved); others apply only to corporations that have alien interests behind them.

Pertinent excerpts from and citations to the laws of individual States are shown in Appendix V.

Ten States (Alabama, California, Georgia, Illinois, Iowa, Kansas, Nebraska, Ohio, Oklahoma, and Wisconsin) told us of proposed legislation, at the time of our review, that would place additional constraints on foreign ownership of their land or would require periodic reporting of such landholdings. Most of these States already have laws containing some restrictions on foreign ownership of land.

Even recognizing the proposed additional legislation, our overall impression is that effective control or monitoring of foreign investments in U.S. farmland through State legislation is a long way off.

Data Collected by States

The States have collected very little data on foreign ownership of farmland. Only two States (Iowa and Minnesota) require nonresident aliens to file annual reports on their agricultural landholdings. These two States and Nebraska also require corporations with agricultural landholdings to file annual reports identifying the names and addresses of alien shareholders. Vermont also provided some information on the amount of farmland purchased by nonresident aliens in certain counties. Data obtained from these four States is as follows.

- Iowa reported that 23 nonresident aliens owned about 7,000 acres in 1977, and that 6 of 13 corporations with at least 5-percent alien ownership owned about 2,100 acres. (Data was not available for the other seven corporations.) The 9,100 acres represents 0.03 percent of Iowa's farmland.

- Minnesota reported that about 28,200 acres (0.09 percent of Minnesota's farmland) were owned or leased in 1976 by nonresident aliens or by business entities with at least 10-percent alien ownership.

- A Nebraska official said that no landholdings were reported under its requirement.

- Based on a limited survey, Vermont reported that nonresident aliens bought 951 acres, or about 20 percent, of the 4,746 acres of farmland that were sold in 4 of its 14 counties during 1976 and 1977.

There is no basis for concluding whether the above data provides a good clue as to the nationwide situation.

Alternative New Approaches

Following are some observations on various approaches that have been suggested for obtaining information on nonresident alien investment in U.S. farmland. Before any system is instituted, a number of related legal, procedural and coordination issues need to be addressed. These are discussed below and in Appendix IV.

1. As a condition for any individual or entity receiving any benefits through Federal rural/agricultural programs, they could be required to first register their alien status and the acreage they own or lease at the county Agricultural Stabilization and Conservation Service office. This approach has the advantage of being an all-Federal system which should reduce legal and coordination difficulties. It also has a built-in compliance factor for those benefiting or planning to benefit from such programs. A disadvantage would be that all foreign owners of farmland may not participate in, and some may choose to disassociate themselves from, such Federal programs.

2. As part of a mandatory process of recording land transfer transactions at the county level, new land owners or their agents could be required to identify on a data processing card the alien status and acreage of such ownership. This information could be routed through the States to a central Federal point for tabulation and annual reporting. This would not provide data on existing land ownership. It would re-

quire close cooperation of all States and counties, changes in State laws and county ordinances, and uniform data collection and reporting systems. A major advantage would be that information would automatically be generated on all purchases by foreigners.

3. Another approach would be to require that all parties customarily involved in real estate transfers report on any land acquisitions involving foreign interests. Major drawbacks would include uncertainty that all foreign acquisitions have been identified, the large number of data collection points, the probability of much duplication, and the probable strong opposition from nearly everyone concerned in collecting the data. Also this would not provide data on existing land ownership.

4. Periodic and extensive surveys, using scientific sampling techniques and centralized controls, might provide data that could be projected on a nationwide basis. The design and implementation of such an approach could present serious problems, and the resulting data may not be entirely satisfactory.

5. Of the alternatives considered, the most feasible and simplest approach may be to federally legislate a nationwide registration system for foreign owners of U.S. land. Such a system could be generally similar to the alien resident registration system currently used by the Immigration and Naturalization Service—which requires card-type reports to be submitted annually by resident aliens through post offices to a central Federal point. Such a system would place the reporting burden on the landowners (or their agents), would require relatively little involvement by State or county governments, would be conceptually simple, and would provide data on current ownership, rather than only subsequent farmland transfers. The usefulness of such a system would depend on the completeness of the information reported.

Any system used would require the resolution of any problems caused by constitutional and legal issues, and also should include the following.
- Standard definitions of terms and clear reporting criteria.
- Stipulations that only data on foreign investments in farmland would be collected.
- Criteria as to the minimum number of acres to be reported.
- Use of a standard card-type form to facilitate data processing.
- Meaningful incentives or penalties to insure submission of full and accurate data.

This article is reprinted from "Limited Impact of State Laws on Foreign Investment in U.S. Farmland," **Foreign Ownership in U.S. Farmland—Much Concern, Little Data**, U.S. Comptroller General, pp. 2-5, 10-12.

THE AVERAGE COST OF A FARM—BY STATE

REGION I	AVERAGE $/ACRE	AVERAGE ACREAGE	AVERAGE PRICE
Connecticut	$1,885	118	$222,430
Delaware	1,460	187	273,020
Maine	424	222	94,128
Maryland	1,505	167	251,335
Massachusetts	1,193	126	150,318
New Hampshire	701	193	135,293
New Jersey	2,025	122	247,050
New York	593	195	115,635
Pennsylvania	1,010	139	140,390
Rhode Island	1,863	92	171,396
Vermont	573	269	154,137
REGION II			
Alabama	$ 454	189	$ 85,806
Florida	805	364	293,020
Georgia	522	246	128,412
Kentucky	644	132	85,008
Mississippi	432	208	89,856
North Carolina	722	114	82,308
South Carolina	553	171	94,563
Tennessee	571	133	75,943
Virginia	716	162	115,992
West Virginia	438	177	77,526
REGION III			
Illinois	$1,508	247	$372,476
Indiana	1,296	180	233,280
Iowa	1,250	266	332,500
Michigan	815	158	128,770
Minnesota	714	268	191,352
Missouri	558	245	136,710
Ohio	1,206	156	188,136
Wisconsin	666	192	127,872
REGION IV			
Arkansas	$ 547	254	$138,938
Louisiana	592	258	152,736
New Mexico	93	3,695	343,635
Oklahoma	379	432	163,728
Texas	294	710	208,740
REGION V			
Colorado	$ 261	1,345	$351,045
Kansas	383	638	244,354
Montana	160	2,712	433,920
Nebraska	392	706	276,752
North Dakota	266	1,002	266,532
South Dakota	214	1,058	266,412
Wyoming	101	4,413	445,713
REGION VI			
Arizona	$ 121	6,167	$746,207
California	693	453	313,929
Idaho	420	580	243,600
Nevada	96	4,286	411,456
Oregon	294	565	166,110
Utah	247	963	237,861
Washington	501	445	222,945

SOURCE:

Average Price Per Acre: Farm Real Estate Market Developments, ERS, USDA, 1/78.
Average Acreage By State: Farm Numbers, CRB, SRS, USDA, 12/29/77.
Robert T. Mullins, Legislative Services, National Farmers Union, Washington, D.C.

Chapter 4

Redirecting Research Priorities

AN ISSUE OF PUBLIC ACCOUNTABILITY

In recent years, nearly every major public institution has come under increasing scrutiny by citizens' organizations across the country. Both private and public agencies have conducted evaluation and monitoring projects which have helped create new channels for public participation. As a result, institutions as powerful as the U.S. General Services Administration and the nuclear power industry have been required to disclose information and become more accountable to public needs.

Yet there is one set of public institutions whose performance, accountability, and access to the public continues to go almost entirely unexamined: the massive, publicly funded state agricultural system known as the land grant complex. Those concerned with issues ranging from food policy and rural development to energy and employment must begin to understand how the land grant system functions, who it serves, and how more responsive and effective use of its vast resources can be accomplished through increased public participation. As the following two chapters demonstrate, the land grant complex affects the lives of nearly every citizen. Unfortunately, this effect has not always been positive. The accountability of the land grant system and increased local participation in the formulation of its programs and policies is one of the most crucial arenas for agricultural policy reform in the United States.

THE LAND GRANT COMPLEX

The land grant university system was established by the *Morrill Act of 1862*. This federal legislation created free, publicly funded colleges of agriculture and engineering for rural and urban working people. The second *Morrill Act of 1890* provided for the endowment of separate but "equal" colleges of agriculture for black students in the South. Today, the land grant complex is funded by over $1.2 billion in federal, state and county taxes per year and is composed of 71 colleges and universities (including 16 black, or "1890" colleges, plus Tuskegee Institute), 15 schools of forestry, 55 state agricultural experiment stations and over 3,000 county offices of the Cooperative Extension Service.

By creating a nation-wide system of tuition-free colleges and unversities, the Morrill Acts aided greatly in the democratization of higher education, which had previously been available only to those who could afford it. The further creation of the Cooperative Extension Service (under the *Smith-Lever Act of 1914*) as a decentralized, locally controlled system, offered additional informational and technical services to the residents of each county in the United States. Yet despite the significance and the magnitude of the land grant system, very few major studies have evaluated performance. As a result, taxpayers do not know how and why their $1.2 billion in land grant taxes are being spent.

AGRICULTURAL RESEARCH

Federal research funds are filtered down to the state experiment stations (created by the *Hatch Act* in 1887) through USDA's Cooperative State Research Service (CSRS). Agricultural research is also supported by state funds and donations from private sources. In 1977, $415 million was allocated out of federal funds for agricultural research. $129 million went to the states through CSRS; over $220 million was allocated from state funds and $58 million in grants from private industry. The impact of privately funded research grants is a serious question. Increasingly, these funds are being given by agribusiness and by food industry corporations. A clear example of this is illustrated by **Example 14, Donations: To the University of California for Agricultural Research**, reprinted from *California Agriculture*, January 1978.

HARD TOMATOES, HARD TIMES

The 1972 study by Jim Hightower, *Hard Tomatoes, Hard Times: The Failure of the Land Grant Complex*, published by the Agribusiness Accountability Project, argued that the land grant complex was providing an overwhelming and unjustified degree of support to large, already successful farmers and agribusiness corporations, while doing less and less to meet the needs of small farmers and American consumers. A selection from the book, *Hard Tomatoes, Hard Times* is reprinted as **Example 15, Introduction: The Obvious Failure**, at the end of this chapter. Despite the fact that both the USDA and the land grant complex are publicly funded institutions, this was the first serious attempt to evaluate and question the direction and priorities of their programs and policies.

The Agribusiness Accountability Project's report took its title from the tough-skinned, tasteless tomato bred especially for mechanical harvesting. California land grant research developed this variety which subsequently made it possible to mechanize tomato harvesting, which is now the cause of serious unemployment of farmworkers in the state. But the "hard" tomato is not the end of the story. The latest chapter is the "square" tomato. The further development of our seemingly infinite ability to make nature conform to corporate needs—regardless of environmental and social costs— is documented in an article from the *New York Times:* **Example 16, And Now California Develops a Square Tomato**.

During the decade of the 1970s, currents of reform have begun to flow in the once still waters of land grant research and extension programs. Some efforts, like that of the Agribusiness Accountability Project, have come at the national level. Others are now beginning to emerge out of the land grant reform movement at the state level. One such effort produced a still unpublished study, *Failing The People*, which documented problems and questioned the priorities of New York state's land grant college—Cornell University.

A more recent effort to alter the priorities of the agricultural research establishment is the work of the California Agrarian Action Project in Davis. A description of their work is included as **Example 17, California Agrarian Action Project**, from the March, 1978 issue of *Workbook*. The Project has specifically focused on the issue of publicly funded research within the University of California which develops new techniques for mechanical harvesting. This trend towards an "industrialized agriculture" is consciously supported by the big California growers and their academic allies. It is a trend that has forced and will continue to force thousands of farmworkers out of jobs. As the United Farmworkers of America and the Agrarian Action

Project have pointed out, machines can't strike. Mechanization is the answer to the labor problems and turmoil faced by agribusiness in California. An excellent report on this issue, **Example 18, No Hands Touch The Land,** by the Agrarian Action Project, is reprinted at the end of this chapter.

LEGISLATIVE MONITORING

The land grant complex is funded by federal, state and county governments, with each state contributing the most substantial portion—at least 60%, and sometimes as much as 90% of the research budget for a land grant college. State and county governments also fund over 65% of the budget for the Extension Service. Yet despite the fact that they continue to appropriate large sums of money to the land grant system each year, most state legislators and county officials have not become involved in the issues of land grant accountability and accessibility. As a result, land grant appropriations are usually approved automatically and with little discussion or evaluation.

The land grant funding process should be opened up—to citizen participation, questioning and accountability. Individuals and organizations at the state level should voice their concerns and demand that their legislators provide them with answers on land grant appropriations and programs. State legislative hearings, as were held in California in 1977, could result; citizens will become increasingly aware of the importance of these issues, and public officials would then begin to address the need for redirecting the priorities and policies of USDA agencies and the land grant system. For as the land grant complex persists in its policy of helping those who need it least, a growing majority of consumers, family farmers and food industry workers are finding it increasingly difficult to survive within a food production system that is dominated more and more by business and corporate interests, rather than by public interests.

Resources

ORGANIZATIONS

Note:

Unfortunately, there are very few organizations whose primary objective is to monitor the agricultural research underway at the U.S. Department of Agriculture and at the Land Grant Universities in every state. However, many of the organizations listed in the Resource Section of this book have done work on this issue, focusing on specific questions such as the relevance and accountability of current research and evaluating the consequences of agribusiness funding of agricultural research.

In addition, numerous individuals and organizations are moving ahead with new research projects, and are doing so with no support (and often opposition) from the USDA/Land Grant system. This is particularly true in the areas of research relevant to small farmers and in the field of "biological agriculture." An excellent example of this trend is the work done on energy use in agriculture by Barry Commoner's Center for the Biology of Natural Systems at Washington University in St. Louis (see Section III).

Perhaps the most visible work evaluating the research done at Land Grant Colleges is being done in California, focusing on U.C. Davis:

California Agrarian Action Project

P.O. Box 464
Davis, California 95616
(916) 756-8518
Paul Barnett, Don Villarejo

California Rural Legal Assistance

115 Sansome Street (9th Floor)
San Francisco, California 94104
(415) 421-3405
Al Meyerhoff

Professor William Friedland
Department of Community Studies
University of California
Santa Cruz, California 95060
(408) 429-2371

Professor Isao Fujimoto
Department of Applied Behavioral Sciences
University of California
Davis, California 95616
(916) 752-1805

BIBLIOGRAPHY

Erickson, Ronald, "Catsup for the President; Agricultural Research at the University of California, Davis." Published for 1st National Conference on Rural America, reprinted from **The Barrister.** Vol. 6, No. 10. King Hall, University of California, Davis. Davis School of Law. April 1973. Article describing the links between Agribusiness and UCD research.

Friedland, William, **Social Sleepwalkers: Scientific and Technological Research in California Agriculture.** Research Monograph No. 13, University of California, Santa Cruz, Department of Applied Behavioral Sciences, College of Environmental Sciences. 1975.

Fujimoto, Isao and Martin Zone, **Sources of Inequitiies in Rural America: Implications for Rural Community Development and Research.** Community Development Research Series, Department of Applied Behavioral Sciences, University of California, Davis. 1976.

Fujimoto, Isao and Emmett Fiske, **What Research Gets Done at a Land Grant College: Internal Factors at Work.** Department of Applied Behavioral Sciences, University of California, Davis. 1975. Discussion of factors contributing to the direction of agricultural research at U.C. Davis.

Hightower, Jim and Susan De Marco, **Hard Tomatoes: Hard Times: The Failure of the Land Grant Complex.** Schenkman Publishing Company, Cambridge, Massachusetts. 1973.

McCalla, Alex, "The Politics of the United States Agricultural Research Establishment: A Short Analysis," **Policy Studies Journal.** Vol. 6, No. 4, University of Illinois, Urbana, Illinois 61801. Summer 1978. Paper arguing the amorphousness of the agricultural research establishment.

Schmidt, Fred, "Issues on Agricultural Research," **Strategies for Rural Action.** Prepared for the Third National Conference on Rural America, 1346 Connecticut Avenue, N.W., Washington, D.C. 20036. A call for appropriate research by the USDA.

Small Farm Viability Project, **Technology Task Force Report.** State CETA Office, Department of Employment Development, 800 Capitol Mall, Sacramento, California 95814. November 1977.

U.S. Senate, Committee on the Judiciary, Hearings on **Priorities in Agricultural Research of the USDA.** Superintendent of Documents, U.S. Government Printing Office, Washington, D.C. 20402. October 1977. Hearings centered around complaints that USDA research is both socially and environmentally irresponsible.

Donations

EXAMPLE
14

The following is a summary of all gifts
to the Division of Agricultural Sciences of the University of California
for agricultural research
during the period July 1, 1976 to June 30, 1977,
by range of the amounts given or pledged.

$1,000 - 1,499
Agway Inc
Alameda Co Mosquito, Abatement
Amstar Corp
Archer Daniels Midland Co.
Berti, Leo A.
Blue Anchor Inc
Bull Foundation, Henry W.
Burnand, Alphonse A.
Cal Aggie, Foundation
California Avocado
California Saw, Knife & Grind
Chapman Foundation
Chevron Chem Co, Ortho Divisio
Ciba Geigy Corporation
Coastside Contractors
Deli, Joseph
Eureka Laboratories Inc
Fisons Corp
Fleet Foundation
General Mills Foundation
Germain's Inc
Grass Growers Inc
Great Lakes Chemical Corp
Gulf Oils Chemical Co
Harwood Products
Holly Sugar Corp
Irvine Co
J.V.P. Citrus
MacMillan Bloedel, Research Lt
Mallinckrodt Inc
Marin Sonoma, Mosquito Abate
Minnesota Mining & Mfg
Minnesota Mining & Mfg Co
Mobil Chemical Co
Mobil Chemical Co
Montedison USA Inc
No Ca Growers Assn
Nor Calif Turfgrass Council
Northrup King & Co
Olive Administrative Comm
Pacific Western Resources

Phillips Foundation
Program of Cultural Coop
Sacramento Foods
Sandoz Incorporated
Sher, Judith K.
Solano Co Mosquito, Abatement
Specialty Brands, Inc
Spreckles Sugar Division
Tafuro, A. J.
Univ of California, Berkeley F
Velsicol Chemical Corporation
Western States Meat Packers
Zoecon Corporation
TOTAL GIFTS 131
TOTAL AMOUNT $136,693
PERCENT OF TOTAL 4.65%

$1,500 - 2,499
Abbott Laboratories
Amchem Products Inc
Amer Cancer So-Ca Div
American Cyanamid
Andco Farms
Artichoke Industries
Assoc of Applied, Insect Ecolo
Basf Wyandotte Corp
Basf Wyandotte
Baxter, J. H. and, Company
Boswell, J.G. Company
Ca Assn of Nurserymen
Cal Farm Bureau Federation
Calif Assoc of Nurserymen
Calif Beet Growers Assn
California Cattlemans Assoc
California Crop Improvement
Central Ca, Tristerza
Chapman
Ciba-Geigy Corp
Distributors Processing Inc
Dow Chemical
EM Laboratories
Fisons Corporation
FMC Corporation
Forest Economics, Fnd
Gamble
Grand Island Biological Co
Grower, Shipper Vegetable
Gulf Oil Chemicals
HLR Sciences
Jackson & Perkins, Co
Jaeger, William P.
Johnson, Bert D.
Johnson & Son Inc S. C.
Lilly and Company, Eli
Maag, Agrochemicals
Mallano, H. M.
Meyer, B.
Michelbacher, Abe E.
Natl. Audubon Society Inc
Natl Dairy Council
Nicholas Turkey Breeding Farm
Northwest Mosquito Abatement
Oxbridge Inc
Pacific Egg & Poultry Assn
Power Refrigeration Co
Research Corp
San Joaq Vlly Cotton P S Dist
San Mateo Cty Carnation Grws
Sandoz Inc
Shell Development Company
Shibamoto, Takayuki
Soilserv Inc
Stauffer Chemical Co
Stauffer Chemical Co
Storkan, R. C.
Sunkist Growers, Inc.

Thomson-Hayward Chemical
Toro Company,
United States Golf Assoc
Upjohn
Var Dons-Vit & Enology
Velsicol Chemical Corp
Wen-Koe Company
West, Eldon Joe
Wilson, Dave Nursery
Zoecon Corporation
TOTAL GIFTS 124
TOTAL AMOUNT $223,477
PERCENT OF TOTAL 7.6%

$2,500 - 4,999
Amer Cyanamid Company
Amer Hoechst Corporation
Bank America NT & SA
BASF Wyandotte Corporation
Berger & Plate Company
Blackwell, Management Co
Calif Beet Growers Assoc
Campbell Soup Company
Chemagro
Chevron Chemical Co (Ortho)
Ciba Geigy
Conrel
Dairymans Cooperative Creamer
Diamond Shamrock Chemical
Dole Corporation, James
Dupont Denemours, E.I.
E.M. Laboratories, Inc.
Eutek, Inc
FM Corporation
Foremost McKesson, Fdn Inc
Foremost-McKesson Foundation
Garrison, Jeanne
Gerber Products Co
Grower-Shipper Vegetable
Gulf Oil Chemicals Company
Hercules
Hudson Lumber Co
ICI United States, Inc
Lake County Mosquito Abatemnt
Lipton, Thomas J. Inc
Lorenz, Fred W.
Louisiana-Pacific, Corp
McCarthy Land Co
McLaughlin Gormley, King Compa
National Research, Development
Parsons, F. G.
Pennwalt Corporation
Pfizer Inc
Pillsbury Madison &, Sutro
Powers, Jack R.
Rohm and Haas Co
Schwabacher, S. Donald
Scott, O. M.
Shell Development Company

Shell Development, Company
Shell Development
Stauffer Chemical, Co
Stauffer Chemical Co
Sun Studs Inc.
Suntory International
Thompson Haywar Co, and Nutril
Thompson Hayward Chemical Co
Time Incorporated
Tri Cal Incorporated
Trical
Various Donors
Visalia Cooperative, Cotton Gi
Weather Tec
Western Rain Bird Sales
Whittaker, Ruth
Young, F. B.
TOTAL GIFTS 100
TOTAL AMOUNT $343,434
PERCENT OF TOTAL 11.7%

$5,000 - 9,999
Allied Chemical Corporation
Arcata Redwood Co
Boise Cascade Corp
Botsai Overstreet &, Rosenberg
Bradley, Mary
Ca Farm Bureau Federation
Ca North Coast Grape Growers
California Beet, Growers Assn
Chevron, Chemical Co
Chevron Chemical Company
DeKalb Agresearch Incorporatd
Dow Chemical
Dow Chemical Company
Dupont De Nemours & Co E.I.
Dupont De Nemours & Co. E.I.
Henderson Foundation
Hoffmann-La Roche Inc
ICI United States Inc
ICI United States Inc
Lilly Research Laboratories
Louisiana-Pacific, Fdn
Masonite Corp
Merck Sharp & Dohme
Monsanto Agricultural Prod
Monterey Co Grape Growers Assc
Monterey Co Growers Assn
Mosquito Abatement, Dist
Natl Cystic Fibro-, Sis Res Fd
Natl Livestock & Meat Board
Nevada Alfalfa Seed, Advisory
Nurserymens Exchange
Olive Administrative Comm
Penwalt Corporation
Richards Canning Co, Th
Rohm & Haas
Rohm & Haas Co
S & J Ranch

Shell Companies Fdn Inc
Simpson Timber Co
So Calif Turfgrass Council
Spring Valley Lake Assoc
State of Nevada
Tee-2-Green Corporation
Transagra Corporation
Union Carbide Corporation
Union Foundation
Upjohn Company
Velsicol Chemical Corp
Walnut Marketing Board
Wasbauer, Marius S.
Western Plant Breeders
Weyerhauser Company, Foundatio
TOTAL GIFTS 96
TOTAL AMOUNT $604,791
PERCENT OF TOTAL 20.6%

$10,000 - 24,999
Boswell Company, J. G.
Ca Sugar Beet Processors
Ca Tree Fruit Agreement
Carnation Company
Chemagro Agricultural Div
Chevron USA

Diamond Shamrock Chemical Co
Fleischman, Fdn, Max C.
FMC Corporation, Agr Chem Div
ICI United States Inc
Kelco
Koppers Company Inc
Krafft Estate, Ernest
Lilly and Company, Eli
Northern Calif Golf Assoc
Olin-Agricultural Division
Olive Administrative, Committee
Pistachio Association
Pistachio Association
Potlatch Forests Inc
Procter and Gamble Company
Runyon-Winchell, Cancer Fund
San Joaquin Valley, Seed Distr
Searle G. D. & Company
Silver Lakes Association
Society Nutrition, Education
Society of American Florists
State of Nev Dept, of Agricult
Union Carbide
Union Carbide Corporation
Union Carbide Corporation
Weyerhauser Co
Witco Chemical

TOTAL GIFTS: 45
TOTAL AMOUNT: $624,731
PERCENT OF TOTAL: 21.25%

$25,000 - 49,999
Beet Sugar Dev, Foundation
Ca Comm on Rel of Elec to Agr
Cal Forest Protect, Assn
California Cedar, Products Co
Ciba-Geigy Corp
Continental Grain Company
Fed-Amer Soc for Exper Biolgy
Ford Foundation
Laird Norton, Foundation
Monsanto Company
Muscular Dystrophy Assn
Procida
Proctor & Gamble Co
Rose Spring Dwarf Res Commite
Sugar Assn Inc
Tuna Research Fdn Inc
UC San Diego Foundation
Walnut Marketing, Board
TOTAL GIFTS: 12
TOTAL AMOUNT: $370,077
PERCENT OF TOTAL: 12.6%

$50,000 - 99,999
Artichoke Research Assoc
Bennett Estate of, James P.
Noyes Foundation, Jessie Smith
Rockefeller, Foundation
Thille, Albert
TOTAL GIFTS: 3
TOTAL AMOUNT: $214,692
PERCENT OF TOTAL: 7.3%

$100,000 or more
Ca Aggie Foundation
Ca Crop Improvement Assn
Cal Planting Cotton Seed Dist
TOTAL GIFTS: 3
TOTAL AMOUNT: $207,438
PERCENT OF TOTAL: 7.06%

GRAND TOTALS
 NO. OF GIFTS: 1157
 AMOUNT GIVEN
  OR PLEDGED: $2,937,400

This article is reprinted from "Donations: to University of California for Agricultural Research," **California Agriculture**, pp. 19-20, January 1978.

Introduction: The Obvious Failure

EXAMPLE 15

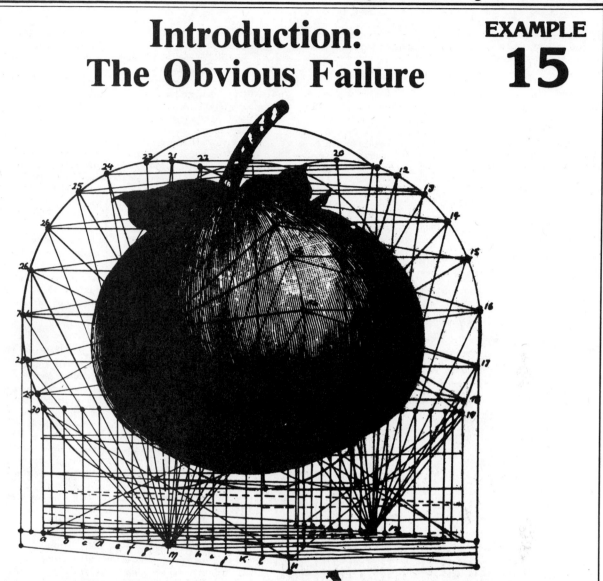

Although agriculture has been and will continue to be the economic and social base of rural America, our rural population is becoming largely a nonfarm one. By 1980, only one rural resident in seven or eight may live on a farm. It is generally agreed that it is neither socially desirable nor economically feasible to try to arrest or even slow down this trend. (emphasis supplied)

—USDA, NASULGC 1966[1]

Although the land grant college complex[2] was created to be the people's university, to reach out to serve the various needs of a broad rural constituency, the system has, in fact, become the sidekick and frequent servant of agriculture's industrialized elite.

Agriculture's preoccupation with scientific and business efficiency has produced a radical restructuring of rural America, and consequently of urban America. There has been more than a "green revolution"[3] out there—in the last thirty years there literally has been a social and economic upheaval in the American countryside. It is a protracted, violent revolution, and it continues today. The land grant college complex has been the scientific and intellectual progenitor of that revolution.

At least since World War II, the land grant colleges of this country have put their tax supported resources almost solely into efforts that primarily have worked to the advantage and profit of large corporate enterprises, particularly the huge corporate farms and ranches, the vertically-integrated and conglomerate corporations in agricultural production, the seed, feed, chemical, credit, machinery and other "in-put"

industries, and the processing, packaging, marketing, distributing, retailing, exporting and other "out-put" industries.

The basis of land grant teaching, research, and extension work has been that "efficiency" is the greatest need in agriculture. Consequently, this agricultural complex has devoted the overwhelming share of its resources to mechanize all aspects of agricultural production and make it a capital-intensive industry; to increase crop yield per acre through genetic manipulation and chemical application; and to encourage "economies of scale" and vertical integration of the food process. It generally has aimed at transforming agriculture from a way of life to a business and a science, transferring effective control from the farmer to the business executive and the systems analyst.

On the one hand, this focus on scientific and business efficiency has led to production (and over-production) of a bounty of food and fiber products, and, not incidentally, it certainly has contributed to the enrichment of an agribusiness few.

On the other hand, there have been far-reaching side effects of the land grant college's preoccupation with the "green revolution." As statistics indicate, and as visits to the countryside make clear, rural America is crumbling. Not just the family farm, but every aspect of rural America is crumbling—schools, communities, churches, businesses and way of life.

RURAL AMERICA IN CRISIS: OFF THE LAND AND INTO THE CITIES

—47.1 percent of the farm families in this country have annual incomes below $3000.

—More than half of the farms in the country have sales of less than $5,000 a year; together, this majority of farmers accounted for only 7.8 percent of farm sales.

—Since 1940, more than 3 million farms have folded, and farms continue to fold at a rate of 2,000 a week.

—The number of black farm operators fell from 272,541 in 1959 to 98,000 in 1970.

—For the first time since the nation was settled coast to coast, about a hundred years ago, the farm population has fallen below 10 million.

—During the 1960's, the proportion of farm people over 55 years of age rose by a third, while the proportion of those under 14 years of age declined by half.

—Hired farm workers in 1970 averaged an income of $1,083 if they did farm work only, while those who also did some nonfarm work averaged an income of $2,461.

—Fourteen million rural Americans exist below a poverty income, with millions more clinging just on the edge of poverty.

—Independent, small-town businesses are closing at a rate of more than 16,000 a year.

—132 rural counties have no doctor.

—30,000 rural communities are without central water systems; 30,000 are without sewer systems.

—2.5 million substandard houses are occupied by rural families; that is 60 percent of the bad housing in America.

—64 percent of all rural counties lost population during the sixties.

—Entire rural communities are being abandoned.

—Since 1940, 30 million people have left their rural homes for urban areas, and this migration continues at a rate of 800,000 a year.

—More than 73 percent of the American people live now on less than two percent of the land.

RESPONSE OF THE LAND GRANT COLLEGE COMPLEX

Despite the obvious need, the land grant college complex, which is the public's primary investment of intellectual and scientific resources in rural America, has failed to respond. Lauren Soth, a close ally of land grant colleges and an editor of the Des Moines *Register and Tribune*, bemoaned this fact in a recent article:

> The land-grant universities continue to devote the overwhelming portion of their research and educational funds to the promotion of agricultural technology and the service of the highest income farmers. They have not yet given anywhere near the attention in either research of education to the problems of the bypassed poor farmers and bypassed rural communities that their numbers justify—to say nothing of help on the basis of need.[4]

In fiscal year 1969, a total of nearly 6,000 scientific man-years were spent doing research on all projects at all state agricultural experiment stations.[5] Based on USDA's research classifications, only 289 of those scientific man-years were expended specifically on "people-oriented" research. That is an allocation to rural people of less than five percent of the total research effort at the state agricultural experiment stations.

The other 95 percent has been concentrated on projects that steadily are creating an automated, integrated and corporatized agriculture. The primary beneficiaries are agribusiness corporations. These interests envision rural America solely as a factory that will produce food, fiber and profits on a corporate assembly line extending from the fields through the supermarket checkout counters.

There is great wealth to be made from rural America. Consumers spent $118 billion for food in 1971. In fact, agriculture is the biggest industry in the country—bigger than the automobile industry, the defense industry, or the electronics industry. With 4.5 million workers in 1969, agriculture employs more people than the combined total of the transportation, steel and automobile industries. One out of every

nine dollars in the Gross National Product is accounted for by the food industry.

But that money is not staying in rural America. Only a third of the consumer's food dollar is pocketed by farmers, and the independent family farmers are getting a small portion of that. The rest of it flows to the cities, with a major chunk going to corporate headquarters in New York, in Atlanta, in Nashville, in Kansas City, in Chicago, in Houston, in Denver, in San Francisco and in other urban centers of agricultural power.

Increasingly, agricultural production is vertically integrated, markets are concentrated and dinner is prepackaged by corporate America. IT&T serves up Gwaltney ham and Wonder Bread. The turkey comes from Greyhound Corporation's Armour division. Dow Chemical brings the lettuce, while Tenneco provides fresh fruits. Count on Boeing for the potatoes and American Brands for Motts apple sauce. Coca Cola serves orange juice and, for dessert, there are strawberries from Purex.

Agribusiness corporations such as Ralston Purina, Del Monte, Tropicana and Safeway are taking control of agricultural production, reducing farmers to contract laborers. Commodity after commodity is being grown under vertically integrated contract, including 95 percent of the broilers, 75 percent of processed vegetables, 70 percent of citrus, 55 percent of turkeys, 40 percent of potatoes and 33 percent of fresh vegetables.[6] Those percentages are increasing every day as corporate power takes hold of rural America, expropriating power and profits.

Profits and power are not all that go to the cities. People go, too. They go unwillingly and they go unprepared. Ironically, they are the waste products of an agricultural revolution largely designed within a land grant college complex originally created to serve them. Today's urban crisis is a consequence of failure in rural America. The land grant college complex cannot shoulder all the blame for that failure, but no single institution—private or public—has played a more crucial role.

The land grant complex has been eager to work with farm machinery manufacturers and with well-capitalized farming operations to mechanize all agricultural labor, but it has accepted no responsibility for the farm laborer who is put out of work by the machine. The complex has worked hand in hand with seed companies to develop high-yield seed strains, but it has not noticed that rural America is yielding up practically all of its young people. The complex has been available day and night to help nonfarming corporations develop schemes of vertical integration, while offering independent, family farmers little more comfort than "adapt or die."[7] The complex has devoted hours to create adequate water systems for fruit and vegetable processors and canners, but 30,000 rural communities still have no central water system for their people. The complex has tampered with the gene structure of tomatoes, strawberries, asparagus and other foods to prepare them for the steel grasp of the mechanical harvestors, but it has sat still while the American food supply has been laced with carcinogenic substances.

It is remarkable that this imbalance continues year after year, while rural America crumbles and urban America seethes, without any public figure taking a hard look at the investment. It is indicative of national leadership's general failure in rural America that this society continues to pour billions of dollars into the land grant complex without questioning the total impact of the expenditure.

In 1966, USDA and land grant spokesmen said: "It is generally agreed that it is neither socially desirable nor economically feasible to try to arrest or even slow down this trend (of a steadily declining farm population)."[8] Who "generally agreed" on this? Did they check with the one million more farmers expected by USDA to fold between now and 1980?[9] What about tens of thousands of small-town businessmen who will have to board up their stores as those farmers pull out?[10] There would not likely be general agreement among the residents of the rural towns that will wither and die, nor by the millions of people who will be rural refugees in alien cities.

Yet, no one in a position of leadership questioned this basic assumption of land grant college policy. In the five years since that statement, half a million farms have gone out of business[11] and some three to four million people have migrated from their rural homes.[12] But the land grant college complex apparently does not perceive this as a crisis.

If those four million people leaving rural America had been four million corn-borers entering rural America, the land grant community would have rung all alarms, scurried into the labs and rushed out with an emergency action program to meet the "crisis."

The American public has a right to expect better from the land grant college complex. The total complex—the colleges of agriculture, the agricultural experiment stations and the state extension services—receive annually an appropriation that is approaching three quarters of a billion tax dollars, including federal, state and county appropriations. The public has a right to expect that those intellectual and scientific resources be more than a subsidy for corporate agribusinesses.

The land grant colleges must get out of the corporate board rooms, they must get the corporate interests out of their labs, and they must draw back and reassess their preoccupation with mechanical, genetical and chemical gadgetry. The complex must, again, become the people's university—it must be redirected to focus the preponderance of its resources on the full development of the rural potential, helping to make the American countryside a place where millions of people can live and work in dignity.

This article is reprinted from Jim Hightower and Susan DeMarco, "Introduction: The Obvious Failure," **Hard Tomatoes**, Hard Times, Schenkman Press, Cambridge, 1973.

[1] USDA and National Association of State Universities and Land Grant Colleges (NASULGC). "A National Program of Research for Agriculture." Report of a study sponsored jointly by USDA and NASULGC for submission to the Senate Committee on Appropriations (October 1966), p. 158.

[2] As used throughout this report, "land grant college complex" denotes three inter-related units, all attached to the land grant college campus:
  A. Colleges of Agriculture, created in 1862 and 1890 by two separate Morrill Acts.
  B. State Agricultural Experiment Stations, created in 1887 by the Hatch Act for the purpose of conducting agricultural and rural research in cooperation with the Colleges of Agriculture.
  C. Extension Service, created in 1914 by the Smith-Lever Act for the purpose of disseminating the fruits of teaching and research to the people of the countryside.

[3] The "green revolution" is the popular label for the increased productivity that has come from hybrid crops, agricultural chemicals, and farm mechanization.

[4] Lauren Soth. "The End of Agrarianism: Fission of the Political Economy of Agriculture." *American Journal of Agricultural Economics*, vol. 52, no. 5 (December 1970), p. 655.

[5] USDA Science and Education Staff. "Inventory of Agricultural Research, fy 1969 and 1970," table IV-D-O, vol. II (October 1970), p. 250.

[6] Don Paarlberg. "Future of the Family Farm." Address before Milk Producer's Federation, November 30, 1971. (USDA), p. 10.

[7] Statement by Dr. Earl L. Butz, former dean of the College of Agriculture at Purdue University, currently U.S. secretary of agriculture. Quoted in The *Record Stockman*, March 10, 1955.

[8] USDA-NASLUGC, *op. cit.*, p. 158.

[9] *The Washington Post*. "Study Sees Huge Drop in Number of Farms," July 12, 1971.

[10] This figure is an estimate based on a National Farmers Union study that showed one small town businessman closing for every six farmers that folded. Thus, if a million farms fold by 1980, some 166,000 small businesses could be estimated to close in the same period.

[11] USDA Statistical Reporting Service. "Trend to Fewer and Larger Farms Continues." Press release from Washington, D.C. office, January 12, 1972. Number of farms in 1966 was 3,239,000; number of farms in 1972 estimated to be 2,831,000—a decline of 508,000 farms in five years.

[12] Based on a non-metropolitan to metropolitan area migration rate that has fluctuated roughly between 600-800 thousand people a year during the 1960's.

EXAMPLE 16 — And Now California Develops a Square Tomato

LOS ANGELES, March 7—Farmers have realized a dream: the square tomato.

To be precise, it is not square like a box but, in the words of William Sims, an agricultural researcher at the University of California-Davis, "it's more square than round."

California growers have begun sowing seeds this year to raise the new tomato, called the UC-82. Researchers say it is hardier and more bountiful than a conventional tomato and—with its squarish shape—is better prepared to survive the bruising of mechanical harvesting and transport from field to cannery in huge glass-fiber containers.

In reduced transit waste alone, Mr. Sims said, the new tomato should save California farmers about $20 million a year.

The square tomato was engineered in much the same way that Detroit creates a new car. There were false starts and a little balancing of this and that to come up with a product that would be more profitable. The UC-82 is the latest in a line of new tomato models introduced by the University of California since it started (in agricultural terms) a production revolution in 1961.

A Matter of Efficiency

Round tomatoes are preferred for the fresh table market. But "they have to be handled like eggs," Mr. Sims noted, and are therefore inefficient for high-volume mechanical harvesting.

In the late 1950's the university's researchers bred a new variety of tomato that had a tough skin. For the first time, a crop could be picked economically by machines without

The New York Times/Sandy Solmon

A conventional tomato, right, beside new square variety

unacceptable amounts of waste. To distinguish this variety from previous tomatoes, the new fruit was called a "processing" tomato for use in canning, juice, soup, ketchup, paste and other sauces.

Mostly because of the efficiencies of mechanical harvesting, California's production of tomatoes for this market increased from 1.3 million tons in 1954 to more than 7 million tons in 1975. California now produces more than half of the world's processing tomatoes. The state's tomato growers last year had revenues of close to $500 million.

The tough-skinned tomato, introduced in 1961, is still the standard here. But it has never been completely satisfactory, as Mr. Sims explained the other day.

Called the VF 145-B7879, the 1961 tomato proved extremely sensitive to temperature variations, its yield per acre was not so good and its shape was not ideal. Too many tomatoes were being damaged during harvesting and transportation to canneries.

Scientists photographed tomatoes of various shapes being picked by mechanical harvesters. They found that elongated tomatoes lined up better when being moved on conveyor belts. And elongated tomatoes bruised less easily.

The trouble with the researchers' first attempts at solving the problem was that humans still preferred round tomatoes. Sorters complained that they could not grab an elongated tomato as easily as a round one. The solution was a compromise—a squarish tomato that is mostly oblong.

The first square-round tomato, called the UC-134, was developed largely by Prof. D. C. Hanna at the university's Davis campus four years ago.

Overly Sensitive to Heat

This variety wasn't fully satisfactory, either. The tomatoes had to be picked too quickly after ripening, they were overly sensitive to high temperatures and many broke off the vines and were lost in harvesting.

The result was the new UC-82, which was developed by a group headed by Allen Stevens of the Davis faculty. He is currently on leave to teach tomato-growing technology in Israel. His chief assistant, Gerald Dickenson, is still at work on the seven-year project.

The Californians' success in harvesting more tomatoes causes a new problem: Now there may be too many of them. A cannery strike and heavy rains last summer narrowed the state's output from an expected 7 million tons to .5.2 million tons. Otherwise, there would likely have been a surplus. If production trends continue, crop analysts say, California could be turning out 12 million tons of tomatoes annually by 1984.

So the industry is looking for new ways to sell tomatoes. Different ways of canning them are being studied in hopes of retaining the flavor of fresh fruit. The possibility of selling frozen tomatoes is being evaluated. And even "tomato chips," something similar to potato chips, are being tested.

This article is reprinted from Robert Lindsey, "And Now California Develops a Square Tomato," New York Times, March 8, 1977.

EXAMPLE 17 California Agrarian Action Project

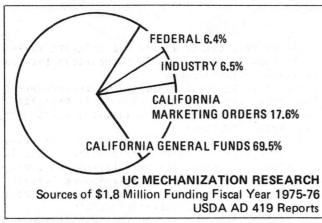

FEDERAL 6.4%

INDUSTRY 6.5%

CALIFORNIA MARKETING ORDERS 17.6%

CALIFORNIA GENERAL FUNDS 69.5%

UC MECHANIZATION RESEARCH
Sources of $1.8 Million Funding Fiscal Year 1975-76
USDA AD 419 Reports

PO Box 464
Davis, CA 95616

Most people believe that the American way of agriculture must be good—look at how much food we have and we still have enough to sell $20 billion worth overseas. Less than 5% of our population is engaged in agriculture, meaning that we can have lots of people in urban areas involved in industry, services, etc. As in many Third World nations, people here are starting to understand that mechanized agriculture isn't completely beneficial. Food quality is a concern, as is an increasing number of small farmers that are priced out of the market by high cost equipment and fertilizer. As a result, an ever more desperate situation exists when more farmworkers become unemployed.

Though less than nine months old, the California Agrarian Action Project has done much research and is pressing for governmental changes to deal with the issue of farmworkers losing jobs as a result of mechanization. California is the nation's largest agricultural state, and the state is spending the most on agricultural research through the University of California system. Yet all this research is going into producing more food—which means heavy mechanization. None of the 1500 agricultural scientists are analyzing the impact of this research. (Nevertheless, appropriate technology could mean high production rates without displacing thousands of farmers and farmworkers.) When will the University of California system start researching appropriate technology?

CAAP is going to the University of California regents and the State Legislature to push for changes in these research methods and priorities. "Proposals for land reform are being developed, with the aim of resettling displaced farmworkers on the land as a long term solution to job loss. Together with job training, this approach offers a realistic solution to job loss." Resources include their newsletter, a slide show ("No Hands Touch the Land") and an excellent pamphlet of the same title (available in English or Spanish for 50¢).

It's a difficult fight because not only do the government and university systems like the present situation, but the situation was created out of pressure from agribusiness for mechanization to avoid the "problem" of farm labor unions and strikes. It's an important struggle however, because the result will affect all of us—in what we eat, who controls food production and what happens to thousands of farmworkers—as well as having international implications related to methods Third World countries use to produce more food and better the lives of the rural majority.

In the northern part of the state, the California Agrarian Action Project has found that thousands of acres of farmland, owned by agencies of the State government, are being leased to large growers, often in "sweetheart" arrangements. The Project is asking that these lands be leased to farmworkers, with priority given to those who have been displaced by mechanization.

Crucial to all of these attempts to re-settle farmworkers on the land is the need for adequate financial and technical assistance. The scarcity of credit has forced many recently established farmworker owned farms out of business.

The taxpayer will be subsidizing whatever change is to come. While it is uncertain that mechanization will lower food prices, it is certain that it requires a public research subsidy to automate the farms, and additional millions of dollars of public assistance to support those who are displaced.

The alternative of resettling farmworkers into productive lives on the land would also require a taxpayer subsidy, but the result would be far more attractive than the influx of thousands more into the ghettos of urban poor. California's farms would not be automated factories, but homes for an autonomous rural people.

—No Hands Touch The Land

This article is reprinted from "California Agrarian Action Project," **The Workbook**, Southwest Research and Information Center, P.O. Box 4524, Albuquerque, New Mexico 87106, Vol. 3, No. 2, p. 53, March 1978.

No Hands Touch the Land

EXAMPLE 18

YOLO FRIENDS OF THE FARMWORKERS • CALIFORNIA AGRARIAN ACTION PROJECT
July 1977

Up until last summer, Flavio Martinez made his living in the cannery tomato fields of the Sacramento Valley. Though he found work thinning and weeding tomato plants, picking apricots, or gathering prunes and walnuts, he earned most of his annual income in the eight weeks of the tomato harvest.

For ten to twelve hours each day, seven days a week, he stood shoulder to shoulder with other workers on the harvest machines, pulling rocks, vines, green and rotten fruit from the deluge of tomatoes that raced by on a conveyor belt. Despite the heat, he wrapped his head in a bandana and a hat, as protection against the noise and swirling dust.

When his family was young, it was a struggle to earn enough to feed six children, but in recent years his two oldest sons joined him on the machines, helping to support the family.

Last July, he returned to the ranch where he had worked for the last eight years. The ranch foreman told him there was no work. The harvest machines had been outfitted with electronic eyes which could sort out the green tomatoes. The sorting crew was being cut from 20 workers to 5.

Martinez spent most of the harvest season driving from ranch to ranch in search of work. Everywhere he heard the same story—no sorters needed because of the electronic eyes.

Electronic eyes sorted tomatoes in the place of 5,000 California farmworkers during the harvest of 1976.[1] Those lucky enough to find work had to accept a 25¢ an hour wage cut.

"In four or five years, every harvester in the state will be equipped with an electronic sorter," predicts Jack Deets, a corporate executive with sorter manufacturer AMF Inc.[2] Priced from $50,000, the new electronic device uses infrared lights and color sensors to tell a green from ripe cannery tomato.

Photo-electric color sorting was first applied to farm machinery by John Powers, a professor of agricultural engineering at the University of California at Davis.[3] In August of 1976, 250 of the unemployed tomato workers picketed UC Davis to protest the public subsidy that supports mechanization research.[4]

Migrant workers were the hardest hit by displacement. Their meagre savings had been spent on the trip north to the tomato harvest. They became trapped, penniless, with dismal prospects for work.

Jobless families moved in with their friends and relatives. In the government run migrant camp at Madison, California, two-thirds of the families were living doubled up, according to Ross Parker, director of the Yolo Housing Authority. With 12 to 15 people living in each 3-room cabin, water and sanitary facilities were pushed to their limit.[5]

Last summer's harvest revealed what may prove to be a serious shortcoming of the electronic sorter. While the sorter worked efficiently at the beginning of the harvest, when most cull fruit was green, human hands and eyes were needed at the end of the harvest when it is over-ripe and rotten tomatoes which must be discarded.

The harvest was still dependent on thousands of migrants, but their work was cut from eight weeks down to one or two weeks of harvest employment. Mar Lynn Ormsby, a demographic analyst for the California Department of Housing, says that mechanization causes "gaps in the traditional south to north itinerary—no longer (are there) 'back to back' harvests to provide continuous work."[6]

With mechanization, the farmworkers' work year is cut, reported UC Berkeley agricultural economist William Metzler, who added, "reliance on Welfare Department assistance has become part of the annual life pattern of many farm families."[7]

"We have worked hard for these growers all our lives," says Flavio Martinez. "When they brought tractors to pull the plows, they cut the horses' necks and ate horsemeat. That might be a kinder end than the future that they are preparing for us."

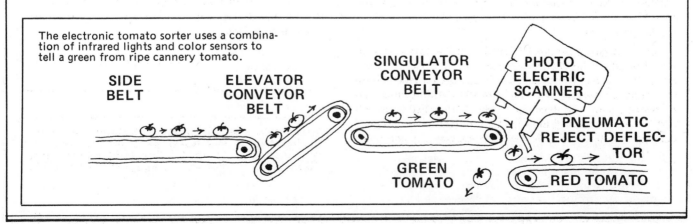

The electronic tomato sorter uses a combination of infrared lights and color sensors to tell a green from ripe cannery tomato.

SIDE BELT   ELEVATOR CONVEYOR BELT   SINGULATOR CONVEYOR BELT   PHOTO ELECTRIC SCANNER   PNEUMATIC REJECT DEFLECTOR   GREEN TOMATO   RED TOMATO

II. Social Sleepwalking

In the heart of the Sacramento Valley processing tomato district is the nation's largest center for agricultural research, the Davis campus of the University of California. UC scientists say their $50 million annual research budget pays for a cornucopia of technology that benefits consumer, farmer, and farmworker alike. The mechanization of the tomato harvest is cited as one of their greatest accomplishments.

The 29 research projects now underway at the University of California threaten 176,000 harvest time jobs in the state.

"Mechanization is one of the chief research missions of the University of California," UC Information Officer Ray Coppock reported to the California legislature in 1966.[1] There are now 22 mechanization projects in progress at Davis, while an additional 7 projects are underway at the UC campus at Riverside.[2]

Public funds pay 93% of the $1.8 million annual cost of these projects, which are aimed at eliminating most of 176,000 harvest time jobs in California. The research involves scientists in several disciplines working in co-operation.

Research to mechanize the cannery tomato harvest conducted in the early 60's is a good example of the multidisciplinary team effort. University scientists bred a thickskinned tomato, devised precision planting systems needed to grow it, tested the chemical that could ripen it, and built the machine to harvest it.[3]

Typical of the engineering studies underway is the development of a mechanical lettuce picker by Davis professor Roger Garrett. The machine uses a gamma ray selector to identify which lettuce heads are mature enough for harvest. A gattling gun packing device wraps the heads in plastic mesh.

New crop varieties are being bred to match the mechanical pickers. Davis geneticist Harold Olmo is trying to breed a new raising grape variety that will dry without being cut from the vine. Says Olmo, "This may lead to direct mechanical harvest and eliminate all hand harvest labor."

University scientists are studying the problems in processing mechanically harvested produce. Wine chemist Cornelius Ough is analysing the "leafiness aroma" in wines made from mechanically harvested grapes. His research will be useful in setting standards for the amount of leaf trash that mechanical grape pickers can be allowed to mix into wine grape loads.

The mechanization developments were criticized at the hearings on the UC budget held by the California Assembly in April. "In a time of such high unemployment, it is inconceivable that the state is spending the taxpayers' money to put more people out of work," UFW spokesperson Michael Linfield told an Assembly committee. He asked that a moratorium be called on labor displacing research until studies are made on the social impact of the projects, and until the state makes provisions to compensate displaced workers.

None of the University's 1500 agricultural scientists is analysing the impact of UC research, admitted James Kendrick, UC Vice-President of Agricultural Sciences. "Our primary mission is concern for the production of food and fiber," he told the committee.

William Friedland, a rural sociologist at UC Santa Cruz, calls the University's approach "social sleepwalking." He wants to study the effects of Garrett's lettuce harvester. The University administration, however, feels that no study of the impact of mechanization is needed, and so will not fund Friedland's work. He has been forced to abandon his research.

III. Tough Tomatoes

Every American consumer knows about the new flavor in canned tomatoes. "They taste like rubber," remarked Calfrornia State Senator Walt Stern (D-Bakersfield) at a recent hearing on the UC budget.

Davis Professor G.C. "Jack" Hanna bred a thickskinned tomato to withstand the rigors of mechanical harvest. Called VF-145, Hanna's tomato was not tough enough. In 1968, he reported that a quarter of the crop, some 1 million tons of VF-145, was damaged with impact cracks contaminated with soil, yeast, and bacteria.[1]

University breeders have developed an even tougher "square round" tomato. To be precise, the tomato is not square like a box, but in the words of tomato specialist William Sims, "it's more square than round."[2] Named UC-82, the new tomato is a thick-walled and juiceless fruit, but it can withstand the high speed operation of harvesters equipped with electronic sorters.

Coby Lorenzon was the Davis engineer who designed the machines that could pick Hanna's tough tomatoes. His harvester was designed for large scale farms. "Usually about 125 acres may be planted per harvest machine for the beginning grower," Sims explained, "and up to 200 acres for the more experienced grower."[3]

The average farmer of the time planted 45 acres of cannery tomatoes. Most could not get the financing necessary to triple their acreage and buy a $25,000 harvester. Within 10 years, the University scientists unwittingly forced 85% of the state's 4,000 cannery tomato farmers out of business.[4]

The remaining growers then expanded their tomato plantings to an average of 350 acres. Once committed to making payments on their new tomato harvesters, they could no longer be flexible in deciding how much to plant. In recent years there has been chronic overproduction in the tomato industry. 1.8 million tons of fruit were left to rot in California fields in 1976 alone.

Large tracts of land are needed to grow tomatoes for machine harvest. Sims advises growers that "row lengths of less than 600 feet seriously decrease harvest efficiency." The larger the field, the less the time lost in turning the machine from one row to another. As a result, mechanization has concentrated the tomato industry in the few California counties with such large tracts of land.

Within 10 years the University scientists unwittingly forced 85% of the state's tomato farmers out of the business.

Pests spread rapidly in the tomato monoculture, necessitating the virtual fumigation of tomato districts with more than four million pounds of pesticides each year.

In the rest of the United States, where there are no huge, uniform tracts of tomato land, tomato acreage is declining. A handful of California canning corporations now pack 85% of the nation's tomato products.

"The mechanized tomato has led to increased corporate concentration in the processing industry," claims consumer advocate Al Krebs. The Western Director of the Agribusiness Accountability Project, Krebs told the California Assembly in April that the state's top four canning corporations now control more than 80% of tomato processing, a situation he termed "tight oligopoly."

It is true that mechanization did cut the cost of producing cannery tomatoes by $7.25 a ton, according to a study made by UC farm advisor Phillip Parsons.[5] Had this savings been passed on to the consumer, mechanization would have lowered the retail price of a can of tomatoes 3%.

But since 1964, the year before the tomato harvest was mechanized, the retail price of canned tomatoes increased 111%, according to statistics compiled by the U.S. Department of Labor. By comparison, the retail price of processed fruits and vegetables went up only 76%.[6]

Between 1970 and 1975, the profits of the processors soared. H.J. Heinz profits went up 104.7%, while Del Monte profits increased 228.9%.

Consumers were not only stuck with high prices and a tough tomato, but as taxpayers they had paid for the research that made it all possible. They continue to subsidize mechanization by paying a number of hidden costs.

One such cost involves a simple failure of the harvest machine, which collects not only tomatoes, but substantial quantities of dirt as well. Dirt and trash removal cost processors $75 million in 1975. The California Tomato Growers Association warns that processing plants will close if municipal sewerage systems do not expand to handle the cannery effluent.[7] California, though hard hit by drought, will still be using millions of gallons of water to wash dirt from machine harvested tomato loads.

Mechanizing the tomato harvest eliminated 32,000 picking jobs in California,[8] and thousands more cannery and farm jobs in Ohio, Indiana, and New Jersey. Tens of thousands more California farmworkers have been displaced in the mechanization of the prune, nut, sugar beet, and wine grape harvests.

Mechanization of the tomato harvest eliminated 32,000 picking jobs in California.

Increased social welfare payments, the migration of jobless farmworkers to American cities, and the decline of small farms and rural communities must be figured as "hidden costs" of mechanization.

"Hard tomatoes and hard times" are the products of mechanization research, wrote the Agribusiness Accountability Project in 1972, adding that "in terms of wasted lives, depleted rural areas, choked cities, poisoned land and maybe poisoned people, mechanization research has been a bad investment."[9]

Footnotes

I. The Electronic Sorter

[1] Estimate based on **Farm Labor Reports 881-A**, a bi-monthly report of the California Employment Development Department.
[2] "Sorting Out the Sorters," **Woodland Daily Democrat**, February 11, 1977.
[3] "Mechanical Tomato Harvest Founders Honored," **Woodland Daily Democrat**, December 29, 1976.
[4] Paul Mapes, "Farmworkers Protest UCD Role in Tomato Sorter," **Sacramento Union**, sec. B, p. 4, August 20, 1974.
[5] Scott Reeves, "'Extra' Families Jam Labor Camp," **Woodland Daily Democrat**, August 5, 1976.
[6] Mar Lynn Ormsby, "Information Report on Agricultural Mechanization," California Department of Housing and Community Development, February 3, 1976.
[7] William H. Metzler, "Farm Mechanization and Labor Stabilization," **Giannini Foundation Research Report** No. 280, University of California, January 1965, p. 57.

II. Social Sleepwalking

[1] **Research on Agricultural Mechanization 1966**, University of California, Division of Agricultural Sciences.
[2] Based on AD-419 reports of the University of California to the U.S. Department of Agriculture.
[3] Wayne D. Rasmussen, "Advances in American Agriculture: The Mechanical Tomato Harvester as a Case Study," **Technology and Culture** 9:531-543, October, 1968.

III. Tough Tomatoes

[1] G.C. Hanna, et al., "Breeding Developments for Fruit Vegetables," **Fruit and Vegetable Harvest Mechanization: Technological Implications**, B.F. Cargill, G.E. Rossmiller (eds.), Rural Manpower Center, Michigan State University, East Lansing, Michigan, 1969, p. 242.
[2] Robert Lindsey, "And Now California Develops a Square Tomato," **New York Times**, March 8, 1977, p. 3.
[3] William Sims, et al., "Mechanized Growing and Harvesting of Processing Tomatoes," University of California Agricultural Extension Service AXT-232, January 1968.
[4] William Friedland and Amy E. Barton, **Destalking the Wily Tomato**, University of California at Davis, Department of ABS, Research Monograph No. 15, June 1975.
[5] Phillip S. Parsons, "Cost of Mechanical Tomato Harvest Compared to Hand Harvesting," University of California Agricultural Extension Service AXT-224, May 1966.
[6] **Handbook of Labor Statistics**, U.S. Department of Labor, Bureau of Labor Statistics, 1970 (Bulletin 1666); 1976 (Bulletin 1905).
[7] "Editorial," **California Tomato Grower**, January 1976, p. 3.
[8] Friedland and Barton, op. cit., p. 41.
[9] Jim Hightower and the Agribusiness Accountability Project, **Hard Tomatoes Hard Times**. (Cambridge, Mass.: Schenkman, 1972), p. 39.

This article is reprinted from **No Hands Touch the Land**, California Agrarian Action Project, Parts 1-4, pp. 1-4, July 1977.

Chapter 5

New Models for Extension and Training

The primary link between publicly supported agricultural research and the farmer is the cooperative agricultural extension work authorized by the *Smith-Lever Act of 1914* which established the Cooperative Extension Service. The Extension Service in each state is, as described in the preceeding chapter, a part of the U.S. Department of Agriculture and the land grant college network. As with agricultural research, extension programs are cooperatively financed by federal, state and local governments. Funds for extension work go through the Federal Extension Service (FES) to the states' Cooperative Extension Service offices (CES). In 1975 USDA gave the Extension Service $179 million in federal funds while state and local governments allocated $270 million towards extension programs.

The basic mission of the Extension Service, as mandated in the Smith-Lever Act, is to help *people* identify and solve their farm, home and community problems through the use of research findings and USDA programs. This "outreach" and technical assistance work is carried out through state and county extension offices throughout the country.

Today, the Extension Service is often criticized for not responding to the needs of many small and family sized farmers and to the problems facing people living in rural communities. Although some publicly supported extension projects have related to the needs of farmers, many county extension agents have formed close ties to the more successful farmers and no longer consider it their responsibility to initiate innovative programs which would improve the economic viability of the majority of farmers.

INNOVATIVE EXTENSION PROGRAMS

In some states, however, there are models for what the Cooperative Extension Service could be doing if it chose to make a concerted effort to offer assistance to a more representative constituency of farmers. Missouri has developed one of the most widely known programs. The Missouri Small Farm Program began in part due to the realization that, according to the 1969 Census of Agriculture, nearly four-fifths of the farms in Missouri had annual sales of less than $10,000. These same farms sold only one-fifth of the state's total agricultural produce.

The Small Farm Program employs paraprofessionals—retired farmers or part-time farmers—to serve as "educational assistants" in their own counties. These outreach workers provide production and management assistance to the farmers participating in the Program. Over 900 small farmers took part in the Program from its beginning, in 1971, through 1975. A description of this innovative Cooperative Extension effort is included as **Example 19, Summary and Recommendations; The Missouri Small Farm Program.**

Several other states have initiated extension programs geared toward the needs of limited resource farmers. The Texas Intensified Farm Planning Program was initiated in 1968 and also uses local farmers as program aides. The program, designed by the Texas Agricultural Extension Service, works with 225 small farm operators in 10 counties. Most of these farmers receive a major portion of their income from farming, although they gross less than $5,000 a year. The Texas Program has since expanded and has also moved into providing marketing assistance. Other states with programs which attempt to work specifically to increase the economic viability of small farmers are Virginia (Virginia Polytechnic Institute), North Carolina (North Carolina A & T) and Maryland. Massachusetts, Rhode Island and Connecticut have jointly sponsored a Tri-State Small Farm Program which is headquartered at the Cooperative Extension Service at the University of Massachusetts in Amherst.

In southeastern Arkansas the state Extension Service in 1972 started a horticulture project that by 1975 was partly responsible for 2,700 gardens which produced $269,000 worth of vegetables for commercial sales. In this project, as in other parts of the state, extension agents have stressed the importance of marketing assistance for small farmers.

NEW MODELS FOR TRAINING AND OUTREACH

The Cooperative Extension Service is not the only vehicle for training and technical assistance to farmers. Because of the unwillingness of many extension programs at the state and local level to work particularly with limited resource farmers, a growing number of non-profit groups and community-based organizations have forged ahead in building imaginative outreach projects and training institutions.

In 1975, for example, the Rural Advancement of the National Sharecroppers Fund began the Frank Graham Experimental Farm and Training Center in Anson County, North Carolina. Another organization in the Southeast which offers management assistance—although more in the area of farmer cooperatives and marketing—is the Federation of Southern Cooperatives. The Federation also runs a Training Center in Epes, Alabama.

Another unique program which deals more broadly with "rural studies" has just been initiated at Southwest State University in Marshall, Minnesota. The program, described in **Example 20, The Nation's First Rural Studies Program Is Launched**, from *Catholic Rural Life*, is now under the leadership of Jon Wefald, a former Commissioner of Agriculture in Minnesota.

An exciting project now in the planning stages is in Massachusetts. A number of people have worked together under the auspices of a group called "Women in Agriculture" to develop a proposal for a New England Small Farm Institute. Although the recent defeat of the Democratic administration in Massachusetts on November 7th, 1978, may well temper the progress of this effort, the organizers of the proposed Small Farm Institute have worked closely with Commissioner of Agriculture Fred Winthrop and many other Department of Agriculture staff members who have been helpful in the planning of the project.

Another model for working with small farmers at the state and local level is that of the Maine Organic Farmers and Gardeners Association (MOFGA) and the New England Organic Farmers Association (NOFA) in Vermont. Both of these membership-based organizations have newsletters, offer advice and assistance in the areas of production, management and marketing, and also provide information on "biological" methods of agricultural production.

A comprehensive view of the training needs of small farmers in one state is provided by the California Small Farm Viability Project's *Training Task Force Report*. The report covers various options and proposals relevant to the Extension Service as well as other training models. An appendix to the report, which is reprinted as **Example 21, Training Task Force: Final Report** from the California Small Farm Viability Project's *Final Report*, includes a model for a state Small Farm Training Center.

CONCLUSION: NEW DIRECTIONS FOR LAND GRANT COLLEGES

Land Grant institutions are structurally and financially the best equipped organizations in this country to explore new ways of helping limited resource farmers, family farmers and rural communities. But the Land Grant system will not realize its potential for constructive and progressive change unless it is convinced to do so by citizens who feel strongly that the resources of the system should be used more equitably and imaginatively. State legislatures and state and local public officials must also exercise their power to redirect the efforts of the Land Grant system. The next decade will be an important time for farmers, concerned citizens and political activists to examine the policies and priorities of land grant institutions and the U.S. Department of Agriculture.

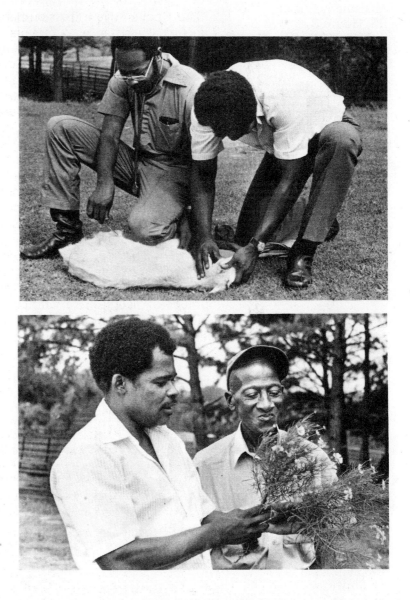

Resources

ORGANIZATIONS

Farralones Institute

Center for Sustainable Agriculture
15290 Coleman Road
Occidental, California 95465
(707) 874-3060
David Katz

Federation of Southern Cooperatives

Rural Training Center
P.O. Box 95
Epes, Alabama 35460
(205) 652-9676
John Zippert, Charles Prejean

Graham Training Center

Rural Advancement Fund
P.O. Box 95, Route 3
Wadesboro, North Carolina 29170
(704) 851-9346
Kathryn Waller

Missouri Small Farm Project

Cooperative Extension
228 Mumford Hall
University of Missouri
Columbia, Missouri 65201
(314) 822-2728
Edward Wiggins, Jerry West

National Extension Evaluation Project

United States Department of Agriculture (USDA)
Room 6435—South Building
Washington, D.C. 20250
(202) 447-4478
Fred Wood, Director; Susan DeMarco

New England Small Farm Institute

Jepson House, Jackson Street
Belchertown, Massachusetts 01007
(413) 323-4531
Judy Gillan, Director

Rural Education Center

c/o Stoneyfield Farm
Wilton, New Hampshire 03086
(603) 654-6077
Samuel Kaymen

Tennessee Valley Authority (TVA)

Small Farm Management Program
Division of Agricultural Development/TVA
Muscle Shoals, Alabama 35660
(205) 383-4631
Roger Woodworth

Texas Intensified Farm Planning Program

A & M University Cooperative Extension Program
Drawer B
Texas A & M University
Prairie View, Texas 77445
(713) 857-2023
Hoover Garden

Tri-State Small Farm Program

Cooperative Extension
University of Massachusetts
Amherst, Massachusetts 01003
(413) 545-1921
(Massachusetts, Rhode Island and Connecticut)
Francis Mentzer,
Extension Farm Management Specialist

Tuskegee Institute

Cooperative Extension
Tuskegee, Alabama 36088
(205) 727-8011
Philip Brown, Director

Small Farm Demonstration Project
Tuskegee, Alabama 36088
(205) 727-8011
Booker T. Whatley, Director

BIBLIOGRAPHY

George, Charlotte, **Lincoln University Small Farm Family Resource Management Program.** Lincoln University Cooperative Extension Service, Jefferson City, Missouri. May 1978.

Hightower, Jim and Susan De Marco, **Hard Tomatoes: Hard Times: The Failure of the Land Grant Complex.** Schenkman Publishing Company, Cambridge, Massachusetts. 1973.

Small Farm Viability Project, **Training Task Force Report.** State CETA Office, Department of Employment Development, 800 Capitol Mall, Sacramento, California 95814. November 1977.

Tuskegee Institute, **Cooperative Extension Service, Tuskegee Institute: 1971-1977.** Alabama Cooperative Extension Service, Tuskegee Institute, Alabama 36088.

U.S. General Accounting Office, **Some Problems Impeding Economic Improvement of Small-Farm Operations: What the Department of Agriculture Could Do.** Superintendent of Documents, U.S. Government Printing Office, Washington, D.C. 20402. August 1975. Report to the Congress; recommendations for improving extension services and the Land Grant College complex so as to benefit small farms.

West, Jerry G., et al., **Missouri Small Farm Project: An Evaluation With a Control Group.** University of Missouri-Columbia, College of Agriculture, Columbia, Missouri. October 1975.

West, Jerry, et al., **Missouri Small Farm Project: Annual Report.** University of Missouri-Columbia, College of Agriculture, Columbia, Missouri. 1977.

Summary and Recommendations

EXAMPLE
19

Results from this analysis show the educational program has been successful

The Missouri Extension Service launched a small farm educational program in 1971. Farmers participating in the program have made numerous changes since 1971 including marked increases in production and sales. This report contains the results of an attempt to assess progress made by

Mr. and Mrs. Bill Haddock, Alton, raise cattle and feeder pigs on their 60-acre farm. Haddock often asks the education assistant for help.

participant farms relative to those who were not participating in the program. A group of farms from which information had been obtained in 1971 were identified for use as a control group in the evaluation of the educational program.

Although both participants and non-participants have made changes in their farming operations, participants have made more progress. Participants had higher farm sales, higher net farm income, larger enterprises, more livestock assets, slightly more efficient resource utilization,

more professional assistance and information, more changes in housing and more stability in level of production. Evidence was not conclusive with respect to relative changes in production practices nor was it obvious that participants had accomplished more of their goals in terms of planned changes than non-participants.

Although participants in the Small Farm Program made considerable progress relative to non-participants, they were still far short of optimum in terms of farm sales or size of enterprise. This would seem to suggest room for further progress with emphasis on more intensive enterprises such as feeder pig production.

Results from this analysis show the educational program has been successful and would warrant expansion to other areas of the state as funds become available. It would appear desirable to develop procedures for showing small farms their opportunities with more intensive enterprises which are adapted to the area. Somewhat greater attention might also be given to improvement of production practices and utilization of resources to help participants achieve some of the planned changes in their farming operations. Participants in the program had a generally favorable reaction towards the program but did not necessarily associate it with the extension service.

Recognition of extension's role is deserved and will be necessary if funds are to be made available for continuation and expansion of the program to additional areas of the state.

This article is reprinted from Jerry West, "Summary and Recommendations," **Missouri Small Farm Program: An Evaluation with a Control Group,** University of Missouri-Columbia, College of Agricultural Economics, Columbia, Missouri 65201, p. 25, October 1975.

EXAMPLE 20 The Nation's First Rural Studies Program Launched

By Karl Ostrom

Southwest State University is developing a new identity for the universities of rural America. It is developing as a cultural resource and exchange center for a regional network of farms, businesses, villages, and small cities where citizens are empowered to shape their social and economic lives.

This new mission to rural America comes at a time when skeptical voices from both countryside and city are asking questions like these:

Can the traditions of independent farmers, small businessmen, cooperatives, community schools, and small towns have a viable place in America's cultural and economic future?

Can rural America's spirit of cooperative, local self-reliance be awakened and mobilized to overcome the cynicism and apathy triggered by the unresponsiveness of giant institutions?

The Rural Studies Program at Southwest State University is saying yes to these questions. Through the languages of art, music, literature, social science, and economic analysis, faculty are joining with students and with the community to revitalize our rural heritage and cultivate its practical promises for the future.

This 4-year technological and liberal arts university is being developed as the hub for a network of rural institutions. Small schools, hospitals, churches, businesses, and local governments are clustered into communities dotting the farmland prairies of southwest Minnesota. Southwest State is undertaking this educational experiment in the context of this rural region.

A contest of social values is at stake in the issue of whether or not these rural institutions can build themselves into a regional network that can control its social and economic destiny. They embody the two-fold value propositions that local responsibility and control in matters of property and labor foster zestful self-investment in one's own surroundings, and that social enthusiasm and responsibility for common welfare and community development is best cultivated through the involvement of citizens in local institutions.

The first proposition finds expression in the traditions of the independent farmer, craftsman, small businessman, cooperative, and employee-owned corporation. The second is embodied in the promotion of voluntary associations and local government institutions.

Values fostered by these rural institutions contrast with lifestyles feasible within the giant corporate and governmental institutions that structure America's urban complexes. Highly centralized institutions tend to foster other-directed sensitivity in place of initiative, and to dependence upon direction from "above" in place of the community effort that makes local self-reliance possible.

The value assumptions of independent farmers and rural communities played vital roles in forming early America's institutions and heritage. Increasingly from the middle of the last century to the present, however, the control of political and economic life has been wrested from local communities and invested in highly-centralized institutions. The idea of community self-reliance has lived on as a myth with little substance, a vestige of an earlier era.

That sector of the economy made up of independent proprietors and farmers has become subservient to the economic sector controlled by the giant corporations that dictate the conditions of the cost-price squeeze endured by farmers. Local governments increasingly have become servant extensions of Big Government rather than vice versa. The changes in American political ideology that accompanied the centralization of our major economic and political institutions created a cultural climate in which the small-scale institutions of rural America could be pushed toward oblivion.

What has developed on the one hand is a strain of political conservatism that places its vested interest in the rights of Big Business to extend centralized controls over vast economic empires with little regard for local autonomy. A strain of political liberalism, at the same time, has invested its interest in government institutions large enough to countervail and control the massive forces engendered by the business world's corporate giants. In a symbiotic two-step dance, these liberals and conservatives sanctioned the development of a corporate-state mind-set in which bigness was to bring happiness and beauty.

Small farms, the small business economy they support, and the small communities with the small schools and hospitals that service them, were to be abandoned, presumably to die, as progress marched on.

And, indeed, rural America began to believe that it must die. Farms were consolidated, small businesses were shut down, railroad tracks were left to rust, and the attention of national government was focused on the problems of making Big Business and Giant Metropolises function. The schools of the countryside were not only consolidated; what they taught also was urbanized. They prepared rural students for urban living and corporate jobs [without a word about rural traditions]. The migration from the countryside that resulted was massive.

It was quite a turnaround, then, when President Jon Wefald, as head of a state-supported university, declared that the time had come "to recognize a new appreciation of our rural values and rural institutions and what they mean to the future of America." Much more is involved in that, however, than a change of direction for a single university in southwest Minnesota.

The middle 1970s have brought a resurgence of rural values triggered by a complex of social forces. The unresponsiveness inherent in giant institutions has contributed to a record level of citizen alienation, apathy, and cynicism toward public institutions; openness to alternatives has become imperative. Crises in energy supply and in the regulation of capital have called into question the stability of highly-centralized, capital-intensive, and energy-intensive institutions. Finally, a shift in values toward increased emphasis on such things as personal identity and self-actualization has resulted in a demand for meaningful participation in social and economic institutions.

Southwest State University will be successful in making rural businesses more prosperous only as its Technical Assistance Center works hand in hand with local and regional business organizations. Its Public Officials Training Board will be helpful to local governments only as it becomes a partner with them and they become partners with each other. The university will be a strengthening agent for family farms, rural schools, churches, and other community institutions only through the forging of a regional network of cooperative rural institutions.

The university does, however, have a unique role in enabling such a network to happen. As a regional institution, it has the opportunity to provide a symbolic center, a people's place that embodies the region's cultural heritage and serves the community's diverse interests.

This article is reprinted from Karl Ostrom, "The Nation's First Rural Studies Program Launched," **Catholic Rural Life**, pp. 21-23, January 1978.

Training Task Force: Final Report

EXAMPLE 21

Because farming is both a science and a business, the family farmer must have a solid knowledge of production processes, management, and marketing. Once he has acquired this basic knowledge, he is obliged to keep constantly abreast of new developments that affect his productivity and efficiency. To do this, he must know how to make use of all available informational resources, including government agricultural agencies and their publications, public and private educational institutions, and technical assistance provided through businessmen and bankers.

Only for in-school youth, from high school through community college and the university, are training resources to prepare for independent farming adequate. For out-of-school adults who would like to enter farming but need instruction in specific production areas, marketing, or management, and for present low-resource farmers who need to sharpen their skills in order to make their farming operation more profitable, training resources are extremely limited. Community colleges, Regional Occupational Centers and Programs, and private, nonprofit, community-based organizations have the greatest flexibility to serve them, but their financial resources and outreach capacity are inadequate.

For the established family farmer, private-sector resources such as lending institutions and commercial operators are important sources of information. The University of California Cooperative Extension Service should be an equally valuable resource, and it does in fact serve those farmers capable of seeking out its agents. Unfortunately, many small farmers are unaware of the services that the Cooperative Extension Service offers, and very few extension agents have the time to identify and seek out the family farmers in their area.

The Task Force believes that all farmers, from the new entrant with limited experience and incomplete knowledge, to the university graduate who needs little or no assistance in keeping abreast of new developments, should have access to the skills and information they need. This implies a general commitment by the public sector to augment the educational services provided specifically to small farmers by three major entities: the University of California Cooperative Extension Service and agricultural research program, the formal education system, and community-based organizations. Comprehensive, intensive training should be available to the least prepared segment of the family-farmer population, and less intensive, more occasional services to the more advanced family farmer. Adoption of such a family-farmer training policy would require the relaxation or revision of the many regulations that currently restrict the innovative use of public funds for small-farmer training.

Where organized training programs are involved, the Task Force makes the following specific recommendations:

- Training programs must be integrated with financing mechanisms for land and production capital and with marketing programs.
- Training must be conceptualized as a long-term undertaking, of at least two or three years' duration.
- Training programs should be designed to provide a subsistance allowance until the farmer's own cash flow from agricultural production becomes adequate to support his family.
- The allowance or stipend system should be coordinated with the existing welfare payment system toward the end of making more positive use of available welfare funds. A family farmer should not be excluded from training or access to subsistance allowances if his income is above the government determined poverty line or if he has an equity investment in land or equipment. Rather, a flexible system of subsistance allowances should be devised that would supplement each participant family's income to the extent necessary in order to provide a total amount representative of a moderate income. A system could be developed involving private-sector bank loans for participants already making moderate incomes and individually determined allowances for low-income participants.
- Training programs should emphasize the need that small farmers have for cooperative action at all levels, particularly in the area of marketing, if they are to compete with large growers.
- Training programs must have a bilingual capacity for the benefit of the non-English speaker.
- A State policy should be established for the preparation and publication of basic, learner verified instructional materials pertinent to the needs of small farmers and published in the native languages of all significant segments of the small-farmer population.
- Increased use must be made of appropriate instructional hardware, along with appropriate software developed locally.
- Because of the present shortage of trainers capable of relating effectively to the client population, programs must be developed to prepare trainers and give them professional status. Consideration should be given to accredited internships and apprenticeship programs and to more extensive use of the peer training concept.

The Task Force's final recommendation is that a mechanism for information collection and dissemination be established for family farmers, supported by public funds. Equally important is the evolution of networking among providers and consumers of training. The existence of such a network would facilitate the exchange of information and would create a power base for advocacy of family-farmer interests and needs.

This article is reprinted from "Training Task Force: Final Report," **The Family Farm in California**, pp. 1-2 (Abstract Appendix A), 113-114 and 153-154, November 1977.

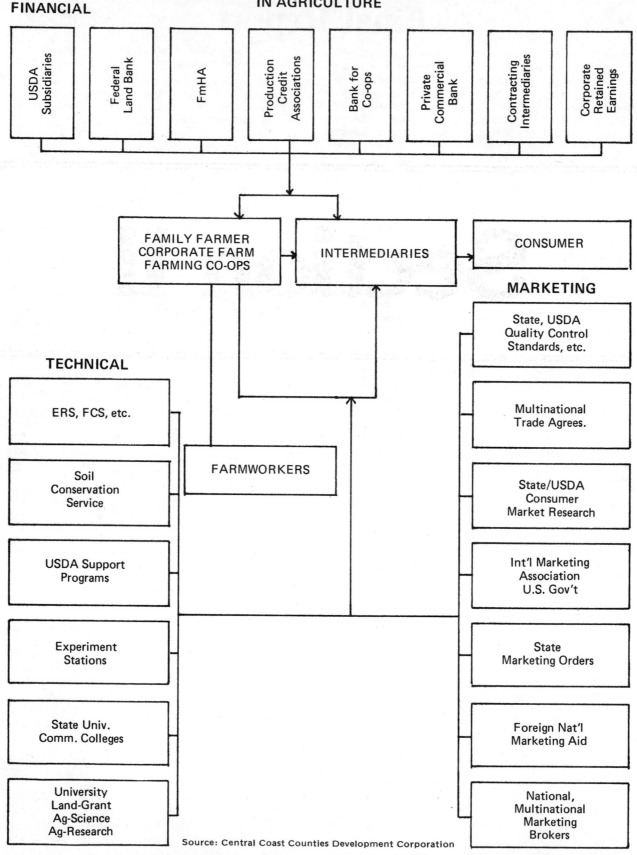

EXISTING AGENCY SUPPORT SYSTEMS IN AGRICULTURE

FINANCIAL

- USDA Subsidiaries
- Federal Land Bank
- FmHA
- Production Credit Associations
- Bank for Co-ops
- Private Commercial Bank
- Contracting Intermediaries
- Corporate Retained Earnings

FAMILY FARMER CORPORATE FARM FARMING CO-OPS

INTERMEDIARIES

CONSUMER

MARKETING

- State, USDA Quality Control Standards, etc.
- Multinational Trade Agrees.
- State/USDA Consumer Market Research
- Int'l Marketing Association U.S. Gov't
- State Marketing Orders
- Foreign Nat'l Marketing Aid
- National, Multinational Marketing Brokers

TECHNICAL

- ERS, FCS, etc.
- Soil Conservation Service
- USDA Support Programs
- Experiment Stations
- State Univ. Comm. Colleges
- University Land-Grant Ag-Science Ag-Research

FARMWORKERS

Source: Central Coast Counties Development Corporation

Section II

Section II

Protecting Farm Land

One of America's greatest natural resources is its farmland. More than any other country, America was blessed with what had seemed like unlimited expansions of the richest and most productive land in the world. This resource, coupled with our democratic traditions and institutions, created a prosperous, productive, and family farm-based agricultural economy.

This democratic agricultural economy is under pressure on a number of fronts. None, however, is more serious than the rapidly accelerating urban sprawl and commercial development pressure which are permanently destroying over 3 million acres of prime farmland each year. The developer's bulldozers, powerlines and stripmines are such that they do not "borrow" prime farmland for temporary development: they permanently destroy its productive ability.

This destruction of farmland is a major loss to the farmers, this country, and to the world. The decrease in tillable land increases the price of remaining land, making it more difficult for new farmers to purchase land to begin farming. America loses the natural resource that has sustained its rural communities which are so essential for the functioning of American democracy. And the world faced with the relentless increase in population loses some of its most productive farmland needed to grow food for millions.

The Federal government has little, if any, authority or control over land use. Both constitutionally and by custom the questions of the use and abuse of land fall solely under the province of state, county, and local governments. Although their response has been slow in coming, state and local governments have recently recognized the seriousness of the land use "crisis" facing this society.

With the same penchant for innovations and experimentation that they have displayed with the problems of supporting the family farm, state and local governments have begun to protect farmland. Major experiments are underway across the country aimed at protecting farmland through such devices as state and local land use plans, innovative zoning concepts, public acquisition of land or development rights, and unique innovations in the property tax structure.

. The major initiatives undertaken by state and local governments in land use planning and zoning techniques are outlined in Chapter 6, *Protecting Farmland Through Planning*, and the major initiatives focusing on changes in the property tax system and other tax policies are described in Chapter 7, *Protecting Farmland Through New Tax Policies*.

Chapter 6

Protecting Farm Land Through Planning

America's cities and suburban sprawl are spreading out relentlessly, threatening to overwhelm rural and farm communities. The commercial development of open and agricultural land poses a desperate crisis for American agriculture.

The annual land loss is staggering. Over 3 million acres of farmland are lost to farming each year. Between 1950 and 1972, this country lost 6% of its total farm acreage. New England lost half of its farm acreage: New Jersey lost 45%.

The rising demand of commercial and residential developers and speculators puts overwhelming burdens on owners of open space and farmers. The wide-open "Market" for such land is accelerating and natural forces seem unable to stop it.

Many state legislatures have decided through one approach or another to prevent the "free market" from making the basic decisions on land use. A number of exciting approaches have been attempted and provide useful models. State governments have been the prime movers on this problem because the U.S. Constitution reserves to the states the right to control uses of land. States, either independently, or acting through county or municipal governments, have taken the lead in protecting farmland and open space from development and speculation.

STATE LAND USE PLANS

One of the major approaches considered by many states, and adopted by some, has been state land use plans. Such state use plans vary widely. The basic principles of a land use plan is that a state divides all the land in that state into different categories based on present use and the quality of the land. The land in the various categories is then restricted to certain narrow uses. State land use plans are, however, designed for a number of objectives including preserving open space, controlling urban sprawl, improving air and water quality, enhancing the local economy, and improving the scenic and visual environment. Meeting those objectives sometimes overlaps with and sometimes conflicts with protecting agricultural land.

One of the nation's strongest land use plans is in the state of Hawaii. It was also one of the first. Passed in 1961, *Hawaii's Land Use Law* created a State Land Use Commission with authority to classify all public and private land in the state into one of four different classifications—urban, rural, agricultural, or conservation. The Commission then established specific boundaries for each zone and proscribed the uses that land could be put to in each district. If an old or new property owner wanted to change the use of his land, he required permission from the Land Use Commission.

Although not as strong as that of Hawaii, *Vermont's Act 250*, which was passed in 1970, established a permit system requiring specific permission for the intensive development of land. Act 250 created a State Environmental Board and a series of District Environmental Boards to hear requests for permits from developers. Permits were required for any development of ten or more acres, and any construction above 2,500 feet of altitude. The 1970 legislation also required the State Environmental Board to prepare a state Land Capability and Development Plan which would have divided the state's land into specific classifications such as those contained in the Hawaiian law. Widespread public opposition to the prospect of "state-wide zoning" eventually killed the Land Capability and Development Plan, but left Act 250 operating and popular.

Somewhat milder than both the Hawaiian and Vermont legislation is that of Oregon. The *Oregon Land Conservation and Development Commission Act of 1973* put that state on the path of controlling development and required that counties develop detailed land use plans within a general framework of state developed guidelines and goals. The 1973 Act also grants wide privileges to the Exclusive Farm Use zones (EFU) which had been permitted in an earlier 1961 law. Oregon was one of the first states to combine land use planning and special tax assessment of farmlands as contained in the EFUs.

Legislators and farm leaders have recognized that state land use plans alone are not adequate to protect threatened farmland. In some states, these groups have pushed for specific land use plans aimed at protecting agricultural land. Two of the most interesting approaches have been proposed in California.

In 1976 California Assemblyman Charles Warren drafted *California Assembly Bill 15* which would have established a powerful state-wide zoning program to protect agricultural land. An Agricultural Resources Council would have been established with power to prescribe the permitted uses of land classified as prime agricultural land. It would also have had the power to review and override local decisions affecting prime agricultural land. Cities and counties would have been required to submit detailed maps of designated prime agricultural land for review and approval. In addition, land designated as prime agricultural would also receive lower assessments from local tax assessors. The bill passed the Assembly but failed in the Senate.

In 1977 attention was focused on another interesting California proposal. *California Senate Bill 1736* was designed to steer development away from prime agricultural lands. A state commission would establish maximum boundaries for municipalities, to be called "spheres of influence." Municipalities would not be permitted to extend roads, sewers, water or public transportation outside its "sphere of influence" after a certain period of time. Denying residentially oriented public services to prime agricultural land would force development to be intensive and within the "sphere of influence" rather than the current pattern of unchecked growth.

A group of Hawaiian Senators tried another interesting approach. They tried to combine the strict land use control regulations created in the 1961 law with the goal of providing low and moderate income housing. The *1975 Hawaiian State Land Bank Bill* would have identified major parcels of Hawaii's land as Land Bank land. The State Land Use Commission then would have been prohibited from changing the classification of that land except on petition of the State Housing Authority. Such legislation would have given low and moderate income housing the first access to any land being developed from agricultural or rural uses.

One should look north to the Canadian Western Provinces for the most comprehensive efforts of land use planning to protect agricultural land. Under the leadership of the New Democratic Party, British Columbia passed the *B.C. Land Commission Act of 1973*. It created Agricultural Land Reserves as a form of zoning aimed at protecting agricultural land from non-agricultural development. The Reserves limit use of the agricultural lands to purposes that will not diminish the ability of the land to produce crops. The Act also allows the province to purchase land directly and lease it back to new farmers. British Columbia's comprehensive approach seems superior to the piece-meal approach of many American states. Excerpts from the report: **Example 22, The B.C. Land Commission—Keeping the Options Open,** describes its authority and programs.

PURCHASE OF DEVELOPMENT RIGHTS PROGRAMS

Another approach a number of states have considered to both help farmers and stop development is to purchase the "development rights" to farmland. Under this type of program, the state or local government purchases from the landowner the right to sell that land for commercial, industrial, or residential development. The farmer continues to own all other rights to the land.

The state or local government pays the farmer for the "development rights" to the land. The value of these "rights" is the difference between the price a developer would pay for the land—the market-value—and the price a farmer would pay if the land was only to be used for farming. Such "development rights" programs are all voluntary. Farmers can either sell or not sell, depending only on their own personal commitment to protecting their land from development and speculation.

One of the first "development rights" programs was the *Maryland Agricultural Preservation Foundation Act of 1974.* This act authorized the state to purchase or accept gifts of easements that restricted the future uses of agricultural and woodland to uses that maintain the existing character of the land. Regrettably, the Maryland Legislature has not yet provided the funding for the program.

The state of Massachusetts recently, however, passed the *Agricultural Preservation Restrictions Act of 1977* which authorizes a $5 million bond to purchase the "development rights" or "preservation restrictions" for farmland. A companion piece of legislation gave Massachusetts towns and cities authority to spend their own money to purchase "preservation restrictions" as part of their own programs. A description of the new Massachusetts legislation published by the Metropolitan Area Planning Council of Boston is included as **Example 23, Notes on the Law: A New Way to Save Our Farmland.** Next door to Massachusetts, the Connecticut House of Representatives also approved a $5 million "pilot" program for that state to purchase the development rights to farmland under development pressure.

The state of New Jersey has also passed a purchase of development rights bill. The four Burlington County townships of Medford, Lumberton, Pemberton and Southampton were chosen as the first sites. The program, funded initially at $5 million is financed from the Green Acres Bond Issue, a large fund used to purchase open space and recreational land for New Jersey.

Perhaps the most well known and largest "development rights" project is the *Suffolk County Farmland Preservation Program.* The initial legislation was approved by the Suffolk County Legislature in 1974, leading the way to voter approval of a $60 million bond issue to finance the program. On September 29, 1977 the first contracts were signed with two farmers, Nathaniel Talmage and George Reeves, to purchase their development rights. The Cooperative Extension Association of Suffolk County published an excellent description of the purpose and procedures of the Suffolk County program which is included as **Example 24, Suffolk's Farmland Preservation Program.**

County officials hope to be able to purchase between 10,000 and 12,000 acres of farmland. Priority would be given to farmer-owned and occupied holdings of at least 200 acres. Besides receiving payment for the development rights, the farmer would also benefit from a reduction of about 80% in property taxes. One of the major problems of the Suffolk County program, as in all development rights programs, is the enormous cost. These high costs will probably result in state and local governments not being able to afford to buy the rights to land near urban areas where development pressures are strongest, but instead to buy the development rights to land which will inevitably face development 10 to 15 years from now.

LAND TRUSTS: A NEW CONCEPT

As a means both to cut the cost of a development rights purchase program and also to keep government out of the land ownership business, some communities have turned to the concept of land trusts. A model *State Land Trust Act* has been drafted by former Vermont State Representative John McClaughry. The Land Trust would be an instrumentality of the state whose primary purpose would be to accept land and interests in land for the benefit of the people of the state. It would not have the power to issue bonds or to exercise eminent domain.

The Trust would accept land or interests in land in two major forms. On the one hand any landowner could donate land, the development rights, or other interests in lands to the Trust. The landowner would get a tax deduction for his charitable contribution. The other major purpose of the Trust would be to permit landowners to lease the development rights or other interests in the land to the Trust for some period of time. The Trust would pay the property taxes on the rights or interests it was then leasing. A slight increase in the state's property transfer tax would cover the cost of financing this program.

THE TRANSFER OF DEVELOPMENT RIGHTS

Another major initiative states have considered to protect agricultural land from development also has the advantage of not costing the public treasury money. This is the concept of "transferable development rights" or TDRs. Illinois has already enacted a limited TDR plan. New Jersey came close to adopting a comprehensive TDR plan, and among the 10 states which considered it last year, a limited TDR plan passed the New York Assembly in 1978. The concept of transferable development rights is well described in the article reprinted from *State Legislatures* which is included as **Example 25, Transferable Development Rights.**

The New York Assembly bill gives cities and localities wider authority under their local zoning and planning process. They would be allowed to set up a system of "transferable development rights" through which a landowner could sell the development rights to the land without actually selling the land itself. That "development right" could be sold to another landowner who wanted to develop one specific parcel of land more intensively than local zoning regulations would permit. The effect of such legislation steers development into certain specified "development areas" of municipalities, while at the same time compensating other landowners for the decreased value of their land caused by the zoning.

Resources

BIBLIOGRAPHY

Block, William J., **Rural Zoning: People, Property and Public Policy**. Cooperative Extension Service, Washington State University, Pullman, Washington 99164. January 1974.

Bosselman, Fred and David Callies, **The Quiet Revolution in Land Use Control**. Prepared for Council on Environmental Quality, 722 Jackson Place, N.W., Washington, D.C. 20006. December 1971. Summaries of state land use plans in Hawaii, Vermont, Minnesota, Massachusetts, Wisconsin, and Missouri; has good theoretical discussion of the role of the state in land use planning.

British Columbia Land Commission, **Keeping the Options Open**. B.C. Land Commission, Burnaby, British Columbia. 1975. Good pamphlet describing goals and provisions of B.C. Land Commission Act of 1973.

Bryant, William and Howard Conklin, "New Farmland Preservation Programs in New York," **Journal of the American Institute of Planners**. American Institute of Planners, 1776 Massachusetts Avenue, N.W., Washington, D.C. 20036. November 1975.

California Land Use Task Force, **The California Land: Planning for People**. Planning and Conservation Foundation, 1225 8th Street, Sacramento, California 95814. 1975.

California Tomorrow, "Land Preservation: Five Bills in Search of a Majority," **Cry California**. California Tomorrow, Monadnock Building, 681 Market Street, San Francisco, California 94105. Summer 1977.

Connecticut Conservation Association, **The Vanishing Land: Agriculture in Connecticut**. Connecticut Conservation Association, Northrop Street, Bridgewater, Connecticut 06572. August/September 1974.

Gale, Dennis and Harvey Yampolsky, "Agri-Zoning: How They're Gonna Keep 'Em Down on the Farm," **Planning**. American Society of Planning Officials, 1313 East 60th Street, Chicago, Illinois 60637. October 1975.

Klein, John V.N., **Report to the Suffolk County Legislature From the Select Committee on the Acquisition of Farmlands**. Select Committee on the Acquisition of Farmlands, County Center, Riverhead, New York 11901. November 1974. Minutes of Committee meetings, and texts of the various contracts designed to purchase development rights in agricultural lands.

Lefaver, Scott, "A New Framework for Rural Planning," **Urban Land**. Urban Land Institute, 1200 18th Street, N.W., Washington, D.C. 20036. April 1978. Introduction to all the issues of rural planning.

Lemire, Robert, **The Economics of Saving Massachusetts Farmland**. Massachusetts Association of Conservation Commissions, Medford, Massachusetts. 1976.

Little, Charles E., **The New Oregon Trail: An Account of the Development and Passage of State Land Use Legislation in Oregon**. Conservation Foundation, Incorporated, 1717 Massachusetts Avenue, N.W., Washington, D.C. 1974. History of issues and passage of Oregon legislation.

Lyman, Gregory, S.J. Meyer, and R. Nelson, "Can Zoning Preserve Farmland," **Practical Planner**. American Institute of Planners, 1776 Massachusetts Avenue, N.W., Washington, D.C. 20036. September, 1977.

McClaughry, John and Richard Lamm, "Two Views on Land Use Planning," **People and Land**. Vol. 2, No. 1, The Land Reform Movement, Center for Rural Studies, 3410 19th Street, San Francisco, California 94110. Summer 1974. Debate over whether state land use planning is the best strategy for preserving agricultural land.

Miner, Dallas, "Agricultural Lands Preservation: A Growing Trend in Open Space Planning," **Management and Control of Growth**. Scott Randall, Editor, Urban Land Institute, 1200 18th Street, N.W., Washington, D.C. 20036.

Miner, David, "Land Banking in Canada: A New Approach to Land Tenure," **Journal of Soil and Water Conservation**. Soil Conservation Society of America, 7515 Northeast Ankeny Road, Ankeny, Iowa 50021. July/August 1977.

Minnesota Department of Agriculture, **A Position Paper on the Preservation of Farmland**. Minnesota Department of Agriculture, State Office Building, Saint Paul, Minnesota. 55155. February 1977.

Myer, Harold, "Exclusive Farm Use Zoning and Farmland Prices," **Journal of the American Society of Farm Managers and Rural Appraisers**. 210 Clayton, P.O. Box 6857, Denver, Colorado 80206. October 1977.

Myers, Phyllis, **Zoning Hawaii: An Analysis of the Passage and Implementation of Hawaii's Land Classification Law**. Conservation Foundtion, 1717 Massachusetts Avenue, N.W., Washington, D.C. 20036.

Nash, Joseph, "Farmcolony: A Development Alternative to Loss of Agricultural Land," **Urban Land**. Urban Land Institute, 1200 18th Street, N.W., Washington, D.C. 20036. February 1976.

National Community Land Trust Center, **Community Land Trusts and Their Relation to Proposals for Purchasing Development Rights from Farmers to Save Farmland**. National Community Land Trust Center, 639 Massachusetts Avenue, Cambridge, Massachusetts 02139.

Pennabecker, James, **Open Space Lands Preservation Techniques: A Literature Review of Innovative Methods**. Council of Planning Librarians, No. 1393, P.O. Box 229, Monticello, Illinois 61856. 1977.

Peterson, Craig and Claire McCarthy, "A Proposal for an Agricultural Land Preservation Program," **Land Use Law & Zoning Digest**. Vol. 29, No. 8, American Society of Planning Officials, 1313 East 60th Street, Chicago, Illinois 60637. 1977.

Solberg, Erling D. and Ralph R. Pfister, **Rural Zoning in the United States: Analysis of Enabling Legislation**. USDA, Economics, Statistics and Cooperative Services, Washington, D.C. 20250.

Sullivan, Edward J., "The Greening of the Taxpayer: The Relationship of Farm Zone Taxation in Oregon to Land Use," **Willamette Law Journal**. Willamette University, Salem, Oregon 97301.

EXAMPLE 22 The B.C. Land Commission —Keeping the Options Open

THE LAND COMMISSION ACT

The Land Commission Act, although primarily intended to preserve agricultural lands for farm use, also contains provisions related to other land uses. For example, it is concerned with the preservation of greenbelt lands in and around urban areas, the preservation of landbanks suitable for urban or industrial development, and the establishment of park-land for recreational purposes.

The essential significance of the Land Commission Act is that its passage marks the coming of age of agriculture in British Columbia. Food production is now an industry of urgent concern to *all* citizens of a province whose farm resources must be husbanded as never before.

The Land Commission, which consists of five members, was appointed by the Lieutenant Governor-in-Council in May, 1973, and reports to the Legislature through the Minister of Agriculture.

The preservation of agricultural land

The Land Commission is empowered to preserve agricultural land for farm use by means of the establishment of protective zones. These zones are shown on maps commonly known as Agricultural Land Reserve Plans. Within a designated Agricultural Land Reserve (ALR), regulations define the type of land-use activity that may take place.

The Commission also has the authority to purchase agricultural land and to hold, manage, lease or sell purchased land at its discretion. These powers are necessary in order that the Commission may act positively to encourage farming and preserve agricultural land for future generations.

Gifts

The preservation of greenbelt land

In general terms, a 'greenbelt' is an area of permanent open space within or surrounding a town or city. Its main purpose is to provide undisturbed natural landscape for the interest and enjoyment of the urban population. Typical greenbelt would include treed areas in the heart of the community, pedestrian and cycling paths alongside waterways, and natural viewpoints overlooking the city. The Land Commission is not empowered to designate land for greenbelt without first purchasing the land. The Commission's objective is to encourage the preservation of natural greenbelt lands by local and regional governments.

The preservation of landbank land

The Land Commission is also empowered to purchase, either on its own or jointly with local and regional governments, certain lands that have desirable qualities for urban or industrial development. It is expected that the Commission will play an increasingly important role in "landbanking" as one means of directing urban development away from farmlands and preserving agricultural lands for agricultural use.

The preservation of parkland

The Land Commission also has a role to play in encouraging the establishment of lands in parkland reserves for recreational purposes. This function is intended to complement and not compete with the activities of Provincial and Municipal park authorities. As in the case of greenbelt and urban landbank land, the Commission has no powers to designate parkland unless the land has been purchased or received as a gift.

The Commission has already received two gifts of land totalling 600 acres.

The Morrell Wildlife Sanctuary was a gift of 275 acres from Mr. W. A. Morrell of Nanaimo. The Sanctuary, dedicated to the protection and study of wildlife, is managed by Malaspina College Council through an advisory committee including Mr. Morrell and members of B.C. Government departments.

Dr. & Mrs. Hugh Campbell-Brown of Vernon donated 300 acres of land along Kalamalka Lake in memory of their parents, who were pioneer farmers in the area. The land is an example of unspoiled natural Okanagan landscape and although a carefully located campsite may be developed at some later date, the Campbell-Brown Park, as it is now named, will be maintained in its natural state.

Land Acquisition

Agricultural Land

Although the Commission is not actively seeking to purchase agricultural land, it has nevertheless acquired a number of properties. Some of these purchases have been of farms close to expanding urban areas; others have involved land in conflict with other resource uses such as wildlife and recreation. In these cases, the Commission has arranged for management studies to determine the best use of the land.

Through its farmland purchases the Land Commission also hopes to assist farmers who wish to retire but are unable to sell their farms on the open market. These farms will be offered to young farmers on a lease arrangement to offset the high cost of establishing new farms.

Once the land has been purchased, and the land-use studies completed, arrangements for tenancy are made by the Property Management Division of the Department of Agriculture in co-operation with other resource departments. Arrangements may involve consolidation with other land parcels or leasing the property as a single farm unit or as an addition to a neighbouring farm.

Greenbelt and Parkland

In co-operation with the Regional Districts and their municipalities, the Commission is also interested in purchasing — or helping local authorities to purchase — greenbelt and parkland in and around urban centres. The initial $5 million set aside for this purpose is being spent on a Regional District per capita basis for properties recommended for purchase by the District. In fact, the Commission will consider the purchase of any type of natural area or park.

The Commission has been given stewardship of greenbelt sites that were purchased by the government in past years. These lands, together with the properties acquired by the Commission, are under the management of the local government authority or the appropriate government department.

The Land Commission's future role

The Land Commission has been described as the coordinator of activity at the boundaries where town and country meet. The Commission anticipates that much of its work will deal with those land-use conflicts that arise where growing communities impinge upon the neighbouring farmland.

The encouragement of family farming is one of the main objectives of the Land Commission Act. In the administration of Agricultural Land Reserves, the Commission will give careful attention to the impact of the regulations on the operations of the active farmer, rancher and orchardist, especially as they affect the family agriculturalist. For example, the Land Commission expects to help farmers adjust property lines and in some cases assemble land (with the co-operation of their neighbours) in order to achieve more viable production units.

The general policy regarding land owned by the Commission will be to place the properties in the hands of farm families who may not have the extensive resources necessary to purchase a farm outright. A career lease is envisioned, with the hope that the operation will be passed on to the next generation of the family in similar tenure.

The Commission also believes that one of the most effective ways of protecting the farming community is by helping cities solve problems which in the past were handled by the naive expedient of encroaching more and more upon the countryside. Techniques to encourage the efficient use of land within towns, methods of projecting patterns of future growth, and other innovative strategies will be publicized to assist regional and municipal decision-makers in planning land use within their jurisdictions. In some instances, direct participation with local government on a partnership basis may be necessary to resolve problems for the mutual benefit of town and country. The Vernon spray irrigation project, designed to divert that city's sewage effluent from Okanagan Lake to otherwise arid lands, is an example of this type of co-operation.

On the broader scale, co-operation with the various departments of the Provincial Government and with the Environment and Land Use Committee of Cabinet will continue to be an important function of the Land Commission.

The Agricultural Land Reserve may be viewed in the long haul as a fail-safe device to conserve countryside for food production. However, much of the land in the Agricultural Land Reserves is suitable for integrated use without compromising the land's food production capability. The identification of such uses will be an important aspect of the work to be done in the future. In some cases, as in high capability forest, wildlife or recreation lands, integration will be essential for better ecological land use planning.

The mandate of the Land Commission is both constructive and extensive. Resolution of land-use conflicts which endanger the material well-being and life style of British Columbians will be the central concern of the Commission.

This article is reprinted from **The B.C. Land Commission—Keeping the Options Open**, B.C. Land Commission, 4333 Ledger Avenue, Burnaby, British Columbia U5G1H1, pp. 8, 12, 14.

EXAMPLE 23

Notes on the Law: A New Way to Save Our Farmland

Chapter 780 of the Acts of 1977 represents the latest effort to halt the abandonment and conversion of Massachusetts farmlands to other uses. This new law creates "agricultural preservation restrictions" (APRs) and provides $5 million to the Massachusetts Department of Food and Agriculture for purchasing such APRs.

An APR is a new kind of conservation restriction especially tailored for farm and forest land. Essentially, the landowner signs a covenant promising the state that the land will not be developed for nonagricultural purposes; when recorded, this covenant will bind all future owners of the land in perpetuity. The land may then be sold or otherwise transferred but it may be used only for farming or forest uses (including dwellings for the owner or his employees). The APR gives the owner more latitude in using his land than does the typical conservation restriction, which may permit nothing more than passive recreation. The statute specifically preserves the other "customary rights and privileges" of the landowner including the "right to privacy and to carry out all regular farming practices." Public access is limited to inspection to make sure the terms of the APR are not violated.

In return for this covenant, the state will pay the landowner a sum not exceeding the difference between the value of the land before it was restricted and its value for farming purposes after restriction. In areas where development pressures have driven up land costs, this price may be too much for the state pilot program to pay. In those areas, cities and towns may vote to contribute some of the cost of the APR.

The region's farmland is slowly vanishing. But can we afford to lose it?

Chapter 780 will be administered by an agricultural lands preservation committee, chaired by the Commissioner of Food and Agriculture, which will be publishing regulations early in 1978. The details of the program will be spelled out in the regulations. The law states that when evaluating proposed purchases, the committee must consider, among other things, the suitability of the land as to soil classification, its development value and its value for farm use, and the degree to which acquiring an APR on that land would preserve the agricultural potential of the Commonwealth. Landowners will apply through the local conservation commission not directly to the committee.

An APR purchased with state funds cannot be released unless the holder, Commissioner of Food and Agriculture and the local selectmen or city council consent after a public hearing, or if two-thirds of the legislature so votes. Furthermore, the owner must pay a sum equal to the market value of the APR at the time of release. This could mean paying back much more than the original price of the APR, if inflation and development pressure have increased the value of the right to build.

So long as the land under the APR is actively farmed, it will be assessed for real estate tax purposes at rates not to exceed the annual guidelines of the Department of Taxation and Corporations for land in the "farm assessment" program, General Laws Chapter 61A. The owner of APR land, however, has additional tax advantages which do not apply to Chapter 61A. For example, state and federal estate taxes will be based on the lower value of land resulting from the relinquishment of development rights.

Additional protection is also supplied by a requirement in the act that if a utility company takes an easement across APR land, the company must pay the owner of the property as much for the easement as if the land were open and not subject to restriction. In addition, the easement must create the "minimum practical interference with farming operations with respect to width of easement, pole locations and other pertinent matters." That last phrase would include maintenance techniques.

In order to be considered for the program, the land must be eligible for "farmland assessment" under General Laws Chapter 61A, although it need not be subject to that program. This means that the property must conform to the requirements of the first five sections of Chapter 61A; that is, it must consist of at least five acres actively devoted to farming or to forestry under an approved forestry plan and it must have grossed at least $500 a year for the past two years. Agricultural uses are defined very broadly in that statute to include growing all kinds of crops, including forest products and raising animals for sale.

Chapter 780 requires the Registries of Deeds to establish by Jan. 1, 1980 special "tract indices" listing all APRs. These indices are needed so that the permanent APR can easily be found by a prospective purchaser searching the chain of title at the registry. Without the index, the APR will not be enforceable unless periodically re-recorded by the holder.

Although this program is sometimes described as involving the sale of the farmer's "development rights," it is not to be confused with the concept of "transferring" development rights from one site to another. The right to develop the land for other than agricultural purposes is simply purchased and held by the state, not transferred to another place.

Since the land will remain in private ownership, the state cannot force the owner to continue to farm. However, since most other forms of development will not be permitted, the land will remain available for farming in future years. If transportation costs should become prohibitive, such a land bank would be crucial to the Commonwealth. Of course, a great deal more than $5 million would be required to secure a substantial base of farmland. The present appropriation represents a pilot program. If it works well, this may be the beginning of an important state program to preserve our agricultural base.

Further information is available from the Division of Conservation Services (727-1552), which handles the funding. □

An agricultural preservation restriction could save farmland now threatened by development.

This article is reprinted from Alexandra D. Dawson, "Notes on the Law: A New Way to Save Our Farmland," Metropolitan Area Planning Council, Boston, Massachusetts, p. 4.

Suffolk's Farmland Preservation Program

EXAMPLE 24

Faced with the rapid and continuous loss of farmlands to non-agricultural uses, Suffolk County has embarked on a unique program to save some of the remaining 60,000 acres. The program, which provides for the purchase of development rights of 12 to 15,000 acres of farmland by the county, was proposed by an Agricultural Advisory Committee after two years of study during which time numerous types of farmland preservation alternatives were considered.

Development rights comprise part of the package of property rights which landowners possess. They are defined as "all the rights, title, and interest except the right of ownership, the right of exclusive possession, and the right to use and sell the land for agricultural purposes."

The value of the development rights is determined by subtracting the agricultural value of the land from its full market value. For example, if the agricultural value is $1,000 per acre and the full market value is $5,000 per acre, the development rights would be worth $4,000 per acre. Or if the agricultural value is $1,500 per acre and the full market value is $15,000 per acre, the development rights would be worth $13,500 per acre.

The County initiates the purchase procedure by sending letters to farmland owners inviting them to submit sealed bids specifying the amount (acreage) of land which is being offered and the asking price. Submission of bids is entirely voluntary and owners of any farmland in the county may make an offer.

All sealed bids are opened by the county on a designated date, read and recorded, and forwarded to a Select Committee for preliminary evaluation. Each parcel of farmland is evaluated relative to its soil, contiguity to other farmland, and price. The Committee compiles a list of those parcels which appear to meet the county's criteria and submits it to the County Legislature along with a similar list of unacceptable bids and reasons for their rejection.

The Legislature, after studying the committee's recommendations, may authorize the County Executive to seek options on each approved parcel for the purpose of making an independent appraisal of both the market value and the agricultural value. The appraisal information is forwarded to the Select Committee which uses it in making the final evaluation of bids.

The Select Committee then prepares a list of those bids for which it recommends the County exercise the option. This list is submitted to the County Legislature which must act on the recommendations. If the Legislature approves the recommendations, the County may exercise the options and sign contracts with the owners of the acceptable parcels. Title searches and any necessary surveys will be carried out and the closing transactions will be concluded within sixty days.

At the closing, the landowner signs the deed conveying the development rights to the County. The County, in turn, pays the owner the cash value of the development rights in a lump sum to the owner or his designee. The County cannot sell any of the development rights without the approval of a majority of voters in a countywide referendum.

The purchase of development rights and the attendant administrative expenses will be financed by the sale of 30-year municipal bonds. A resolution authorizing the sale of bonds must be passed by a 2/3 majority of the County Legislature.

The statute which allows the County to undertake this program is Section 247 of the General Municipal Law. This authorizes local governments to acquire full or lesser title to land for the purpose of open space preservation. Suffolk County Local Law No. 19-1974 enacted by the County Legislature authorized the implementation of the farmland program.

The county program is designed to relieve some of the economic pressures which force farmers out of business. Selling development rights will prevent the forced liquidation of the farm assets to pay federal estate taxes on the death of the owner since most of the assets will not be in the form of land. Local property taxes will be based on the agricultural value of the land rather than on the full market value which includes the value of development rights. Farmers who participate in the program will have money to reinvest in their farming operations and/or to purchase additional land to expand the operation.

This article is reprinted from "Suffolk's Farmland Preservation Program," New York Cooperative Extension, 246 Giffing Avenue, Riverhead, New York 11901.

EXAMPLE 25

Transferable Development Rights

A new land management concept is promising state and local governments a way to preserve historic, agricultural or environmentally sensitive areas at no public cost, without financial loss to owners and without sacrificing future growth.

It's called Transferable Development Rights (TDR) and it's gaining attention across the country. Illinois has already enacted a limited TDR plan, eight other states considered the measure last year and more are expected to introduce TDR this session.

The basic premise of TDR is that a property owner can sell the right to develop his land just as he can sell a right of way for a power line or the right to drill for oil. The major difference, however, is that he sells the development rights for use on a different piece of property.

A simplified TDR plan might work like this:

Rising land values are threatening farmland at the edge of a community. The farmers who own the property know that if they sell their land for the development of a high-rise complex, they will realize a financial gain far above their return from farming.

The city, however, is interested in preserving the land as farmland, so it designates the property as a "preservation zone," protecting it from any change in use. At the same time, the city designates a lucrative site, which can accomodate the new growth, as the "transfer zone."

By allowing higher density development in the transfer zone than in the rest of the community, the city gives builders an incentive to develop there. But the developers can only build on the land at the higher, more profitable density if they buy "development rights" from the farmers in the "preservation zone."

Because farmers can sell their development rights at the going market price, they are not penalized by the preservation plan; neither is the developer, who can build the high-rise complex in the transfer zone.

The community also benefits. It is able to concentrate development where roads, schools, sewers and other public facilities and services are most available and easiest to upgrade. In addition, the community can achieve its planning goals at much less public expense.

By using private marketplace forces to compensate landowners whose property is to be preserved, TDR eliminates some of the problems common to other new land management techniques. "Because TDR offers a way to preserve historic or environmentally-sensitive properties while accomodating growth and develop-

ment, it is a way to have your cake and eat it too," says John Helb of the New Jersey Legislative Services Agency.

But TDR has its opponents. New Jersey has come the closest to enacting a comprehensive TDR law, but the plan has come under attack from several quarters.

Builders worry that it may turn out to be just another procedural roadblock in a business already bridled with permits and certificates. Although real estate interests would be able to sell development rights just as they do actual property, they also oppose TDR, claiming it might foster exclusionary zoning and interfere with "normal development." Farmers, too, have been concerned that the "development rights" certificates might turn out to be so much devalued paper.

"One key question is whether the TDR certificate is a marketable commodity," says Assemblyman John Doyle, a sponsor of the New Jersey bill. Since the worth of the certificate is based on the difference between the property's agricultural or open space value and its full market value for future development, demand for construction in the transfer zone would affect demand for certificates.

To avoid ending up with a buyer's market for TDRs, staff and sponsors of the New Jersey bill are now studying ways to allow municipalities to phase in the creation of TDR certificates to keep the supply from outrunning the pace of development in the transfer zones.

Although the New Jersey bill would require interested communities to conduct extensive planning and market studies before designating preservation and transfer zones, there are bound to be disputes, and some of them will wind up in litigation.

"We expect court challenges to the New Jersey enabling act," Doyle says. "But it is my hope that a court will decide to defer judgment until the TDR has been implemented in a few places."

TDR may not be suited to all municipalities; it only makes sense for communities that have areas worth preserving as well as areas that can support more intensive development, he points out. "But for those communities, it's an experiment that may help them better guide their own destinies." C.D.

"The basic premise of TDR is that a property owner can sell the right to develop his land just as he can sell a right of way for a power line or the right to drill for oil."

This article is reprinted from "Transferable Development Rights," **State Legislatures,** NCSL Communications Department, 1405 Curtis Street, 23rd Floor, Denver, Colorado 80202, p. 24, April/May 1977.

Chapter 7

Protecting Farm Land Through New Tax Policies

State legislatures have been devoting considerable time to restructuring their property tax systems. These actual or proposed changes are aimed at overlapping problems. One of the major problems is responding to the rapidly rising property tax burden of working farmers and another is the rising property taxes affecting all owners of open space, woodland, and farmland.

Many state legislatures have moved forward and have introduced direct tax relief for farmland. From the first farmland tax relief bill passed in Maryland in 1956, this approach has become increasingly popular. By the year 1969 a total of 22 states had similar laws, and as of 1976, 42 of the 50 states passed some significant form of farmland tax relief.

State farmland property tax relief varies enormously in a number of crucial public policy areas. All of the legislation has as its avowed purpose the modification of the property tax system to provide incentives for maintaining land for agricultural use. Many legislators are convinced that property taxes on farmland are much too high in relation to farm income. Tax reduction efforts also seem much more acceptable politically than state wide zoning or land use controls.

The states have chosen to modify their property tax systems by permitting that agricultural land be assessed at its use-value rather than its market-value. The use-value taxes are lower. The use-value of land is its value to produce food and fiber, while the market-value reflects its potential worth if developed as an industrial park, a golf course, a shopping center or home sites. Up until recently, most states required that assessments be based on market-value, thus forcing the farmer to pay much higher taxes, especially in counties where development pressures are increasing each year.

State legislatures have experimented with three basic types of systems for property tax relief through use-value assessments. The first is a simple "preferential assessment" in which agricultural land is assessed at its current use-value. No restrictions are placed on whose land is eligible and under what conditions. The second basic system is "deferred taxation" in which land is again assessed at its use-value, but if the land is later developed the tax relief provided must be paid back to the local or state government in some manner. Finally, the third system is the so-called "restrictive agreement" in which, in exchange for lower tax assessments, the government and the landowner sign a formal contract restricting the land to agricultural use for some designated period of time.

PREFERENTIAL ASSESSMENT

The nation's first farmland tax relief program is a good example of "preferential assessment." *The Maryland Preferential Assessment Law of 1956* makes all agricultural and open land eligible for assessment at use-value rather than market-value. Any landowner is eligible for the program, be they farmer, executive, or developer. A problem with this legislation is that there are no income limitations and also no requirements for payback if the land is eventually developed. Landowners, particularly near developing areas, can get large financial benefits from the program.

Criticism of the Maryland law has been growing. Developers, rather than working farmers, are getting the major financial benefits from the program. Developers are buying farmland they intend to develop, but while waiting for the market to rise, they graze a few cows or rent land out to local farmers and thus qualify for the lower assessment. Since there are no penalties if the land is later developed, the developer loses nothing from converting the agricultural land into a shopping center or suburban development. The weakness in the Maryland Farmland Assessment Law, and similar laws in other states, is well described in the report from the Montgomery County Council which is reprinted as **Example 26, The Farmland Assessment Law: A Proposal for Reform.**

DEFERRED TAXATION

Both the Massachusetts and the Pennsylvania laws meet some of the deficiencies of the Maryland law. Both are good examples of the system of "deferred taxation." *The Massachusetts Farmland Assessment Act of 1973* provides for taxation of both farmland and forestland at use-value. This is similar to the Maryland law. However, if the land is converted to uses other than agriculture, a conveyance tax is assessed on the sale price of the land. In addition, the seller of the land must pay "roll back" taxes equal to the difference between what the taxes would have been on the land at market-value and the actual taxes paid. The roll back taxes would cover the current and four preceding years.

The Pennsylvania Farmland and Forest Land Assessment Act of 1974 is similar to the Massachusetts bill. However, the roll back tax penalty is even more severe. If a landowner eventually develops land that had received lower taxes under this Act, he must pay the unpaid taxes for the current year and six previous years, plus 6% interest on those unpaid taxes. In addition, the roll back taxes become a lien on the property until paid.

RESTRICTIVE AGREEMENTS

The California Land Conservation Act of 1965, also known as the "Williamson Act," is an example of the "restrictive agreement" system. Basically, the act permits local governments to contract with landowners who agree to use their land only for agricultural purposes. In exchange, the landowners are taxed at use-value rather than market-value. The normal term of these contracts is ten years, renewable annually unless specifically cancelled by either party. If the landowner develops the land while the contract is in effect, he pays a substantial penalty. If he decides not to renew the 10 year contract, the assessment on his land gradually increases to market value.

On its surface the "Williamson Act" appears successful as contracts cover over 4.4 million acres of land or 40.4% of California's taxes. A recent study, however, revealed that the great majority of the land enjoying the lower taxes is far from the major cities and is not seriously threatened by development. Corporate farms and large land owners appear to have been the major beneficiaries of the law. The inadequacies of the Williamson Act are detailed in an article from the March 1977 issue of *California Agriculture* which is reprinted here as **Example 27, Use-Value Assessment and Land Conservation.**

One of the major problems of all farmland tax relief programs has been the question of who ends up paying the taxes that farmers no longer will be paying. Most states' farm tax relief programs, in effect, turn over the operation and financing of these programs to local governments. By reducing property taxes on farmland or open space, counties or towns are in fact increasing property taxes on homeowners or on industrial or commercial property. The increased property tax payments by homeowners has been a major source of popular opposition to local government's implementation of farmland property tax relief proposals.

The Vermont Land Use-Value Taxation Act of 1978 takes the burden for financing farmland relief off the local homeowner. Under the Vermont law, local officials assess qualified farmland on use-value and market-value. The farmer pays taxes on use-value. The state of Vermont then reimburses the town for the difference between what the farmer actually pays and what the market value is. This interesting plan of shifting the burden of local farmland relief to a more progressive state tax structure may well become a viable model for other states.

CREATING AGRICULTURAL DISTRICTS

Superior to enacting property tax relief alone is to draft an overall program that includes farmland tax relief as one component. One of the best models is the *New York Agricultural District Act of 1971*. New York state farmers may petition their county government to create an "Agricultural District" as long as it includes more than 500 acres. If approved, the farmers only have to pay taxes on the use-value of the land. If the land is subsequently developed, the farmer must pay back taxes covering the previous five years.

The Agricultural District, however, gives the farmer a number of other benefits. Land within a District is strongly protected against eminent domain from any state agencies or departments. Certain local ordinances or regulations that might restrict farming are not applicable to land within agricultural districts. And farmers in the Districts do not have to pay any taxes for new public expenditures that would encourage development. The New York bill has served as a model for a proposed *Pennsylvania Agricultural District Act* which was introduced into the General Assembly in early 1978.

CAPITAL GAINS TAXES

States have also been willing to experiment with other elements of the tax structure to give tax relief to farmers. One of the most interesting innovations being watched closely by other states is the *Vermont Tax on Gains from the Sale or Exchange of Land*. Passed by the Legislature in 1973, the law's purpose is to reverse the trend of inflationary property values and to thereby slow down the increases in the farmer's property taxes caused by the significant, short term land speculation in Vermont.

Under the Vermont law, anyone buying and selling land within a period of six years must pay a capital gains tax on the profits from that sale. Individual homes and small lots of land are exempt. For example, if land is bought and then sold at a higher price within six months, the state tax is 70%. The rate of taxation declines annually, reaching zero at the end of six years. Speculators have protested that the law does not give them any incentive to buy and sell land for development.

The Vermont statute has encouraged legislators in a number of states to introduce similar bills. *The Montana Act Imposing an Additional Tax on the Capital Gains Realized in the Speculative Sale of Land* was introduced in 1975 by State Representative Ora Halversen. This bill also taxes capital gains from land purchases and sales starting at a high rate and declining to zero at the end of six years. However, the Montana bill provides even higher taxes in each category based on the percentage of profit the speculator made on each transaction. Legislators in other states have also introduced the *Virginia Land Gains Tax of 1976*; the *Oregon Tax on the Gains from the Sale or Exchange of Land in Oregon of 1975*; the *Washington Land Sales Excise Tax of 1975*; the *California Recreation Fund and Unearned Value Tax Act of 1972*; and the *Illinois Land Gains Tax of 1975*.

With the single exception of Vermont, no other state has a capital gains tax on land speculation aimed at protecting farmers. In this respect the United States is considerably behind other English speaking countries. Australia, New Zealand, Great Britain and Canada have used such taxes extensively to hold down speculation and thus keep rural land values from rising so rapidly. One of the most recent developments in this area was the passage by the Ontario Provincial Assembly of the *Ontario Land Speculation Act of 1974*.

PROGRESSIVE PROPERTY TAXES

Some states are also considering a "progressive" property tax. Under such a system, owners of large land holdings would be required to pay property taxes at a higher rate than owners of less land. At the encouragement of their respective Farmer's Unions, the states of Minnesota and North Dakota have been discussing what they call a "graduated" property tax. In North Dakota, Byron Dorgan, the elected State Tax Commissioner, is in the forefront of those discussions. Excerpts from a discussion paper he prepared is reported as **Example 28, The Progressive Land Tax: A Tax Incentive for the Family Farm.**

Another important area for innovation is in the overall structure of property tax rates. Most states have either constitutional prohibitions or statutes requiring that all property be assessed at the same percentage of value. Such prohibitions prevent counties, cities or towns from assessing commercial or industrial property at a higher rate than, say, residential or agricultural property.

Four states and the Canadian province of Alberta have "classification" property tax systems permitting the assessment of different types of property at different rates. The four states of Minnesota, Arizona, Alabama, and Tennessee are joined by two other states, Montana and West Virginia, which achieve the same effect by different means. In Arizona, for example, there are a number of different property tax classifications. Farm and residential property is assessed at 18%, commercial and industrial property at 25%, utility property at 40%, mining, railroad and airline property is at 60%, and producing oil and gas wells at 100%.

The obvious advantages of a sympathetic classification system have led a number of farm organizations and homeowners' associations to try to get their states to adopt classification systems. In Vermont, State Representative Norris Hoyt introduced the *Maximum Assessment of Agricultural, Forest and Open Land Act of 1975*. This bill would have required that all agricultural, forest, and open land would be assessed at 20% of fair market value, while all other property would be assessed at 50%. Massachusetts Fair Share, a state-wide community organization, is strongly supporting a state referendum to allow the state to adopt some type of classification system to help residential homeowners and farmers.

ADDITIONAL TAX PROPOSALS

The states of Michigan and Wisconsin have tried another innovative method of using tax policy to assist farmers. Michigan has adopted a variation on the property tax "circuit-breaker" that had hitherto been used primarily to provide property tax relief to low-income and elderly homeowners. Under the Michigan law, a farmer is entitled to a credit on his income tax if his property taxes rise above 7% of his income. The other requirement to receive the tax credit is that the farmer enter into a ten year development rights contract ensuring that the land is not developed.

Wisconsin's *Farmland Preservation Act of 1977* is even more ambitious. State income tax credits are offered to farmers who are willing to participate in a detailed and extensive program aimed at preventing development of agricultural lands. The size of the income tax credit depends both on the household income of the farm family and the degree of their, and their county's, participation in the effort to protect agricultural land. More and more states will be intensively examining the Michigan and Wisconsin laws as possible models for legislation to protect farmland. The Wisconsin law is described in detail in a pamphlet published by the University of Wisconsin's Cooperative Extension Program which is reprinted as **Example 29, Wisconsin's Farmland Preservation Program**.

Finally, although no longer an active legislative proposal, the North Dakota Farmer's Union drafted a bill in the early 1970s which would help new farmers through their most difficult period of financial stress due to the enormous capital investment required to begin farming today. This program was modeled on a similar five year tax forgiveness given to new industries by most states.

Resources

BIBLIOGRAPHY

Atkinson, Glen, "The Effectiveness of Differential Assessment of Agricultural and Open Space Land," **American Journal of Economics and Sociology**. 50 East 59th Street, New York, New York 10021. April 1977.

Bailey, Mary L., **Farm Real Estate Taxes 1976**. Economic Research Service, USDA, Washington, D.C. 20250. December 1977.

Barrows, Richard L., **Use-Value Taxation: The Experience of Other States**. Staff Paper Series, No. 73. Department of Agricultural Economics, University of Wisconsin, Madison, Wisconsin 53706. March 1974.

Barrows, Richard L. **Wisconsin's Farmland Preservation Program**. Extension Program, University of Wisconsin, Madison, Wisconsin 53706. May 1978.

Barrows, Richard L. and Marvin B. Johnson, **Farmland Tax Relief in Wisconsin: Use Value Assessment vs. Income Tax Credits**. Agricultural Economics Staff Paper Series/Cooperative Extension Programs. University of Wisconsin, Madison, Wisconsin 53706. February 1977.

Bell, Michael, "Use-Value Assessment and the Agricultural Value of Farmland," **Assessors Journal**. International Association of Assessing Officers, 1313 East 60th Street, Chicago, Illinois 60637. June 1977.

Conklin, Howard E. and William G. Lesher, "Farm-Value Assessment as a Means for Reducing Premature and Excessive Agricultural Disinvestment in Urban Fringes," **American Journal of Agricultural Economics**. November 1977.

Dorgan, Byron, **The Progressive Land Tax: A Tax Incentive for the Family Farm**. Conference on Alternative State and Local Policies, 1901 Q Street, N.W., Washington, D.C. 20009. 1978. $1.50, $3.00 institutions.

Economic Research Service (ERS), **State Programs for the Differential Assessment of Farm and Open Space Land**. Agricultural Economic Report No. 256, ERS, USDA, Washington, D.C. 20250. April 1974.

Gustafson, Gregory and L.T. Wallace, "Differential Assessment as Land Use Policy: The California Case," **Journal of the American Institute of Planners**. American Institute of Planners, 1776 Massachusetts Avenue, N.W., Washington, D.C. 20036. November 1975.

Hady, Thomas F. and Ann Gordon Sibold, **State Programs for the Differential Assessment of Farm and Open Space Land**. Agricultural Economic Report 256. Economics, Statistics, and Cooperative Services, USDA, Washington, D.C. 20250. April 1974.

Hagman, Donald G. and Dean Misczynski, "Special Capital Gains and Real Estate Windfall Taxes," **National Tax Journal**. December 1975. Surveys developments in capital gains taxes in Canada, Australia, New Zealand, England, and United States.

Holland, David M., **An Economic Analysis of Washington's Differential Taxation Program**. Circular 578. College of Agriculture Research Center, Washington State University, Pullman, Washington 99164. December 1974.

Hopeman, Alan, **Green Acres Law: The Use of Differential Assessment in Minnesota**. Research Department, House of Representatives, State Capitol, St. Paul, Minnesota 55155. February 1978.

International Association of Assessing Officers (IAAO), "Classified Property Tax Systems," **IAAO Newsletter**. IAAO, 1313 East 60th Street, Chicago, Illinois 60637. June 1974.

International Association of Assessing Officers (IAAO), "Property Tax Incentives for Preservation: Use-Value Assessment and the Preservation of Farmland, Open Space and Historic Sites," **Proceedings of the 1975 Property Tax Forum**. IAAO, 1313 East 60th Street, Chicago, Illinois 60637.

Keene, John, et al., **Untaxing Open Space: An Evaluation of the Effectiveness of Differential Assessment of Farms and Open Space**. GPO No. 041-011-0031-9, Superintendent of Documents, U.S. Government Printing Office, Washington, D.C. 20402. 1976. 401 pages.

Kolesar, John and Jaye Scholl, **Saving Farmland**. Center for Analysis of Public Issues, Inc., 92-A Nassau Street, Princeton, New Jersey 08540.

Lapping, M.B. and R.J. Bevins, "Differential Assessment and Other Techniques to Preserve Missouri's Farmlands," **Missouri Law Review**. Summer 1977.

Montana Department of Community Affairs, **Differential Taxation and Agricultural Land Use**. Helena, Montana 59601. January 1978.

Rolleston, George, **Real Property Taxation on Commercial Farms in New York State**. New York State Cooperative Extension Service. Warren Hall, Cornell University, Ithaca, New York 14853. February 23, 1979.

Berry for the NEA

'We, in Washington, see prosperity just around the corner for the family farm. All you have to do is survive until the suburbs reach you, and you'll make a fortune in real estate!'

The Farmland Assessment Law: A Proposal for Reform

EXAMPLE 26

The farmland assessment law (Maryland Code Article 81, Section 19 (b)) provides for farm-value assessment of land used as a farm, regardless of its market value. It was sold to the voters in 1960 on grounds that it would preserve farming and open space. It has not done so, as is shown by a number of surveys of the land changes which have occurred in the last 15 years. The Report of the State Department of Agriculture's Committee on Preservation of Agricultural Land stated the situation as follows in 1974:

> Since 1949, more than 1.2 million acres have been withdrawn from agricultural use. The rate of decline has averaged 62,600 acres per year. It is projected that an additional 1.5 - 1.8 million acres will be removed from farms by the turn of the century leaving from 1.0 to 1.3 million acres in agricultural use.

The fact is that the reduced tax due to this law has practically no effect on the rate of land conversion or development. When the opportunity for development arrives, there is much to be made in development, and the tax concession cannot offset more than a small fraction of the gains to be made. Nor does the rate of development depend on taxes paid by either farmers or speculators. Neither homebuyers nor businesses move to our State or County in response to the tax paid or not paid on farms or speculative holdings. They act on the basis of employment and business opportunities, not someone else's taxes.

Neither logic nor the history of recent years give any basis for believing that the farmland assessment law is a useful instrument for preserving agriculture or open space.

Does Farmland Assessment Help Poor Farmers?

The argument is made that farmers are helped to stay on their land by the low taxes provided by the "farmland assessment" law. The trouble with this argument is that most farmers' land is worth little more than what it will yield in income from farming, so they get little advantage from the farmland assessment law. For them, assessment at market value is farmland assessment--and the law is not necessary to give them that assessment. This is true for the rural counties of the State, and for the rural areas — the real farm areas — of Montgomery County and other suburban counties.

Some farmers have experienced suburban development in their vicinity, however, and the value of their land has increased many-fold. Most of these have cashed in on their land profits, and have either retired from farming or bought more and better farm land elsewhere, with the proceeds of their sale. A few have themselves gone into residential or commercial/industrial development activity.

The people who get the big advantages from farmland assessment are those who own the most valuable land — wealthy investors in land, and developers holding land for future development.

A farmer in the rural area between Clarksburg and Damascus might have 200 acres worth $1,000/acre. The assessment on his land based on 50% of market value, would be $100,000. The "farmland assessment" (Article 81, Section 19 (b) (1)) would be about $30,000. He gets an assessment reduction of $70,000 — worth about $2500 a year in taxes.

On the other hand, land in the Gaithersburg, Rockville, and Potomac areas is worth $10,000 - $100,000 per acre. Two hundred acres would be assessed at $1,000,000 to $10,000,000, based on 50% of market value, but at only the same $30,000 under "farmland assessment." Thus the investor in these areas of intense development gets a reduction of between $970,000 and $9,970,000 in his assessment. That is worth between $36,000 and $360,000 to him annually, as an addition to his profits.

This reduction in taxes for wealthy investors shifts additional tax burdens onto the average homeowner (and the farmer, as well), who is generally _less_ able to carry the burden than those whose tax burdens are shifted onto him.

The reduction in taxes for the investors and speculators also increases the profits from holding land, thus increasing investors' demands for developable land, and raising the price of building lots and housing.

The biggest tax reductions do not provide any help to preserving farmland or open space because the owner would lose far more by failing to sell or develop his land when opportunity offers, than by paying taxes on market value. For example:

Much land in Montgomery County's developing areas is worth $25,000 per acre or more. The tax at regular, market-value assessment is a little less than 2%, or about $400 a year. The net average annual income from sale or development, however, is about 8% of the $25,000, or $2000 a year, generally more than $1900 a year greater than the income per acre from farming. The investor would make a much larger sacrifice if he decided not to develop than if he paid taxes on regular, market-value assessment. The "farmland assessment" reduces his taxes 98%, and helps him financially, but it is not large enough to induce him to keep his land undeveloped, in open space.

In the non-developing areas, (the real rural, farm areas) on the other hand, the speculative value of the land is minimal. The opportunities to develop the land are few, and the sacrifice in holding the land in open space is small. The tax loss is small, but farming is preserved, for lack of development opportunities.

Thus the farmland assessment results in tax reductions for those who are not likely to continue farming, and only small or zero tax reductions for those who are likely to continue farming. Real farmers get little or nothing, while the profits of speculators and developers are greatly increased, both by reduced taxes and increased land prices.

The fact that landholders in developing areas do not intend to preserve their farms is shown by the failure to maintain their barns, their equipment, and their fields. Investment for future farming activity doesn't pay, and is reduced accordingly.

How Can Farms and Open Space be Preserved?

Public controls (zoning, sewering, etc.) and contracts (convenants, or public purchase of the land or its development rights) are the only means of permanently preserving farming or open space. Temporary open space, without controls, lasts only until the right opportunity for development arrives. The open space is preserved only as long as it would be without farmland assessment.

This conclusion, which both logic and recent experience confirm, is set forth in a number of recent studies, including an April 1976 publication, "Untaxing Open Space" by the Federal Council on Environmental Quality, and a June 1976 Study, "Farmland Retention in the Washington Metropolitan Area" by Dallas Miner for the Washington Area Council of Governments. These studies conclude that farmland assessment makes little or no contribution to preserving farmland.

To make farmland assessment serve its original purpose of preserving farms and open space, it must be based on a commitment to farming or open space. Otherwise, the large public revenue losses yield nothing in return. Rural zoning and/or the formation of Agricultural Districts are the logical means of securing the commitment.

Proposal of the Montgomery County Council

The Montgomery County Council is requesting the Legislature to enact a bill which will provide relief to average taxpayers and improve the equity of the tax system, while creating a real incentive for the preservation of farming. It limits farmland assessment to lands which are either in the Rural Zone (principal permitted use, agriculture; residential permitted only with minimum 5-acre lot size) or in an Agricultural District. Agricultural Districts are to be defined as in the measure (House Bill 783) recommended to the Legislature in 1975 by the Legislative Council, or in a County bill which has been developed along the same lines, in lieu of enactment of the State bill. Lands in Agricultural Districts are to have a 20-year commitment against development, and development will be permitted only after repayment of tax concessions and any payments received for development rights. The repayment provisions do not apply to Rural Zone properties.

In addition to Rural Zone and Agricultural District lands, the Montgomery County bill permits deferral of market-value taxes on farms owned and operated by farmers, defined as those who live on a farm and earn a living (at least to the extent of 50%) from farming. Farmers receiving this deferral would have to pay the deferred taxes when they sell their farms (but not when they transfer by gift or inheritance), or themselves engage in development. This provision enables farmers in developing areas to continue enjoying the benefit of present low assessments, so they will not be forced to sell by a shortage of cash resulting from assessments based on speculative value of their land. When they or their heirs sell the farm, however, the cash to pay taxes is in hand, and the back taxes should be paid.

In these times of real hardships for poor and even average taxpayers, it is unreasonable to burden them with millions of dollars of tax burden which can better be carried by the wealthy individuals and corporations who own development lands. These taxpayers not only have more ability to pay, but are in business to make profits from land sales rather than farming. Only if a durable commitment to farming is made is there any equity or public purpose to be served by giving farmland assessment to valuable development lands.

"Now THAT'S what we call effective land use."

This article is reprinted from "The Farmland Assessment Law: A Proposal for Reform," Montgomery County Council, Maryland.

EXAMPLE 27 Use-Value Assessment and Land Conservation

There is no evidence that the California Land Conservation Act of 1965 has "conserved" agricultural land.

Hoy F. Carman ■ Cris Heaton

Concern over conversion of agricultural land to other uses led to passage of the California Land Conservation Act of 1965 (CLCA). Also called the Williamson Act (after its author, Assemblyman John C. Williamson) this program has three major objectives:

■ To preserve a maximum amount of available agricultural land to maintain California's agricultural economy and ensure an adequate food supply for the nation's future.

■ To discourage premature and unnecessary conversion of agricultural land to urban uses.

■ To maintain farmland in developing areas as valuable open space for existing and pending urban developments.

The California Land Conservation Act is enabling legislation that provides for binding contracts between local governments (counties or cities) and landowners. Local governments are not required to participate in the program; contracts are usually initiated by landowners. The landowner agrees to restrict his land to agricultural or related use for at least 10 years in return for use-value assessment for property taxes. Because agricultural use-value of California land is typically lower than market value, the landowner can reduce property taxes by temporarily forfeiting development rights.

The basic contract has several important features. Although the minimum length of contract is 10 years, it may be longer; Sacramento County, for example, has a 20-year contract. Contracts are automatically renewed each year, unless one party gives notice of nonrenewal. Notice of nonrenewal results in a programmed return to market-value assessment for the remaining life of the contract. Cancellation can be requested by either party to the contract but, to become effective, must be approved by all parties and by the State Director of Agriculture. Contract cancellation obligates the landowner to pay a penalty equal to 50 percent of the new assessed value of the property (12½ percent of market value) unless waived by the Director of Agriculture as being in the public interest.

Progress of the Act

County data on the rate and level of sign-ups for fiscal year 1975-76, as compared with earlier years, indicate that many counties are nearing a ceiling in land that is likely to be placed under the California Land Conservation Act. Thus, substantial amounts of prime land are, and will continue to be, subject to urban development.

The CLCA has been a source of controversy since its inception, and the ability to accomplish its objectives is questioned. The problem, briefly stated, is: Can a voluntary program that offers property tax reduction secure participation in the face of highly profitable development expectations? An accumulation of data on the Act permits some tentative conclusions.

After a slow beginning, landowner and county participation in the CLCA increased substantially. There were only 200,000 acres in six of California's 58 counties participating in the Act during the 1967-68 fiscal year (table 1). This increased to some 4.2 million acres in 37 counties in fiscal 1969-70 and to 14.4 million acres in 47 counties during fiscal 1975-76. The 1975-76 level of participation represents approximately 40.4 percent of California's total land in farms and 45.9 percent of available farmland in the 47 participating counties.

CLCA provisions emphasize enrollment of the most productive, or prime, agricultural land. Although definition of land productivity is difficult and subject to change through time, the Act has established several criteria for classifying prime land. Using these criteria, the California Department of Water Resources estimated that California had 12,621,700 acres of prime land in 1974. Prime land has represented more than 30 percent of total land enrolled under the Act since 1972-73 (table 1). The 4.37 million acres of prime land enrolled in 1975-76 represented just over one-third of total prime land available and almost 41 percent of the prime land available in participating counties.

There is substantial county-to-county variation in the percentage of farmland and prime land enrolled under the CLCA. Only 21 of the 47 counties participating have more than one-half of available farmland enrolled, and only seven counties have more than one-half of available prime land enrolled (table 2). A comparison of the percentage of total land under the Act with the percentage of prime land under the Act in each county indicates a lag in the inclusion of prime land. The percentage of prime land sign-ups is equal to or greater than the percentage of total farmland sign-ups in only nine counties.

Empirical analyses also raise questions concerning the performance of the Act. A case study of land under contract in 11 central California counties found that farmland near incorporated areas was much less likely to be under contract than was more remote land. Another study found that initial land sign-ups were concentrated in below-average, nonprime agricultural land located some distance from incorporated areas. Much of the land under contract was in little or no danger of being converted to nonagricultural use, whereas much land not under contract is viewed by its owners as having development potential.

Because many participating counties are nearing a ceiling in sign-ups of land, annual increases in participating acreage will decrease in these counties and in the state.

Property tax reductions under CLCA can have a significant fiscal impact on local government and school districts, because these property taxes are either lost or shifted to other taxpayers. The tax revenue difference to counties as a result of land being placed under the Act in 1975-76 was almost $22 million. The estimated total tax difference (city, county, school, and other district taxes) was $69 million. This was less than 1 percent of total property taxes levied in the participating counties in fiscal year 1975-76. The impact, however, was quite variable. For example, the tax revenue difference due to the Act was 15.6, 12.3, and 11.0 percent, respectively, in Kings, San Benito, and Tulare counties. Estimated per-acre tax shifts ranged from $.01 in Monterey County to $111.51 in San Bernardino County (table 2). California does provide subvention payments to school districts and to local governments to offset partially the fiscal impact of the Act. Reimbursements amounted to $14.4 million in 1974-75.

California has had a decade of experience with a voluntary program to preserve agricultural land. Although CLCA has undoubtedly provided property taxation consistent with long-term agricultural use in many areas, there is no evidence to indicate that it has "conserved" agricultural land. Substantial amounts of California's best agricultural land will continue to be subject to development, despite the significant public investment in this program.

TABLE 1. LANDOWNER AND LOCAL GOVERNMENT PARTICIPATION IN THE CALIFORNIA LAND CONSERVATION ACT OF 1965, 1967-68 TO 1975-76

Fiscal year	Total acres under contract	Acres of prime land	Counties participating
1967-68	200,000	Not available	6
1968-69	2,081,988	131,273	23
1969-70	4,249,374	572,611	37
1970-71	6,234,062	1,863,716	39
1971-72	9,582,658	2,622,648	42
1972-73	11,476,416	3,428,437	44
1973-74	12,719,389	3,914,988	45
1974-75	13,742,978	4,179,762	47
1975-76	14,427,087	4,371,027	47

TABLE 2. THE CALIFORNIA LAND CONSERVATION ACT: LAND UNDER CONTRACT BY CATEGORY AS A PERCENT OF LAND AVAILABLE AND ESTIMATED TAX SHIFTS BY COUNTY, 1975-76 FISCAL YEAR

County	Total land	Percent of farmland	Prime land	Percent of prime land	Estimated tax shift for land under the Act
	acres		acres		$ per acre
Alameda	164,080	56	7,408	20	9.62
Amador	87,555	34	2,015	34	2.33
Butte	126,837	23	39,696	18	2.40
Calavaras	115,300	47	1,463	31	1.13
Colusa	199,388	41	0	0	.06
Contra Costa	79,617	25	4,744	6	10.75
El Dorado	182,830	81	1,748	25	1.49
Fresno	1,421,171	84	935,489	75	5.22
Glenn	254,836	48	33,167	17	.55
Humboldt	91,351	12	0	0	.85
Kern	1,644,419	62*	792,634	46	3.50
Kings	607,337	85	487,041	83	5.58
Lake	42,602	24	4,194	12	2.27
Lassen	56,440	9	11,120	11	.29
Los Angeles	40,033	7	0	0	19.19
Madera	436,621	57	163,416	61	1.87
Marin	89,985	51	9,532	28	8.90
Mendocino	1,050,790	57*	15,030	35	.85
Monterey	618,234	42	47,291	19*	.01
Napa	62,435	28	7,114	8	1.09
Nevada	2,310	3	0	0	4.20
Orange	71,184	39	8,810	14	22.72
Placer	130,084	62	15,313	39	3.20
Plumas	92,792	73	0	†	1.23
Riverside	73,011	12	48,553	10	34.01
Sacramento	223,199	43	90,398	48	8.96
San Benito	535,856	74	51,719	61	1.76
San Bernardino	12,940	1	10,211	2	111.51
San Diego	115,301	19	17,433	9	9.84
San Joaquin	452,415	52	303,758	46	9.45
San Luis Obispo	577,724	37	57,507	39	2.30
San Mateo	45,223	54	1,572	18	10.50
Santa Barbara	460,791	48	51,057	28	7.69
Santa Clara	349,262	73	19,316	28	9.34
Santa Cruz	12,239	20	2,201	9	18.73
Shasta	101,525	19	9,680	20	1.65
Sierra	35,337	69	0	†	.74
Siskiyou	259,635	34	23,150	10	1.14
Solano	250,269	70	100,357	58	5.99
Sonoma	243,985	37	15,842	15	7.12
Stanislaus	570,678	75	182,348	43	5.45
Tehama	643,231	58	34,818	32	1.57
Trinity	6,816	7	0	0	1.57
Tulare	973,069	73	469,113	67	7.19
Tuolumne	199,893	63*	0	†	1.89
Ventura	135,785	31	42,638	32	31.58
Yolo	435,006	77	244,435	72	2.35
Total Counties	14,381,421	46	4,363,331	41	4.69
Cities	45,666		7,696		38.57
Total	14,427,087		4,371,027		4.79

Source: Data on total land and prime land under contract from the California Resources Agency, data on land in farms from the U.S. Bureau of Census; and data for total prime land from the California Office of Planning and Research.

* Based on total private land rather than on land in farms.
† No prime land in the county.

This article is reprinted from "Use-Value Assessment and Land Conservation," *California Agriculture*, University of California, Division of Agricultural Sciences, pp. 12-14, March 1977.

The Progressive Land Tax: A Tax Incentive for the Family Farm

EXAMPLE
28

INTRODUCTION

A mere mention of the "graduated land tax" will still make the blood boil in many North Dakota citizens who have participated in the sometimes bitter political debates on that subject in past decades. It was, according to some, a strategy for the preservation of family farms -- and yet, to others, it was a radical scheme that would penalize farmers who were doing well.

The purpose of this paper is not to initiate a new heated political debate on that issue. However, a dialogue must begin somewhere on what to do about the continued disappearance of the family size farm, and this paper is offered as a vehicle to begin that discussion. To that end, the pages that follow contain an explanation of how the economy of an agricultural state suffers when family size farms decrease in number; a discussion of the disappearance of the family size farms in North Dakota; a review of the philosophy and history of using property tax incentives to assist in arresting the decline of the small family farm; a discussion of the progressive land tax concepts and how they have been used around the world; and some observations on the need for North Dakota to begin evaluating a progressive land tax system.

The Rural Life Style

Family farming is more than just a business. It is a way of life -- a rural lifestyle. Adam Smith's description of old England as a nation of shopkeepers could be used to describe North Dakota's economy. Our towns and cities are made up primarily of small businesses, and the economy of these towns and cities is supported by and tied directly to an agricultural economy made up of thousands of family farm units that dot the prairies.

These family farm units support small towns and cities and together they create a rural lifestyle. For several decades, this lifestyle was considered dull and undesirable by many, and yet

Large Concentrations of Landholdings

However, in addition to the natural growth of the size of the average farm, there is evidence that the frequency distribution curve charting the size of farms has become skewed to the right with larger and larger concentrations of landholdings.

With more and more land being held in fewer and fewer hands, the average family size farm is having to compete with the awesome economic power of some landowners who perhaps have forty, eighty or even one hundred twenty quarter sections of land.

The sad fact is that family farmers always lose in that kind of competition because they don't wield the economic clout to bid for the next quarter of land to add to their existing unit if they are bidding against someone who already has a hundred twenty quarter sections of land.

The Census of Agriculture is conducted every five years, but it does not report landholdings in sufficiently detailed categories

to provide conclusive proof that the concentration of landholdings is serious. However, there is evidence from the Census of Agriculture that provides some clues about the shifting of landholdings. A review of the data from 1959, 1964, 1969 and 1974 shows the following about the number of farms in North Dakota and their acreage during specified years.

	1959	1964	1969	1974
Farms under 1000 acres	43,561	35,628	31,881	27,589
Farms 1000 - 1999 acres	9,278	10,635	11,343	11,332
Farms over 2000 acres	2,089	2,573	3,157	3,789
Total Farms in North Dakota	54,928	48,836	46,381	42,710*4

It can be seen that while the total number of farms in North Dakota has declined from almost 55,000 in 1959 to about 42,700 in 1974, a decrease of about 25%, the number of farms of over 2,000 acres has risen dramatically from less than 2,100 in 1959 to almost 3,800 in 1974, an increase of over 80%. At the same time, the number of farms in the 1,000 to 1,999 acre size range has increased by only 22%, from 9,278 to 11,332. In other words, it appears that the larger farms, those over 2,000 acres, are growing at a faster rate than those closer to the statewide average size of just over 1,000 acres.

PROVIDING AN ECONOMIC INCENTIVE FOR THE SMALL FAMILY FARM: A PROGRESSIVE LAND TAX APPROACH

While there are many factors influencing farming that are outside of the direct control of state government, the development of a property tax system that influences the growth of family farming is controlled by state government. Therefore, some argue that North Dakota should demonstrate, by the force of example, its commitment to the future of family farming by using this element of policy which is under our direct control to encourage the family farm unit.

Currently, the property tax, because it is a flat rate tax, offers no disincentive to large accumulations of land and no incentive to the family farm size unit. For example, under the present property tax system in North Dakota, if two farmers own property of identical value, but one owns ten times more land than the other, he or she pays ten times more in property taxes. The tax rate does not increase as the size of the farm unit increases. If, however, the large farming operation were subject to twelve times as much in taxes on ten times as much land, then there obviously would be a property tax disadvantage to accumulating more and more land.

In the United States our experience with progressive tax rates has been accomplished almost exclusively with the income tax, and not the property tax. A progressive tax in the income tax area is justified by the "ability to pay concept." There are some who argue that this same concept would not apply to the property tax because, although the possession of income directly reflects the ability to pay, the possession of property does not necessarily reflect the ability to pay. In some cases, that is a valid argument; however, there is certainly some relationship between the ability to purchase and accumulate large landholdings and the ability to pay taxes. In fact, the goal of a progressive property tax is to intercede in the decision by large landowners to use income gained from previous property owned to purchase more and more property.

Mechanics of a Progressive Land Tax

A graduated or progressive land tax would establish progressively higher tax rates on larger landholdings than on family sized farmland holdings. That way, the large farm operation not only would pay more tax than a small farm unit, but it would also pay a higher rate of tax.

A property tax system could provide tax discounts to the basic homestead unit while calling for progressively higher taxes on larger concentrations of land. In this manner, the system would not only provide a disincentive to the very large concentrations of land, but it would provide a direct incentive to the family size farm unit.

To illustrate how progressive land tax rates might apply, I have developed the following set of sample rates:

ILLUSTRATION OF HOW A PROGRESSIVE PROPERTY TAX RATE STRUCTURE MIGHT LOOK:

1. Up to $500,000 in fair market value of property, 98% of the standard rate for the county would apply.
2. From $500,000 to $1,000,000 in market value the tax would be the amount from No. 1 + the standard rate on everything over $500,000.
3. From $1,000,001 to $1,500,000 in market value, the tax would be the amount from No. 2 + 105% of the standard rate on everything over $1,000,000.
4. From $1,500,001 to $2,500,000 in market value, the tax would be the amount from No. 3 + 115% of the standard rate on everything over $1,500,000.
5. Over $2,500,000 in market value, the tax would be the amount from No. 4 + 130% of the standard rate on everything over $2,500,000.

[I have included the above example for illustration purposes only. The specific levels and rates for a progressive land tax would have to be studied at great length before enactment. A program, to be effective, must be flexible enough to allow reasonable expansion of family farm units without the threat of tax penalties, but it also must be tight enough to discourage the very large concentrations of land owned by one farming unit.]

In Theory, Progressive Tax Rates Reduce Land Prices

The economic argument for using a progressive property tax structure to encourage family size farming is that the higher property tax rate reduces the value of land, which reduces the price of land, making it more readily available for purchases by new or small farmers who otherwise could not afford to purchase the land. The large landholder is discouraged from adding that next quarter or section of land to his or her farm operation because the high tax rate makes the land less attractive as an investment. Theoretically, the price of land is reduced because "the capital value of an asset equals the discounted value of the expected net income stream."*6

Said another way, a progressive land tax should make land less expensive by changing the existing supply and demand relationship for land by serving as a disincentive for the large operator to bid on another expansion tract. As the large landowner's demand for more land diminishes, the supply and demand relationship for land is altered. When the normal supply demand relationship is altered by a progressive tax, land becomes more available to family size farming units with less economic competition from the large landholders.

Of course, property taxes are not the only influences on land values. Many other factors may work to increase the value of all farm land at the same time the progressive property tax exerts some downward pressure on land prices.

Nonetheless, while a progressive property tax may fail to reduce the price of land in real terms, it may still succeed in its goal of discouraging larger accumulations of land by making persons who own those accumulations compete on more even terms for expansion tracts with the smaller farmers.

CONCLUSION — IT'S TIME FOR NORTH DAKOTA TO CONSIDER THE PROGRESSIVE LAND TAX

The title of this paper calls for a "discussion" — we have discussed the broad subject of progressive land taxes; we have discussed the characteristics of farmland ownership and the destructive capacity that concentrated land ownership has on the survival of the family farm unit; and we have discussed in brief form the experiences that some other countries have had with the use of the progressive land tax.

As you have seen in this report, the progressive land tax concept has had little practical use in the world, and consequently its success in discouraging large concentrations of land is as yet, inconclusive. However, that does not mean that a progressive land tax system cannot successfully reestablish some economic equilibrium between family size farms and the very large concentrations of farmland.

It is my opinion that North Dakota should begin a serious evaluation of the progressive land tax issue to determine whether such a tax system could be effective in aiding family farms in their struggle for esistence. If that evaluation concluded that a progressive property tax system should be tried, then it should be initiated in a very slow and cautious manner in order to probe the capacity of that approach to assist family size farms.

To be acceptable, an experimental progressive land tax program would have to be implemented in a way that focuses only on those concentrations of land that are clearly threatening the family size farm units. For example, the individual who owns 110 quarters of land and is bidding on another quarter should find that a progressive land tax will offset the natural economic advantage he or she would otherwise have in acquiring that property when bidding against smaller farmers.

The question of what is a family sized farm would be one of the most difficult features of the progressive land tax legislation to determine. It is said that a big farm is always one quarter more than you own. The family size farm is not a monolithic term that can be applied to all farms in North Dakota. Different types of farming conducted in different locations of the state require different quantities of property in order to sustain a living for the farm family.

Most of us might agree that concentrations of land that approach 60, 80, or 100 quarter sections should be subjected to a marginally higher property tax than smaller farm units because of the natural economic advantage they already enjoy. However, when you move down the scale of ownership, the line is not as clear. I have not attempted in this paper to define the family farm, but I don't agree with those who say it can't be done.

Given some time, policy makers in the executive branch or the legislative branch could come up with a pretty good definition of what is a family size farm unit in North Dakota, using valuation as a criterion.

A progressive land tax would not prevent concentrations of landholdings from existing or even from becoming larger, but it would provide certain economic disincentives to offset the natural economic advantages that large landholders already have over the family farmers. I look at it as "evening things up."

Certainly, there would be difficulties in initiating the progressive property tax system, but the difficulties are not insurmountable. If we believe it is an important element of public policy to preserve the family farm, we must take the important steps to provide economic encouragement to the family size farm units. The message of Thomas Jefferson in the Foreword of this paper is as relevant today as it was in 1785 — "The small landholders are the most precious part of a state."

We have lost a fourth of our small family farms in North Dakota in less than 20 years. We cannot wait an additional 20 years or a decade before we investigate every possibility for helping the family size farm, including exploring the progressive land tax. An evaluation of this tax system should begin today.

This article is reprinted from Byron L. Dorgan, "The Progressive Land Tax: A Tax Incentive for the Family Farm," North Dakota Tax Commission, April 1978.

EXAMPLE 29

Wisconsin's Farmland Preservation Program

On June 29, 1977, Wisconsin's Farmland Preservation Act became law. The purpose of the new law is to help local governments that want to preserve farmland through local planning and zoning, and to provide tax relief to farmers who participate in the local programs.

This pamphlet summarizes the law—both the initial program and the permanent program. Then, the meaning of the new law for farmers and city people is discussed.

THE INITIAL PROGRAM

In the first five years, 1977-1982, farmers can voluntarily sign contracts: the farmer agrees not to develop his land and in exchange is eligible for state income tax credits.

The Contract

To qualify for a contract, the farmer must have 35 acres or more, and must have earned $6000 in gross farm profits in the last year or $18,000 in the last three years (Line 28 on the IRS Schedule F). Also he must either have an SCS farm plan or request that a plan be prepared. The farmer applies to the county board for a contract. The county approves or rejects the application, but the farmer can appeal a rejection to the state Agricultural Land Preservation Board. If the county approves the application, the state must sign a contract with the farmer if the land is qualified under the law.

Under the contract, no development is allowed unless it is for farm use. Farmers are eligible for income tax credits, and are exempt from special assessments to provide urban-type public services such as sewer and water. The contract follows the land, even if the land is sold. The initial contract expires on September 30, 1982.

Tax Credits

The income tax credit is based on *household income*. Household income includes net farm income and all money earned off the farm by the husband, wife, and dependent children, plus *property taxes* (up to $4000). The tax credit is calculated by a very detailed formula. Only property taxes up to $4000 are eligible for relief, the maximum credit is $2600, and households with incomes over $35,000 are not eligible for any credits under the formula. Basically, the higher the property tax the higher the credit, *and* the lower the income the higher the credit. The table below shows the *maximum* tax credit. Farmers with initial contracts receive 50% of the maximum credit.

MAXIMUM TAX CREDIT SCHEDULE**

| Household Income plus property taxes (up to $4000)* | Property Taxes: | | | |
	1,000	2,000	3,000	$4,000 or more
0	800	1,500	2,100	2,600
5,000	680	1,395	2,010	2,525
10,000	480	1,220	1,860	2,400
15,000	200	975	1,650	2,225
20,000	0	600	1,325	1,950
30,000	0	0	0	800
34,000	0	0	0	160

*Household income as defined for the Homestead tax credit program.

**Actual credit received by farmers: initial contract = 50% of these amounts; credit under permanent program depends on action of local governments.

A contract expires naturally in 1982. If a farmer is not eligible for the permanent program because the county board failed to qualify him, then he pays back the last two years of tax credits. If the farmer *is* eligible but chooses not to participate any longer, he must pay back all the tax credits received plus 6% interest from the time the contract expires. If a contract is terminated early, the landowner must pay back all the tax credits plus 6% interest from the time the credit was received. **If the farmer signs a new contract or is in an exclusive agricultural zone, there is no repayment of tax credits.**

THE PERMANENT PROGRAM

Tax credits after 1982 depend on what the local government does. In order for farmers to remain eligible for tax credits, counties must take some action. Counties are not required to do *anything,* but tax credits depend on some county action. Counties could act earlier if they wish, but by October, 1982:

1. Urban counties—counties over 75,000 population or adjacent to counties with over 400,000 population must have exclusive agricultural zoning ordinances.
2. Rural counties—counties with 75,000 population or less must adopt either a farmland preservation plan or an exclusive agricultural zoning ordinance.

Exclusive Agricultural Zoning ordinances must provide that farmland cannot be developed, and no residences can be built unless occupied by the farmer, his parents or children, or a person working on the farm. Other than for these exceptions, the minimum parcel size for a residence is 35 acres. Special exceptions and conditional uses, such as a roadside stand, must be compatible with farming. Rezonings must be based on the availability of public services and protection of the local environment. Agricultural Preservation Plans must contain farmland maps, policy statements, and a proposed program to preserve farmland. Plans are not binding on counties or landowners.

Local Option

No county is required to have zoning or planning. However, after 1982, tax credits will be available to farmers only if their land is in a county plan preservation district or in an exclusive agricultural zone. Even if the county acts, town government and landowners still have some options. County preservation plans are not binding on landowners or governments, and the plan can be modified if there is good reason. Contracts are voluntary for farmers.

Zoning is optional for the county and town governments, but any local zoning is binding on the landowner. Under the law, in a rural county, any town board can reject the county's exclusive agricultural zoning ordinance *for that town.* In an urban county, a majority of towns can veto the county's exclusive agricultural zoning ordinance if they wish. Finally, zoning is not forever, and can be changed if there is a need to use the land for development.

Tax Credits

In rural counties, farmers in a preservation district under the county's plan may voluntarily sign contracts. The contract is similar to the initial contract except that it is for 10-25 years and the farmer is eligible for 70% of the maximum tax credit. If the rural county has exclusive agricultural zoning instead of the plan, farmers in agricultural zones receive 70% of the maximum credit. If the county has both zoning *and* a plan, farmers are eligible for 100% of the maximum credit. Under some special conditions, if *towns* adopt exclusive agricultural zoning, farmers in the zones could qualify for 70% of the maximum credit.

In urban counties, farmers are eligible for tax credits only if the county board puts their land in an exclusive agricultural zone. Zoning would qualify them for 70% of the maximum credit, but if the county has both exclusive farm zoning and a preservation plan, farmers are eligible for 100% of the maximum credit.

When a contract expires or when land is removed from an agricultural zone, the farmer is liable for some of his past tax credits. If a farmer continues in the program by signing a new contract, or the land remains in an agricultural zone, no back credits are due. In any case, the credits must be paid only when the land is developed or sold. As long as the land remains in farm use, no credits need be paid back. If a farmer's contract expires at the end of its term and he doesn't renew it, he pays back all tax credits for the past 20 years, plus 6% compound interest from the time the contract expires. If the contract is terminated early, he pays back all credits for the last 20 years, plus

6% compound interest from the time the credit was received. Other farmers may have received tax credits because the land was zoned only for agriculture. If the zoning is later changed, the farmer is liable for the tax credits for the past 20 years, plus 6% compound interest from the time of the rezoning. Again, the payment is due when the land is sold or developed.

Administration

Both the initial and the permanent programs will be administered by the Wisconsin Department of Agriculture, Trade and Consumer Protection. A special State Agricultural Lands Preservation Board is created to *certify* exclusive agricultural zoning ordinances and preservation plans, act on requests for early termination of contracts, act on appeals from farmers who were denied contracts by the county, and approve spending of funds for counties to develop preservation plans. The Board is composed of the secretaries of the State Departments of Agriculture, Trade and Consumer Protection; Administration; Local Affairs and Development; and two public members.

Effect on Farmers

The new law will affect farmers in two ways. First, local planning and zoning can protect farm operations from interference from urban land uses. When farm and urban land uses are mixed, land use conflicts often arise over farm odors, noise, or dust, and there are sometimes conflicts over fence maintenance and trespass. Exclusive agricultural zoning by local governments could help reduce these conflicts by separating farm and urban land uses. Farmers are also protected from special tax assessments for sewer, water, or other urban public services. Exclusive agricultural zoning will also help reduce the cost of public services and keep farm property tax assessments from rising as rapidly as they would if nearby farmland were being developed.

Farmers are also eligible for tax relief, but two points must be noted. First, the tax relief depends on the farm family's income. When income is low, tax credits will be high; when income is high, tax credits will be low. In effect, the tax relief is more like an *insurance policy* than a pure across-the-board tax cut. The tax relief program is insurance against a bad crop year or any other event that reduces farm income.

Second, the tax relief is a pure tax break only if the land stays in farming. The program offers only tax *deferral* if the land is developed. As long as the land stays in agriculture or open space use, no tax credits are repaid. So if the land stays in farming, the program offers a tax break. But if the land is removed from the contract or zoning, and is then sold or developed, tax credits for the last 20 years must be repaid. In effect, the property taxes were *deferred* until the land was sold or developed. In this case the tax relief amounts to an interest-free loan for the period the land is zoned or under contract (or a loan at

6% interest if a contract is terminated early). So, the new law offers a pure tax break only to those who keep their land in farming. To others, the law offers only tax deferral.

Effect on City People

The Farmland Preservation Act may benefit urban residents by preserving open space, by helping to preserve farmland for the future, and by helping to control urban sprawl and reduce the cost of extending public services to new developments. Since the tax credit does not affect the property tax collected by the local government, the program will not increase property taxes for urban people. However, everyone in the state will pay for the program since it offers farmers a credit against the state income tax. However, the total cost of the program is likely to be quite small, especially in the early years when there are few contracts signed. In the end, controlling urban sprawl may save more taxes for urban residents than the cost of farmland tax credits.

SUMMARY

The Farmland Preservation Act was passed to assist local people who want to preserve farmland, and to provide tax relief to farmers who participate in the local programs. The success or failure of the program rests in the hands of farmers, local citizens, and local elected officials. There are many options for local government under the law, and the state will not dictate local planning and zoning policies—those policy choices are the proper business of local citizens and local government. The Farmland Preservation Act will assist local governments in what they decide to do, but the decisions must be made by local citizens.

For more information on the Farmland Preservation Act, contact your county office of University of Wisconsin-Extension, usually located in the county courthouse; or write the Wisconsin Department of Agriculture, Trade and Consumer Protection, 801 West Badger Road, Madison, Wisconsin, 53713.

This article is reprinted from Richard Barrows, "Wisconsin's Farmland Preservation Program," Cooperative Extension Programs, Wisconsin Department of Agriculture, Trade and Consumer Protection, November 1977.

Resources

ORGANIZATIONS

The following bibliography lists key organizations and published resources for both chapters six and seven. The resource sections at the end of each chapter provide a more detailed list of readings specifically related to each issue.

The American Land Forum, Inc.

1025 Vermont Avenue, N.W.
Washington, D.C. 20005
(202) 347-4516
Charles Little

Connecticut's Office of Legislative Research

Legislative Office Building
18-20 Trinity Street
Hartford, Connecticut 06115
Lawrence Furbish, Research Analyst

Conservation Foundation

1717 Massachusetts Avenue, N.W.
Washington, D.C. 20036
(202) 797-4300
Robert Healy

Connecticut Conservation Association

Northrop Street
Bridgewater, Connecticut 06572
(203) 354-9325
Robert Kunz, Executive Vice-President

Council on Environmental Quality

722 Jackson Place, N.W.
Washington, D.C. 20006
(202) 395-5832
Charles Warren, Director

Environmental Protection Agency

401 M Street, S.W.
Washington, D.C. 20024
(202) 755-0442
John Gustafson

The National Agricultural Lands Study

722 Jackson Place, N.W.
Washington, D.C. 20006
(202) 395-5832
Bob Gray, Director

National Association of Conservation Districts

1025 Vermont Avenue, N.W.
Washington, D.C. 20005
(202) 347-5995
Neil Sampson, Executive Vice-President;
Charles Boothby, Executive Secretary

National Association of County Officials (NACO)

1735 New York Avenue, N.W.
Washington, D.C. 20006
(202) 785-9577
Bob Weaver

National Conference of State Legislatures

444 North Capitol Street
Washington, D.C. 20001
(202) 624-5400
Bob Davies

National Governors' Association

444 North Capitol Street
Washington, D.C. 20001
(202) 624-5335
Susan Seladones, Research Assistant,
Center for Policy Research

Natural Resources Defense Council

1725 I Street, N.W.
Washington, D.C. 20006
(202) 223-8210
Tom Barlow

Office of Congressman James Jeffords

429 Cannon House Office Building
Washington, D.C. 20515
(202) 225-4115
Roger Allbee, Legislative Staff

Resources for the Future

1755 Massachusetts Avenue, N.W.
Washington, D.C. 20036
(202) 462-4400
Pierre Crosson

Soil Conservation Service/USDA

Environmental Services Division
P.O. Box 2890
Washington, D.C. 20003
(202) 447-3839
Norman Berg, Associate Administrator;
Darwyn Briggs, Research Staff

Urban Land Institute

1200 18th Street, N.W.
Washington, D.C. 20036
(202) 331-8500
Ronald Rumbaugh, Executive Vice-President

BIBLIOGRAPHY

Babcock, Richard F., and Duane Feurer, "Land as a Commodity 'Affected With a Public Interest,'" **Urban Land**. Urban Land Institute, 1200 18th Street, N.W., Washington, D.C. 20036. November 1977. Good article on the private interests involved in land-use planning.

Belden, Joe, and Bob Davies, **A Survey of State Programs to Preserve Farmland**. Council on Environmental Quality, 722 Jackson Place, N.W., Washington, D.C. 20006. June 1979.

Blobaum, Roger, "The Loss of Agricultural Land," in **Change in Rural America: Causes, Consequences and Alternatives**. Rodefeld, et al. C.V. Moseby and Company, St. Louis, Missouri. 1978.

Brown, Lester R., **The Worldwide Loss of Cropland**. Worldwatch Paper 24. Worldwatch Institute, 1776 Massachusetts Avenue, N.W., Washington, D.C. 20036. December 1978.

Catholic Rural Life, "Farmland Preservation Issue," **Catholic Rural Life**. Vol. 28, No. 6. NCRLC, 4625 N.W. Beaver Drive, Des Moines, Iowa 50322. June 1979.

Council of State Governments, **State Agricultural Land Issues**. Council of State Governments, Iron Works Pike, Lexington, Kentucky 40578. August 1978.

Cotner, M.L., et al., **Farmland: Will There Be Enough?** ERS-584, Economics, Statistics and Cooperative Service, USDA, Washington, D.C. 20250.

Coughlin, Robert D., *et al.*, **Saving the Garden: The Preservation of Farmland and Other Environmentally Valuable Land**. National Science Foundation, 1800 G Street, N.W., Washington, D.C. 20006. August 1977.

Council on Environmental Quality, **Environmental Quality The Ninth Annual Report of the Council on Environmental Quality**. CEQ, 722 Jackson Place, N.W., Washington, D.C. 10006.

Dideriksen, Raymond I., *et al.*, **Potential Cropland Study**. Statistical Bulletin No. 578. Soil Conservation Service, USDA, Washington, D.C. 20250. October 1977.

Environmental Protection Agency, **Background Paper in Support of an EPA Policy to Protect Environmentally Significant Agricultural Lands**. Environmental Protection Agency, 401 M Street, S.W., Washington, D.C.

Esseks, J.D., "Politics of Farmland Preservation," **Policy Studies Journal**. Vol. 6, No. 4, 361 Lincoln Hall, Illinois University, Urbana, Illinois. Summer 1978. $2.50. Overview of four techniques to preserve agricultural land: Differential Assessment; Agricultural districting; Purchase of development rights; restrictive zoning.

Fletcher, Wendell W., **Farmland Protection Legislation**. Issue Brief IB78013, The Library of Congress, Congressional Research Service, Washington, D.C. 20540. May 5, 1978. Review of national legislation.

Healy, Robert, "Rural Land: Private Choices, Public Interests," **Conservation Foundation Letter**. Conservation Foundation, 1717 Massachusetts Avenue, N.W., Washington, D.C. 20036. August 1977.

Lapping, Mark, "Policy Alternatives for the Preservation of Agricultural Land Use," **Journal of Environmental Management**. Environmental Program and School of Natural Resources, University of Vermont, Burlington, Vermont 05401. Revised January 1977.

Lee, Linda K., **A Perspective on Cropland Availability**. Economics, Statistics and Cooperative Service, USDA, Washington, D.C. 20250. 1978.

League of Women Voters, **Preserving America's Farmland**. League of Women Voters, 1730 M Street, N.W., Washington, D.C. 20036. Undated.

Little, Charles, ed., **Land and Food—The Preservation of U.S. Farmland**. American Land Forum Report No. 1. American Land Forum, Inc., 1025 Vermont Avenue, N.W., Washington, D.C. 20005. Spring 1979.

Little, Charles, Neil R. Sampson and Robert E. Coughlin, **Protecting Agricultural Lands: Workshop Papers**. Prepared for an informal Workshop on the Importance of the Agricultural Land Base. Library of Congress, Washington, D.C. 20540. February 8, 1977. Paper on case for retaining prime lands; paper on the present agricultural land situation; paper on methods to protect agricultural lands.

Maine Consortium for Food Self-Reliance, **Report on the Loss of Farmland**. Maine Consortium for Food Self-Reliance, c/o Richards Land, Freeport, Maine 04032.

Massachusetts Department of Food and Agriculture, **To Save the Farms Interim Report of the Agricultural Land Preservation Committee**. 100 Cambridge Street, Boston, Massachusetts 02202.

Schumde, Keith, "A Perspective on Prime Farmland," **Journal of Soil and Water Conservation**. Soil Conservation Society of America, 7515 Northeast Ankeny Road, Ankeny, Iowa 50021. September/October 1977. Issue devoted to Farmland Preservation.

Soil Conservation Service, **Prime and Unique Farmlands: Important Farmland Inventory**. 7 CFR Part 657, Superintendent of Documents, U.S. Government Printing Office, Washington, D.C. 20402. 1977. Proposed rules issued by USDA; Soil Conservation Service.

Soil Conservation Society of America (SCSA), **Journal of Soil and Water Conservation**. SCSA, 7515 Northeast Ankeny Road, Ankeny, Iowa 50021. September/October 1976. Six articles on farmland preservation.

Steiner, Frederick. **Agricultural Land Preservation: Alternatives for Whitman County (Washington)**. Whitman County Regional Planning Council, Colfax, Washington. October 1, 1979.

Toner, William. **Saving Farms and Farmlands: A Community Guide**. American Society of Planning Officials, 1978.

Urban Land Institute, "Preservation of Prime Agricultural Land," **Environmental Comment**. Urban Land Institute, 1200 18th Street, N.W., Washington, D.C. 20036. January 1978.

Whyte, William, **Securing Open Space for Urban America: Conservation Easements**. Technical Bulletin No. 36, Urban Land Institute, 1200 18th Street, N.W. Washington, D.C. 20036 1979.

Section III

Section III

Conserving Energy and Natural Resources

Energy, soil, water and other natural resources are of vital importance to agriculture. Their importance becomes ever more apparent in the face of rising food demands and dwindling supplies of these critical natural resources.

American policy makers often point with pride to the fact that today's farmers produce food for many times the people they did 50 years ago. In fact, this trend has become even more dramatic in recent years. In 1950 one farmer raised enough food for 16 conssumers, while in 1972 he was raising enough for 52 consumers.

This enormous increase in agricultural production has not been a consequence of an increase in the number of farmers or in the amount of land under production—both have been rapidly declining. This dramatic increase in productivity has been the consequence of accelerated exploitation of basic natural resources such as energy supplies, soil, and water, and a rapid increase in the "industrialization" of agricultural production. The strain caused by the exploitation of these natural resources, and the ruinous impact of certain new technologies, are major threats to American farmers, consumers and to the environment.

Although these problems are extremely serious, policy makers have been slow to respond. At the national level, federal officials continue to ignore these problems—which past policies of promoting the exploitation of natural resources and the use of technology have done so much to create.

At the state and local level, public officials have not recognized the seriousness of these problems and are not responding as quickly as they have to such issues as the need for adequate capital and credit, the need to protect farmland; and the need to open up new markets. Regrettably, part of the reason is the traditional American belief that natural resources are endless and are there to be exploited.

However, many states and cities are beginning to take the needed first steps. One powerful advantage they have is the unprecedented public interest and experimentation in conserving natural resources and energy. Many of these projects should become the basis for the development of innovative public policies at the state and local level in the 1980s.

Chapter 8, *Protecting Soil and Water Resources*, outlines state and local initiatives aimed at conserving soil and water resources in agriculture. Chapter 9, *Conserving Energy and Adopting New Technologies*, outlines state and local initiatives as well as those taken by private citizens and organizations aimed at conserving energy in agriculture.

Chapter 8

Protecting Soil and Water Resources

Conservation of natural resources essential to agriculture has become increasingly important in a world of ever more precarious food and energy supplies. Soil and water are the principal resources needed for farming. In this chapter fertilizer is also included because of its importance as a soil conditioner and also because it is often a source of water pollution. A crucial question for the future of our current food system is whether we can continue to use huge amounts of synthetic, petroleum-based fertilizers. In the long run, the environmental and energy costs may be too great.

SOIL AND FERTILIZER

Loss of topsoil due to wind and water erosion in the United States is now far outstripping natural formation of new soil. Topsoil loss from farmland is approximately 12 tons per acre each year, while replacement through formation of new topsoil occurs at a rate of about 1.5 tons per acre annually. Over the last two centuries, about one third of the topsoil in the United States has been lost. Government conservation programs have improved the soil picture since the severe losses of the earlier part of the twentieth century, but the problem continues. It was aggravated during the early 1970s by fencerow-to-fencerow planting, and aided and abetted by Nixon-Ford-Butz agricultural policies, which encouraged excessive cultivation in order to take advantage of high grain prices in 1973 and 1974. An article on the continuing problem of soil erosion is included in this chapter: **Example 30, Industrialization of Farms Threatens U.S. Topsoil.**

Agricultural production requires fertilizer, whether of synthetic or natural sources. Use of synthetic nitrogen fertilizer has increased enormously since the end of the Second World War. In 1950, 976,000 tons of nitrogen were used as fertilizer. Use in 1960, 1970, and 1975 was up to 2.7 million tons, 7.4 million tons, and 8.6 million tons respectively. But with the price of natural gas from which the fertilizer is manufactured rising in the 1970s at an accelerating rate, use of nitrogen has begun to level off. From 1974 to 1975 nitrogen fertilizer use actually declined. Constraints on energy supplies may make synthetic fertilizers increasingly expensive and impractical in the future.

Petroleum-based fertilizers deserve much of the credit for great advances in U.S. agricultural productivity. But in recent years increasingly large increments of fertilizer have had to be applied to the land in order to keep yields rising at steady rates. And because nitrogen fertilizer is harmful to the organic life in healthy soil, farmers are beginning to look more seriously into using organic fertilizers and composted manures. Studies at the University of Missouri and Washington University-St. Louis have shown that crops raised on organic fertilizers can produce yields or incomes equal to those of "conventional" methods.

Organic fertilizer in its best form is not simply manure applied to the land but composted waste. Composting of manure or other wastes piled and turned periodically produces a substance much like topsoil. Both direct application and composting of sewage sludge and other urban wastes have attracted the attention of local governments. This trend has come as environmental regulations mandate cleaner water and thus less ocean and river dumping of sewage. Many city and county sanitation districts such as those in Chicago and Milwaukee have instituted programs to apply sludge and wastewater to the land.

One of the most fascinating and ambitious programs was introduced in Massachusetts by State Representative Mel King. His proposed *Massachusetts Compost Bill* (HB 2811), 1977, would establish a state authority to collect and process organic wastes through the composting process, and then sell the resulting product—a rich fertilizer—to the state's farmers on a preferential basis. A good description of the proposed Composting Authority is included as **Example 31, Something for Nothing**, Issue 19 of the *Massachusetts Farm Bulletin*. King followed up on this proposal with a less ambitious bill, designed to get a foot in the door. HR 4908, 1978, would establish a Compost Division within the Massachusetts Bureau of Solid Waste Disposal. This new Division would be responsible for organizing and managing local and regional composting projects.

Another reason why innovative farmers and policy makers are turning to more use of organic fertilizers is because nitrogen fertilizers can seriously pollute local water supplies. An excellent case study of nitrate pollution in Holt County, Nebraska can be found in **Example 32, Nitrates: An Insoluble Problem.**

WATER

Water is essential to food production, especially in the drier climate of the Western United States. Irrigation in California has turned a semi-arid landscape into one of the nation's principal food producing areas. Conservation of water resources is needed for future productivity, but struggles are continuing over who will control irrigated land and access to water. Both federal and state governments are involved.

Total water use in the United States between 1940 and 1975 rose from 136 billion to 371 billion gallons, an increase of 173%. Much of this change was due to irrigation. In 1940, 71 billion gallons were used for irrigation; in 1975 this level of use was up to 179 billion gallons. Federally subsidized "cheap" water has led to considerable waste. The U.S. General Accounting Office found that more than half the water supplied to American farms by the Interior Department's Bureau of Reclamation in 1973 was lost as waste.

This loss of water could be at least partially avoided. In Arizona, for example, per capita water consumption is twice as high as the national average. Arizona's irrigated farms use about 5 acre-feet of water per acre each year. (An acre-foot is the amount of water needed to cover one acre to a depth of one foot.) Neither the state nor the federal government imposes any restriction on this use.

Arizona's neighboring state, New Mexico, has, on the other hand, been a model of responsible water use for decades. Its state water conservation program requires permits before significant amounts of water can be diverted for private use. Set up in 1907 for surface water and applied to ground water in 1931, this program is run by a state engineer. As a result of the state's emphasis on conservation, farmers in New Mexico use three acre-feet to irrigate one acre of hay, while Arizona farmers use twice as much.

One of the most serious causes of this problem of wasting water resources is that most Western states grant water rights on an unrestricted, first come-first served basis. New Mexico's extensive statutes have controlled this to some extent. A similar effort has been underway in Montana, through HB 491, 1975. This bill would have required a public determination that applications for permits to use more than 10,000 acre-feet of water per year were in the public interest.

One of the most fascinating local programs aimed at conserving water used in agriculture is taking place in Northglenn, Colorado, a suburb of Denver. Northglenn has worked out an arrangement with local farmers in which the highest quality water would be diverted immediately from irrigation to domestic uses, then after being used and treated, with nutrients remaining in it, the water would be pumped back out to agricultural areas for irrigation use. This unusual cooperative scheme between farmers and residential users is described in excerpts from *Nature Is, Man Becomes*, the City of Northglenn's brochure on the program, which is reprinted as **Example 33, A Miracle of Cooperative Planning.**

Overshadowing waste of irrigation water is the issue of whether small family farmers or corporate and large-scale farmers should have preferential access to federally subsidized water. The federal *Reclamation Act of 1902* requires that irrigation assistance should go only to individuals owning 160 acres or less. The law has never been adequately enforced, and today irrigated holdings in such areas as California's Westlands Water District average 2,400 acres. Court victories by small farmers and groups such as National Land for People forced the Interior Department in 1977 to respond.

The Interior Department's plan would limit federal water to 160 acres owned and 160 acres leased for each farm husband, wife and lineal descendent. Even this moderate and inadequate plan stimulated intense opposition and lobbying from the large farmers, ranchers and agribusiness interests in the Western states. The conflict surrounding federally-subsidized water in California is laid out in the May 1977 issue of *Catholic Rural Life* which is reprinted as **Example 34, How Corporations Violate Family Farm Water Rights.**

These interests have argued that 160, or even 640 acres is an insufficient size for an economically viable farm. But the U.S. Department of Agriculture released a study in early 1978 showing that substantial profits would be possible even for the moderate-sized farms envisioned by Interior's proposals. Farms of 640 acres could make net incomes of $23,000 to $125,000, compared with a 1976 average net income for all U.S. farms of $7,900.

Example 35, The Family Farm Water Act, an initiative proposed in Washington state, is one local effort to accomplish the same objective—to bar the biggest holders from monopolizing irrigation rights. The initiative defines family farms as consisting of no more than 2,000 irrigated acres. Only family farms or land being "developed" into family farms would then be eligible to receive water permits. The major problem with the proposal is that the 2,000 acre maximum would keep out only the very largest holders of farmland.

Some other, more recent technological developments in dry land farming also favor highly capitalized agriculture and thus corporate and large-scale, farm-related interests. An example is "center pivot" irrigation, a mechanical system consisting of an approximately one-quarter mile long raised pipeline rotated around a central anchor. The Center for Rural Affairs, in its 1976 study, *Wheels of Fortune*, found that a single center pivot system (capable of irrigating about 133 acres) costs around $60,000 for the well and equipment alone, exclusive of land and operating costs. This level of capitalization means that again, absentee investors, corporations and the wealthiest farmers will be the most able to profit from this new development in irrigation technology.

Resources

ORGANIZATIONS

Agricultural Resources

1838 Wyoming Avenue, N.W.
Washington, D.C. 20009
(202) 797-9119
David Weiman
160-acre limitation issues.

Clearinghouse for Enforcement of the Reclamation Laws

1346 Connecticut Avenue, N.W.
Fifth floor
Washington, D.C. 20036
(202) 659-2800
Peggy Borgers, Coordinator

Center for Rural Affairs

P.O. Box 405
Walthill, Nebraska 68067
(402) 846-5428
Marty Strange, Co-Director

Environmental Policy Center

317 Pennsylvania Avenue, S.E.
Washington, D.C. 20003
(202) 547-6500
Louise Dunlap, Director

National Land for People

2348 North Cornelia
Fresno, California 93711
(209) 237-6516
George Ballis, Director

Natural Resources Defense Council

1725 I Street, N.W. (Suite 600)
Washington, D.C. 20006
(202) 223-8210
Tom Barlow, Director

Soil Conservation Service

U.S. Department of Agriculture
P.O. Box 2890
Washington, D.C. 20013
(202) 447-3839

PUBLISHED RESOURCES

Baldwin, Andrew, Anne Bartz and Tom McKenna, "The San Felipe Story," **Friends of the Earth.** Vol. 7, No. 2. 620 C Street, S.E., Washington, D.C. 20037. November 1977. Economic and social implications of the proposed San Felipe project, which would bring water into Santa Clara county at an enormous cost.

Carter, Luther J., "Soil Erosion: The Problem Persists Despite the Billions Spent on It," **Science.** Vol. 196, No.

4288. April 22, 1977. Article following recent alarm of CAST report on increasing soil erosion.

Center for Rural Affairs, **Wheels of Fortune.** Center for Rural Affairs, P.O. Box 405, Walthill, Nebraska 68067. January 1976. In depth study of center pivot irrigation systems in Nebraska.

Ecology Action of the Mid-Peninsula, **Resource-Conserving Agricultural Method Promises High Yields.** Ecology Action of the Mid-Peninsula, 2225 El Camino Real, Palo Alto, California 94306. January 1976. Article publicizing recent results of French intensive method of soil preparation and resultant high crop yields.

Economics, Statistics, and Cooperative Staff, **The U.S. Department of the Interior's Proposed Rules for Enforcement of the Reclamation Act of 1902: An Economic Impact Analysis.** Economics, Statistics, and Cooperative Service, USDA, Washington, D.C. January 1978.

Faber, Harold, "Albany Is Requiring the Conservation of Soil and Water by Landowners," **New York Times.** Sunday, April 17, 1977. Description of law requiring all landowners owning more than 25 acres to apply for a soil conservation plan from the state.

Goldstein, Jerome, **Sensible Sludge: A New Look at a Wasted Natural Resource.** Rodale Press, Emmaus, Pennsylvania. 1977.

Howard, Sir Albert, **The Soil & Health.** Schocken, New York. 1972.

Hyams, E., **Soil and Civilization.** Harper & Row, New York. History of man's relation with soils.

Ludlow, Lynn and William Hearst, **The Paper Farmers.** Examiner News Staff, San Francisco Examiner reprint. 1976. Investigation of effectiveness of National Reclamation Act of 1902.

Margolis, Philip, "Land Reclamation Laws: An Overview," **Rural America.** Vol. 2, No. 7. 1346 Connecticut Avenue, N.W., Washington, D.C. 20036. May 1977. List of highlights in the history of land reclamation legislation.

National Catholic Rural Life Conference, **Catholic Rural Life.** Vol. 26, No. 5. 3801 Grand Avenue, Des Moines, Iowa 50312. May 1977. Issue devoted to water.

National Farmers Union, **20 Misconceptions on the 160-Acre Legislation.** National Farmers Union, 1012 14th Street, N.W., Washington, D.C. 20005. November 1977. Myths of the effectiveness of the Reclamation Act of 1902.

New Land Review, Staff, "No One Knows the Value of Water," **New Land Review.** Center for Rural Affairs, P.O. Box 405, Walthill, Nebraska 68067. Spring 1976. Description of social and ecological problems caused by center pivot irrigation systems in Nebraska.

Richard, John, "The Scramble for Water: Agriculture Versus Other Interests in Wyoming," **Policy Studies Journal.** Vol. 6, No. 4. Policy Studies Organization, 361 Lincoln Hall, University of Illinois, Urbana, Illinois 61801. Summer 1978.

Smith, Charles, Bibliography: **160 Acre Anti-Monopoly Water Laws.** National Land For People, 2348 North Cornelia, Fresno, California 93711.

Industrialization of Farms Threatens U.S. Topsoil

EXAMPLE 30

AMERICA'S "green revolution" may be over.
The intense 30-year industrialization of the nation's farm lands, during which crop yields more than doubled through the introduction of complex harvesting machinery, petrochemicals and genetically engineered crops, appears to be at an end.

"We are bumping against the ceiling of applied technology," reports John Timmons, professor of natural resources at Iowa State University. "Unless we are able to develop new technologies our productivity is not going to go up."

A survey of major crop yields in the last decade shows that, while production has continued to rise as unused farm land is brought back into production, the yields per acre of major grains have dipped and swung in patterns unmatched since the Dust Bowl years of the mid-1930s.

According to the Department of Agriculture, statistics for 1977 show corn and wheat below the yields attained in 1972.

But what is of increasing concern to many agronomists and agricultural economists is that recently developed farm technology may have masked, or even contributed to, serious problems, particularly the decline in the quality of the nation's soil.

The most serious problem, they believe, is increasing erosion, particularly in the Midwest Corn Belt.

Scientists contend that the heavy use of fertilizers has allowed crop yields to stay at relatively high levels. They warn, however, that this could be a short-term effect. Unless topsoil erosion patterns are not corrected, they say, yields will drop considerably and productions costs will increase dramatically.

"We're Going To Be in Trouble"

OTHER MAJOR problems include: increased sedimentation as topsoil and fertilizers run off into streams and reservoirs; depletion of irreplaceable supplies of ground ter in the Missouri Basin and sections of Texas; compaction of soil through use of heavy machinery, and use of high-quality farmland for urban development.

"We've been generating tremendous productivity," says Timmons. "But if we continue to interfere with soil and water quality we're going to be in trouble."

In a report to Congress last February, the General Accounting Office warned that, because of excessive erosion, farms in the Great Plains, Corn Belt and Pacific Northwest are losing topsoil at a rate which threatens productivity.

Topsoil is crucial to crop production because it contains most of the organic matter and a major share of the nutrients required by plants. Topsoil thickness varies from a few inches to several feet. Corn Belt lands have a topsoil thickness of 6 to 16 inches.

As a general measure, scientists say losses of 5 tons per acre are acceptable in areas of good quality soil. But in a random study of 283 farms, the GAO found that 83 per cent had losses higher than that. Some farms' losses ran two to three times that rate.

The GAO found that the Department of Agriculture's soil conservation programs, costing several hundred million dollars per year, have been ineffective in establishing enduring conservation practices and in reducing erosion to tolerable levels.

The GAO quoted a report by the Council for Agricultural Science and Technology (CAST) which indicated that Corn Belt farmers were less effective in controlling erosion than they were 15 years ago. CAST, which has its headquarters at Iowa State University at Ames, directs task forces of research scientists and collects and publishes material of interest to the agricultural industry.

The CAST report found that the United States was losing 4 billion tons of topsoil a year in 1972 as compared to 3 billion tons in 1934.

Farmers "Plowed Up Everything"

MUCH OF THE BLAME for increasing erosion in the Midwest has been laid to farmers who rushed to get more land into producton to take advantage of rising grain prices following the 1972 U.S.-Russia wheat deal.

The CAST report estimated that, between 1973 and 1974, 51 million acres were taken out of the federally subsidized soil bank program and converted into crop land. Much of this acreage, known as the "fragile lands," was planted without soil preparation.

Soil losses as great as 50 tons per acre occurred in south Iowa, and erosion of as much as 200 tons per acre was recorded on the sloping cultivated fields in Illinois.

"It was a shortsighted thing they did," says Timmons. "But we got an exhortation from Washington to increase yields, so farmers went out and plowed up everything."

Increased use of fertilizers has allowed a shift away from soil-conserving corp rotations and has allowed farmers to make more intense use of the land through single-cropping or rotating major cash crops such as corn and soybeans.

The GAO noted that, based on the 1974 market value of fertilizers, it would have cost $1.2 billion to purchase the chemicals needed to replace nutrients lost through erosion in that year.

Genetic engineering, the ability to create single strains of fast-growing, reliable food crops, is one of the cornerstones of modern agriculture. But such high-yielding crops also can have little resistance to unforeseen diseases and are often susceptible to pest infestation. In 1970, leaf blight destroyed at least 15 per cent of Iowa's corn crop.

Even the most noticeable facet of the new industrial age in agriculture, the harvesting machines, may have reached their zenith. It appears doubtful that crop yields will be further increased by new machinery.

"Machines are at a very high stage right now," explains Roger Garrett, chairman of the Agricultural Engineering School at the University of California at Davis. "The efficiencies are pretty high; we capture up to 95 per cent of the grain already. It's hard to imagine being able to improve upon that."

"Farmers are going to have to take a serious look at our continuing exploitation of resources," says Iowa State's Timmons. "Unless we either change some practices or develop new technology, the windfalls from which we have benefited will be depleted."

This article is reprinted from Paul Shinoff, "Industrialization of Farms Threatens U.S. Topsoil," Washington Post, January 5, 1978.

EXAMPLE
31 Something for Nothing

For thousands of years, Asian farmers hauled their toilet wastes out to the fields for fertilizer, presumably without a second thought. So did the rest of the world, before the days of chemical farming. In fact, second thoughts didn't occur until the 19th century, when "modern sanitation methods" were introduced into Victorian England's cities. The re-invention of the flush toilet then (the Romans had used water for waste carriage) sat well with Victorian pruddery, and soon, body wastes became, at least in the urban mind, something unspeakable, to be rid of by a pull of the chain. Meanwhile, in the countryside, farmers continued to use animal manure for fertilizer.

By the mid twentieth century, well over half of all Americans were hooked up to central sewers, and were furiously washing their toilet wastes downstream, diluted into a 98 percent water solution. The federal government poured, and continues to pour, tens of millions into sewer construction, in relentless warfare against that Victorian curse, our own body wastes.

Unfortunately, like so many gigantic enterprises, this one does not work, and we only find out after it has failed. Once collected at the central treatment plant, the wastes must be separated from the water, a very expensive process, not to mention the cost of getting the sewage there. Today, next to the cost of your home and your auto, the most costly item you will ever pay for is that system of pipes and valves, settling tanks and all the other hardware down at the treatment plant. This wet B-1 bomber, this nuclear-power-plant-sized disaster has only recently been recognized for what it is, as small towns across the country begin to simply refuse to build central sewer systems. Costs-per-home runs to thousands of dollars, and human interest stories are now being picked up in the press; stories of impoverished older people under threat of losing their homes because they can't pay the sewer assessment; of waterbodies, as small as local rivers and as large as Moosehead Lake in Maine, being polluted by discharges from central treatment plants.

Not only are the systems expensive, they just don't work. Sludge squeezed out of the sewage contains all sorts of dangerous industrial chemicals, because the sewers pick up not only home sewage along the way, but every variety of commercial and industrial waste as well. Once combined, there is no way yet known to separate out the treatable from the untreatable chemicals. What the central treatment plants deliver as sludge is a chemical menace. Just getting rid of the sludge has become a national problem, some cities dump it in the ground (where it pollutes the ground water), others haul it out to sea (where it floats back onshore, to the shock of bathers and the anger of fishermen).

Many towns in Massachusetts have not yet been punished with central sewers, we still have septic tanks. When these are pumped out, the wastes (called "septage") are hauled to town dumps or quietly emptied into the woods. These dumping grounds are vile places, unloved by their neighbors, and suspect by the local health officers, as being sources of disease-bearing organisms. And that brings us to the present, a present which hopefully will not be our future.

Massachusetts may be the first state in the union to take a positive step toward solving this problem of what to do with sludge and septage. House Bill 2811 would create a Compost Authority, within the state government, with powers and money to create and support local and regional composting facilities.

The idea is to haul these wastes to a central location, and to subject them to composting, along with other wastes such as sawdust or wood chips or leaves, most any material that is cheap, high in carbon content, and capable of absorbing water (sludge is dry enough, but septage is still quite wet).

Rather than abandoning these wastes, they will be re-used, made into a compost which is valuable as fertilizer. The fertilizer will then be sold, or given away to local gardeners, nurseries, farmers, and golf courses.

The proposed Authority would be self-financing. Receipts from sales of fertilizer, and payments received from the treatment plants and septage haulers will pay the cost of the compost facilities. No state appropriation is asked for aside from $200,000 to get the Authority in business. Even this money must be repaid from the first revenue bond issue that the Authority will issue.

Sponsoring this bill in the legislature is Mel King, the representative from Boston's South End. King is an unusual urban politician, for his long record in support of legislation benefiting rural Massachusetts. He has been active in such programs as Development Rights, gardening on public land, and the new community development finance corporation. He sits on the Natural Resources and Agriculture Committee of the legislature, whose staff member, June Murphy, drafted the compost authority bill. This committee favorably passed along the bill last month, and Ways and Means

has the next crack at it. Thus far, no organized opposition has surfaced.

Much of the credit for the idea is due a private citizen—Pio Lombardo, an environmental engineer in Boston. Lombardo believes that "it can be demonstrated that composting is the cheapest way to handle the sludge and septage problem," and that there are no significant scientific or technological questions that still have no answers. He told me of several facilities already in operation which now treat sludge and septage by composting. At Beltsville, Maryland, the USDA takes sludge from the massive Blue Plains sewage treatment plant (serving the Washington, D.C. area); Durham, New Hampshire has a smaller facility which uses its compost for highway plantings and landscaping on public lands. In the state of Washington, a privately owned facility has been composting septage for three years, and seems to be financially solvent.

Here in Massachusetts, three southeastern towns (Rehoboth, Swansea, and Seekonk) are well along in their planning of a compost facility to serve some 30,000 population. An 8 acre plot is being considered to serve the facility, and the cost of this land, plus paving and materials handling equipment, make up the estimated $200,000 needed to launch the facility.

Septage is first pumped from the trucks into a holding tank. Air is then pumped through the septage to create aerobic conditions (favoring oxygen-using microorganisms which accomplish the composting action). At this stage, the septage is no longer smelly, and it can now be mixed, out-of-doors, with sawdust or some similar material, in a compost pile. Two to three weeks later, the compost is done, but will be aged another 8 weeks or so before sale. While it is too early to say for sure, the price may be around $5 a ton—which is very cheap for high quality organic fertilizer.

But if septage composting has already been proven to work, composting municipal sludge is still an open question. As mentioned earlier, because municipal wastes are such a mixture of home, industrial and commercial, they often contain chemicals which defy breakdown by composting. Until the chemistry of finished compost containing sludge can be worked out, any Massachusetts Composting Authority will probably stick to composting septage.

This Authority seems like a very sensible idea. It does more than simply make something from nothing, it makes something useful from something now judged a positive nuisance. Farmers and gardeners, nurserymen, public parks officials, and public works departments should all be interested in this bill, for it may result in their obtaining a local source of cheap organic fertilizer. Public health officials should like it, because it rids them of their town dump problems with septage. Environmentalists should like it because it preserves and returns to the soil valuable nutrients, instead of washing them into rivers via sewage treatment plants or into groundwater via town dumps. Taxpayers should favor it, because it solves a public problem without public money. And, finally, even the Arab oil sheiks should like it.

Pio Lombardo fantasizes the day when all those tankers will return to the Persian Gulf laden with compost to fertilize the barren desert. He says that "oil and compost are the same thing, oil is just older." □

This article is reprinted from "Something for Nothing," Farm Bulletin, Issue 19, pp. 1, 3, 4, March 22-April 12, 1977.

Nitrates: An Insoluble Problem?

EXAMPLE 32

The writer lives on an irrigated Angus cattle ranch northwest of O'Neill, Nebraska. A native of Holt County, Norma Jane has written for several big city dailies on the East Coast, and presently works part-time for the Norfolk Daily News.

Last spring, it looked to a number of local officials as if Holt County was going to have a problem. There were mumbled mentions of poisoned aquifers, possible restrictions on nitrogen fertilizers, and long-term epidemics of nitrate-caused cancer.

The cause?

Well, it seemed as if one of the many unforeseen by-products of intensive center pivot irrigation in northern Holt County was going to be nitrate poisoning of the underground water supply.

A lot of people were worried.

For one thing, there was the heavy use of fertilizer.

Dr. Roy Spalding and Mary Exner, water quality experts from the University, had reported in no uncertain terms that there had been an increase from 13,000 tons to 22,500 tons of nitrogen applied to Holt County farms last year alone. In other words, irrigators had almost doubled their use of fertilizer from 1975 to 1976, and everybody knew they'd been using it heavily enough for more than ten years.

Then Dr. Spalding informed the joint meeting of Upper and Lower Elkhorn NRDs (which had hired him in the first place) that nearly 50 percent of the nitrogen was being leached directly into the groundwater supply.

People were startled, to say the least.

How can this happen? they asked.

Well, he explained, when fertilizer is applied at any time other than early growing season—when the plants have just come up—it is largely wasted. Nitrogen cannot be converted into life-giving fertilizer unless the seeds have sprouted and roots are out there to draw it in.

Otherwise, spring thaws and rains simply leach the nitrogen away and when the plants come up, most of the fertilizer is already gone. Furthermore, a lot of the nitrogen is applied too heavily even when it is applied at the proper time, so that leftovers get leached into groundwater by irrigation water.

What happens to the nitrates when they get to the groundwater?

Good question.

The answer is that they stay there. Nitrates do not break down of their own accord unless taken in by a growing plant (or animal, or human). Dr. Spalding referred to the work of Paul Fishbach to illustrate what he meant about nitrate storage.

He said that Fishbach found he could get the same effect from the nitrate-laden irrigation water he pumped up onto his test fields that he got from the original nitrogen applications. He said that if you have a concentration of 30 parts per million of nitrogen in your water, you can get the same yield by pumping that water onto your crops as if you used 200 pounds of fertilizer.

Dr. Spalding went on to point out that the nitrate-nitrogen concentrations in Holt County's underground water was increasing 1.1 mg. per liter, per year, in direct correlation to the increased amounts of fertilizer being used on center pivot irrigated cornfields.

He was hesitant to talk about what this might mean to human health in the area. He did, however, point out that 20 percent of the irrigation wells in the Atkinson-O'Neill area had concentrations of nitrogen well above the board of health limit of 10 mg per liter.

Doctors in the area were not so hesitant to discuss it. Dr. James Ramsey of Atkinson and Dr. William Becker of Lynch, both stated that they had treated a number of patients afflicted with nitrate poisoning. Although infants were the most susceptible, they said that adults as well as farm animals can be seriously affected, too.

Dr. Henry Lynch, who is chairman of the department of preventive medicine and public health at Creighton University in Omaha, supplied considerable background information to the problem.

He explained that nitrates react with hemoglobin in the blood to inhibit its oxygen-carrying capacity. Thus, victims of nitrate poisoning are usually starved for oxygen, which is why it's termed the "blue-baby syndrome" in infants. Particularly vulnerable, he said, are babies less than 10 weeks old.

Adults are not exempt from painful reactions, though. He said that they may suffer everything from severe headaches, dizziness, nausea, and general fatigue to fainting and coma from nitrate poisoning. In some cases the nitrates cause a disease in the blood which is known as methemoglobenemia, according to Dr. Lynch, and it is treated with hemo-dialysis—which involves changing the victim's blood completely.

He said that the maximum safe level for adult ingestion of nitrates is 45 parts per million, and that the maximum safe level for farm animals is 100 ppm.

Farm animals drinking contaminated water react to poisoning by showing a poor weight gain, decreased milk production, reduced reproductive capabilities and deterioration of the linings of the entire gastrointestinal and respiratory tracts, according to Dr. Lynch. He added that nitrates also interfere with the proper absorption of vitamins A, E, B12, and K.

Needless to say, Holt Countians paid attention.

Dr. Spalding's water quality survey showed several wells in excess of 300 and 400 ppm of nitrate, and a number of domestic and stock wells with more than 100 ppm in the water.

All signs seemed to point toward trouble. The bitter drought, which had led to federal disaster relief funding in neighboring Boyd County, and would have caused the same thing in Holt County, were it not for the preponderance of irrigated farms, was an increasing worry.

Officials reasoned that if the nitrates couldn't be dissolved, perhaps at least they could be diluted. But, if the drought didn't break, dilution was a slim hope.

Grimly, a lot of people sent off samples of well water for testing at the state health laboratories. They listened to doctors theorize that since nitrites have been positively linked to cancer, couldn't it be possible that nitrates were also . . .? Two studies, in fact, had reportedly demonstrated that adults who ingested water with 10 to 20 mg. per liter of nitrogen in it over a period of 20 years were apt to develop cancer of the stomach and bladder.

With all the other exposes of contaminated, cancer-causing agents in our food and clothes and air, it seemed reasonable to assume the worst about the water.

Meanwhile, the rains came. The summer of 1977 wiped the dust off everybody's raingauges, more than doubling the amount of moisture received in 1976, and even though there was a certain amount of water table decline from irrigation pumping, it was nothing like it had been, the people relaxed.

Marshall Logan, Holt County Extension Agent, now says that of the 120 water testing bottles sold from his office over the summer, only 15 percent came back with reports of nitrate-nitrogen concentrations over the safe level of 10 ppm.

John Blofser, at the state health department laboratory in Lincoln, reported almost the same thing.

After going through his extensive records of private well testing in Holt County, Blofser found that 18 out of 126 wells showed levels over 10 ppm. That's 14.2 percent contamination in private water.

Dr. Spalding had found 20 percent of the irrigation wells containing water with unsafe levels of nitrate-nitrogen. He also found that the unsafe wells were almost always located in areas of intensive center-pivot irrigation, and that the contaminated domestic or stock wells were either in the same sort of area or close to a feedlot or septic tank.

There was always, in other words, an obvious explanation for the problem.

Blofser and Logan are barred by laws of confidentiality from releasing the identities or the locations of Holt Countians whose private well tests came back this summer with reports of unsafe water. They are also reluctant to speculate on the possible connection this 15 percent might have with Dr. Spalding's 20 percent.

However, as explained by the water quality study last spring, a suspiciously large number of the contaminated wells were located within the same general area that the heaviest concentrations of center pivot irrigation, just north of Atkinson and O'Neill, are found in. As Dr. Spalding put it before the NRD boards, the two maps have a similarity which cannot be

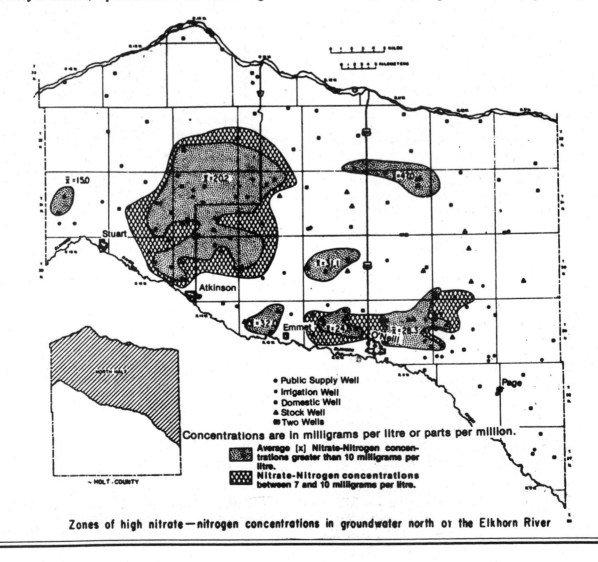

Zones of high nitrate—nitrogen concentrations in groundwater north of the Elkhorn River

overlooked, especially since fertilizer is a potent and logical source of nitrate contamination.

Yet, the ruckus seems to have died down.

People seem to have been lulled into a sense of security about their water by the heavy summer rains. Not even state department officials were especially concerned (or even aware, until asked for a compilation of results!) that 15 percent of private well tests in Holt County showed nitrate contents higher than the 10 mg per liter level of safety.

If corn production experiences any slowdown whatsoever in Holt County this year, it will be solely because of disastrous prices, and not for reasons of health or public safety. A Water Short Course held Sept. 1 in O'Neill drew only 40 participants—most of whom were NOT farmers—and resulted in very little discussion about nitrates, or even water quality in general.

Much greater concern was exhibited at the meeting for federal water policy, state legislation and NRD authority. In fact, the state Water Resources Association, which sponsored the short course, offered as its keynote concern a speech about how little voting impact the 17 western states have in the House of Representatives or the Senate.

Dr. Les Sheffield, irrigation specialist from the University of Nebraska, told the group that this state is now the third largest irrigator in the nation. Only California and Texas are "ahead", and Nebraska shows signs of being able to catch up easily, since it is also the fastest growing agricultural producer in the nation . . .

He said that Nebraska farmers have converted over 6 million acres from dryland to irrigated crops in the last 30 years, and the signs are indicating no slowdown. Dr. Sheffield estimated a total economic impact, statewide, of $4.7 billion from the irrigation phenomenon. He told his audience that over 80 percent of Holt County's corn-producing fields are now irrigated—that's 97,925 acres—and are providing 93.3 percent of its total corn sales.

Only 24,083 acres are still in dry-land production, he said, and those fields average only 34.6 bushels per acre. Irrigated fields yield an average of 118.8 bushels per acre.

Dr. Sheffield did express his concerns about the dangers of a blind monoculture of corn, however. He recommended that farmers pay serious attention to the possibilities of alternate crops, alternate methods of irrigation (besides center pivot systems), soil quality, water quality and water quantity.

However, subsequent discussion centered largely around the problem of NRD "power". The question seemed to be, does the NRD have any?

State Senator John DeCamp, who was one of the scheduled speakers that day, in O'Neill, stated that he believed the Natural Resources Districts were created for the purpose of "solving local water problems". He indicated that he thought NRD boards were empowered with the legal right to "vote-in a control area", (an area where water quality or quantity is being endangered to the point of public outcry), and then establish enough restrictions to restore the water to its previous levels.

DeCamp admitted that those powers had yet to be tested for constitutionality in state courts and he also said that he didn't know of any cases yet where an NRD board had actually invoked a "control area".

DeCamp then went on to explain that he, personally, is opposed to extensive restrictive legislation from either a state or federal level, and that he has blocked and intends to continue blocking any "proposals from Omaha" which might place too many restrictions on farming under the guise of environmental protection.

After some other discussion of NRD powers, the upshot seemed to be that nobody knows who is in charge of water quality or quantity because nobody's ever had to protect it before. Holt County's NRD boards are reluctant to move in any dramatic way toward restrictive measures because they lack authoritive guidelines for any such move.

Brock Reynoldson, manager of the Upper Elkhorn NRD, has said several times that he believes the NRD boards will have to get a lot more backing from state legislation before they can do much controlling. He says that as things stand now, his office can educate and advise and monitor, but it cannot force a farmer to cut down his use of fertilizer.

And that, water drinkers everywhere, is how things stand. ◆

PROBLEMS WITH THE HOUSE WATER? NAW. WE USE IT ALL THE TIME. JUST CAN'T LET THE BABY DRINK IT. OUR REAL PROBLEM IS THE COST OF CROP PRODUCTION.

This article is reprinted from Norma Jane Skjold, "Nitrates: An Insoluble Problem?" New Land Review, The Center for Rural Affairs, pp. 10-11, Fall 1977.

EXAMPLE 33   A Miracle of Cooperative Planning

A common need — An uncommon coalition. A surprise is taking place in Northglenn: a farm-city coalition is supporting a water resources management program. This suburb of Denver, a city of about 35,000 people, has a crucial problem. In a climate where water is the lifeblood of survival, a municipality must be able to control its own destiny.

Farmers need water too. Condemnation proceedings by other communities threaten 40,000 acres of prime irrigated land. Under Colorado law, domestic needs for water have a higher priority than agricultural needs. In this part of Colorado, which is semi-arid, water is absolutely essential to the productivity of the farmers. Irrigation is necessary because many of the farms are too small for profitable dry land farming.

A startling plan. As a result of these common needs, Northglenn has a new and startling plan: a water exchange and recycling system mutually shared by the city of Northglenn and the Farmers Reservoir and Irrigation Company. Designed to simultaneously satisfy municipal demands while keeping agricultural land in production, the

system will divert water owned by FRICO to Northglenn, where it will be treated and delivered for domestic use. Afterward, the nutrient-enriched water will be treated, stored, and returned to the farmers for irrigation of croplands. Thus, through cooperation, the rural-urban link will be preserved and continued crop production will be assured.

A $31 million bond issue was passed two to one by Northglenn citizens who believe in . . .

A daring model for the west . . .
and for the nation. This model of rural-urban shared planning is a precedent-setting answer to the water-deprived West. The rewards are many: self-sufficiency, control of water rates, improved water service, better quality of water, continued food production, zero discharge of pollutants, including urban runoff, conservation of nature's resources, control of a mutual destiny.

The problem is clear, the solution is both imaginative and practical. An idea has come alive in Northglenn, Colorado. We need your help to make it work.

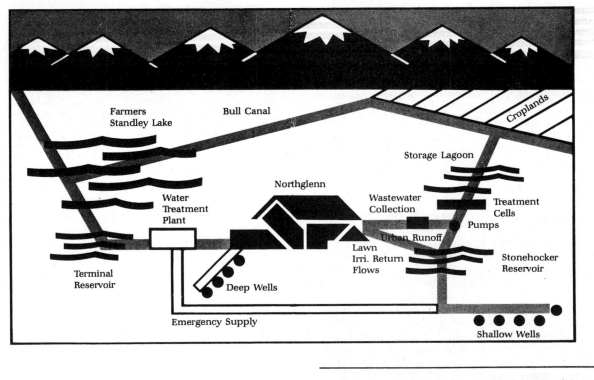

This article is reprinted from "A Miracle of Cooperative Planning," **Nature Is: Man Becomes,** City of Northglenn, Colorado 80234.

How Corporations Violate Family Farm Water Rights

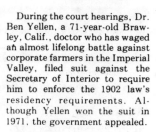

EXAMPLE 34

'No right to the use of water for land in private ownership shall be sold for a tract exceeding 160 acres to any one landowner unless he be an actual bona fide resident on such land, or occupant thereof residing in the neighborhood . . .'

By A. V. Krebs

Few federal laws have been so systematically subverted and flagrantly violated as the 1902 Reclamation Act, passed specifically to open western land to small farmers.

Today, 75 years later, renewed efforts are underway by grassroots groups, legislators, legal experts, and others to get this law enforced.

The law has three main provisions:

160-Acre Limitation. One owner may obtain no more than 160 acres worth of subsidized water. Under subsequent administrative decisions that limit was extended to include 320 acres for a wife and one child for a total of 480 acres.

Anti-Speculation Provision. An owner may irrigate more than 160 acres by contracting with the Bureau of Reclamation to sell this "excess land" within 10 years in parcels of 160 acres or less and at a price which does not take into consideration the value of the water.

Residency. Owners of the land must live on it or in the neighborhood.

In trying to get this law enforced throughout some 11 million acres of irrigated farmland in 16 western states, the 160-acre advocates have focused their attention on the 600,000-acre Westlands Water District in California's San Joaquin Valley.

Inhabitants of this district, the nation's largest, include Southern Pacific Co. [110,000 acres], J. G. Boswell Co. [23,500 acres], Standard Oil of California [10,000 acres], and Bangor Punta [10,000 acres]. Other companies with important Westlands ties include Travelers Insurance, Anderson-Clayton, and Prudential Insurance. All farm and receive water under the 1902 Reclamation Act.

Westlands is part of the Central Valley Project in which, according to government figures, irrigation farmers repay 17 percent of the project's costs while taxpayers and electric power users repay 83 percent. The Westlands water subsidy, in cash terms, amounts to about $40 per year per acre.

A 1975 study by the University of California at Los Angeles showed that the entire Westlands Project is replete with subsidized federal dollars, estimated at between $366 and $448 million

over a 40-50 year period. This is far more than is commonly acknowledged. One of these subsidies, present in all reclamation projects, is the interest-free repayment of an estimated $111 to $154 million in costs of the distribution system.

Due to a peculiarity in the Westlands contract, landowners are not required to pay for the system until it is completed, even though most of the district's landowners are presently receiving water. Thus, any large landowners who have signed a recordable contract under provisions of the "excess land" clause and have sold the land by 1982, when the project is supposed to be completed, will not have paid for any of the system.

The study points out that future landowners, who will be small because of recordable contract provisions, will be paying a higher assessment rate than they would otherwise pay to the extent current large excess landowners escape capital charges.

"Altogether the interpretation and administration of the Reclamation Law has substantially favored the large landowner," the study concluded, **"while the initial objectives of the Reclamation Law—to assist the small-scale farmer and foster the family farm—are not being achieved."**

It has only been in the last three years, after extensive research by the Fresno-based National Land for People, joint public hearings by the Senate Small Business and Interior Committees, a Grand Jury investigation, and a handful of lawsuits, that a few Westlands owners have begun making "paper sales" of their excess land holdings.

Russell Giffen, who at one time owned more than 77,000 acres, has made such a paper liquidation sale. Anderson-Clayton, a diversified multinational and the world's largest cotton marketing firm, also sold its 30,000 acres. Both sales included many illegal and questionable transactions that simply transferred the land to family members and business associates of Giffen and Anderson-Clayton.

National Land for People researchers investigated some 50

such Bureau of Reclamation-approved excess land sales and all contained violations of the law. Despite these revelations, however, a new contract between the Westlands Water District and the Bureau of Reclamation awaiting U.S. Senate approval states that "excess land under a recordable contract may be sold as excess land to any purchaser."

Interior Secretary Cecil Andrus has indicated he intends to make a complete review of the new contract. Meanwhile, the Bureau of Reclamation is under court order to use public rule-making procedure in an effort to put a stop to all package deals and general illegal sales. There also is an injunction on further sales.

Based on their 1975-76 Senate Committee hearings, Chairmen Gaylord Nelson and Floyd Haskell have proposed a Reclamation Lands Family Farm Act. The proposal states that "the administration of a substantial amount of the acreage currently affected by Reclamation Law has not accomplished, and is not likely to accomplish, the statutory policy of settling family farmers on the land."

While this issue is being considered in the Congress, several significant legal actions are pending in court.

South of the San Joaquin Valley is another rich California agricultural area, the 500,000-acre Imperial Valley. Half of its land holdings are of 1,000 acres or more and nearly two-thirds of the land is absentee-owned. In 1968 the Interior Department, after issuing a 1964 desist order, filed suit in U.S. District Court in San Diego to keep the Imperial Irrigation District from selling water to owners of more than 160 acres. The government lost the case in 1971 and the Justice Department refused to appeal.

During the court hearings, Dr. Ben Yellen, a 71-year-old Brawley, Calif., doctor who has waged an almost lifelong battle against corporate farmers in the Imperial Valley, filed suit against the Secretary of Interior to require him to enforce the 1902 law's residency requirements. Although Yellen won the suit in 1971, the government appealed.

Yellen later persuaded a U.S. Court of Appeals to allow him to take over the government's lost 160-acre suit and join that with his own residency appeal suit. The joint suit is awaiting a long overdue Court of Appeals ruling. A ruling favorable to Yellen could at last lead to the vigorous enforcement of the Reclamation Law that its originators intended.

Meanwhile, by a recent 8-1 vote, the U.S. Supreme Court held that water limitation laws apply to all land serviced by dams built by the Corps of Engineers. The court refused to review an Appeals Court decision upholding the law specifically on the Pine Flat-Kings River project near Fresno.

Of the million acres in the Pine Flat service area, more than one-third is excess land owned by many of the same operators who farm the Westlands district. Pine Flat was completed in 1954 and, although legal battles have been in progress since that time, water has been delivered to its large landowners for more than 22 years.

In Fresno, the first indictment under the 1902 Reclamation Law ended in a guilty plea by John Bonadelle, a local land speculator and subdivider. He accused the Bureau of Reclamation of operating on a double standard and engaging in selective prosecution. He pleaded one of his corporations guilty to a conspiracy charge and was fined $10,000.

This article is reprinted from "How Corporations Violate Family Farm Water Rights," **Catholic Rural Life,** pp. 11-13, May 1977.

EXAMPLE 35 The Family Farm Water Act

Official Ballot Title:

Shall new appropriations of public water for non-public agricultural irrigation be limited to farms of 2,000 acres or less?

Statement for

WHY INITIATIVE 59?

Initiative Measure 59 addresses the question of future development of irrigated farmland in Washington State. Washington has almost 1½ million acres of irrigated land. Prior to 1966 almost all irrigation development occurred in public reclamation projects which provided water to family-size farms. In recent years, large corporations have been withdrawing public water to irrigate thousands of acres of land. Three to 4 million acres are still available for irrigation development in Washington State. Initiative 59 asks: Will these acres be developed in family-size farms for the public good, or in large corporate farms? Ordinary family farm corporations are not affected.

A VOTE FOR INITIATIVE 59 WILL BE A VOTE FOR THE FAMILY FARM

Family farms are the basis of a stable, low cost food supply. Family farms support local communities. Family farm earnings stay in the area, supporting local businesses and creating permanent jobs for area residents. Family farms are the foundation of rural society. Family farms ensure the preservation of churches, schools, civic organizations and traditional rural values.

THE ALTERNATIVE IS LARGE CORPORATE FARMS

Most large corporate farms are governed by boards of directors in distant cities and worked by transient and commuter laborers who have no ties to local communities. Large corporations involved in both the growing and processing of agricultural products can acquire the ability to manipulate and influence prices for food products.

INITIATIVE 59 WILL ENSURE THAT PUBLIC WATER IS USED IN THE PUBLIC'S INTEREST

Initiative 59 will guarantee that the use of public water will benefit the maximum number of people. Initiative 59 will ensure that water available for irrigation will go to family farms.

Rebuttal of Statement against

DON'T BE MISLED! Initiative 59 will NOT: restrict development, cost thousands of jobs, or raise food prices. Initiative 59 grants individuals and corporations the *same* water rights.

FACTS: A study by the Senate Select Committee (Arvin-Dinuba) shows that Family Farms create more jobs and businesses than corporate farms. Family Farms provide the base for a stable, low-cost food supply. The independent family farmer has historically produced an abundant food supply.

WE DON'T NEED LARGE CORPORATE FARMS TO HAVE A STRONG AGRICULTURAL ECONOMY!

Voters' Pamphlet Statement Prepared by:

RAY HILL, Grange Committee to Support the Family Farm Water Act; GEORGETTE VALLE, State Representative; NAT WASHINGTON, State Senator.

Advisory Committee: JACK SILVERS, Washington State Grange; JOE DAVIS, Washington State Labor Council, AFL-CIO; NANCY THOMAS, Washington Environmental Council; WENDELL PRATER, Washington State National Farmer Organization; DAMON R. CANFIELD, Former State Senator.

Statement against

LET'S KEEP GROWING WITH OUR INCREASING DEMAND FOR JOBS

Washington needs all the jobs farming can give it. Initiative 59 will cost us thousands of potential jobs by restricting the irrigation development upon which Washington's agricultural industry depends for survival. In one area alone, such irrigation development offers the potential of some 17,000 new jobs, 1,700 new businesses, 108 million dollars in new annual payrolls and a 70-fold increase in the community tax base.

. . . WITH A STRONG FARMING COMMUNITY IN A FREE ENTERPRISE SYSTEM

Strong, progressive agriculture depends on a free market economy. Initiative 59 attempts to dictate the size of farming operations by granting unlimited water rights to some farmers and denying all water to others. Farms are operated like any other business—government should not be allowed to mandate how large or small a business should be.

. . . WITH OUR INCREASING NEED FOR FOOD PRODUCTION

The American farmer's ability to provide a plentiful supply of food is unmatched anywhere in the world. Initiative 59 threatens this capability by arbitrarily restricting the water Washington's farmers need to keep on producing.

. . . WITH OUR NEED FOR ECONOMIC STABILITY BASED ON AGRICULTURE

Agriculture is our state's most important economic factor. Initiative 59 threatens all business and industry which depends on a free, healthy farming industry.

. . . WITH OUR NEED TO KEEP THE PRICE OF FOOD DOWN

Initiative 59 imposes unfair, unnecessary and burdensome restrictions. It benefits no one and, in the end, the consumer will pay for increased production costs.

Initiative 59 restricts agricultural development by arbitrarily limiting water rights for irrigation to farms of 2,000 acres or less. It is an unjustified proposal which the people of the state of Washington simply cannot afford.

DON'T STOP OUR AGRICULTURAL INDUSTRY—VOTE NO ON INITIATIVE 59!

Rebuttal of Statement for

INITIATIVE 59 DOES NOTHING FOR FAMILY FARMS!

Talking about "family farms" is just a clever attempt to get at public emotions while clouding the real issue: Initiative 59 does nothing more than limit the size of *all* irrigated farms whether they are owned by individuals, families or corporations.

Initiative 59 does nothing for our water resources. It simply dictates that some farmers are to have *unlimited* water while others shall have none at all. This is not only grossly unfair, but it is aimed at artificially restricting the size of certain businesses in this state. Aren't farmers, after all, in the *business* of producing food?

VOTE AGAINST ARBITRARY ECONOMIC RESTRICTIONS — VOTE "NO" INITIATIVE 59.

Voter's Pamphlet Statement Prepared by:

MAX E. BENITZ, State Senator; FRANK "TUB" HANSEN, State Representative; HUBERT F. DONOHUE, State Senator.

Advisory Committee: CHARLES D. KILBURY, State Representative; WILLIAM POLK, State Representative; JIM MATSON, State Senator.

COMPLETE TEXT OF

Initiative Measure 59

AN ACT Relating to the withdrawal of public waters for use in irrigation of agricultural lands; establishing family farm permits and other water permit classifications; and adding a new chapter to Title 90 RCW.

BE IT ENACTED BY THE PEOPLE OF THE STATE OF WASHINGTON:

NEW SECTION. Section 1. This chapter shall be known and may be cited as the "Family Farm Water Act".

NEW SECTION. Sec. 2. Nothing in this chapter shall affect any right to withdraw and use public waters if such rights were in effect prior to the effective date of the act, and nothing herein shall modify the priority of any such existing right.

NEW SECTION. Sec. 3. The people of the state of Washington recognize that it is in the public interest to conserve and use wisely the public surface and ground waters of the state in a manner that will assure the maximum benefit to the greatest possible number of its citizens. The maximum benefit to the greatest number of citizens through the use of water for the irrigation of agricultural lands will result from providing for the use of such water on family farms. To assure that future permits issued for the use of public waters for irrigation of agricultural lands will be made on the basis of deriving such maximum benefits, in addition to any other requirements in the law, all permits for the withdrawal of public waters for the purpose of irrigating agricultural lands after the effective date of this act shall be issued in accord with the provisions of this chapter.

NEW SECTION. Sec. 4. For the purposes of this chapter, the following definitions shall be applicable:

(1) "Family farm" means a geographic area including not more than two thousand acres of irrigated agricultural lands, whether contiguous or noncontiguous, the controlling interest in which is held by a person having a controlling interest in no more than two thousand acres of irrigated agricultural lands in the state of Washington which are irrigated under rights acquired after the effective date of this act.

(2) "Person" means any individual, corporation, partnership, limited partnership, organization, or other entity whatsoever, whether public or private. The term "person" shall include as one person all corporate or partnership entities with a common ownership of more than one-half of the assets of each of any number of such entities.

(3) "Controlling interest" means a property interest that can be transferred to another person, the percentage interest so transferred being sufficient to effect a change in control of the landlord's rights and benefits. Ownership of property held in trust shall not be deemed a controlling interest where no part of the trust has been established through expenditure or assignment of assets of the beneficiary of the trust and where the rights of the family farm permit which is a part of the trust cannot be transferred to another by the beneficiary of the trust under terms of the trust. Each trust of a separate donor origin shall be treated as a separate entity and the administration of property under trust shall not represent a controlling interest on the part of the trust officer.

(4) "Department" means the department of ecology of the state of Washington.

(5) "Application", "permit" and "public waters" shall have the meanings attributed to these terms in chapters 90.03 and 90.44 RCW.

(6) "Public water entity" means any public or governmental entity with authority to administer and operate a system to supply water for irrigation of agricultural lands.

NEW SECTION. Sec. 5. After the effective date of this act, all permits issued for the withdrawal of public waters for the purpose of irrigating agricultural lands shall be classified as follows and issued with the conditions set forth in this chapter:

(1) "Family farm permits". Such permits shall limit the use of water withdrawn for irrigation of agricultural lands to land qualifying as a family farm.

(2) "Family farm development permits". Such permits may be issued to persons without any limit on the number of acres to be irrigated during a specified period of time permitted for the development of such land into family farms and the transfer of the controlling interest of such irrigated lands to persons qualifying for family farm permits. The initial period of time allowed for development and transfer of such lands to family farm status shall not exceed ten years. Such time limit may be extended by the department for not to exceed an additional ten years upon a showing to the department that an additional period of time is needed for orderly development and transfer of controlling interests to persons who can qualify for family farm permits.

(3) "Publicly owned land permits". Such permits shall be issued only to governmental entities permitting the irrigation of publicly owned lands.

(4) "Public water entity permits". Such permits may be issued to public water entities under provisions requiring such public water entity, with respect to delivery of water for use in the irrigation of agricultural lands, to make water deliveries under the same provisions as would apply if separate permits were issued for persons eligible for family farm permits, permits to develop family farms, or for the irrigation of publicly owned land: PROVIDED, HOWEVER, That such provisions shall not apply with respect to water deliveries on federally authorized reclamation projects if such federally authorized projects provide for acreage limitations in water delivery contracts.

NEW SECTION. Sec. 6. (1) The right to withdraw water for use for the irrigation of agricultural lands under authority of a family farm permit shall have no time limit but shall be conditioned upon the land being irrigated complying with the definition of a family farm as defined at the time the permit is issued: PROVIDED, HOWEVER, That if the acquisition by any person of land and water rights by gift, devise, bequest, or by way of bona fide satisfaction of a debt, would otherwise cause land being irrigated pursuant to a family farm permit to lose its status as a family farm, such acquisition shall be deemed to have no effect upon the status of family farm water permits pertaining to land held or acquired by the person acquiring such land and water rights if all lands held or acquired are again in compliance with the definition of a family farm within five years from the date of such acquisition.

(2) If the department determines that water is being withdrawn under a family farm permit for use on land not in conformity with the definition of a family farm, the department shall notify the holder of such family farm permit by personal service of such fact and the permit shall be suspended two years from the date of receipt of notice unless the person having a controlling interest in said land satisfies the department that such land is again in conformity with the definition of a family farm. The department may, upon a showing of good cause and reasonable effort to attain compliance on the part of the person having the controlling interest in such land, extend the two year period prior to suspension. If conformity is not achieved prior to five years from the date of notice the rights of withdrawal shall be canceled.

NEW SECTION. Sec. 7. (1) At any time that the holder of a family farm development permit or a publicly owned land permit shall transfer the controlling interest of all or any portion of the land entitled to water under such permit to a person who can qualify to receive water for irrigation of such land under a family farm permit, the department shall, upon request, issue a family farm permit to such person under the same conditions as would have been applicable if such request had been made at the time of the granting of the original family farm development permit. If the permit under which water is available is held by a public water entity prior to the transfer of the controlling interest to a person who qualifies for a family farm permit, such entity shall continue delivery of water to such land without any restriction on the length of time of delivery not applicable generally to all its water customers.

(2) The issuance of a family farm permit secured through the acquisition of land and water rights from the holder of a family farm development permit, or from the holder of a publicly owned land permit, where water delivery prior to the transfer is from a public water entity, may be conditioned upon the holder of the family farm permit issued continuing to receive water through the facilities of the public water entity.

NEW SECTION. Sec. 8. The department is hereby empowered to promulgate such rules as may be necessary to carry the provisions of this chapter. Decisions of the department, other than rule making, shall be subject to review in accordance with chapter 43.21B RCW.

NEW SECTION. Sec. 9. This chapter is exempted from the rule of strict construction and it shall be liberally construed to give full effect to the objectives and purposes for which it was enacted.

NEW SECTION. Sec. 10. If any provision of this act, or its application to any person, organization, or circumstance is held invalid or unconstitutional, the remainder of the act, or the application of the provision to other persons, organizations, or circumstances is not affected.

NEW SECTION. Sec. 11. Sections 1 through 10 of this act shall constitute a new chapter in Title 90 RCW.

The Law as it now exists:

Under existing law, the exclusive process available for the establishment of new water rights for commercial agricultural irrigation purposes is the permit system of the water codes of 1917 and 1945. These codes provide that the Department of Ecology shall issue a permit if, after investigation, it finds that there is water available for use, and the use as proposed in the application will not impair existing rights or be detrimental to the public welfare. Additional general policy directions for processing water right permit applications were given to the Department of Ecology in the Water Resources Act of 1971 and the State Environmental Policy Act of 1971.

Initiative Measure No. 59 was submitted to the Legislature for consideration at its 1977 session. Because the Legislature did not enact the initiative, the State Constitution requires the initiative measure to be submitted to the voters at the 1977 general election for their approval or disapproval.

The effect of Initiative 59, if approved into Law:

Initiative Measure No. 59 contains additional directions to be followed by the Department of Ecology in the issuance of permits authorizing new withdrawals of public waters for irrigation of agricultural lands. If the initiative is approved, the Department of Ecology is directed to issue permits authorizing the use of public waters for agricultural irrigation purposes only in four classifications, two of which are:

1. "Family farm" permits. Permits of this class shall contain no conditions limiting the period of effectiveness, such as a fifty year term. However, with limited exceptions, these permits shall restrict the holder to the use of public waters to lands constituting not more than one "family farm":

". . . a geographic area including not more than two thousand acres of irrigated agricultural lands, whether contiguous or non-contiguous, the controlling interest in which is held by a person having a controlling interest in no more than two thousand acres of irrigated agricultural lands in the state of Washington which are irrigated under rights acquired after the effective date of this act."

2. "Family farm development" permits. These permits may be issued without limitation on the number of acres of land involved. The authorization to use waters is conditioned upon the holder developing the lands into "family farms" and transferring the controlling interest in these farms to persons qualified to hold "family farm" permits within an initial time period not exceeding ten years from the date of issuance of the permit and a possible additional period of up to ten years. Purchasers of irrigated land developed under a family farm development permit in parcels of two thousand acres or less would receive water rights without any time limitations.

The other two classifications of permits are (1) permits which may be issued only to governmental entities for the purpose of irrigating publicly owned land, and (2) permits which may be issued to public water entities, such as irrigation districts, for distribution of water for agricultural irrigation under the same provisions as would apply if separate permits were issued to persons eligible for a family farm permit, a permit to develop family farms, or a permit for publicly owned lands.

None of the provisions of the initiative shall effect any right to use public waters in effect prior to the effective date of the initiative.

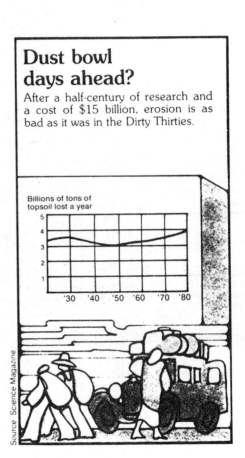

Dust bowl days ahead?

After a half-century of research and a cost of $15 billion, erosion is as bad as it was in the Dirty Thirties.

Billions of tons of topsoil lost a year

'30 '40 '50 '60 '70 '80

Source Science Magazine

This article is reprinted from "The Family Farm Water Act," Initiative 59 (1977), Legislative Research Council, Olympia, Washington.

Chapter 9

Conserving Energy and Adopting New Technologies

The industrialized agriculture practiced in the United States and in many other countries today depends heavily on inputs of energy and technology—machinery, biocides, chemical fertilizers, fuel, and electricity. Fertilizers are covered in the preceding chapter, while the other technological and energy requirements of food production and distribution are the subject of this chapter.

In 1920 there were 6.4 million farms in the United States; today there are only slightly more than one-third of that number. Average farm size has increased—up even between 1960 and 1977 from 297 to 393 acres. A smaller farm labor force now produces more food for more people because of the rapid development of technological inputs. Energy and technology have replaced labor, and thousands of people from once vibrant rural communities have, for better or worse, moved to the city. The social consequences of this dramatic rural to urban shift are considerable, but they are not the subject of this chapter. Of at least equal significance (and potential danger) are the consequences for the environment and for future natural resource supplies.

Few would suggest that a return to the mule and plow is the answer to problems posed by our technological fix. But what might be both wise and increasingly necessary would be to begin to move toward some middle ground between new and old practices. We may feel further impelled along such a course when we consider that big agribusiness corporations dominate the farm inputs industries. The four largest firms in each industry have shared monopoly control over more than four-fifths of U.S. tractor sales, three-fourths of chemicals, and two-thirds of petroleum products.

Farming itself takes up only about one-fifth of the energy expenditure for the entire food system. The rest is used for processing, packaging, transportation, and the other steps between the farm gate and the consumer's table. As our food becomes more and more highly processed and packaged, there is an even greater energy requirement. Most food in the U.S. is transported by truck, although rail transit is four times as energy efficient as trucking. Poultry and eggs are moved an average of about 1,200 miles to a final market destination; fruits and vegetables travel an average of 2,000 miles. In some cases these long shipping distances are necessary, but others are the result of centralization of commodity production into certain areas of the country. Overall more than six units of energy (most of it based on fossil fuels) are put into the food system for each one unit of food energy that is produced.

Agriculture itself may not be as big an energy user as other sectors, but the methods of farming that have been widely adopted over the last three to four decades are very energy intensive. One estimate, by researchers at Cornell University, is that if the U.S. model of industrialized agriculture were used throughout the world, if petroleum were the only fossil fuel, and if petroleum supplies were used only for food production, known oil reserves would be exhausted in less than 30 years. This is a grim scenario. Much closer to home for the American farmer is the inescapable fact of soaring prices for energy inputs—farm chemicals, fuel and electricity.

MODELS FOR CHANGE

Some individuals and groups (although unfortunately few agencies at local, state, or federal levels) have begun working to reverse the trend toward ever greater use of costly energy and technology. One of the most interesting efforts is the Small Farm Energy Project, a research and demonstration effort involving farmers in Northeastern Nebraska. An article describing the work of the Project is **Example 36, Energy: New Directions for Farm Research.** Initially the work of the Small Farm Energy Project was opposed by the agricultural research establishment at the University of Nebraska. But the Project's research is in fact just the sort of exploration that state and local governments (research and extension are supported by both state and federal funds) should be undertaking. Instead most farm research is narrowly focused on increasing production and efficiency, regardless of the social and environmental costs. An example of the often devastating consequences of such technologies—for example, the development in California of harvesting machinery that puts farmworkers out of their jobs, can be found in Chapters 5 and 10.

The use of insecticides and herbicides is an area of agricultural technology that threatens to create increasingly severe economic and environmental problems. Pesticide use in American agriculture has been rising rapidly in recent years; it has more than doubled in the last 15 years to an annual level of 600,000 tons. In many cases the chemical saturation has killed off natural predators of the pests. New pests have arisen with resistance to the older poisons and without natural enemies in the fields. This has led to a treadmill of even larger applications of chemical insecticides.

Many farmers are exploring the organic path with little or no use of chemical fertilizers or pesticides. Integrated pest management (IPM) is something between purely organic and "conventional" (i.e., chemical) practices. IPM uses pesticides sparingly. As **Example 37, Big Farms Adopt Organic Methods to Control Pests** shows, even large farmers—for purely economic reasons—are now becoming interested in integrated pest management.

Seeds are an agricultural input not often thought of as a "technology," yet they are among the most basic elements of farm science. In the last three and one-half decades new "miracle" seed varieties have been developed, replacing older seeds. There now exists the danger that some of the older, more genetically sound varieties may disappear. This issue is discussed in a report: **Example 38, Seeds of Life or Destruction** by the Agricultural Marketing Project.

Many observers fear that modern agriculture may be reaching a scientific dead end. Application of huge doses of increasingly complex technology has made American farming highly productive in terms of output, but inefficient in other ways. **Example 39, Farmers Think Small, Earn Big Profits**, from the Center for Rural Affairs' magazine, *New Land Review*, describes how small and medium-sized farmers are using simpler technologies *and* earning a living. This is not to suggest that we can do without machinery or fossil fuels. Obviously we cannot. But circumstances will probably force increasing recognition of the advantages of decentralization and diversity to our highly centralized and energy- and capital-intensive system of food production and distribution. This is a crucial area for new public policies, research and model programs. State and local governments have yet to make strong and concerted efforts to support the development of these alternatives. Everyone—farmer, consumer and environmentalist—can benefit.

Resources

ORGANIZATIONS

Environmental Action

1346 Connecticut Avenue, N.W.
Washington, D.C. 20036
(202) 833-1845

Environmental Defense Fund

1525 18th Street, N.W.
Washington, D.C. 20036
(202) 833-1484

National Center for Appropriate Technology

P.O. Box 3838
Butte, Montana 59701
(406) 723-6533

Rodale Press

Organic Park
Emmaus, Pennsylvania 18049

Small Farm Energy Project

P.O. Box 736
Hartington, Nebraska 68739
(402) 254-6893
Dennis Demmel

BIBLIOGRAPHY

Center for Studies in Food Self-Sufficiency, **Research Report on Developing a Community Level Natural Resource System.** Center for Studies in Food Self-Sufficiency, Vermont Institute of Community Development, 90 Main Street, Burlington, Vermont 05401. 1976.

Commoner, Barry, **The Closing Circle.** A.A. Knopf, New York. 1971.

Commoner, Barry, **The Poverty of Power.** A.A. Knopf, New York. 1976.

Editors of Organic Gardening and Farming Magazine, **Organic Farming Yearbook of Agriculture.** Rodale Press,

Energy, Research & Development Administration (ERDA), **Solar Energy for Agriculture and Industrial Process Heat.** ERDA, Division of Solar Energy, Washington, D.C. June 1977.

Esbenshade, Henry, **Farming for a Social & Ecologically Accountable Agriculture.** Alternative Agricultural Resources Project. Citizen Action Press, Davis, California. June 1976.

Goldstein, Jerome, Editor, **The Least Is Best Pesticide Strategy.** J.G. Press, Incorporated, Box 351, Emmaus, Pennsylvania 18049.

Integrative Design Associates, **Appropriate Technology and Agriculture in the United States.** Superintendent of Documents, U.S. Government Printing Office, Washington, D.C. 20402. 1977.

Kay, June and Gail Yoakum, "Pesticides: War in the Fields," **Arizona Daily Star.** Tucson, Arizona. October 23-26, 1977.

Lappé, Frances Moore, and Joseph Collins, "Pushing Pesticides," **Food Monitor.** No. 2. P.O. Box 1975, Garden City, New York 11530. December 1977.

Lockeretz, William, et al., **Organic and Conventional Crop Production in the Corn Belt: A Comparison of Economic Performance and Energy Use For Selected Farms.** Center for the Biology of Natural Systems, Washington University, St. Louis, Missouri. June 1976.

Melick, Lowell, **Improved Natural Agriculture.** Institute for Community Services, Edinboro State College, Edinboro, Pennsylvania.

National Catholic Rural Life Conference, **Catholic Rural Life,** "Special Energy Issue." Vol. 25, no. 1. National Catholic Rural Life Conference, 3801 Grande Avenue, Des Moines, Iowa 50312. January 1976.

National Science Foundation, **Appropriate Technology— A Directory of Activities and Projects.** National Science Foundation/Research Applied to National Needs. National Technical Information Service, Document Sales, U.S. Department of Commerce, Springfield, Virginia 22161.

Office of Industrial Programs, **Energy Conservation in the Food System: A Publications List.** Office of Industrial Programs, Federal Energy Administration, Washington, D.C. 20461. May 1976.

O'Malley, Becky and Norman Wirt, "How the University of California Organized the Pesticide Lobby," **The Elements.** Public Resource Center, 1747 Connecticut Avenue, N.W., Washington, D.C. 20009. February 1978.

RAIN. 2270 N.W. Irving, Portland, Oregon 97210. Features articles on appropriate technologies for the rural sector.

Zwerdling, Daniel, "Can U.S. Farmers Kick the Petrochemical Habit," **New Times.**

EXAMPLE 36

Energy: New Directions for Farm Research

Last winter, when temperatures got down below forty degrees, Rick Pinkelman finally had to turn on his fuel oil furnace. But even then, he didn't have to work that furnace very hard to keep his Cedar County, Nebraska home warm enough for himself, his wife Mary, and their two children.

This young farm family can stay warm with less oil thanks to two strange wooden boxes leaning against the windows on the south side of the Pinkelman home. Though they look like miniature playground slides, they are really simplified solar energy collectors, and they provide enough heat to take a big chunk out of the Pinkelman fuel oil bill. And they cost Rick Pinkelman about $10 to build.

The solar window boxes are part of the Pinkelmans' participation in a federally-funded Small Farm Energy Project sponsored by the Center for Rural Affairs. The project is trying to find economical ways for small farmers to save energy. The idea is to "work up" energy innovations right there on the farm, using low-cost, practical approaches that any farmer can apply on his own farm.

The solar window boxes are a good example. The wood frame boxes collect solar energy on a masonite sheet painted black. The heat is trapped by a piece of glass about three inches above the collector surface and simply rises out of the box into the house through the window in which the box is set. Cold air from the floor of the room circulates into the box through a vent under the collector surface for reheating.

Rick Pinkelman built his solar window boxes out of scrap material lying around the farm. He had to pay about $10 for insulation to lay in the sides of the box to prevent heat loss.

His success with the boxes was impressive to his neighbors, many of whom are also participants in the project. So, on a hot August Tuesday, a dozen of them got together at the lumberyard in Hartington, Nebraska, and built their own.

In all, 25 cooperating small farmers in Cedar County are participating in the project. Each of them plans to adopt at least two energy "innovations" ranging from solar heating of farm buildings to composting farm wastes for fertilizer. Careful records are being kept by each cooperator to determine the effect various innovations have on energy use and farm income.

Another group of similar farmers who do not adopt innovations are also keeping records so the two groups can be compared.

The project has gained plenty of attention both because of its emphasis on alternative energy uses on the farm and because it addresses the needs of small farmers. Requests for information about the project have poured into its Hartington, Nebraska office, and project staff recently were asked to testify about the project before Congressman Rick Nolan's (D., Minn,) Subcommittee on Family Farms and Rural Development.

Some of the agricultural establishment hasn't thought much of the project, though. Glenn LeDioyt, an Omaha-based farm manager openly attacked it in a letter to the Omaha **World Herald** in which he said it duplicated the University of Nebraska's farm research. But Congressman Nolan remarked pointedly after hearing testimony on the project that it was

With plywood, fiberboard, fiberglass, insulation, nails and paint from your local lumber yard and used press plates from the newspaper, you can build one of these cost effective units in a day's time.
With plans available from the Small Farm Enerhy Project, you can make one for yourself for about $45.00

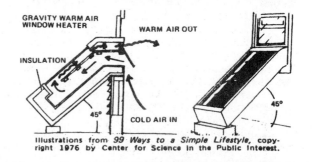

GRAVITY WARM AIR WINDOW HEATER
WARM AIR OUT
INSULATION
COLD AIR IN
45°
45°

Illustrations from *99 Ways to a Simple Lifestyle,* copyright 1976 by Center for Science in the Public Interest.

It didn't cost $50,000 like its commercial counterparts, but this homemade compost turner helps cooperator Edgar Wuebben produce compost fertilizer from manure, sawdust and other organic matter. He built it from an old auger, gear box and other "junk" around the farm. The Small Farm Energy Project emphasizes energy innovations that small farmers can adopt without heavy expense.

interesting that such an innovative approach to farm research was not being funded by the United States Department of Agriculture, which is supposed to help farmers through its land grant university system. It is funded instead by the Community Services Administration, the federal anti-poverty agency.

The project is different from conventional agricultural energy research for three reasons. First the project uses farms, not laboratories as the testing ground for practical innovations that can be adopted on any farm. That's to help convince farmers that energy saving innovations can pay off now in their own operation. Solar window boxes would probably not be more than an interesting idea to Cedar County farmers if Rick Pinkelman hadn't demonstrated that they work.

Second, the project stresses low-cost energy innovations which any farmer using a little ingenuity and materials available on the farm or in any small town can adopt on his own farm. Instead of increasing farmers' dependence on purchased energy inputs, this project puts them in the business of producing their own.

And third, the Small Farm Energy Project works with small farmers, with low or moderate incomes and limited land and capital, not the big farmers or the so-called "top management" farmers that agricultural research and extension specialists frequently serve.

A cooperator can receive up to $500 from the project to share in the cost of an innovation. This helps to cut the risk of financial loss in the event an innovation does not pay off. In exceptional cases if an innovation shows great promise, but carries substantial risk, the cost share can increase to $1,000.

So far, the project has approved 17 cost-share projects ranging from insulation of farm buildings to solar heating of a farrowing barn.

The most ambitious innovation has been proposed by Rick Pinkelman, whose propane and electrical bills

have taken a big gouge out of his hog operation. Convinced by his window box experiment, Pinkelman wants to heat his farrowing barn with solar heat. Project staff and consulting engineers think it's a good idea. His southern facing corrugated tin roof will be converted into a solar collector by painting it black and covering it with translucent greenhouse fiberglass. The collected heat will be stored in washed rock from the local gravel pit laid in the hay loft, and at the expected 40% efficiency rate, Pinkelman plans to heat the entire farrowing barn with solar energy. And he will pocket the money he would have laid out for the 1,000 gallons of propane it took to heat the barn last year.

The whole unit is expected to cost about $1200, and the Small Farm Energy Project has approved Pinkleman's request for $730 cost-share.

Not all of the energy innovations are as dramatic. Some are more basic. Benny Kaiser, for instance, recently got approval for a cost share request to insulate his farrowing barn. Kaiser figures it will cost about $800 to do the job, but says he should be able to cut his heating fuel cost in half. He also thinks that the insulation will boost production because the sows will be less likely to wander away from the building to have their litters in the open field, a practice which frequently results in the loss of baby pigs.

Some innovations encourage new farming practices that chip away at the farmer's dependence on the commercial fertilizers and pesticides which currently account for about one-third of the energy use in production agriculture.

Edgar Wuebben, who has farmed east of Wynot for 23 years, started composting almost immediately after a project speaker explained how he uses compost on his own Iowa farm as a substitute for fertilizer. Compost is decomposed organic waste such as maure, sawdust, grass clippings. It is used as a soil conditioner and fertilizer. Typically, the decomposition is accomplished by bacteria that require oxygen, so the raw waste material being composted must be "stirred up" to expose more of it to the air.

Commercial compost turners are available on the market, but they have been designed for large scale operations such as commercial feedlots who see compost as a way to convert their waste problem into a money making product. Those manufactured turners can turn 50 tons of compost per minute but they cost $50,000 or more, much more than the small farmer can afford.

Wuebben solved the problem by building his own simple compost implement to attach to his chore tractor. He used an old auger out of his silo as the churning device, mounted it on a tool bar from a retired anhydrous ammonia applicator, and connected the auger to the tractor power take off with an old gear box salvaged from other used farm equipment. Everything in the homemade implement was laying around the farm waiting to be used.

Wuebben's 500 foot compost windrow is supplying his farm with valuable fertilizer and soil conditioner, and as a result, he has eliminated the use of anhydrous ammonia as a nitrogen fertilizer. And he points out that since the composting process takes place at high temperatures, weed seeds frequently carried in raw manure are killed, reducing his need for herbicides, another big energy expense.

To make sure his compost is "working" at the right temperature, Wuebben has 48 thermometer checkpoints in his compost windrow, and he is carefully watching the effect which turning the pile and added moisture have on the temperature.

Neither Edgar Wuebben's compost operation nor Rick Pinkelman's solar window boxes are going to make a big dent in the national energy picture, even if all farmers started using them.

Farmers use a very small percentage of the nation's energy—only about three percent according to the United States Department of Agriculture.

But farmers depend very much on the energy they do use. Everything from fertilizer to temperature controlled livestock buildings have become important to modern commercial farming operations, and while the price of those purchased energy inputs has risen dramatically in recent years, the price the farmer gets for his products hasn't. As a result, energy price increases on the farm have meant lower farm income. And as the price of corn drops steadily this summer and fall, farmers are casting a worried eye on energy prices.

The Small Farm Energy Project is trying to find ways farmers can break their energy chains by developing farm technology that will help decrease the farmer's dependence on purchased energy, put him in the business of "producing" his own energy, and protect his income from the energy treadmill. To the participants in the project, the energy crisis is an income opportunity, an opportunity tailored to the needs of the small farmer.

At the August solar window box workshop, the cooperators and project staff took an afternoon break for lunch. After, discussion turned to project business. Several farmers reported on a recent visit to Mead, Nebraska where the University's field laboratory is testing a composting operation using one of the commercially manufactured compost turners which

are well beyond the means of these practical small farmers. But it sure could turn compost, one of them who had been there remarked with a grin.

"Maybe you could get one and do custom work for all the cooperators who compost," suggested one of the project staff.

"Yeah," the grin broadened, "If everybody here gets a GREAT big compost pile."

Everybody laughed and went back to work on the solar window boxes, which they had to finish before chores. ◆

Cooperator Martin Kleinschmit staples aluminum press plates from last week's local newspaper to his solar window box. Painted black, the aluminum plates make an excellent solar collector surface. The window box, which is made entirely from locally-available materials, was built in a day.

This article is reprinted from Marty Strange, "Energy: New Directions for Farm Research," New Land Review, The Center for Rural Affairs, pp. 6-7, Fall 1977.

Big Farms Adopt Organic Methods to Control Pests

EXAMPLE
37

VISALIA, Calif. — Huge agribusiness combines in the San Joaquin Valley, the richest and most densely cultivated agricultural region in the nation, are fast adopting "organic" methods of pest control and drastically reducing their use of chemical sprays because they've discovered it saves them a lot of money.

The growers range from the 45,000-acre J. G. Boswell Corp., the largest irrigated farming operation in the United States, and Prudential Insurance Co.'s huge Dudley Ridge Ranch to small family-owned plots.

The farmers are turning to a loosely defined concept known as "integrated pest management," or IPM. IPM techniques, developed by university-trained advisers, combine traditional concepts of crop rotation with sophisticated bug traps and computer analysis of insect life cycles that show best how to interrupt them. IPM uses chemical poisons only as a last resort.

While "organic" or chemical-free farming is often promoted by city-bred environmentalists, the most enthusiastic proponents of IPM scoff at the suggestion that they are being moved by a change of social philosophy. "We're motivated by economics, pure and simple," explained Mike Shannon, a third-generation crop farmer whose family-owned S-K Ranch owns or has interest in some 30,000 acres.

"None of us in farming wants to spend a dime on anything—whether it's machinery, labor, or spray," he said.

Indeed, Shannon maintains that it is the large grower who is best able to put so-called "natural" methods, such as crop rotation, into practice. "It doesn't hurt us, it helps. But small farmers can't let their land lie fallow."

According to the U.S. Environmental Protection Agency, 80 per cent of the 1 billion pounds of pesticides used by American farmers each year are petroleum-based and thus have gotten dramatically more expensive in recent years. In addition, insects have developed natural resistance to many pesticides, and health hazards to humans have led to government bans on others.

Shannon said the S-K Ranch has been able to reduce its pesticides use by two-thirds while "getting the same production we got in our peak periods of 30 years ago."

And Shannon is not alone. Although more land in the area is coming under cultivation, making use rates difficult to compute, an estimated 30 per cent of the valley's farmers now use IPM methods.

The S-K Ranch owns a pesticide supply company and a crop-dusting service, but Shannon says he'd rather not spray. "It costs money," he says. "We have the planes, but I'd rather not touch them."

Shannon says he has little regard for statements by Secretary of Agriculture Bob Bergland, who, he says, suggested that farmers are resisting alternatives to massive pesticide use.

"Bergland talks like we never heard of it [IPM]. We get the impression that they think all farmers are stupid, waiting for every chance to spray."

Shannon acknowledges he was first introduced to IPM by Richard Clebenger, a 36-year-old agronomist who grew up on a small farm nearby. Coincidentally, Clebenger, one of the few IPM advisers in this area, first began work as a pesticide salesman for a large chemical company.

Then, about a dozen years ago, Clebenger was hired to manage a small farm. There he got his chance to put to use some of the principles he had learned in his agronomy training. Despite good results, however, others were hard to convince.

Clebenger says there was great resistance at first to IPM techniques. "There were—and still are—a lot of farmers we call 'dusty,' guys who can't sleep right unless they have given their fields a good spray."

In 1970 Shannon set aside a 200-acre cotton patch on which Clebenger could try his new techniques. "That was my big break," Clebenger recalled. "I proved it to him in dollars and cents."

Since then Clebenger has gone from working "out of my back pocket" to a $400,000-a-year IPM consulting business, in which he uses a Beechcraft Bonanza to call on his more than two dozen clients.

Driving down a rutted, rain-washed road, Clebenger and Shannon pointed out one application of IPM. On one side was a new planting of alfalfa; on the other, the land lay fallow, waiting for a spring planting of cotton.

By early spring, Clebenger will have a series of electric insect traps spotted among the alfalfa. Using deep purple light bulbs as lures, the traps, five-foot-high cylinders, will catch bugs for a daily count.

Keeping a tally of the numbers and types of bugs present, and matching that against computer analyses of pest movement and mortality patterns, Clebenger can determine the balance of parasites and their predators and what he is likely to have trouble with and when. In an extreme case, his data may tell him he needs to spray, but more often there is an organic remedy.

In the case of the cotton, he will leave a wide strip of alfalfa as a border when that field is cut. It is a costly gamble because hay is now bringing $80 a ton and up, but the strip will attract bugs that would otherwise jump the road onto the ripe cotton buds.

"If we cut it all down the lygus bugs would jump to the cotton," says Clebenger. "We'd have to spray the cotton and kill everything, including the beneficial—the pirate bugs, the ladybugs. After that, we'd have a boll worm buildup, a mite problem, or some other critters. It would never stop."

From the air, the pressure on agricultural production in this valley is clearly illustrated. Stretching from the granite foothills of the Sierra Nevadas, the land resembles a giant checkerboard of green and rich brown. Giant oaks once dotted these plains, a sanctuary for birds which kept many insects in check. But the trees proved a barrier to machinery and they were rooted out, except for isolated stands kept by sentimental landowners as shelter from the hot summer sun.

In the old days, says Clebenger, good farmers did better than their neighbors because of their will to work and their knowledge of the crop. Today, chemicals are the great equalizer. "Pesticides can be the farmer's pacifier. Mine, too.

"I'm not an environmentalist, but the study of the environment is what this is all about. Look, we jerked out the weeds and the trees, along came the bugs which ate everything up," he said.

"I am what I started out to be, a field checker, someone who talks to farmers. We make a lot of educated guesses. We got insects that are alive and moving."

This article is reprinted from Paul Shinoff, "Big Farms Adopt Organic Methods to Control Pests," *Washington Post,* January 9, 1978.

EXAMPLE
38 Seeds of Life or Destruction

For years families have sat down together on cold February nights to pore over the Burpee Seed catalog and make plans for their summer gardens. The less ambitious gardeners among us have usually waited to be sure warm weather was really coming before heading down to the local hardware store or garden center to examine the Ferry-Morse or Northrup King seed rack. Either way, we would scarcely have guessed that these seed companies were anything but independent, old family businesses—the company names are so familiar and reassuring. Recently, however, seed companies have become attractive targets for corporate take-overs, especially by big chemical and drug firms. Purex Ltd. now owns Ferry-Morse Seed Co. Sandoz Inc. has acquired Northrup King. And Burpee is a subsidiary of General Foods, makers of Jell-O, Maxwell House Coffee, Bird's Eye Foods and Gravy Train dog food.

In barely a hundred years, the U.S. seed business has undergone remarkable transformations. Not so long ago, farmers and city gardeners alike saved the seeds from their best plants for use the following year. Small family-run seed businesses grew out of these efforts but were quickly dwarfed by a number of large, national seed companies that came to dominate certain areas of the business. Half of the hybrid corn seed, for example, is supplied by just two firms—Pioneer and DeKalb. ACCO, Coker, Stoneville, and Delta and Pineland dominate cotton seed sales.

Now many seed companies are being bought by multinational corporations. Twenty or more seed companies have sold out in recent years and there are at least six serious merger negotiations underway at this time.

The $3.5 billion seed industry with its profit rate of over 15% is an attractive one to parent multinational corporations. It is a business that "lends itself to worldwide commercialization," according to an industry expert. But internationalization of the seed business (and modern agriculture in general) is beginning to cause concern in many quarters. You should know why. Your future may depend on it.

Something new is something different In 1943, the Rockefeller Foundation launched a new era in seed breeding by establishing a center in Mexico for research into high yielding varieties of wheat and corn. After much cross-breeding and selection, such varieties were developed in their test fields and greenhouses. These new plants, and the ones that followed differed in three important aspects from traditional varieties:

1. The extra-high yield resulted from and was dependent on the plants' ability to respond to more fertilizers and water—and the farmers' ability to pay for these inputs.
2. High yielding varieties of many crops are "hybrids," i.e., the offspring of two distinct varieties. Generally hybrids either cannot reproduce or

their offspring are of very poor quality. Thus, farmers using hybrid seed cannot save their seed—they must buy new seed each year. Though high yielding non-sterile varieties could be developed, the seed companies have little incentive to do so.
3. The new varieties are extremely limited genetically because of the intense inbreeding necessary to fix certain qualities found in the plants.

Why should this concern us? Many of the new "miracle" seeds can be used in poor countries only by rich farmers, because only they can afford the seeds as well as the fertilizers, pesticides and irrigation equipment necessary to make them work. Therefore, although the new seeds might offer increased yields, their bounty has not benefitted the poor who need it the most. In fact, poor farmers unable to use the new technology have found it increasingly difficult to compete with the big farmers and have gone "out of business." In many areas of the world, this has literally meant starvation for the peasant. Ironically, many areas where food crop yields have grown the fastest have the fastest growing malnutrition rates. Meanwhile, large landholdings devoted to the new seeds have grown even larger.

As the new seeds have spread across the world, they have replaced the old, traditional seeds. Where thousands of varieties of wheat once grew, only a few can now be seen. Herein lies the danger. Each variety of corn, for example, is genetically unique. It contains genetic "material" not found in other varieties. If, because of genetic limitations, which result from inbreeding, new varieties are no longer resistant to certain insects or diseases (conceivably even insects or diseases never before known to attack corn), then real catastrophe could strike. And this is precisely what happened in 1970 when the corn blight struck the South, where farmers had planted their fields with a variety of corn defenseless against that disease. You may remember the Dutch elm disease which is another recent example of this phenomenon . . . and there are more.

When plant varieties are lost, their genetic material is lost—and lost forever. Without existing seeds which carry specific genes conferring resistance, it may not be possible in the future to breed resistance back into corn—or any other crop.

As the following chart shows, U.S. agriculture is alarmingly vulnerable to catastrophic disease epidemics.

100% of all the millet in North America is from 3 varieties of seed.
96% of all peas comes from 2 varieties of seed.
76% of all snap beans comes from 3 varieties of seed.
72% of the potatoes comes from 4 varieties of seed.
71% of the corn is from 6 varieties of seed.
69% of the sweet potatoes comes from 1 variety of seed.
60% of all dry beans comes from 2 varieties of seed.
56% of the soybeans comes from 6 varieties of seed.

53% of the cotton comes from 3 varieties of seed.
50% of all wheat comes from 9 varieties of seed.

(Information in this chart comes from a report made by the National Academy of Sciences and was assembled in this form by The Plain Truth magazine.)

Potentially available varieties of most of these crops far exceed the number in use. In some cases literally thousands of varieties exist. To avoid losing the genes these plants carry, the genetic material on which present and future world food supplies totally depend:

1. A more concerted effort must be made to collect and store the thousands of seed varieties that are being lost. The U.S. government agency assigned this task did not receive a budget increase in its first 15 years of existence. Its collection is inadequate at best. One expert asserted, "If you are willing to entrust the fate of mankind to these collections you are living in a fool's paradise."

2. Seed development must not be concentrated in a few corporate hands. Corporations whose main line of business is fertilizer and pesticide production may have no economic interest in breeding disease—and pest-resistant plants or in preserving the genetic material that makes resistance possible.

3. The government should require seed companies and other agribusiness companies to file environmental impact statements when their exports to other parts of the world might threaten the existence of old, traditional varieties of crops.

4. Encourage your grocer to stock different varieties of fruits and vegetables. Blackberries, loganberries, gooseberries, and other foods have nearly disappeared. Though in no danger of extinction, many varieties of apples—the Grimes Golden, the Pippin, the Cortland, the Baldwin and others—are no longer to be found in the stores. A whole generation is growing up thinking that Delicious and Winesap are the only apples around. If your grocer can't help, ask the farmers at the Food Fair for a "different" kind of apple—you'll be in for a pleasant surprise. — by Cary Fowler

For more information contact —
Agricultural Marketing Project, Station 17
Vanderbilt Medical Center, Nashville, TN 37232
(615) 322-4773

This article is reprinted from "Seeds of Life or Destruction," Agriculture Marketing Project, Nashville, Tennessee, 1977.

EXAMPLE 39 Farmers Think Small, Earn Big Profits

Today many people believe the maxim, "bigger is better," applies to farming. As an example of that kind of "success", *Newsweek* magazine recently featured a man who farms 1,200 acres in Iowa and who vacations in Europe.

Yet, here in Nebraska, another group of farmers is making a comfortable living by ignoring much of the wisdom filtering down to them from magazines, advertising and extension agents. Instead of buying new, large machinery, some design or rebuild their own. Instead of applying expensive pesticides and chemical fertilizers, they buy "organic" products, recycle animal wastes from their own livestock, or simply rotate crops. And all of the five interviewed for this article run small or medium sized farms. They may never make the pages of *Newsweek*, but they're making money.

Consider Vincent Kramper of rural Dakota City. The 1,200 acre farm, (which in partnership with two brothers comes out to 400 acres per owner), is the largest of those owned by this group of individualists.

"My brothers and I belong to a minority," he says. "We use the old way of rotating crops and use no commercial fertilizer." The Kramper brothers first plant a field with alfalfa and a cover crop of oats. After two to three years they switch to one corn crop, then soybeans, and sometimes a second corn crop, before ending the five or six year cycle and returning to alfalfa.

"The greatest advantage to rotations is the humus it puts back into the soil," Vincent Kramper points out. The buildup of organic matter in the soil makes it more workable and helps it absorb moisture better.

Kramper does use modern equipment to harvest a large alfalfa hay crop, but his thoughts on commercial fertilizer are more conservative. "I have experimented several years with commercial fertilizers. In my trials, I have found that for every dollar I spent on fertilizer, I received one dollar worth of product back."

"I don't believe many people figure in the cost of harvesting the extra yield," he adds, "that is, in fuel, wear and tear of transporting it, drying, and possibly storing it. We want the highest *net* return, and we are not out to impress anyone with yields only." Kramper reports that the latter seems to be most important to some of his neighbors.

Kramper, who has no livestock, might be considered unusual. Organic farming, an old form of agriculture now catching the interest of many farmers due to the rise in fertilizer prices, emphasizes the use of animal waste and such natural soil builders as compost. But Vincent Kramper uses neither. He succeeds with only rotations. Occasionally he harvests as much as 100 bushels of corn to the acre, but more importantly, the Kramper brothers don't borrow annual operating loans from the bank. Their farm accounts are solidly in the black.

Unlike Kramper, Herman Hovendick, who farms 120 acres southwest of Blair has been a full-fledged organic farmer since he began in 1945. He tried anhydrous ammonia on part of his farm in the 1950s, but was not impressed with the results. Instead, he adds rock phosphate and gypsum to the soil and rotates corn, oats and alfalfa. While his neighbors who use chemical fertilizers may get higher yields per acre, Hovendick thinks his financial return per acre is just as good.

Although Hovendick bought three small Harvestore storage units to store silage and haylage, he

SELF-MADE MAN . . . Herman Hovendick with the feed bunk he designed and built.

STUDENT OF THE SOIL... Marvin Ruenholl inspects his chisel plow, a useful tool in building workable soil.

built his own bunk line feeding systems. The innovative farmer combined old electric motors, elevator chain and lumber to fashion the two systems. One feeds 40 stock cows during the winter. The other system, which feeds 40 yearlings, has a reciprocating carrier running half the length of the feed bunk. The carrier is unloaded by stationary paddles as a reversible motor moves it back and forth over tracks the length of the bunk. Hovendick says an equipment firm now has a similar unit on the market.

Hovendick reared a family of three children on his small farm and believes his 120 acres are enough. When asked if a young person could get started in farming on his own today, Hovendick says that one could buy older, less expensive equipment and succeed. Since used machinery requires some maintenance, the beginning farmer would have to be mechanically inclined to attempt such a task, he explains.

Renting instead of buying land at first also helps make it easier to start out. Hovendick adds, "Buying land is almost out of the question with land selling for $1,500 an acre."

One problem with renting, Hovendick says, is that today landowners prefer farm tenants with large, new equipment, which they think is more efficient. But Hovendick sees changing attitudes ahead. "With the energy crisis," he says, "people are going to have to think more about smaller scale farming and self-sufficiency."

Personal savings helped Marvin Ruenholl start farming 240 acres near Syracuse, Neb., 20 years ago. At the time, the topsoil on the farm was gone and the remaining subsoil was found to have a high magnesium content. It was hard, and when stirred, would run back together. Ruenholl frequently broke shanks on the cultivator when going over the hardest spots.

He uses no pesticides or chemical fertilizers and does most of his earliest tilling with a chisel plow. For most crops he chisel plows in the spring, pulling a harrow behind to conserve moisture. Soybean ground is chiseled in the fall for oats the following year.

Although many of Ruenholl's methods are those of the past, he uses the latest soil testing technology. At one time he had his soil tested by a New York firm which recommended adding potash. A different test by another firm indicated the soil had too much potash and lacked calcium. Ruenholl made the recommended change, a dose of fine ground lime, with good results. He now uses calcium phosphate and a foliar spray of kelp and trace minerals.

The Ruenholl family also raises about 300 laying hens, another unconventional practice for the average farm. They have made the operation profitable by selling eggs directly to a Lincoln cooperative, Open Harvest, and to two health food stores in that city.

Another organic farmer, K.C. Livermore of Valley Neb., started out in farming with a big operation that got smaller, and more profitable. At one time he farmed 800 acres using conventional pesticides and fertilizers, but five years ago he gave that up when he acquired his uncle's farm—160 acres of cropland and 100 acres of pasture. His uncle had returned to organic methods five years before that after deciding "he was giving his money away to the fertilizer companies,"

Livermore recalls. Livermore has stuck with his uncle's methods.

"I'm a lot better off and I feel much more secure," he says of the smaller organic farming operation. Without the use of chemical fertilizers and pesticides, investment and risk in each crop is lower.

Livermore has tried a variety of organic fertilizers. This year he's using two: a liquid made from whole fish and fish oils and composted paunch manure produced in Council Bluffs, Iowa. This spring he applied the manure to some of his corn and soybean fields at the rate of 1,000 pounds per acre, which he says will "pay off more than commercial fertilizer, because the value of compost will carry over for quite a few years."

Like Ruenholl, Livermore uses soil testing, crop rotation, and minimum tillage to get the most from his soil. And, although seed companies press for earlier planting of hybrid-corn, Livermore relaxes in the spring and is one of the last to the fields. This year he started planting on May 26. Last year his corn was up three days after planting. "I plant late for better weed control," he says. In addition, Livermore feels that warmer soil temperatures at later planting improve germination and initial growth. Therefore, the amount of seed per acre, especially alfalfa, is reduced.

On an even smaller scale than Livermore, Larry Krell farms 40 acres near Union, Neb. A former housing contractor, Krell built a cluster of homes for three families on the farm. His home reduces energy costs by using a combination wood and gas stove and six inches of insulation. During the winter his greenhouse along the south wall of the home is used to grow vegetables and to collect solar heat for the rest of the house. Krell also plans to use a wind generator soon to pump water and, eventually, to generate 100 volt electricity.

Krell doesn't think the 800 acre farms of today are family farms. "They have to be that size because they are big businesses," he says. He believes society would be better off with more people on the land, producing their own food. That's why he's interested in "setting up a prototype small family farm" which can be more self-sufficient.

The Krells are primarily truck farmers, raising a wide variety of vegetables sold locally and in Omaha. They raise some soybeans and alfalfa and Krell is developing a small herd of livestock to use some of those soil-bulding crops and to provide manure for fertilizer.

Since organic farming isn't as productive during the switch from chemicals to natural methods as later on (full production takes four years or more) Krell thinks it's difficult for the beginning farmer to start organically. Only those farmers who have most of their land and equipment paid for can afford the lower returns during the transition.

Krell has discovered other problems for the small producer. "You can't find two-row equipment or parts any more," he says. In spite of such problems, though he is optimistic about the future of his model farm.

Such faith in small farms and self-sufficiency seems to fly in the face of overwhelming trends toward larger and more technological food producing systems. But, as Krell, Vincent Kramper, Herman Hovendick and others like them show, Nebraska has its share of farmers who are asking critical questions about agricultural trends. At the same time, these farmers are selective in combining some of today's technology with older methods. Who knows? These unconventional farmers may be paving the way for future food production and wholesome rural living.

This article is reprinted from Dennis Demmel, "Farmers Think Small, Earn Big Profits," New Land **Review,** The Center for Rural Affairs, p. 5, Summer 1976.

Section IV

Section IV

Supporting Low-Income Farmers, Farm Workers, and Farm Women

The following three chapters document the need for state and local governments to make serious efforts to respond to the problems of low-income farmers, farm workers and farm women. A progressive agricultural policy must include a commitment to support these individuals. In all three cases, state and local governments have only begun to become more responsive by considering new legislation; by amending current, harmful laws or by redirecting the priorities of state agencies and local programs.

Low-income and minority farmers are pressured by many of the same problems which confront family farmers. However, the degree to which they are affected by these problems is even more dramatic. Access to land, capital and credit, stable marketing outlets and to technical assistance and training opportunities is severely limited. 46% of all black-owned farms have annual sales of less than $1,000. Chapter 10, *Support for Low-Income Farmers*, outlines the most critical issues for state and local action. Also described are new approaches and concrete models which point the way to the needed changes in public policies affecting low-income and minority farmers.

Chapter 11, *Protecting Farm Workers*, discusses the need for—and models of—state legislation which extends health, welfare, employment and social service benefits, and improves both wages and the shocking working and living conditions of farm laborers. The chapter also deals with one of the most crucial issues facing farm workers—the fact that they are not covered by the *National Labor Relations Act* (NLRB) and are therefore excluded from the rights which have been held by all industrial workers in the U.S. since 1935. Consequently, farm worker organizations and their supporters are turning to state legislatures in an effort to pass legislation guaranteeing to agricultural workers the right to organize and join unions which are then able to represent them in labor/management relations and disputes.

Chapter 12 describes the recent and tremendously energetic organizing by farm women around the issue of estate and inheritance tax discrimination. State legislatures are the targets of this growing movement made up of increasingly politically active farm women and wives. A number of states have responded to the need for tax reform by passing new bills or by drafting amendments to existing state laws.

The increasing efforts to organize around the issues affecting low-income farmers, farm workers and farm wives—and the strengthening of the organizations which represent these individuals—will clearly make state and local governments more aware of the serious problems which now exist. The next step is to draft, introduce, and lobby for the legislation which is needed to support these grassroots efforts.

Chapter 10

Support for Low-Income Farmers

As farming in the United States becomes increasingly industrialized, farmers are forced to expand their land holdings in order to raise production levels. By doing this, they are attempting to keep up with the rising level of capital investment required for larger and more expensive farm equipment, inflationary operating costs and land taxes. This trend has accelerated since the 1940s—making it impossible for all but the most successful and sophisticated farmers to earn decent livelihoods from agriculture.

According to the U.S. Department of Agriculture, two-thirds of the nation's 2.6 million remaining farms are classified as "small farms," having annual gross sales of less than $20,000. In 1975, realized net farm income for these same farmers averaged about $2,300. Small farmers account for only 10% of total farm sales and 75 % are forced to earn additional income from off-farm jobs. Although there are low-income farmers in every region, 70% live in Southeast and North Central states.

Low-income farmers face many of the same problems which are outlined in Section I, *Strengthening the Family Farm*. These include limited access to land, capital and credit; lack of stable and accessible markets; the unavailability of training, outreach, technical assistance and research relevant to the needs of small farmers, and increasing corporate control over both farm land and the agricultural economy. In **Example 40, Black Agriculture in the Seventies,** Manning Marable summarizes the negative effects of this situation on black political and economic development in the South.

These larger, structural problems are aggravated by the absence of public policies and institutions at the federal, state and local levels which support small and low-income farmers. Although there are exceptions, the most creative approaches and effective models for assisting low-income farmers are being initiated by community development corporations (CDCs), non-profit and community-based organizations.

ACCESS TO LAND

Acquiring or retaining agricultural land is one of the most critical problems facing low-income and minority people in the United States. As land prices continue to rise, access to productive land ownership becomes increasingly impossible for individuals without inherited wealth or substantial assets.

The two minority groups who have historically owned land are Native Americans and Blacks in the South. The Emergency Land Fund (ELF) provides legal, financial and technical assistance to black landowners, in hopes of reversing the trend of black land loss in Southeastern states. In 1910, five million black farmers—70% of the total black population of that time—owned over 15 million acres of land in the South. By 1970, only six million acres remained in black ownership. Black land loss has been occurring at the rate of over 6,000 acres a week and ELF estimates that if this trend continues, there will be no black landowners by 1990.

The major causes of declining black land ownership are the legal problems due to confused and "clouded" titles involving an absence of wills and multiple, shared ownership of land. In **Example 41, A Blight Hits Black Farmers**, Attorney Scott Graber clearly describes the legal complexities associated with what is known as "Heirs Property." Graber estimates that over one-third of all black-owned land in Southeastern states is directly affected by this problem—which inevitably leads to foreclosures by the state and involuntary tax and partition sales at the county level.

Only two states have considered legislation to assist black landowners in "clearing" title to their property. In 1974 the South Carolina Legislature introduced a bill which would have authorized the state Housing Authority to underwrite suits in order to clear title to land involving 15 acres or less and having a market value of less than $15,000. Black people with land problems are most likely unable to afford the expensive legal services required to clear title to their property and the South Carolina bill offered potential assistance. The Mississippi Legislature will consider a bill in 1979 to assist black landowners with the complex legal problems which continue to cause the loss of black-owned land at the rate of 333,000 acres each year.

There is a growing movement within the farmworker community towards leaving the "migrant stream," where farm workers face an endless cycle of dependency, low wages and deplorable living and working conditions. Many farmworker families are trying to buy land, either individually or cooperatively, and are beginning their own farm operations. An article by Jim Draper, **Example 42, How Co-ops Help Migrant Workers Get Farm Land**, describes the role of the Central Coast Counties Development Corporation (CCCDC) in Aptos, California, in assisting a group of farmworker families to begin farming. CCCDC used its leverage to obtain a lease to a tract of land from Santa Cruz County, to secure bank loans and in addition offered training and technical assistance in the areas of production techniques, management skills and marketing.

The Cooperativa Central, a farmworker-owned and -operated farm in Salinas, California, supports over fifty ex-farmworker families who are earning annual incomes of $17,000 per family from the production of strawberries. The Co-op recently bought 700 acres of prime farmland in the Salinas Valley. The California Agrarian Action Project has found that the state government now leases thousands of acres of state-owned land to large growers. CAAP has recommended that the state give priority to working out lease arrangements with farm workers—especially those who have been displaced by the onslaught of mechanization in California agriculture.

A second proposal which would make farm land available to farm workers and small farmers involves the enforcement of the *1906 Federal Reclamation Law* which would limit land holdings to 160 acres per family member in the numerous water districts throughout the Western states. Because the Law has never been enforced, large growers and agribusiness firms own thousands of acres of federally-subsidized irrigated farm land. National Land for People, based in Fresno, California, has led the fight to enforce the 160 acre limitation clause which would then open up access to valuable farm land to both farm workers and small farmers.

FINANCIAL AND TECHNICAL ASSISTANCE

Without access to credit, working capital and to training and management assistance, low-income and minority farmers cannot hope to develop economically viable farm operations. Chapter 5, *New Models for Extension* and Training, described the most innovative and effective programs offering technical assistance to small, limited-resource farmers. Several of these programs have been initiated by the Cooperative Extension Services out of the Land Grant Colleges and the 1890 Black Land Grant Schools such as Texas A & M, the University of Missouri, Virginia Polytechnic Institute (VPI), the University of Arkansas, Tuskegee Institute and elsewhere. However, many of these programs are denied substantial funding at the state and county level. In particular, state legislatures in the South have often approved higher levels of appropriations out of state funds to the state Land Grant Colleges than to the 1890 Black Land Grant Schools which have made more frequent attempts to assist low-income farmers.

Many of the most successful models for providing training in the areas of production techniques, bookkeeping, accounting and management skills and marketing assistance are again the CDCs and non-profit organizations. Local agencies such as the state Departments of Agriculture, Land Grant Colleges and County Extension Services should look more carefully at the programs initiated by groups like the Federation of Southern Cooperatives, the Rural Advancement Fund's Graham Training Center and Agricultural Teams' Farm-to-Market Project in the Southeast; CCCDC and the West Side Planning Group in California; the Center for Rural Affairs' Small Farm Energy Project in Nebraska and the efforts of the Maine Organic Farmers and Gardeners Association in New England. A pamphlet on the National Council of La Raza's Project AGRED is reprinted as **Example 43, AGRED: The Assistance Group for Rural Economic Development.** The pamphlet describes AGRED's efforts to assist Chicano organizations and individuals in the Southwest in the area of agriculturally-related economic development enterprises. **Example 44, Improve Your Farming: A Directory of Services to the Small Farmer of Illinois**, was issued by the Illinois State Economic Opportunity Office and provides a concrete example for what every state could easily do to inform small farmers of the technical and financial assistance available to them at the state and local level.

ACCOUNTABILITY OF PUBLIC OFFICIALS AND INSTITUTIONS

The bottom line is that low-income and minority farmers must organize to hold public officials and institutions accountable to their problems and responsive to their needs. One successful action was taken by the recently organized National Association of Landowners (NAL), a county- and state-wide, membership-based organization of black farmers in the South which grew out of the work of the Emergency Land Fund. **Example 45, Alabama Landowners Protest FmHA Nomination**, describes NAL's opposition to the nomination of Thurston Faulkner as the State Director of the Farmers Home Administration, based on his past record of racial discrimination while working in the Alabama State Board of Education. NAL's campaign against Faulkner's nomination revolved around the larger issue of the insensitivity of the FmHA to black farmers. In 1974, the proportion of FmHA loans to black farmers in eleven southern states was a mere 12.1% of total loans disbursed. In Mississippi, where 42.8% of all farmers are black, FmHA loaned only 7.7% of its total 1974 appropriations to black farmers. In 1976, Emergency Land Fund researchers discovered that of 237 FmHA Loan Specialists in the U.S. only 14 were black, and that only 1% of all FmHA District Directors were black.

Resources

ORGANIZATIONS

Black Land Services

P.O. Box 126
Penn Community Center
Frogmore, South Carolina 29920
(803) 838-2669
Joseph McDomick, Director

Center for Rural Affairs
Small Farm Advocacy Project

P.O. Box 405
Walthill, Nebraska 68067
(402) 846-5428
Gene Severens, Attorney; Chuck Hassebrook,
Field Organizer

Central Coast Counties Development Corporation

7000 Soquel Drive
Aptos, California 95003
(408) 688-9000
Miguel Barragan

Cooperativa Central

Technical Assistance Project
53 Russell Road
Salinas, California 93906
(408) 449-3996
Gabino Marquez, Director

Emergency Land Fund
and
National Association of Landowners

564 Lee Street, S.W.
Atlanta, Georgia 30310
(404) 758-5506
Joseph Brooks, Director

Federation of Southern Cooperatives

P.O. Box 95
Epes, Alabama 35460
(205) 652-9676
John Zippert, Charles Prejean

National Rural Center

Small Farm Policy Project
1828 L Street, N.W.
Washington, D.C. 20036
(202) 331-0258
John Cornman, President; Heather Tischbein,
Project Coordinator

National Rural Development
and Finance Corporation

1300 19th Street, N.W. (#360)
Washington, D.C. 20036
(202) 466-6950
Alfredo Navarro, Director

Rural Advancement Fund/
National Sharecroppers Fund

2128 Commonwealth Avenue
Charlotte, North Carolina 28205
(704) 334-3051
Kathryn Waller, Director

Southern Cooperative Development Fund

1601 Surrey Street
Lafayette, Louisiana 70501
(318) 232-9206
Reverend McKnight, Director

Southern Rural Policy Congress

915 South Hull
Montgomery, Alabama 36104
(205) 263-1397
Bill Harrison, Director

BIBLIOGRAPHY

Bildner, Robert, "Hard Times for Southern Famers," **In These Times.** 1509 North Milwaukee Avenue, Chicago, Illinois 60622. December 21-27, 1977.

Brooks, Joseph, "Loss of Black Owned Land Continues in Rural South," **Catholic Rural Life.** National Catholic Rural Life Conference, 3801 Grand Avenue, Des Moines, Iowa 50312. March 1976.

Browne, Robert S., "**Only Six Million Acres: The Decline of Black Owned Land in the Rural South.**" Emergency Land Fund, 836 Beecher Street, S.W., Atlanta, Georgia 30310. 1973. $2.50.

Central Coast Counties Development Corporation (CCCDC), **Program Profile.** CCCDC, 7000 Soquel Drive, Aptos, California 95003. 1978.

Christian, Virgil, and P. Adamantius, "Farm Size and the Displacement of Black Farm Families in Southern Agriculture," **Human Resource Development in the Rural South.** A Report of the Center for the Study of Human Resources, University of Texas, Austin, Texas. 1971.

Colette, Arden W., and Gail Eastley, **A Bibliography: The Role of Communications and Attitudes in Small Farm Programs.** Rural Development Series Number 4, Southern Rural Development Center, Box 5406, Mississippi State, Mississippi 39762. $3.00.

Comptroller General of the United States, **Some Problems Impeding Economic Improvement of Small Farm Operations: What the Department of Agriculture Could Do.** Report to Congress, General Accounting Office, 4th and G Streets, N.W., Washington, D.C. 20548. August 15, 1975.

Emergency Land Fund, **40 Acres and a Mule.** Emergency Land Fund, 233 East Hamilton Street, Jackson, Mississippi 39205. Newsletter, $2.00/year.

Emergency Land Fund (ELF), **Implications for Black Land Loss: Federal Financing for Black Rural Development. A Report on Minority Credit Barriers in Eleven Southern States.** ELF, 836 Beecher Street, S.W., Atlanta, Georgia 30301. 1977. $1.00.

Emergency Land Fund (ELF), **The Black Land Base: A Public Policy Perspective.** ELF, 836 Beecher Street, S.W., Atlanta, Georgia 30301. 1977. $1.00.

Emergency Land Fund (ELF), **To Save Our Land.** ELF, 836 Beecher Street, S.W., Atlanta, Georgia 30301. Annual Report of ELF.

Graber, Scott, "A Blight Hits Black Farmers," **The Nation.** March 11, 1978.

Institute for Southern Studies, "Our Promised Land," **Southern Exposure.** P.O. Box 230, Chapel Hill, North Carolina 27514. Fall 1974. $3.50. Newsletter; entire issue.

Ladewig, Howard, and Vance Edmonson, **The Effectiveness of Nonprofessionals in Cooperative Extension Education for Low-Income Farmers.** Texas A & M University, College Station, Texas 77843.

Marable, Manning, "Black Agriculture in the Seventies," **In These Times.** 1509 North Milwaukee Avenue, Chicago, Illinois 60622. January 25-31, 1978.

Marshall, Ray, and Allen Thompson, **Status and Prospects of Small Farmers in the South.** Southern Regional Council, 75 Marietta Street, N.W., Atlanta, Georgia 30303. 1976. $4.50.

McCurry, Dan, "Losing Ground," **Sustenance.** The Action Center, 1028 Connecticut Avenue, N.W., Washington, D.C. 20036. April 1978.

McGee, Leo and Robert Boone, "Black Rural Land Ownership: A Matter of Economic Survival," **The Review of Black Political Economy.** Fall 1977.

National Sharecroppers Fund (NSF), **The Condition of Farmworkers and Small Farmers: 1977.** NSF, 2128 Commonwealth Avenue, Charlotte, North Carolina 28205.

Salaman, Lester M., **Black Owned Land: Profile of a Disappearing Equity Base.** Office of Minority Business Enterprise, Department of Commerce, E and 14th Streets, N.W., Washington, D.C. 20230. 1974.

Salaman, Lester M., **Land and Minority Enterprise: The Crisis and the Opportunity.** Office of Minority Business Enterprise, Department of Commerce, E and 14th Streets, N.W., Washington, D.C. 20230. June 30, 1976.

Southern Cooperative Development Fund (SCDF), **Annual Report.** SCDF, 1006 Surrey Street, Lafayette, Louisiana 70501. 1978.

Southern Regional Council (SRC), **Increasing the Options: A Report of the Task Force on Southern Rural Development.** SRC, 75 Marietta Street, N.W., Atlanta, Georgia 30303. 1974. $5.00.

Southern Regional Council (SRC), **Map: Rural Population as Percent of Total Population.** SRC, 75 Marietta Street, N.W., Atlanta, Georgia 30303. 1974. $1.00. Map covers counties of 15 southern states.

Southern Rural Development Center (SRDC), **Rural Development Research at Land Grant Institutions in the South.** Publication No. 2, SRDC, P.O. Box 5406, Mississippi State, Mississippi 39762. January 1977.

Southern Rural Development Center (SRDC), "Small Farms: Feature Issue," **Rural Development Research and Education.** SRDC, P.O. Box 5406, Mississippi State, Mississippi 39762. Summer 1977.

Tuskegee Institute, **Cooperative Extension Service, Tuskegee Institute: 1971-1977.** Alabama Cooperative Extension Service, Tuskegee Institute, Alabama 36088.

Washington Post, "U.S. Policy Handcuffs Small Famers," **Washington Post.** October 5, 1971.

Wiggins, Edward and Duane Dailey, **Missouri Small Farm Program Report.** University of Missouri, Extension Division, Columbia, Missouri. 1974.

Black Land Ownership 1900 - 1970

Millions of Acres

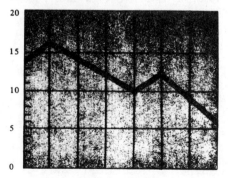

1900 1910 1920 1930 1940 1950 1960 1970

Emergency Land Fund

EXAMPLE 40 Black Agriculture in the Seventies

The black farmer, once the backbone of the black American economy, is facing extinction. The economic system in America, called "free enterprise" by those who profit from it and "monopoly capitalism" by its critics, has given birth to great hopes and even greater frustrations for thousands of small Southern farmers. The illusion that has persisted up to the '70s that small black and white farmers could survive the introduction of big business into Southern agriculture has finally collapsed.

On the surface, Southern farming seems to be a growing, thriving avenue for potential black economic advancement and achievement. In the 30 years after 1940, for example, the percentage of Alabama land owned by blacks increased over 50 percent. The average number of acres per farm increased 128 percent between 1940 to 1969, and average farm net incomes increased sharply.

These rosy statistics do not reveal the basic cancer at the heart of Southern agricultural development—the domination of a handful of corporations over the recent development of farming in the region.

Here are some startling statistics on Alabama that seldom reach the back pages of Southern farm journals or newspapers:

Since 1940, the total number of farms in Alabama has declined to only 60,000, a 75 percent drop within a single generation.

The top 5 percent of Alabama farms account for 53 percent of agricultural sales.

The bottom 60 percent of Alabama farms, with annual sales of less than $3000, account for approximately 5 percent of farm sales.

By 1971, the best timber growing land in Alabama was owned by five giant corporations: Kimberly Clark, 432,000 acres; International Paper, 380,000 acres; Gulf States, 355,000 acres; Scott Paper, 302,000 acres; St. Regis Paper, 280,000 acres. The total land owned by the giant paper corporations was in excess of 3,200,000 acres.

The domination of giant corporations over produce farming is especially apparent. In the chicken and egg industry, Alabama's leading agricultural business, independent farmers have been forced out of business at an alarming rate. Companies like Ralston-Purina and others purchase about 95 percent of all chickens. These companies dole out small change to farmers from which all their operations must be financed. Today, most chicken farms are lucky to net $1.60 an hour.

Black farmers own less than 5 percent of all farm acreage. Between 1950 and 1971, the number of black-operated farms in the South dropped from 560,000 to 98,000. Since 1954, black folks have been losing Southern land at the rate of 333,000 acres per year.

Statistics in the other Southern states are similar to those for Alabama. Since 1959, the percentage of acres owned by blacks has declined in Texas and Louisiana by 33 and 29 percent respectively. About half of all the farmers in Georgia account for 2 percent of all agricultural sales in any given year, while the top 10 percent of Georgia's farmer-capitalist elite reap 60 percent of total sales. Small farmers are becoming as rare as honesty from one's senators and representatives.

The expansion of capitalism into the Southern states after World War II effectively destroyed the possibility of an agriculturally based, Southern black middle class. Blacks who for generations had owned large homesteads were forced off the land by corporations, and were forced to migrate north or to work in Southern boomtowns like Charlotte, Birmingham, Atlanta, Memphis or Jacksonville. From 1954 to 1969, black farm owners declined in number in Alabama from 18,408 in 1954 to 7,226, a 60 percent decrease. From 1959 to 1969, the number of acres owned by black Alabamians declined by 50 percent, from 1,262,583 acres to 636,859. The rapid transformation of the South's economy toward corporation-controlled agriculture has important political consequences. Land owning blacks provided a major force for the rural civil rights movement during the '50s and early '60s. Black farmers were active in voter registration campaigns, are more likely to run for public office than non-landowning, rural black people, and consistently provided a solid electoral base for independent black political activism, such as the Mississippi Freedom Democratic party. Blacks throughout the South owned less than six million acres by 1974, and own perhaps only five million acres today. The destruction of a black agricultural base has, in turn, led to the demise of rural black political power and influence, and has tended to create black urban-oriented politicians who are little aware of rural problems.

The civil rights movement and the subsequent rise and fall of black power did little to stop the expulsion of black property-owners from the countryside and the mushrooming problems of black flight to Southern cities. Stressing political style and rhetoric over an analysis of changing economic conditions, black politicians were ill-prepared to comprehend the dilemma of black land loss.

Neither the Carter administration's pious sermons on black employment nor apologies from liberal representatives of the agricultural-corporate establishment can rebuild the promise of black rural economic development. Under existing economic rules in the U.S., the rugged, hard-working farmer will become just another worthless cog in the corporate means of production. Until the rules of the game are changed, there will be no such thing as black economic equality, either in the cities or on the land. ■

This article is reprinted from Manning Marable, "Black Agriculture in the Seventies," In These Times, p. 16, January 21-25, 1978.

EXAMPLE 41

A Blight Hits Black Farmers

Photo by Post

In 1865 John Boles, a freedman, bought 10 acres of land in Beaufort County, South Carolina. A part of America's promise is the opportunity to own land; to buy it and build on it, and enjoy the security that land bestows. But for some people this promise brings with it problems —legal problems that often make ownership meaningless. One-third of the land held by blacks in the rural South cannot be bought, sold, or traded away. The same land cannot be used as collateral for housing or for agriculture. Commonly called Heirs Property, it is almost without market value. Tens of thousands of black farm families are affected, but the best way to understand what has happened is to look at the Boles family's long relationship with the land.

John Boles, for our purposes the first of his line, had belonged to a planter named Tom B. Chaplin and the 10 acres he bought had once been a part of Chaplin's plantation. As soon as Boles got title (from the Freedman's Bureau) he planted cotton, okra and collards; he also raised a family. When Boles died in 1915 he left three boys: John Jr., James and Hezekiah.

Boles left no will designating one child heir to his 10 acres. In Beaufort County, and generally among blacks in the rural South, wills. were rare. When a man died his land usually passed, by statute, to his wife and children. When the wife and children died the land passed to the grandchildren. Two or three generations later 100 people could be part owners of 10 acres.

In the case of Boles's children, Hezekiah had left for New York and a new life in 1880. James followed five years later, when Hezekiah told him that steady, predictable work was to be had with the railroad. John Jr., the eldest, stayed on the Beaufort land and farmed it, as his father had done before him. But staying on the land was not easy. There were hurricanes and there were years when the rains failed. In 1919 the boll weevil put an end to cotton farming in Beaufort County. The depression was as hard on John and his family as it was

on the South in general. But he managed to hang on, partly because during World War II he could get part-time work at a nearby military base. In 1950 he turned the farm over to his oldest son, Frank, and Frank has been working it for the last twenty-five years.

Frank lives in the frame house his grandfather built in 1865. It is dark and damp; Rachel, Frank's wife, is weary of the house and has been insisting for several years that it be rebuilt or abandoned.

The Farmers Home Administration (FmHA) is the federal agency responsible for getting rural people of marginal resources out of shacks and into modest homes; it has put thousands of blacks into small houses. Believing, therefore, that the FmHA would help him build a new house, Frank went to the county supervisor in Beaufort County. The supervisor told him he would need "clear title" and recommended a lawyer who would "quiet title." The lawyer told Frank that he would need "quitclaim" deeds from all the heirs, and from any other persons having an interest in the 10 acres. Frank got "quitclaim" deeds from his own brothers and eventually he got deeds from Hezekiah's three children (all living in Stamford, Conn.). But Frank never knew his Uncle James and never heard if James had married or had children. In spite of his best efforts, he could not find James or any trace of his children.

Frank went back to the FmHA and explained his problem. "I can't find no trace of the man. He didn't come home for my daddy's funeral and none of my people in New York know anything about James." The FmHA supervisor then told Frank that this missing interest was considered a "cloud on the title," and meant there could be no title certificate or title insurance. "The best thing for you to do is to find some other land— or get yourself a doublewide."

Although mobile homes ("doublewides") are an acceptable alternative for many people, Frank wants something permanent. Unfortunately, he can get no help at the Farmers Home Administration. He will discover that the "missing interest" will discourage every bank and every lender, and that both bankers and bureaucrats will urge him into a mobile home, because it can be financed without a mortgage.

We are not talking about a problem that is peculiar to South Carolina. Although Heirs Property is estimated to involve 8 percent of the land in that state, it afflicts one-third of black-owned land from North Carolina to Mississippi. Heirs Property is most acute in rural counties, those counties that are still untouched by heavy industry, suburban home building, oil exploration or resort development; counties where agriculture is still the principal source of income and land can be purchased for less than $500 an acre.

What is really wrong with shared ownership? The land can be lived on and farmed by any of its owners. What's wrong with that? The land can be lived on and farmed, but that's about the extent of it. Because ownership is uncertain or scattered, this land cannot be mortgaged, or put up as collateral to finance farm equipment, or used in any other way to generate credit. But the biggest problem is not credit; the biggest problem is the likelihood that the property will be lost by those who own it. To understand this danger, one must understand what happened to the Southern black family as it "grew" and migrated from the South.

It was predictable that some of the family, some of these displaced heirs, would lose interest in paying taxes and keeping fences tidy. These children and grandchildren were leading lives that would eventually alienate them from the land. But something else was happening to these people: as the family grew, individual interests in the land were getting smaller.

In 1932, C.V. Kiser, who was writing a book called *Sea Island to City*, interviewed a number of black migrants in New York City. When he asked these recent emigrants if they owned land, they would invariably say that they owned an "interest in some." Kiser wrote, "The number of individuals nowadays having an 'interest' in land may be ascertained somewhat by the eighteen quitclaim signatures which a recent purchaser of a small tract of land secured in order to obtain a clear title."

Thirty-five years after Kiser wrote about the problem created by eighteen heirs, a tract of land in Mississippi (one believed to be above oil) required 1,000 signatures. and 1,000 heirs provide 1,000 targets to a "developer" who really wants the land. A person bent on acquisition can purchase the interest of any single heir—any fractional interest—then demand that "his" interest be partitioned from the tract. If the land cannot be easily subdivided, and very often that cannot be done equitably, the court will order a sale of the land and a division of the proceeds. It is not uncommon for the person triggering the sale to purchase the entire tract, that having been the plan.

Land in South Carolina's Sea Islands (a popular coastal resort) and tracts in the Citronelle Oil Field (north of Mobile, Ala.) were forced on the market by this device. These involuntary sales are a serious and continuing problem in Alabama. The Emergency Land Fund—a nonprofit organization created to slow black land loss in the South—spends a great deal of its time trying to rally heirs, raise enough money to purchase the endangered property, and keep those heirs who live on the land in their homes. The Alabama office of the ELF participated in at least seventy partition suits during 1977. It estimates that between 150 and 200 partition sales, involving land in Alabama's Black Belt, occurred that year. The total of such sales throughout the South is not known, for the records are scattered in county courthouses across the whole region. Alabama lawyers receive a 10 percent nonnegotiable fee for handling a partition action that results in a sale. While no one has drawn a direct relationship, this fixed sum can only encourage sales and discourage division.

Tax sales can be an equally serious consequence of multiple ownership. Usually one heir, the one still living on the land, has been paying the taxes. Thus, his death precipitates a crisis. Which heir will assume the tax burden? Who will return home and maintain the land? Sometimes the family discovers that no one is interested in farming or paying the taxes. If the family is small, it may be able to consolidate the interests and sell, but that kind of cooperation is difficult when twenty, forty, or more people are involved.

While there are many reasons for black owners to lose their land—including voluntary sales—Heirs Property accelerates this loss. With two or three exceptions, every county in the South having significant minority land ownership "lost" a large part of that ownership between 1969 and 1974. Barbour County, Alabama is a good example. In 1969 the Agricultural Census reported 17,901 black-owned acres; by 1974 blacks held only 10,687 acres in this county. According to the same census, black holdings in Mississippi dropped by 500,000 acres in these years, and in Alabama, the blacks lost 300,000 acres. For Georgia the figure was 230,000 acres; for South Carolina, 200,000 acres; for North Carolina, 100,000 acres. While the census figures may not be precise, they do indicate erosion. If it continues, one can reasonably assume that black land ownership in the South will be insignificant by 1985.

Another problem—the one confronting Frank Boles—is credit. The Farmers Home Administration has a well-intentioned housing program designed to put lower-income families under a decent roof, but when it comes to security for a loan, the agency is stiff-necked. It wants a clear title and nothing less will do.

The Housing Act of 1949 (the Act that created the FmHA's program) does not insist on clear title. The language requires security "upon the applicant's equity in the farm" that will reasonably assure repayment of the debt. There is even language in the FmHA regulations that would allow the use of a "partial interest" to secure a housing loan, when that interest is large enough to cover the value of the loan. But despite this language and although Frank can show a two-thirds interest in the 10 acres, it is unlikely that the FmHA will make him any kind of loan. It is also unlikely—in the five Southern states that I surveyed—that the FmHA will finance Frank's attempt to find James or his children. But the chances are very good that the FmHA will encourage Frank to find another piece of property on which to build or to purchase a mobile home.

This kind of advice removes thousands of acres from use as collateral, and it eliminates thousands of acres that could be used as sites for new homes. More important, this practice means that thousands of families, large families, have been forced into mobile homes that were not designed for families or for long use. In short, this federal policy simply defers the problem of rural housing for blacks until these mobile homes disintegrate.

Scattered ownership creates other problems. For example, those who live on Heirs Property cannot in most states qualify for the homestead exemption. But the reality is the continuing failure to recognize and label Heirs Property for what it is—a serious, debilitating handicap that prevents economic activity on millions of acres of Southern farmland. Many blacks still believe that Heirs Property is a blessing, that this confused ownership protects them from developers. But in fact Heirs Property is no obstacle to anyone who wants to trigger a partition sale.

There are lawyers who argue that Heirs Property is *not* widespread, and that in any event existing statutes are adequate to deal with the problem. North Carolina lawyer Herbert Toms says, "There is no property that cannot be cleared." "The existing laws can deal with the heir situation in Alabama," says Jerry Austell in Mobile. "We shouldn't make any changes . . . at least the law is comprehensible now."

In one respect, these lawyers are correct. The existing statutes are logical and can be made to deal with almost any situation, assuming you can pay the legal costs. A "quiet title" action—even one that involves no more than two or three heirs—is expensive. After the heirs have been located, they must be persuaded to consolidate what they own. This takes time, money, persistence; and in the end one stubborn heir, or an heir who cannot be found, can destroy a well-conceived effort.

Recognizing this problem, the South Carolina legislature in 1974 introduced a bill that would have authorized the state housing authority to underwrite suits to clear title on land involving 15 acres or less and having a market value of $15,000 or less.

The bill might have released thousands of acres in South Carolina from title bondage. Unfortunately, the legislature adjourned before action was taken, and the legislator who pushed for passage has since retired. But at least some people in South Carolina realized that the state (not to mention its black citizens) would benefit if these properties were in a position to be built upon (and fully taxed). But South Carolina is the only Southern state that has made any move to that end, although Mississippi is considering legislation. Organizations like the Emergency Land Fund are without funds, without staff adequate to deal with the massive amount of acreage involved. The people who recognize Heirs Property for what it is have no ability whatsoever to remedy the problem.

Although there is no functioning program at the FmHA that would help people like Frank Boles, there is a proposed amendment to Senate Bill 1150 that could make FmHA housing available to folks with Heirs Property. This amendment would authorize the Secretary of Agriculture to make loans on land even though there are "remote outstanding claims." While this language would have obvious application in the South, the amendment would also be important in New Mexico, where Spanish land grants have clouded titles. It would make the FmHA housing program available to Indians and Eskimos in Alaska. In Maine, litigation by Indians has clouded title to thousands of acres.

Gloria Tinubu, who wrote her masters thesis on Heirs Property in South Carolina, found that the "inability to agree" was the primary reason why Heirs Property remained Heirs Property. The proposed amendment speaks directly to this problem. The distant cousin in Cleveland who will not cooperate or even acknowledge that he has a 1/64th interest would not be allowed to block the loan, since it is hoped that the amendment would identify such an interest as "remote."

At this writing the FmHA is trying to define "remote." State offices are asking the county supervisors what kind of "remote claims" prevented loans in the past. Obviously the definition of "remote" is as critical as the amendment itself.

To return to Frank Boles, what is the likelihood that James, or his children, will show up and attack the title? How long has it been since anyone has seen James? Questions of that sort must be answered if the FmHA is realistically to assess "risk." If it is unlikely that James or his heirs will return, then that missing interest, even though it is one-third, is a "remote interest."

For the first time there is an opportunity at the federal level to untangle this legal mess. The Farmers Home Administration has demonstrated a willingness to assume a certain degree of risk in an attempt to put millions of acres back into productive use. It will be a tragedy, a quiet tragedy, if the Congress fails to seize this chance. ☐

C. Scott Graber is a writer and attorney in Beaufort, S.C. This article is based on research underwritten by the Legal Services Corporation, Washington, D.C.

This article is reprinted from C. Scott Garber, "A Blight Hits Black Farmers," **The Nation**, pp. 269-272, March 11, 1978.

How Co-ops Help Migrant Workers Get Farm Land

EXAMPLE

42

A member of Rancho La Fe, a cooperative affiliated with Central Coast Counties Development Corporation, trains European cucumbers to grow along a wire nine feet above the ground in a greenhouse.

Tereso Morales, in blue coveralls, looks quickly across his perfectly-manicured strawberry field, expert eye casting for missed weeds and drying plants. This has been a year virtually without rain, so more sprinkler irrigation than usual has been

'Then the day came when the development corporation said if you can do it with zucchinis, we think you can do it better with strawberries'

necessary along California's central coast.

A month from now, six of his children will hurry off the Watsonville schoolbus, help their mother with the work necessary in a family of 12 children, have an early dinner, and then do their homework. Next day they'll be up early, picking strawberries into flats of six-pint baskets and watching for the return of the schoolbus.

When a flat is full it goes to the end of the row for loading into a truck, which goes to a cooler six miles away where the field heat is removed. A carefully-operated forklift moves a pallet of berries to

a refrigerated truck, which by noon is being unloaded into the cavernous cargo of an airliner at the San Jose or San Francisco airports.

Next morning, just 24 hours out of the field, the berries will be selected by a housewife who lives a block off Park Avenue in New York.

This story began seven years ago when Morales and five other families asked the Central Coast Counties Development Corporation of Aptos to help them become farmers and escape the capricious wage slavery of migrant farmworker life.

The development corporation said it would try. The first step was leasing a 7-acre piece of bottomland from the Santa Cruz County government. It was suitable for raising zucchini squash, a high-yielding, labor-intensive and staple crop with ready acceptance in West Coast markets.

Weekend work. And nights. Zucchini, like strawberries, have to be picked every other day during their peak. There had to be meticulous record keeping, with every cent of income and expenses counted. And the hours had to be recorded as well, so there could be equitable distribution of money.

Then the day came when the development corporation said if you can do it with zucchinis, we think you can do it better with strawberries. Along with this vote of confidence came word that a $100,000 grant was a strong possibility.

"Together, we'll go to the bank, show them your records of work and income from the parttime work you've been doing, and borrow $200,000 more on the strength of that $100,000 deposit," members of the group were told.

"But there will have to be 30 families; it will take that many for the economies of scale you'll need to pay for management, bookkeeping, plants, equipment, and so on."

Looking back, Morales says in his Spanish-flavored English that "the hardest thing for me was to vote to approve hiring a man to sit at a desk and write figures in a book for $12,000 a year. We'd been getting by — each family — on about $4,000 a year. But it worked, and that's the important thing."

There were classes at night, two a week, in English as a second language, in cooperative management, in basic bookkeeping, in cooperative organization, in parliamentary procedure, "and English and English and English," Morales remembers.

Now the organization, Cooperativa Campesino, is an independent entity, conducts negotiations with the bank for annual operating funds, and looks back with understandable pride at having paid back the start-up loan ahead of schedule and putting in-

comes of the families into the $15,000 range.

Morales, now a development corporation board member, drops by to see its Agricultural Training Center, established on the old zucchini field and 10 additional acres. There is instruction in greenhouse construction and operation, cooperative practices and management, basic accounting, "and common sense," in the words of one of the trainees.

With another production cooperative, in the formative stage on part of a 112-acre tract near John Steinbeck's Salinas, the development corporation is putting together an organization to build a strawberry cooler, using federal and other funds. This will add 15 cents a flat to the income of cooperative members near the cooler, a little less for others farther away.

This vertical integration may enable the cooperative members to do their own marketing, too, bypassing expensive brokers. Also there can be assistance for other farmworkers and sharecroppers hoping to enter the field of cooperative farming/cooling/shipping/marketing.

President and chairman of the development corporation is Manuel Santana, who with a handful of other people organized the non-profit community development group in response to community needs. "You can't have community development without individual development," he said, "and that goes for board and staff and everyone."

Alfredo Navarro, the corporation's determined executive director, is a national leader in community development, housing, alternate energy, non-traditional education, and in as-

saulting the agricultural extension and land grant bastions. He and Santana are both convinced an entire community has to shift mental and operational gears "if you're going to really help poverty-battered people change their economic, cultural, educational, and political lifestyles."

There are no shortcuts, Navarro warns, either in the time required or in the complicated process.

"We've managed to combine physical facilities with welfare-oriented training programs funded by the federal government — and time — with the leveraging of bank loans to bring people out of the migrant stream to a place where they can control and manage the institutions and conditions that affect their lives," he says.

"A great many other organizations are trying the same things, but a lot of them have tried to cut corners and as a result, there have been a great many failures."

Santana and Navarro both are critical of vacuums in federal and state programming for rebuilding rural areas and they have taken a lead in trans-regional efforts to end geographical and ethnic rivalries.

"The problems we face are closely related to Indian problems and to the problems of blacks in the rural South," Navarro added.

"The real difficulties are in Washington and the state capitals where irresponsible programs are being administered by unresponsive and unimaginative officials. There is not nearly enough input from longtime community developers in either the administrative or the legislative process."

Strawberries must be tilled carefully so plant damage is minimal and so irrigation water will flow evenly. The tractor operator is a member of Rancho La Fe, a cooperative associated with Central Coast Counties Development Corporation.

This article is reprinted from "How Co-ops Help Migrant Workers Get Farm Land," **National Catholic Rural Life**, pp. 17-20, March 1976.

EXAMPLE 43

AGRED: The Assistance Group for Rural Economic Development

A Project of

The National Council of La Raza

Goal

AGRED's goal is to provide technical assistance in forms of management, marketing, and finance to existing enterprises engaged in rural economic development via agriculture, agribusiness, and/or recreation. This assistance will be provided to enterprises that, while lacking development, have definite future potentials, and will be provided on a long term basis. Primary emphasis on AGRED technical assistance will be placed upon firms engaged in agriculture/agribusiness/recreation which have an impact upon the local economy. A cooperative with many members, or a corporation hiring local residents are examples of entities with an impact upon the local economy. Entrepreneurs engaged in other rural economic development having no impact as measured by the above criteria, will also be considered potential candidates for AGRED assistance.

For the purpose of discussing its activities, AGRED has made the following definitions:

1. **Rural** - Rural can be described by population size (towns of 25,000 or less), or by economic activity (farming, ranching). AGRED has combined both definitions, since non-rural areas by population, rarely encompass rural economic activities.

2. **Agriculture** - The economic activity of farming (grains, vegetables), ranching (beef cattle, dairies, sheep production), poultry, pigs, and animal specialties.

3. **Agribusiness** - Economic activities which directly complement agricultural endeavors, such as beef packing and slaughtering plants, agricultural supplies and services, custom harvesting of grains and farm products, forestry and wood products, and cattle feedlots.

4. **Recreation** - The provision of leisure time activities in a rural setting. Such activities could include camping, hunting, fishing and other directly complementary business activities.

Objectives

In providing its technical assistance, AGRED has two primary objectives: 1) avoid duplication of efforts, and 2) provide assistance on a long term basis to clients. In an effort to avoid duplication of assistance already being provided, and in an effort to maximize utilization of AGRED's skills, AGRED will concentrate primarily on assisting existing enterprises and entrepreneurs engaged in rural economic development which are: 1) problem-ridden, but possessing future business viability, 2) in need of expansion capital, and/or 3) companies seeking to expand market outlets for their products.

AGRED feels that sources of technical assistance to new entrepreneurs and to enterprises which perform non-rural economic activities, are already in existence, and the skills of these sources should be capitalized upon.

It is expected that most of AGRED's clients will be economically underdeveloped but potentially viable enterprises. As such, these clients will need long term technical assistance before their potentials are realized. AGRED believes that it can work with fifteen to twenty such clients at any one time, and be able to do justice to these clients. Long term technical assistance is defined as assistance constantly being provided over a period of at least one year.

Strategies

To realize the potentials of a client, and to fully meet a client's needs, the AGRED-client relationship must grow to become a special relationship, where each works to the mutual benefit of the other. This is especially true with clients seeking long term technical assistance from AGRED. Such a relationship can be established only by mutual respect and trust by one party for the other. Full disclosure of all relevant information is an integral part of this mutual respect and trust. It is emphasized that AGRED in its desire to further rural economic development via agriculture, agribusiness, and/or recreation, will keep client information in the very strictest of confidences. The confidentiality of client information is further protected by law.

A primary requirement in obtaining AGRED assistance is that the client be involved in rural economic development via agriculture, agribusiness, and/or recreation. Clients should also: 1) have an impact upon the local economy and/or desire the continued preservation and development of presently owned lands; 2) be an existing business; 3) located in Utah, New Mexico, and Texas, the region served by AGRED; and 4) be minority oriented and/or minority owned. An emphasis is placed on impact upon the local economy.

Once eligibility is established, AGRED staff will visit the potential client as many times as necessary to establish a relationship, and to determine AGRED's capabilities to assist the potential client. Should AGRED be unable to meet client needs, AGRED will suggest other resources capable of providing the desired assistance. When AGRED and the potential client have determined that a working relationship can be established, the client must formally request in writing AGRED's assistance. Upon receipt of such a request, AGRED will familiarize itself thoroughly with the client's history, including corporate and financial history. The assistance process will then commence, and will be continued until the client's goals are met.

All assistance provided by AGRED to its clients is provided at no cost to the clients.

Staffing

AGRED is staffed to meet the three basic needs of most enterprises: marketing, management, and finance. Heading AGRED is Ray Lopez, Group Director, who was for five years the Executive Director of the Home Education Livelihood Program, Inc. (HELP); HELP, a non-profit corporation, provides health and social services to rural economically deprived residents, and was involved in water and sewer development projects, and community economic development.

Marketing and Resource Developer- The Marketing and Resource Developer will be responsible for indepth marketing assistance, which includes identifying and marketing new products, expanding existing product markets, and implementation of public relations and advertising techniques. Additonal responsibilities would include assistance in market studies, and developing market and sales techniques.

Cooperative and Management Specialist- The Cooperative and Management Specialist will provide assistance in cooperative organization and aid the manager in more effectively performing his functions. Additional responsibilities include assistance in improving membership participation, aiding the client in determining managerial needs, and expanding cooperative services to the general membership.

Financial Analyst and Business Packager- The Financial Analyst and Business Packager will provide such assistance as preparation of cash flow projections, improvement of existing accounting systems, and assist in securing additional monies as needed by ventures to insure adequate capitalization. To a limited extent, the Analyst and Packager will also package loans.

Conclusion

In the foreseeable future, agriculture will remain: 1) the mainstay of the rural Southwest, and 2) the predominant skill possessed by most of the rural Southwest's population. If rural economic development is to be speeded up, and the problems of the rural minority (continuing decay of the economic base and worsening non-participation in the economic mainstream) is to be stemmed, existing industry and existing skills must be capitalized upon. AGRED stands ready to address itself to these problems. Clients desiring further information and/or interested in obtaining assistance need but write:

Mr. Ray Lopez, Group Director
NCLR/Assistance Group for Rural
 Economic Development
2403 San Mateo NE, Suite S-14
Albuquerque, New Mexico 87110
We look forward to your inquiry.

This article is reprinted from **AGRED: The Assistance Group for Rural Economic Development**, The National Council of La Raza, pp. 2-5, 1978.

EXAMPLE
44
Improve Your Farming

A Directory Of Services Available To The Small Farmer Of Illinois

FOREWORD

Illinois is an agricultural state and a significant portion of the agricultural communties consists of small farm families.

Traditionally, small family farmers have not always known about or availed themselves fully of the technical and financial assistance available to this segment of our community.

This booklet is designed to provide comprehensive information about assistance available to Illinois small farmers from two sources: 1) Federal and State Programs; and 2) Private Resources. More importantly, the use of this booklet will provide a better understanding of the opportunities, requirements and guidelines of particular agencies and organizations concerned with agricultural development in the State of Illinois.

Your local Community Action Agency will help you locate all agencies and organizations listed in this booklet.

FEDERAL AND STATE PROGRAMS

I FARMERS HOME ADMINISTRATION (FmHA)

The Farmers Home Administration (FmHA) of the United States Department of Agriculture provides credit to farmers, rural residents and communities. It helps borrowers gain maximum benefit from loans through counseling and technical assistance.

A. Farm Ownership Loans

PURPOSE: To buy land, refinance debts, construct, repair or improve buidlings, improve farmland, develop water facilities, and establish business enterprises to supplement farming income.
FOR: Eligible operators of not larger than family farms.

B. Farm Emergency Loans

PURPOSE: To repair, replace, or restore farm property and equipment, including essential home furnishings and personal possessions damaged by a natural disaster or to reimburse for expenses incurred for these purposes. In case of severe production losses, farmers may borrow to cover expenses and repay from future earnings.
FOR: Eligible farm operators in designated emergency loan areas.

C. Recreation Enterprise Loans

PURPOSE: To develop recreation areas, including swimming, fishing, boating and camping facilities.
FOR: Individual farmers planning income-producing outdoor on-farm recreation.

D. Home Ownership Loans

PURPOSE: To buy, build, improve repair, or modernize rural homes and related facilities, including water supplies and waste disposal facilities. (Loans are also available to remove health and safety hazards in dwellings occupied by very low income owners who cannot afford new or modernized homes.)
FOR: Farmers and other rural residents who need housing but are unable to obtain terms they need from private or cooperative lenders.

E. Grazing Association Loans

PURPOSE: To help association members acquire grazing land for livestock.
FOR: Nonprofit corporations owned, operated and managed by neighboring members who are family farmers or ranchers.

F. Soil and Water Conservation Loans

PURPOSE: To finance land and water development measures, woodland drainage, irrigation, pasture improvement and related land and water use adjustment.
FOR: Any eligible owner, tenant, leaseholder, partnership, or corporation.

G. Farm Labor Housing Loans

PURPOSE: To buy, build or repair housing and related facilities for domestic farm labor.
FOR: Farm owners, associations of farmers, broadly based non-profit organizations, non-profit organizations of farm workers and public agencies.

II SOIL CONSERVATION SERVICE (S.C.S.)

The Soil Conservation Service (S.C.S.) provides technical assistance in establishing soil and water conservation programs and practices. The S.C.S. technician can advise the farmers as to what practices he should or could use and how he can implement them. There is no charge for S.C.S. technical assistance.

A. Soil and Water Conservation

PURPOSE: To provide technical and consultative assistance to individuals, groups, and units of government in planning and carrying out a national soil and water conservation program, and provide leadership in conservation, development, and productive use of the nation's soil, water and related resources.
FOR: Owners and operators of private lands, units of state, county, and local government, zoning and planning bodies, etc.

B. Soil Surveys

PURPOSE: To provide published soil surveys of counties or other comparably sized areas for wide-spread use by interested agencies, organizations, and individuals.
FOR: All individuals and groups who have a need for soil maps and interpretations.

III AGRICULTURAL STABILIZATION AND CONSERVATION SERVICE (A.S.C.S.)

The Agricultural Stabilization and Conservation Service (A.S.C.S.) administers conservation programs and disaster payments. The conservation programs are cost-sharing programs in which technical assistance is provided and the cost of implementing the conservation measures is divided between the United States Department of Agriculture and the farmer. The disaster payments are paid directly to the farmer for losses incurred due to natural disaster, such as flood, etc. These are not loans.

A. Agricultural Conservation Program (ACP)

PURPOSE: To encourage producers to apply lasting soil and water conservation practices on their farms. This program will cost-share with farmers from 50 to 75 percent of the cost in carrying out approved conservation practices.
FOR: Any eligible person who as owner, landlord, tenant or share-cropper on a farm or ranch bears a part of the cost.

B. Emergency Conservation Measures

PURPOSE: To rehabilitate farmlands damaged by natural disasters in counties designated as disaster areas by the Secretary of Agriculture.
FOR: Any eligible owner, landlord or tenant on a farm who bears part of the cost for improvement on a farm in a declared disaster area.

C. Forestry Incentives Program

PURPOSE: To encourage and assist private timberland owners in carrying out measures to increase the production of timber products.
FOR: Private timberland owners who are willing to work with the local forester in developing and following a timber management plan in planting trees and improving existing stands of timber.

IV   THE EXTENSION SERVICE

The Cooperative Extension Service is a three-way partnership. The University of Illinois, The U.S. Department of Agriculture, and your county share in planning and financing extension work. Local people participate in planning county programs by serving voluntarily on councils. Extension program councils help plan, implement and evaluate programs in each county in the state.
Extension advisers assist farmers and managers of agricultural businesses through education and information on the best way to grow, market, process, and use farm products. They suggest how to adapt scientific methods to individual needs and to adjust farm businesses to changing economic conditions. Skilled Extension specialists and Extension advisers help farmers solve everyday problems of:
a. crops and soil
b. livestock and poultry
c. farm machinery and building
d. forestry
e. safety and the safe use of pesticides

Home owners can get educational information on problems of lawn, gardens, landscaping, and insect control. Extension also assists farmers' cooperatives and the wholesalers and transporters of farm goods. Special programs are being implemented to help low income farmers move into the economic mainstream. (In addition to helping the farmer improve his income, The Cooperative Extension Service conducts programs directed to the entire farm family activities. Programs in Home Economics, 4-H Clubs and other youth activities are such an example.)

V   ILLINOIS DEPARTMENT OF AGRICULTURE

The Illinois Department of Agriculture is primarily a regulatory agency. It does, however, offer some services directly to the individual farmer. These programs are:

A. Illinois Rural Rehabilitation Act Loans

The Illinois Rural Rehabilitation Act Loans are long term and have low interest rates. The amount of the loan is determined by the Illinois Department of Agriculture and, in some cases, the U.S. Department of Agriculture.
1. The loans are made to individual farmers for acquisition, enlargement, development or improvement of soil and water development on farms to be operated by the farmer.
2. Loans are made to members of the Future Farmers of America, Future Homemakers of America, 4-H Club, and similar organizations to carry out agriculturally-oriented projects sponsored and supervised by such organizations.
3. Loans are made to individual farmers for providing waste management control or disposal systems to be used for dairy and other farm enterprises.
4. Loans are made to individual farmers for purchase of livestock, poultry, fur-bearing and other farm animals, fish, bees, farm machinery and equipment, milk base, feed, seed, fertilizer, insecticides, and other farm supplies; payment of cash rent; purchase of essential home equipment and furnishing; or for meeting family subsistence needs.
5. Loans are made to individual farmers to buy membership or stock in farm purchasing and marketing associations or farm services type cooperative

associations to enable them to carry on a successful farming operation.
6. Loans are made for carrying on pilot project farming operations to determine the feasibility of introducing new crop, livestock, poultry, or other farm enterprises; or for improving such enterprises in the state. The loans may be made on the basis that they will become total or partial non-recourse loans (as determined by the state) in the event that, through no fault of the borrower, the enterprise is unprofitable.
7. Loans are made to individuals who formerly were farmers or members of farm families to enable them to become reestablished on farms and to engage in farming, or to carry on pilot project farming operations described above.
8. Loans are made: 1) to individual farmers or members of their families cr to farm laborers for on-the-job training, intern or educational training programs, vocational school, college or university, to improve their skills in farm service employment; or 2) to other parties for use in assisting such persons in accomplishing such objectives.
9. Loans are made to assist farmers in obtaining medical and dental services for themselves and their families. Loans also are made to provide medical and dental services through rural medical clinics, services of resident physicians, summer medical student internship, and related record-keeping and other services.

B. Agriculture Hot Line

If a farmer has any questions or problems relating to agriculture he should call:
(217) 782-2898

C. Market Information

The department sends out a free weekly market report, Illinois Grain and Market News. To be put on the mailing list, simply write to:

Illinois Department of Agriculture
Division of Marketing and Agricultural Services
Bureau of Markets
Emmerson Building
State Fairground
Springfield, Illinois 62706

This article is reprinted from "Improve Your Farming," A Directory of Services Available to the Small Farmer of Illinois, Illinois State Economic Opportunity Office, 1978.

EXAMPLE 45

Alabama Landowners Protest FmHA Nomination

by Karen Spellman

In an apparent move to test the open door policy of the Carter Administration, members of the newly organized National Association of Landowners (NAL) (See *ruralamerica*, March 1977) met on March 25 with Secretary of Agriculture Robert Bergland to seek reorganization of the Alabama Farmers Home Administration and to oppose the nomination of Thurston L. Faulkner to head that agency.

Six members of the Alabama NAL, joined by Alabama State Senator Jerry Powell and Emergency Land Fund Executive Director Joe Brooks, cited instances of racial discrimination in hiring and lending practices within FmHA and protested the controversial nomination of Faulkner.

NAL's opposition to Faulkner comes as a result of his 7-year scandal-ridden career as State Director of Alabama's Vocational and Technical schools. As State Director Faulkner has been the object of repeated public investigations which have led to charges of fiscal misappropriation, administrative impropriety and racial discrimination.

In 1975, Faulkner and the State Board of Vocational Education were sued by two black students attending Patterson Vocational College in Montgomery who charged the Board with operating segregated classes in the school's cosmotology department.

Faulkner's most celebrated scandal, however, came in 1975 when an investigation into Faulkner's program expenditures revealed that he had made unauthorized use of nearly $200,000 in state education funds to purchase and maintain a private airplane.

Informed political sources credit T.L. Faulkner's nomination to a series of post election political maneuverings between Alabama's two U.S. Senators, Sparkman and Allen, and the Alabama State Democratic Party.

NAL accused Faulkner of possessing a "plantation mentality" and cited his insensitivity to the needs of minorities. "His personal history of racial discrimination, and his well-documented professional record denying blacks equal access to employment promotion and training make him totally unacceptable and incapable of holding down such an influential position."

Alabama FmHA; Too Little, Too Late

During the Bergland meeting, NAL also focused on the record of discrimination in hiring and lending practices amassed by the Alabama Farmers Home Administration. NAL members described personal experiences with discriminatory practices when applying for housing and operation loan assistance from FmHA.

To correct the situation, NAL recommended that Alabama FmHA be required to (1) restructure the selection system for County Committees to insure minority representation on the county selection boards that screen local farmer loan applications, (2) establish a State Commission on Agriculture that would review FmHA programs and practices and hear grievances and complaints from state farmers.

No Word Yet On Faulkner

As a result of the meeting, the Agriculture Department has begun an investigation into Faulkner's qualifications. While unwilling to comment on the result of the investigation, Alex Mecure, Assistant Secretary for Rural Development did say that all future FmHA Directors would be required to have "a solid track record on the question of affirmative action".

An Ad-Hoc Committee Against the Faulkner Confirmation has begun a letter writing campaign to oppose Faulkner's candidacy. They request persons to write or call Robert Bergland, Secretary of Agriculture, U.S. Department of Agriculture, Washington, D.C. 20250, 1 800-325-5300.

This article is reprinted from Karen Spelman, "Alabama Landowners Protest FmHA Nomination," **Rural America**, May 1977.

OFF-FARM AND TOTAL INCOME PER FARM OPERATOR FAMILY

By Value of Sales Class, Selected Years

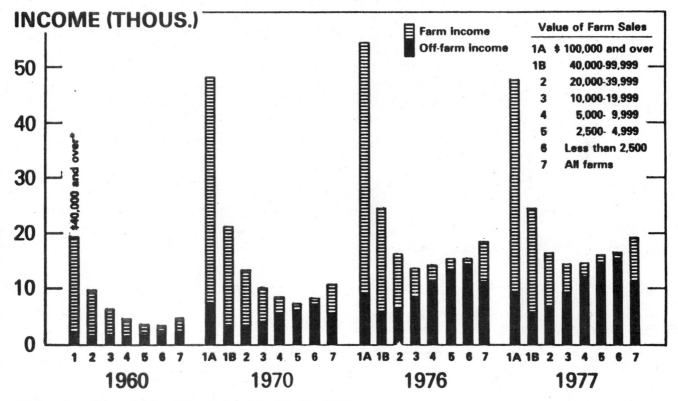

INCOME (THOUS.)

Farm income
Off-farm income

Value of Farm Sales	
1A	$ 100,000 and over
1B	40,000-99,999
2	20,000-39,999
3	10,000-19,999
4	5,000- 9,999
5	2,500- 4,999
6	Less than 2,500
7	All farms

1960   1970   1976   1977

Sales class 1A and 1B not separately identified in 1960.

Chapter 11

Protecting Farm Workers

Farmworker organizations and their supporters have struggled for decades to improve wages, health and welfare benefits and working conditions for migrant farm laborers in the United States. The "hired farm working force" stabilized at 2.8 million individuals during the 1970s. A 1976 study by USDA documented that the average annual income of hired farmworkers was only $1,652 and that over 50% were employed solely in farm work and had no other source of earnings.

One of the most serious problems facing farmworkers is that they have historically been excluded from federal laws regulating labor management relations. The *National Labor Relations Act* (NLRA), which was passed by Congress in 1935, was designed to place labor and management in substantially equal positions to insure that both sides in a labor dispute would have equal bargaining power. The strongest opposition to the NLRA was from southern agricultural interests. To avoid possible defeat, Congress was forced to make a concession to the bill's southern opposition, and the new collective bargaining law for the protection of American workers was passed— excluding from its coverage all agricultural workers.

Secondly, at the state level, much of the legislative effort of farmworkers and their supporters is spent lobbying against bills and state laws which discriminate against efforts to unionize farmworkers. They have specifically opposed "Right to Work" legislation which provides that workers don't have to join a union or pay union dues and prohibits closed union shops. In Arizona (a "Right to Work" state) a bill was passed in 1972 which outlawed all strikes and boycotts. The Farm Bureau pushed similar bills in 32 other states although only those in Arizona, Kansas and Idaho passed. In 1978 an attorney from The United Farmworkers of America (UFW) successfully worked to get the Arizona legislation declared unconstitutional, based on the first amendment—the freedom of speech.

IMPROVING WAGES, BENEFITS AND WORKING CONDITIONS

New Jersey was one of the first states to respond to the shocking living and working conditions of its migrant farmworkers. Efforts to enact needed legislation began in 1967 when controversy erupted after New Jersey farmers chased VISTA workers out of farm labor camps for allegedly organizing migrants into labor unions. The national publicity around this issue and the reports of the unlawful working conditions led to a package of reform legislation in 1967. But improvements were minor; wages were raised, but only to $1.50 per hour minimum, and the enforcement procedures were extremely lax.

In 1970, the State Department of Community Affairs proposed legislation which guaranteed access to New Jersey migrant labor camps for antipoverty officials and other qualified persons seeking to provide migrant workers with legal and medical assistance and social services. The legislative package also proposed a special state welfare fund for migrants and much stiffer penalties for farmers who refused to comply with the state's sanitation and housing regulations for farm labor camps. However, the 1970 reforms stopped short of recommending a higher minimum wage for farmworkers and it also refrained from supporting efforts to organize farm labor unions in New Jersey. A *New York Times* article describes the New Jersey legislation and is included as **Example 46, Aid for Migrants Urged by Cahill.**

Wisconsin passed a bill in 1977 (Assembly Bill 404) which established a State Council on Migrant Labor within the State Department of Industry, Labor and Human Relations. The bill provided the Council with much improved standards for wage rates, working conditions, the maintenance and inspection of migrant labor camps and on recruitment and hiring procedures for farmworkers. The bill also guaranteed the right of free access to all migrant labor camps in Wisconsin to insure that migrant workers and their families are not isolated from the larger community and from social, legal, medical and other services to which they are entitled. The legislation required that the Council members would be made up of six representatives of migrant workers and their organizations, six representatives of farmer/employers and two members each from the State Senate and the State Assembly.

Although, like New Jersey, Wisconsin's effort is a step in the right direction, there are many problems inherent in such liberal reforms. The Council's enforcement procedures are extremely vague and penalties for farmer/employer violations are too lenient: insignificant fines of $10 to $100 per day and a 15 day "grace period" in which to correct violations of state regulations. The Wisconsin legislation also does not address the need of extending to farmworkers the right to union representation and to collective bargaining rights.

CALIFORNIA: LEGISLATIVE VICTORY FOR FARMWORKERS

Because the most serious of the numerous problems facing farmworkers in the United States is that they are excluded from coverage under the National Labor Relations Act (NLRA), farmworker organizations and their supporters, who have for years focused on changing federal policy with little success, have recently changed their political strategy. They are now beginning to turn to state legislatures in an effort to enact progressive state agricultural labor relations acts.

On June 5, 1975, California enacted the first comprehensive farm labor legislation to provide a mechanism for regulation of the collective bargaining process in the nation's principal farm state. By enacting the *Agricultural Labor Relations Act* (S. 1140.2), the state extended to farmworkers the same right of all other workers to full freedom of association and the right to designate representatives of their own choice for the purpose of collective bargaining and mutual aid or protection.

Requiring an employer to recognize and bargain with a representative of his employees' choice is the first step toward providing a just and equitable context within which labor and management can function peaceably and effectively. California's ALRA establishes procedures for secret ballot elections so that—for the first time—farmworkers may choose whether they wish to be represented by a union for the purposes of collective bargaining. An Agricultural Labor Relations Board was created to conduct elections, investigate unfair labor practice charges and to determine the appropriate bargaining unit.

Another significant provision of the ALRA includes the regulation of the secondary boycott without completely restricting its utilization. A secondary boycott is an economic tactic against an innocent employer with whom the labor organization does not have a dispute (the secondary employer) in order to coerce that employer to stop doing business with the party with whom the labor organization does have a dispute (the primary employer). The California ALRA is even less restrictive on this issue than the federal NLRA as it permits picketing which has the effect of requesting the public to cease all purchasing from a secondary employer.

To pass this historic state labor legislation the United Farmworkers Union (UFW), led by Cesar Chavez, aligned itself with the labor movement by joining the AFL-CIO and gained strong and active support from church leaders, students, citizen's groups and the Democratic Party. In the 1974 gubernatorial election the UFW led a massive voter registration drive; registering 350,000 California voters. Brown won and subsequently the first bill introduced in the 1975 legislative session was the proposed Agricultural Labor Relations Act.

In 1976, under intense lobbying pressure by California agribusiness and the Teamsters Union, the State Legislature refused to reappropriate funds for the Agricultural Labor Relations Board whose office subsequently closed. The UFW was forced to go around the legislature and introduce a state-wide initiative (Proposition 14) which was designed to put the ALRA in "cement" and restore funding to the Agricultural Labor Relations Board. Proposition 14 is described in a California Ballot Title as **Example 47, Agricultural Labor Relations: Initiative Statute.** The initiative lost, but the effort helped politically to get the California Legislature to pass compromise legislation which refunded the Board, subject to an annual re-evaluation.

TEXAS ORGANIZING FOR COLLECTIVE BARGAINING RIGHTS

Farmworkers in Texas, as in every other state with the exception of California, do not have the right—long held by all industrial workers—to bargain with their employers for better wages and working conditions. In 1977 the Texas Farmworkers Union gained active support from religious and community organizations and labor union locals to obtain collective bargaining rights for farmworkers. The *Texas Agricultural Labor Relations Act* (SB 1057) was introduced in 1977 by State Senator Truan and in the House (HB 1325) by Representatives Barrientos, Moreno and Garcia. The Texas Legislature concentrated instead on bills which would grant workmen's compensation and unemployment insurance to farmworkers in the state.

Workmen's compensation is a step in the right direction, but farmworkers would still be earning poverty-level incomes. Extending unemployment insurance benefits to farmworkers is also a positive step, but again the problem is that the insurance rate is based on a small percentage of what one earns. In 1976 the median income for a farmworker family of six in the Rio Grande Valley was $3,990.

Other states have introduced legislation which extends benefits to farmworkers. Washington now grants workmen's compensation to farm laborers and both Florida and California grant unemployment and disability insurance benefits to farmworkers. This sort of legislation is one way to test the "political waters" at the state level as in California, where it was a prelude to the more effective and comprehensive ALRA passed in 1975.

IMPACT OF MECHANIZATION

The improved wages and working conditions won recently by organized farmworkers in California has in a very real sense created a backlash—accelerating the development of agricultural mechanization which has forced, and will continue to force, thousands of farmworkers out of jobs. The UFW contends that if unchecked, increased use of mechanical harvesting equipment will lead to the loss of 100,000 of the 250,000 farm labor jobs in California in the next ten years. The impact of publicly-funded agricultural mechanization research carried out at the University of California is now being addressed by the union, citizen action and public interest research groups in California.

In 1964, over 50,000 workers found jobs in the tomato harvest. By 1972, after the U.C.-Blackwelder tomato harvester was developed and introduced, 32,000 workers had lost their jobs. When confronted with the effects of U.C. research on mechanization, the University and agribusiness interests replied that this trend is necessary to keep consumer food prices low. But as Cesar Chavez, UFW president, points out in his article, reprinted as **Example 48, Square Tomatoes and Idle Workers: The Farm Workers' Next Battle**, the price of a can of tomatoes has risen 111% since 1964.

In 1976 a "rider" was attached to the California Assembly's version of the University Budget requiring that a "social impact" report be prepared to assess the effects of labor-displacing agricultural research. After strong lobbying by the University, the rider was deleted.

In 1977 the UFW worked with Assemblyman Art Torres to draft two bills. One measure required that social impact studies be conducted before public money could be spent for mechanization research. The second bill would have created a state fund to assist and compensate farm workers displaced by mechanization. The revenue for this fund would have been collected through a tax on those who directly profited from mechanization.

Although both bills were defeated in committee, public concern throughout the state pressured the University Board of Regents to schedule a hearing in 1978 on U.C.'s role in developing machines specifically to replace harvest labor. Pressure from the UFW, organized citizen's groups and from several concerned state legislators also forced a special investigation by the state's Auditor General focusing on the role of agribusiness in supporting agricultural research done at the University of California. The end result was that the UFW and its supporters requested that a Governor's Blue Ribbon Commission be established to report on U.C. research on farm mechanization and its impact on both farmworkers and consumers.

Resources

ORGANIZATIONS

American Friends Service Committee

1501 Cherry Street
Philadelphia, Pennsylvania 19102
(215) 241-7133
Domingo Gonzalez, National Representative
for Farm Laborers and Rural Affairs

California Agrarian Action Project

P.O. Box 464
Davis, California 95616
(916) 756-8518
Paul Barnett, Don Villarejo

Farm Labor Organizing Committee

714½ St. Clare
Toledo, Ohio 43609
(419) 243-3456
Beldemar Velasquez, Chairperson

Mexican American Legal Defense & Educational Fund

28 Geary Street
San Francisco, California 94108
(415) 485-9110
National Headquarters. Vilma Martinez, Director

1411 K Street, N.W.
Washington, D.C. 20005
(202) 393-5111
Al Perez, Director

Migrant Legal Action Program

806 15th Street, N.W.
Washington, D.C. 20005
(202) 347-5100
Rafael Gomez, Director

National Association of Farmworker Organizations

1332 New York Avenue, N.W.
Washington, D.C. 20020
(202) 347-2407
Tom Jones, Director; Sue Hoechstetter, Food and
Rural Development Advocacy

National Council of La Raza

1725 Eye Street, N.W.
Washington, D.C. 20006
(202) 659-1251
Raul Yzaguirre, President

AGRED

2403 San Mateo Boulevard, N.E.
Albuquerque, New Mexico 87110
(505) 268-2421
Ray Lopez, Director
La Raza's project; Assistance Group for Rural
Economic Development

Texas Farmworkers Union

P.O. Box 876
San Juan, Texas 78589
(512) 787-5984
Antonio Orendain, Director

United Farmworkers of America AFL-CIO

Box 67
Keene, California 93531
(805) 822-5571
Headquarters of the Union
Cesar Chavez, President

BIBLIOGRAPHY

Alvarez, Sal, **The Legislative History of the UFW**. United Farmworkers of America, Box 67, Keene, California 93531.

Alvarez, Sal, **The Legislative Struggle of the UFW**. Quinto Del Sol Publications, P.O. Box 9275, Berkeley, California 94709. 1973. $1.95.

Barnett, Paul, "Tough Tomatoes," **The Progressive**. Vol. 41, No. 12, December 1977. Questions accountability of agricultural research at U.C. Davis and the impact on farmworkers in California.

California Agrarian Action Project (CAAP), **Newsletter**. CAAP, P.O. Box 464, Davis, California 95616.

California Agrarian Action Project (CAAP), **No Hands Touch the Land**. CAAP, P.O. Box 464, Davis, California 95616. Also available in Spanish.

Central Coast Counties Development Corporation (CCCDC), **Program Profile**. CCCDC, 7000 Soquel Drive, Aptos, California 95003.

Chavez, Cesar, "Square Tomatoes and Idle Workers: The Farmworkers' Next Battle," **The Nation**. March 25, 1978.

Draper, James, "How Co-ops Help Migrant Workers Get Farmland," **Catholic Rural Life**. National Catholic Rural Life Conference, 3801 Grand Avenue, Des Moines, Iowa 50312. March 1976.

Friedland, William and Amy Barton, "Tomato Technology," **Society**. September/October 1976.

Levy, H.M., "Agricultural Labor Relations Act of 1975: La Esperanza de California Para El Futuro," **Santa Clara Lawyer**. Santa Clara Law School, Santa Clara, California. Summer 1975.

McWilliams, Carey, **Factories in the Fields: The Story of Migratory Labor in California.** Little, Brown and Company, Boston. 1939.

National Association of Farmworker Organizations (NAFO), **An Analysis of the Department of Labor's Services for Farmworkers.** NAFO, 1332 New York Avenue, N.W., Washington, D.C. 20020 $10.00.

National Child Nutrition Project (NCNP), **Food Action.** Vol. 2, No. 3, NCNP, 46 Bayard Street, New Brunswick, New Jersey 08901. May/June 1978. Entire issue.

National Sharecroppers Fund (NSF), **The Condition of Farmworkers and Small Farmers: 1977.** NSF, 2128 Commonwealth Avenue, Charlotte, North Carolina 28205.

Portes, Alejandro, "Return of the Wetback," **Social Science and Modern Society.** Vol. II, No. 3, Transaction Press, Rutgers University, New Brunswick, New Jersey 18903. March/April 1974.

Rosenthal, Clifford, "Meeting Migrant Needs," **Food Action.** Vol. 2, No. 3, National Child Nutrition Project, 46 Bayard Street, New Brunswick, New Jersey 18901. May/June 1978.

Rural America, "Where Have All the Farmworkers Gone," **Rural America Research Report.** No. 1. Rural America, 1346 Connecticut Avenue, N.W., Washington, D.C. 20036. September 1977. Report on the deficiencies of statistical methods used to estimate number of farmworkers in the United States.

Smith, Leslie and Gene Rowe, **The Hired Farm Working Force.** Report No. 405, Economics, Statistics and Cooperatives Service, USDA, Wasington, D.C. 20205. July 1978.

Texas Farmworkers Union (TFWU), **El Cuhamil.** TFWU, P.O. Box 876, San Juan, Texas 78589. TFWU's Newsletter.

Union for Radical Political Economics, "Farmworkers Face Mechanization Battle," **Dollars & Sense.** 234 Sommerville Avenue, Sommerville, Massachusetts 02143. March 1978.

U.S. Department of Labor, **Handbook of Labor Statistics.** Bulletin 1666, Bureau of Labor Statistics, U.S. Department of Labor, 441 G Street, N.W., Washington, D.C. 20210. 1978.

Aid for Migrants Urged by Cahill

EXAMPLE

46

Governor Recommends Plan for the Farm Workers

By RONALD SULLIVAN
Special to The New York Times

TRENTON, Nov. 7 — Gov. William T. Cahill, acknowledging that New Jersey had failed to do enough in behalf of the state's migrant farm workers, proposed a series of recommendations today aimed at guaranteeing them better living and working conditions.

"Our society cannot tolerate such disregard for fairness and human dignity," the Republican Governor declared in a policy statement issued here.

The Governor's recommendations were a response to controversy late this summer in which Federal antipoverty workers charged that a number of South Jersey farmers were perpetuating squalor and deprivation in their migrant labor camps and were using threats and intimidation to prevent them from helping the 20,000 black and Puerto Rican migrants who follow the harvest to New Jersey every year.

Among his proposals, the Governor said, is one ordering the state Attorney General to draft legislation that would knock down trespass signs and thus guarantee free access to migrant labor camps. Last August, two antipoverty workers were arrested on trespass charges by the state police when they refused to leave a migrant camp.

"Refusals to permit Federal and state antipoverty, health and education officials to visit migrant labor camps," Mr. Cahill said, "have too often frustrated attempts to improve the lives of seasonal workers."

In addition, Mr. Cahill said he had ordered his administration to "explore" legislation that would provide all migrant farm workers with the higher wage and living guarantees now given to Puerto Rican workers under contracts negotiated with the Commonwealth of Puerto Rico.

The two recommendations are expected to generate heated opposition from farming interests, although the New Jersey Farm Bureau said it would withhold comment until it had studied the recommendations in full.

With this in mind, Mr. Cahill said his proposals were primarily aimed at "a heedless minority who have ignored many legal requirements and who have used devious means to evade others."

"In doing so," he said, "they have caused many of our seasonal workers to labor and live in substandard conditions while receiving less than minimum wages."

The Governor's other recommendations, which were based on a study by the state Department of Labor and Industry, also include the following:

¶Legislation that would make the farmers primarily responsible for guaranteeing the health and welfare of migrant workers, and a crackdown on those who refused to conform to the state's sanitation and housing regulations.

¶New requirements for providing fresh water and sanitary facilities in the work fields and new, stiffer regulations governing the role of migrant crew leaders.

¶A requirement that workers receive the equivalent of $1.50 an hour, the state minimum wage, when working at piece rates.

¶A requirement that Puerto Rican migrants have quick access to Spanish court interpreters and Spanish-speaking lawyers when they become involved with the law.

The Governor stopped short of recommending a higher minimum wage for farm workers and he also refrained from expressing any support for recent efforts to organize farm workers into labor unions.

Max B. Rothman, the director of the farm workers division of Camden Legal Services, Inc. a federally financed antipoverty agency, said the recommendations "reflected the recognition by the Governor that something must be done."

Mrs. Irene Smith, the president of the State Conference of the National Association for the Advancement of Colored People, said the Governor's report was "good." But she contended there was no time left for "exploration" and urged the immediate implementation of Puerto Rican contract guarantees to black migrant farm workers.

This article is reprinted from Donald Sullivan, "Aid for Migrants Urged by Cahill," **New York Times,** November 8, 1970.

EXAMPLE 47

Agricultural Labor Relations-Initiative Statute

Ballot Title

AGRICULTURAL LABOR RELATIONS. INITIATIVE STATUTE. Repeals Agricultural Labor Relations Act of 1975; reenacts as Agricultural Labor Relations Act of 1976. Makes technical amendments to maintain status quo under 1975 Act, except requires new appointments to Agricultural Labor Relations Board. Additional amendments require: access for union organizers to property of employers for certain periods; minimum of 50% of employees to petition for decertification of union; Legislature to provide appropriations necessary to carry out the Act; Board to provide employer-supplied lists of agricultural employees to persons involved in elections. Permits Board to award treble damages for unfair labor practices. Financial impact: Proposition would result in minor, if any, increased costs to the state.

Analysis by Legislative Analyst

PROPOSAL:

Background:

The Agricultural Labor Relations Act of 1975, which became effective August 28, 1975, gives agricultural workers the right to select and join unions of their own choosing for purposes of bargaining collectively with their employer and to participate in lawful union activities. These rights are similar to those given to nonagricultural workers in private employment under the National Labor Relations Act.

The Agricultural Labor Relations Act of 1975 created a General Counsel and a five-member Agricultural Labor Relations Board. The board holds elections for agricultural workers to select the union of their choice. The counsel takes legal action against unions or employers which engage in unfair labor practices prohibited by the act such as discriminating against an employee for exercising his free choice to join a union and the failure of either party to bargain in good faith.

The board establishes rules and regulations for implementing the act. It also settles disputes regarding the holding of elections and charges of unfair labor practices. The board has the power to prescribe remedies in unfair labor practice cases and may direct the offending party to compensate injured parties for certain losses. Such remedies may include job reinstatement and restoration of lost wages. The board enforces its orders by court proceedings.

The board established under the 1975 law ran out of money in February 1976. Its program was stopped for the remainder of the 1975–76 fiscal year because no additional funding was provided. Funding after July 1, 1976 is now included in the 1976 Budget Act.

This proposition repeals and reenacts the Agricultural Labor Relations Act, retaining most of its basic features with the following modifications:

1. Provides for the appointment of a new Agricultural Labor Relations Board with new terms of office.
2. Authorizes union organizers to enter an employer's property for purposes of campaigning for an election. The period of access would be limited to three hours per day at specified times. This provision is similar to a regulation, established by the existing board, which has the effect of law.

3. Provides that a new election cannot be held if, in addition to other conditions, an election was held under existing law within the twelve months immediately preceding the filing for the new election.
4. Requires the board to make lists of employees available to persons who file notices of intention to petition for elections. The board obtains such lists from employers to determine workers' eligibility to participate in an election to select a union.
5. Allows the board to order payment of treble damages as a penalty for an unfair labor practice.
6. Makes it more difficult to hold an election to remove a union which has previously won an election and which has been certified as the official bargaining representative of a designated group of workers. Petitions for holding such elections would require the signatures of 50 percent rather than 30 percent of the workers.
7. Directs the Legislature to appropriate sufficient funds to allow the board to fulfill its responsibilities. The Legislative Counsel advises that this provision is directory, not mandatory upon the Legislature and does not constitute an appropriation. Therefore, regardless of its intent, it would not bind the Legislature to appropriate any specific amount of money.

FISCAL EFFECT:

The Budget Act of 1976 appropriates $6,688,000 from the General Fund for the administration of the Agricultural Labor Relations program during the 1976–77 fiscal year. Because this proposition largely reenacts provisions of existing law, it would not result in any significant increased cost to the state. Some features which differ from existing law would result in minor increased state costs, and others would result in savings. Any net increased cost could be absorbed within the amount currently budgeted to the board.

Because the proposition would not legally bind the Legislature to appropriate any specific amount of money for the board, the level of funding in future years would be determined by the Governor and Legislature through the state's regular budget process. In summary, the proposition would result in minor, if any, increased costs to the state.

Argument in Favor of Proposition 14

The right to vote is one of our most cherished rights. And yet, as we celebrate our bicentennial, the right to vote is still at issue for the quarter million men, women and children in California who harvest the food we eat.

In 1935, when Congress granted working people the right to organize and choose their representatives by secret ballot elections, agribusiness persuaded lawmakers to deny those rights to farm workers.

Last year, Governor Brown decided to end forty years of discrimination by granting farm workers the same rights as other workers. So he sponsored the Agricultural Labor Relations Act which was endorsed by agribusiness, the Teamsters Union and the United Farm Workers.

The law was passed by the legislature—and it worked!

Gone were the bloodshed and violence which were part of California agribusiness since the turn of the century. There were no strikes or strife in the fields; more than 400 elections were held.

Yet within five months—after losing 93 per cent of the elections—agribusiness demanded crippling changes in the law before legislators provided funds necessary to continue the voting.

The Teamsters Union, which had won only one-third of the elections, also lobbied to halt the balloting.

The California legislature was not strong enough to stand up to agribusiness-Teamster power and to permanently guarantee all of the people the most sacred American right—the right to vote.

The farm workers' only alternative was to bypass the politicians in Sacramento and to go directly to you, the people. They ask you to permanently guarantee their right to vote.

You can guarantee an end to the terrible hardships farm workers and their families have suffered. You can end squalid labor camps, malnourished farm worker children, and hazardous working conditions in the fields. Then farm workers need no longer face a life span far shorter than those of other Americans.

Proposition 14 asks you, the people of California, to act so that those who work in our fields are never again deprived of their right to vote. Your "yes" vote for Proposition 14 will assure that.

CESAR CHAVEZ, *President*
United Farm Workers of America, AFL-CIO

MERVYN DYMALLY
Lieutenant Governor of California

RICHARD ALATORRE
Member of the Assembly, 55th District
Coauthor, Agricultural Labor Relations Act

Argument Against Proposition 14

Proposition 14 is a hastily conceived and fiscally irresponsible abuse of your initiative process. California law (the Agricultural Labor Relations Act of 1975) already provides for the gains which the proponents of the initiative seek, subject to the responsible oversight and budgetary control of the legislature.

This initiative repeals the existing law, removing all legislative controls over it and mandating the legislature to spend whatever money necessary to administer the new law, notwithstanding any fiscal irresponsibility demonstrated by the Agricultural Labor Relations Board. The terms of the ALRA of 1976 could be changed only by repeating the expensive and cumbersome initiative process.

A NO Vote is imperative for the following reasons:

Inflexibility. The governor, legislators and the past chairman and current members of the ALRB have all acknowledged that the current law will have to be changed, perhaps often, to meet the needs of employees, employers and labor organizations. This initiative prevents the legislature from making such changes, since any modifications in the law require additional initiatives which can be presented only every two years or by a costly special election held at the direction of the governor. Such inflexibility is fatal because labor relations legislation must respond to the changing needs and relationships of all parties. This has been true of all other federal and state labor relations laws.

Fiscal Irresponsibility. The initiative contains the following language:

"SEC. 3. The Legislature shall appropriate such amounts to the Agricultural Labor Relations Board as may be necessary to carry out the provisions of this part."

This apparent attempt at "blank check" financing for the agency which grossly overspent its 1975–1976 budget in less than six months could mean cuts in other vital state programs and would have an indeterminate effect on the tax bill for California's citizens.

Basic Property Rights Would Be Destroyed. The initiative makes the infamous "access rule," a regulation still under judicial challenge before the U. S. Supreme Court, a permanent part of the law. Thus, nonemployee union organizers could trespass on private property, enter dairies, greenhouses, poultry production facilities, farms or other agricultural private property for up to three hours every working day without permission of the property owner, regardless of risks to health, safety and sanitation. The initiative allows this invasion of private property even though organizers engage in "disruptive conduct"—a frightening and dangerous precedent leading to the further erosion and destruction of property rights of all citizens.

Duplication. The issue here is not whether farm workers should have the right to decide which union, if any, should represent them. That right exists under present law. The issue is whether the existing law will continue under the responsible substantive and budgetary control of elected representatives.

Food production is too vital to California and the nation, and agriculture too essential to the state's economy to permit such a cumbersome and impractical method of resolving agricultural labor relations issues.

KENNETH L. MADDY, *Republican*
Member of the Assembly, 30th District

JOHN GARAMENDI, *Democrat*
Member of the Assembly, 7th District

HARRY KUBO, *President*
Nisei Farmers League

This article is reprinted from "Agricultural Labor Relations—Initiative Statute," California Legislature, Sacramento, California, pp. 52-55.

EXAMPLE 48 Square Tomatoes and Idle Workers: The Farm Workers' Next Battle

On February 16, the United Farm Workers appeared before a rare public meeting of the University of California Board of Regents to plead the case of thousands of farm workers who had been displaced by machines developed through U.C. research. Our union does not oppose progress, we told the regents; we do not even oppose mechanization. The university should be congratulated on its tremendous breakthroughs in mechanization technology. No one can deny that U.C. has had success in its research programs. They've done a very good half of the job.

But we believe the progress should be complete. The other half of the job is to use this wonderful technology to develop complementary programs for the workers who are losing their jobs. Research should benefit everyone, workers as well as growers.

It is no secret that there is a deep disagreement between the union and the university on the practical results of its research. U.C. claims to have had little, if any, impact on workers; we know mechanization affects workers because we see them unemployed and begging for welfare. So we urged the regents to join with us in asking Governor Brown to appoint an independent blue-ribbon committee to conduct a thorough and impartial study on the effects of U.C. research, if any, on the farm workers, and to issue appropriate recommendations. Governor Brown received a telegram on February 16 from us urging him to name the blue-ribbon panel, and he has not yet responded.

What was the reaction to our initiatives? "The university is an agent of change," said U.C.'s vice president for agriculture, J.B. Kendrick Jr. "It does not decide public policy or compensate losers among conflicting societal interests."

It is difficult to understand how anyone can tag as losers men and women who have had no voice in a headlong rush into mechanization. The farm workers call the machines "los monstruos"—the monsters. They see them as mechanical behemoths that threaten to decimate the farm labor work force and turn California into another Appalachia, with an underclass of unemployed workers as poor as any to be found in Kentucky or West Virginia.

Kendrick calls them losers in an impersonal process of change, but in the workers' view it is a cruel irony that the rapid spread of machines—bringing hardship and suffering to countless thousands of displaced men and women—is spearheaded by one of the great institutions of public education in the nation.

In the harvest of thirteen crops alone, more than 120,000 farm worker jobs will be lost to machines and for most of the crops the university is developing farm equipment at an increasingly swift pace. U.C. research projects already underway or nearing completion will mechanize the great majority of such labor intensive crops as wine grapes, raisin grapes, lettuce, fresh tomatoes, peaches, apricots, cherries, melons and celery, to name only a few. Kendrick dismisses the workers as losers, but we believe the university has a moral and social responsibility to the farm workers and to others who are adversely affected by its programs.

History will judge societies and governments—and their institutions—not by how big they are or how well they serve the rich and powerful but by how effectively they respond to the needs of the poor and helpless.

In our boycotts, we always assumed that supermarkets and other corporations must take seriously the needs of society, and especially the needs of the poor, even though they are answerable only to their stockholders for the profits that they earn. We often asked, if individuals and organizations did not respond to poor people who are trying to bring about change by nonviolent means, then what kind of democratic society would we become? And some corporations did respond by joining with millions of Americans in honoring the farm workers' boycotts.

If corporations and other social institutions can recognize their moral responsibility, how much more should we expect from a great university that is supported by all the taxpayers, including the farm workers, particularly when that university is a direct cause of hardship and misery for the poorest of the poor in our society? It is appropriate for the people to expect that an institution responsible for educating their children will be an example to the young by demonstrating through its policies and deeds its commitment to a just and peaceful world. How can the university teach justice and respect for the freedom and dignity of all people when it practices the

Renault, Sacramento Bee

"It Uses the Short-Handled Hoe and Won't Join the United Farm Workers."

opposite with its money and its people by refusing to live up to its own moral and social obligations?

Contrast these obligations to U.C.'s record in developing farm technology and its anti-farm-worker bias.

Last summer the electronic-eye tomato sorter was widely used for the first time in California tomato fields. The state Assembly's Office of Research, after a thorough study, projected that at least 7,500 farm workers would be displaced by the sorter last year alone.

Displacing the work force in the tomato harvest or industry is an omen for all farm workers in the age of U.C. mechanization research. In 1964, some 50,000 farm workers found jobs in the harvest. By 1972, after implementation of the U.C.-Blackwelder tomato harvester, 32,000 workers had lost their jobs and the work force shrank to 18,000. By 1976, the number of workers had risen to 27,000 as a result of increased tomato acreage, but by then U.C.'s electronic-eye sorter had been introduced. Each sorter reduces the number of workers on a harvest machine from fifteen to twenty to two to six, a 66 to 90 percent displacement. Soon, if the sorter continues to be adopted, only 3,000 farm workers will be left in processing the tomato harvest, a loss of 24,000 jobs from the 1976 level.

When confronted with the effects of its research on farm workers, the university responds that its programs are needed to keep down prices for consumers. But does the consumer really benefit? The mechanization of the tomato harvest appears actually to have increased their price to consumers. Since 1964, the price of a can of tomatoes has risen 111 percent, while the price of all foods went up only 90 percent, and the costs of all other produce only 76 percent.

U.C. agricultural engineers have been able to develop their machines only with the enthusiastic assistance of other U.C. scientists. Most fruits and vegetables are too fragile to withstand the rigors of machine harvesting, so the university has genetically reprogrammed the plants to the needs of the machine. The "square-round" tomato developed at U.C., Davis, and in general the new varieties of tasteless, pulpy, nutritionless fruits and vegetables are the result.

The public underwrites agribusiness' research. Of U.C. mechanization research funding for fiscal years 1975-76, only 6.5 percent was supplied by the agricultural industry. The rest of the money came from public funds: 69.5 percent from the state general fund, 6.4 percent from the federal government, and 17.6 percent from marketing order money.

The taxpayer pays twice for state-supported farm research. He pays, first, when public funds are used to develop the machines with no thought for the men and women whose jobs are wiped out; he pays again when these once gainfully employed workers turn to the state for support and the public is forced to absorb the social costs of mechanization.

The displacement of 120,000 farm workers due to mechanization will raise the California unemployment rate by 1.2 percent. Recent studies and testimony before the Joint Economic Committee of Congress and the House Subcommittee on Crime tie an unemployment rise of 1 percent to an increase in a myriad of social problems, including suicides, mental hospital admissions, crime, alcohol abuse, cardiovascular disease, infant and maternal mortality, automobile accidents, and a substantial loss of state and federal revenue.

Mechanization has been a problem for farm workers for many years. The first shock came in cotton more than twenty-five years ago. As early as 1950, a third of California's cotton crop was harvested by machines. By 1964, 97 percent of the state's crop was mechanized.

Some 100,000 workers found jobs in the cotton fields, more than were employed in cotton than in any other single crop. By the late 1950s, thousands of families who relied on cotton harvesting for their livelihood were left without jobs or a future. Today, in such west San Joaquin Valley farm communities as Corcoran, Hanford, Huron and Mendota, there are thousands of workers who were laid off by the cotton machines and never able to find new jobs. Their children, an entire generation, were raised in these hamlets of unemployment, unable to find work and subsisting on welfare.

Sugar beets, almonds and most of the field crops were also completely mechanized, leaving in their wake thousands of farm workers with nowhere to turn and nothing to look forward to except lives of misery and poverty. These workers learned that mechanization grabs your dignity as well as your job.

We knew mechanization was a serious problem, but the union was too busy trying to get organized and fighting for its life against agribusiness to tackle the mechanization question. But after the California Agricultural Labor Relations Act was passed in 1975, and collective bargaining gains were slowly made, the leadership of the union began to see the mechanization issue as the most inevitable battle.

First we tried to deal with the problem in contract negotiations, but there was no uniformity, and it was difficult to expect an employer who agreed with us to compete with other growers in the industry. Next we tried to talk to growers about their responsibility to the workers who contribute so much to building up the wealth of their ranches but are often left stranded when machines are imported. We were unsuccessful.

Then we tried legislation. In the spring of 1977 we introduced two bills written by state Assemblyman Art Torres. One measure required that social impact studies be conducted before public money was spent for mechanization research. A companion bill created a state fund to assist and compensate farm workers displaced by machines. Revenue would be collected through a tax on those who directly profit from mechanization. Both bills were defeated in committee.

An administrative requirement on U.C., similar to the social impact study legislation, was vigorously opposed by the university in legislative budget hearings. The bills will be reintroduced in revised form during the current legislative session.

At the union's Third Constitutional Convention last August in Fresno, the delegates unanimously passed a resolution committing the union to an all-out drive on mechanization. After the convention, the UFW National Executive Board developed a plan to implement the workers' resolution.

We kicked off the campaign with four daylong union-sponsored conferences organized throughout the state in February. More than 2,000 union members and active supporters attended the seminars. They heard union leaders and staff detail the extent of the problem and participated in workshops where they contributed their ideas on how the UFW could best implement its campaign. At each conference, farm workers and city supporters alike pointed to the need to focus attention on U.C.'s research role.

The year after passage of the 1975 Farm Labor Law, U.C.'s Division of Agricultural Sciences produced a pamphlet entitled "Labor Management in California Agriculture: A Practical Guide." Questions posed and answered by the pamphlet included: "Stopping the union is a big job. How could we go about it?" "What about making sure I don't hire pro-union workers?" "All this [the law] is a lot of trouble for the short time every year I need a lot of labor. Maybe I should just mechanize and forget labor problems?"

The pamphlet carried a note saying it was designed for growers who had been unable to attend U.C. Division of Agricultural Sciences classes on the new law.

U.C. Extension offered a class to growers in 1977 on the union and the legal aspects of union representation elections. The *Woodland Daily Democrat* reported (March 31, 1977): "A group of California growers . . . got a lesson in combatting unions at U.C. Davis Extension. Farm Employers Labor Service Manager George Daniels explained how to wage psychological warfare against farm workers' unions battling for the vote of agricultural workers in union certification elections. . . . Daniels explained how to get around ALRB (Agricultural Labor Relations Board) rules if growers found it necessary."

Given this history, was the university's rapid drive to mechanize California farms triggered by the recent successes of the farm workers' movement? In the two and a half years since passage of the law, our union, after winning secret ballot elections, has signed more than 100 contracts with growers. Negotiations, at varying stages of progress, are underway at another 100 ranches, and our union is awaiting certification as bargaining agent at yet another fifty companies. Despite problems with enforcement and maladministration of the Act, the law is alive and functioning, and free collective bargaining is a reality for farm workers, at least in California.

Since it was founded nearly sixteen years ago, the union has achieved some success in raising wages and improving working conditions for farm workers in California. More important, we have destroyed the myth of grower invincibility; farm workers are no longer afraid to stand up for their rights.

The University of California's Kendrick is not the first person to call the farm workers losers. The workers have met such contempt before when they faced seemingly insurmountable odds. And they managed not only to survive but to prevail. □

This article is reprinted from Cesar Chavez, "Square Tomatoes and Idle Workers: The Farm Workers' Next Battle," **The Nation**, pp. 330-332, December 1977.

Chapter 12

Preventing Tax Discrimination Against Farm Women

Farm women are significantly affected by both federal and state inheritance tax laws which require proof of financial contribution to an estate in order to assess ownership for tax purposes. Each state has its own inheritance tax laws and the federal law applies to property owners in all states. Every property owner must pay both federal and state inheritance taxes.

The federal estate tax law—and most state statutes which have been modeled on it—has until recently treated any property held in joint tenancy as belonging to the deceased spouse unless the surviving spouse can prove that he, or more often she, has actually contributed "money or monies' worth" to the purchase or development of the property. In most cases, farm wives have not directly made financial contributions but they have increased the overall value of the farm through long hours of physical labor. In addition they often do most of the accounting and participate in the management of the farm around production and marketing decisions.

Joint labor in an unincorporated business has not been recognized by IRS and state tax assessors as sufficient evidence of joint ownership for estate tax purposes. This is a serious problem as 12 million of the 14 million—or 85% of all family farms and small businesses in the United States are unincorporated. If a farm is incorporated, the percentage of stock held by the widow is evidence of joint ownership. Therefore, it is the women who work on the smallest, family-run operations who are most severely affected by this problem. The inequitable consequence is that the death of the wife may result in no tax to her husband while a widow, who may have worked a farm for years with her husband, is faced after his death with a tax bill from both the state and the federal government based on the total value of the farm property. The problems inherent in the estate tax structure are outlined in an article by North Dakota Tax Commissioner Byron Dorgan which is reprinted as **Example 49, The American Estate Tax: A Death Penalty.**

FEDERAL ESTATE TAX REFORM

In the last few years, controversy over this so-called "widow's tax" has led to reforms in estate tax legislation. An initial step at the federal level was made in 1976. Section 2002 of the *Tax Reform Act* provided that if title to property is held as a joint tenancy there will be no consideration of financial contributions made by either spouse for the purposes of assessing estate taxes. However, the same statute provided that the joint tenancy be created subject to the federal gift tax. This was an improvement for most women because the gift tax is lower than the rates for the inheritance tax, but the legislative assumption remained that only the spouse who had made a direct economic contribution to the property would be considered the owner.

The 1976 reform had two serious shortcomings for farm families. First, it benefits only those farmers who are affluent and sophisticated enough to obtain tax-planning advice and assistance. An indication of how many thousands of farm families do not receive such legal assistance can be found in a 1976 study by the Wisconsin Farmers Union of their county officers which revealed that fewer than 50% had wills. Secondly, if the joint tenancy is created by the husband and wife when they are older, the farmer is required to pay a gift tax based on the current value of the property. The phenomenal increase in land values over the last 25—or even 5 years—results in extremely high taxes if the land is assessed on current market-value.

In April 1978, Senator Gaylord Nelson (D-Wisconsin) introduced a bill to eliminate the "widow's tax" for the owners of family farms and small businesses. The Nelson bill (S. 2865), which was passed by Congress later in 1978, allows the surviving spouse to be considered the owner (for estate tax purposes) of up to 50% of jointly-held farm or small business property if she (or less frequently, he) has actually participated in the operation. Consequently, a farm wife may "earn" an estate tax credit of 2% a year, up to a maximum of 50%. By working on a farm for 25 years, a woman can now be considered to own 50% of the farm for estate tax purposes. Upon her husband's death, the federal tax would apply to only one-half of the farm property value. A press release issued by the U.S. Senate's Select Committee on Small Business describes the legislation and is included as **Example 50, Nelson Bill to Eliminate the Widow's Tax.**

STATE TAX REFORM

At the state level, efforts to reform tax laws which now unfairly discriminate against farm women and other surviving spouses are beginning to gain momentum. An article in *The Farm Journal* by Laura Lane, which is included as **Example 51, Farm Women: You Have Fewer Property Rights Than You Think**, describes the numerous property and inheritance tax problems which exist in current state laws.

In 1976 the Wisconsin Legislature passed a tax reform bill (SB 113) which provides up to a 50% inheritance tax exemption for surviving joint tenants. This replaced a law which required the surviving spouse to prove actual financial contribution in order to qualify for an automatic exemption. The State Legislature announced that this legislation provides a $1.6 million annual inheritance tax break which will primarily benefit Wisconsin women who help to build their families' farms, homes and businesses. The Wisconsin Revenue Department estimates that the new law will benefit over 9,800 widows each year. The benefits of the bill are described in an article in the *Wisconsin Farmers Union News*, reprinted as **Example 52, Lucey Signs Inheritance Tax Reform Measure.** A more technical description of the bill can be found in an article from *The Wisconsin Agriculturalist* which is reprinted as **Example 53, Law Change Avoids Double Taxation.**

In Montana, a bill passed by the State Legislature (SB 223) provides for simplified filing procedures to enable the surviving spouse to obtain full title to the farm property without going through the expensive and time consuming process of legal advice. The Montana Legislature will be in session January 1979 for the first time in two years. Encouraged by progressive and politically active women's organizations, state legislators plan to introduce a bill which proposes equal ownership, using the coal severance tax as the resource to make up the loss of state revenues.

A 1976 Minnesota law (SB 633) increases state inheritance tax exemptions and removes sex distinctions from inheritance tax laws. It also provides an alternative method of determining the assessment of a surviving spouse's inheritance tax by allowing a marital exemption of 50% of the property, up to $250,000. To aid those who inherit a family farm or small business, the new law permits payment of inheritance taxes over a five-year period.

Nebraska enacted legislation in 1976 (LB 585) which exempted jointly-held property from inheritance taxes with each spouse being considered as having equally contributed to the property. Similar legislation has recently been passed in Ohio and South Dakota.

Changing state laws to prevent unfair inheritance tax burdens on women involved in family farms (and small businesses) is an important issue for progressives at the state level to address. Added to the already severe economic pressure on family farms, high inheritance taxes force thousands of farm wives to sell their land in order to pay taxes after their husbands die. A brief summary of this problem in the words of one farm wife is reprinted from a special newsletter published by Common Cause as **Example 54, ERA and State Property Laws**.

The tax reform issue is probably the most pressing issue for farm women to organize around at the state level. Other important issues involve farm credit discrimination and access to training in agricultural production and marketing. A relevant article by Frances Hill in *Catholic Rural Life* is reprinted as **Example 55, Why Women Deserve More Opportunity in Farming.** The bottom line is for rural women to become more politically active and to join broader coalitions of individuals and organizations working for farm, land and food policy reform at the state and local level.

Resources

ORGANIZATIONS

American Agri-Women

Estate Tax Issues Committee
Springfield, Nebraska 68059
Doris Royal, Coordinator

National Farmers Union

1012 14th Street, N.W.
Washington, D.C. 20005
(202) 628-9774
Ruth Kobell, Legislative Staff

Rural America

1346 Connecticut Avenue, N.W.
Washington, D.C. 20036
(202) 659-2800
Peggy Borgers, Legislative Staff

Rural American Women

1522 K Street, N.W.
Suite 700
Washington, D.C. 20005
(202) 785-4700
Jane Threatt, President

Women's Family Farm Project

United Methodist Church
475 Riverside Drive
New York, New York 10027
(212) 678-6161
Ruth Gilbert, Coordinator

Women Involved in Farm Economics (WIFE)

Box 484
Osceola, Nebraska 68651
Betty Majors, National President

Box 316
Roundup, Montana 59072
Gay Holliday, National Officer

BIBLIOGRAPHY

American Agri-Women, **Newsletter**. c/o Trenna Grabowski, Route 1, Dubois, Illinois 62831. Bi-monthly, $5.00 year, members; $10.00 year non-members.

Beaudry, Ann, **Women in the Economy: A Legislative Agenda**. Conference on Alternative State and Local Policies, 2000 Florida Avenue, N.W., Washington, D.C. 20009 $5.00. Chapter on inheritance tax revisions, pages 58-61.

Common Cause/ERA, **The Equal Rights Amendment and Property Laws**. Common Cause/ERA, 2030 M Street, N.W., Washington, D.C. 20036.

Council of State Governments (CSG), "Selling the Farm for Taxes," **State Government News**. CSG, P.O. Box 11910, Iron Works Pike, Lexington, Kentucky 40511. June 1976.

Country Women, **Newsletter**. Box 51, Albion, California 95410. $4.00/year.

Farm Journal, **Estate Planning Idea Book**. Farm Journal, Box 1927, Philadelphia, Pennsylvania 19105. 1978.

Hill, Francis, "Why Women Deserve More Opportunity in Farming," **Catholic Rural Life**. Vol. 27, No. 4, National Catholic Rural Life Conference, 3801 Grand Avenue, Des Moines, Iowa 50312. April 1978.

International Women's Year Commission, **The Legal Status of Homemakers**. Superintendent of Documents, U.S. Government Printing Office, Washington, D.C. 20402. One booklet for each state and the District of Columbia. Deals with the rights of women under state law during marriage, divorce and widowhood.

Lane, Laura, "Farm Women: You Have Fewer Rights Than You Think," **Farm Journal**. June/July 1978. Legal biases against farm women and what can be done to correct this discrimination.

Ott, Carol, "Rural Women Fight for Rights: Farm Women Lead Coalition," **Working Women**. June 1978.

Robbins, William, "Women in Agriculture Fight for Their Families and Their Farms," **New York Times**. November 14, 1977.

Rural America, **Women in Rural America**. Rural America, 1346 Connecticut Avenue, N.W., Washington, D.C. 20036. December 1977. $.50.

Rural American Women (RAW), **Newsletter**. RAW, 1522 K Street, N.W., Washington, D.C. 20005. Bi-monthly, $10.00/year, includes membership.

Salamon, Sonya and Ann Keim, "Land Ownership and Women's Power in a Midwestern Farming Community," **Journal of Marriage and Family**. To be published February 1979.

Strasser, Judy, "Farm Women: Fighting to Survive," **In These Times**. 1509 North Milwaukee Avenue, Chicago, Illinois 60622. December 21-27, 1977.

Wisconsin Legislative Council, **Major Provisions of Wisconsin and Federal Inheritance Estate and Gift Taxes**. Research Bulletin 77-1. State Capitol, Madison, Wisconsin. February 9, 1977. Text of legislation which gives women tax breaks if they have farmed with their husbands jointly.

The American Estate Tax— A Death Penalty

EXAMPLE
49

THE AMERICAN PUBLIC has begun sending loud messages to the United States Congress and the State Legislatures that there desperately needs to be some changes made in our estate or death tax laws. The American public is right. The estate tax is weary with age and no longer relates successfully to today's economy with its exemptions and rates. That is the major reason the U.S. Congress is considering proposed changes to the estate tax law. Political observers predict that this is the year the changes might happen.

ANTIREVOLUTION TAX

Some years ago when I was studying economics, and more specifically the field of taxation, I perceived that the estate or death tax system in this country was part of a grand plan in the American system to redistribute wealth. Idealistically, I thought the estate tax was an "antirevolution tax." Basic history lessons tell us that many other societies in the world have invariably had to experience violent revolutions in order to redistribute wealth when that wealth became concentrated in the hands of a few. It appeared the United States, through a system of taxing transfers of estates, was engaging in a method of redistributing concentrations of wealth peacefully through our tax system. Philosophically, that has made a lot of sense.

In 1935, President Franklin D. Roosevelt emphasized the relationship of the federal estate tax system to this concept of redistribution of wealth. According to Roosevelt:

> The desire to provide security for one's self and one's family is natural and wholesome but it is adequately served by a reasonable inheritance. Great accumulations of wealth cannot be justified on the basis of personal and family security. In the last analysis such accumulations amount to a perpetuation of great and undesirable concentration of control in a relatively few individuals over the employment and welfare of many, many others. Such inherited economic power is as inconsistent with the ideals of this generation as inherited political power was inconsistent with the ideals of the generation which established our government.

Notwithstanding these reflective thoughts expressed by President Roosevelt, the redistribution of wealth effect was only a by-product of the major reason for the initial imposition of estate taxes. In fact, estate taxes historically have been imposed and increased in order to finance war efforts by this country.

HISTORY

For example, in 1862 the first estate tax was enacted in order to help defray the cost of the Civil War. In 1870, however, a distinguished member of the U.S. House Ways and Means Committee named "Pig Iron" Kelley led the charge to abolish the estate tax. Actually, he proposed to abolish the Internal Revenue Service completely, but had to accept the death of the estate tax as a consolation prize. For the next 28 years the United States government had no federal estate tax. In 1898 another House Ways and Means Committee member, Representative Dingley, proposed an estate tax ranging to 15 percent to help finance the Spanish American War. Since 1916 the present estate tax has been part of the federal taxation system. In 1917, the estate tax rates were raised to a maximum of 25 percent to help finance World War I.

There have been a lot of minor changes in between, but in 1941 during World War II the estate tax rates were fixed from 3 percent to 77 percent and in 1942 the estate exemption was raised to $60,000. That is essentially the same estate tax that the American public now lives and dies with in 1976.

As we can see, history casts only a small shadow on the "redistribution of wealth" ideal. Nevertheless, while the estate tax has been primarily a revenue measure during times of national crises, the tax is still well grounded philosophically and can operate as a pressure relief valve to redistribute wealth through an orderly process in our society.

The fundamental problem of the estate tax in 1976 is that it's antiquated. It does not reflect today's economic realities. If the image of the estate tax was bruised yesterday because its revenue financed wars, its image is far more damaged today because we are tampering with the fundamental importance of estate taxation as a means to redistribute concentrations of great wealth. In practice the estate tax has become increasingly traumatic to the family of modest means.

We need an estate tax in this country that will prevent the transmission from generation to generation of vast fortunes by will, inheritance, or gift because such a transmission of concentrated wealth seems inconsistent with the ideals of the American people. At the same time, however, we do not want an estate tax to behave as a punitive tax that destroys the average family's ability to retain a small family farm or business. We do not want an estate tax that destroys the continuity of the economic unit owned by persons of modest means who would like to pass that heritage to either their spouse or lineal descendants.

CHANGING TIMES

Times change, and so should tax laws. Unless tax laws change with the times, that which is transcendentally true can become existentially false. A good example of this principle is the $60,000 basic exemption in the federal estate tax system. In 1942 that exemption would have allowed the transfer of a farm with well over 1,000 acres without any estate tax obligation. At that time, the size of the average farm in this country was far below 1,000 acres. Today, for example, in North Dakota the size of the average family farm is slightly over 1,000 acres and yet at today's prices the transfer of that family farming unit can and does incur a substantial estate tax obligation. The same principle is true with the moderately successful small business or, in the wage earner's case, a home and lifetime accumulation of savings or assets. In 1942 all of these could be passed on to the spouse or to a lineal descendant without estate tax liability. However, because the tax law has not changed with the times and because we have had unprecedented economic changes, particularly inflationary price level changes, now the average family farm cannot be transferred without a substantial estate tax obligation. Nor can a small business or a moderate accumulation of assets by a wage earner be transferred without an estate tax obligation.

We need to increase the estate tax exemption in our federal estate tax system in order to reflect today's economic standards. A $200,000 basic estate tax exemption that has been widely proposed is proper for all estates of farmers, businessmen, and wage earners. This would not be any substantial departure from past policy, since it would approximate and be relative to the estate tax enacted in this country in the 1940s.

In addition to increasing the basic exemption, we must study and change the estate tax rates, particularly in the low- and middle-sized estates. The rate structure, like the exemption, must change with the times or it too will effect an unplanned change in the incidence of taxation.

For example, if in 1942 a family estate had a taxable estate tax base of $30,000, that family would have paid $3,000 in estate tax or an effective taxable estate tax rate of 10 percent. If, as a result of price level increases and the decline of purchasing power of the dollar due to prolonged periods of inflation, the head of that same family would have a taxable estate of $100,000 today, then the estate tax would be $20,700 or 21 percent of the taxable estate. Although the average family unit has the same purchasing power relative to all other families in our society, it is now paying an estate tax that is several times higher than the estate tax paid by the average family 30 years ago. While the real money value of the estate might have remained approximately the same, inflation has pushed the inflated market value of the estate upward over time and pushed that estate into a higher tax bracket. This is a hypothetical case used to illustrate the effects of inflation on the incidence of the estate tax itself. A football analogy seems most appropriate here. The dollar, much like the football, is moving in value. The down markers (in this case the estate tax rates) must be moved also in order to maintain an accurate measurement at any given point in time.

CHANGING THE WIDOW TAX

Even if we raise the basic exemption and lower the tax rates, the estate tax will not have received a complete overhaul unless its reform includes recognition of a surviving widow's contribution to the family estate. The present estate tax law discriminates against women in cases where property is owned jointly by husband and wife, as it implies that a housewife makes no monetary contribution to the accumulation of a family's estate. For example, upon the death of one spouse, the law dictates that the surviving spouse must pay a death tax on the full estate (if owned jointly) unless it can be proved that he or she contributed in actual dollars to the building of that estate. A widower can easily prove contribution because he has probably earned a wage all of his adult life.

Unfortunately, a widowed housewife cannot prove contribution so easily. She is not paid a salary and, consequently, the law assumes that her contribution to the estate is without value.

We live in a decade when law after law is being changed to recognize a woman's self-worth. The estate tax law must change as well, to recognize and assume that a woman contributes to the building of an estate on an equal basis with her husband. Specifically, when property is owned jointly by a husband and wife, and the estate is passed on to the surviving spouse, one half of that estate must be automatically exempt from taxation on the presumption that the surviving spouse, whether male or female, whether wage earner or housewife, has contributed to one half of the entire estate. Any further deduction, such as the marital deduction, should be considered after this automatic division of property.

REFORM NECESSARY

As Tax Commissioner of North Dakota, I believe my State epitomizes the urgent need for estate tax reform. North Dakota is one of the most rural States in America. It is also a State with a relatively high per capita income (we rank 15th in the Nation) and our economy, while very healthy, resembles Adam Smith's description of early England, when he pictorialized the intermingling of small agricultural units amid a nation of shopkeepers. We have about 42,000 farms in North Dakota that support a large number of small towns and a lot of small merchants. We have a law in North Dakota prohibiting corporate farming and therefore the farms in North Dakota are family owned and operated and still maintain a base of support for small towns which are the hubs of economic activity for rural living. There are not many large estates that show massive accumulations of wealth in North Dakota. Most estates reflect the accumulation of the assets of a small farm, small business, or a wage earner's investments over a lifetime. In 1942 most of these accumulations would have been allowed to pass to descendants without economic interruption. Because the estate tax law has not kept pace with changing times, these estates and the economic units they represent are now being interrupted by an estate tax.

Philosophically, most Americans support the notion that an estate tax or inheritance tax could and should be used to fragment the immense collection of wealth over long periods of time in this country. However, the estate tax should not interrupt the continuity of the individual family units that make up our type of economy and should not impede the ability of average Americans to pass a modest accumulation of assets to their heirs without burdensome estate taxes.

This article is reprinted from Byron Dorgan, "The American Estate Tax—A Death Penalty," **State Government**, North Dakota, pp. 6-9, Spring 1976.

EXAMPLE 50

Nelson Bill to Eliminate the Widow's Tax

WASHINGTON, D.C., Sept. 27—The Senate Finance Committee approved a bill today that would largely eliminate the threat of the "widow's tax" and give women credit for their contribution to the family farm or small business.

Sen. Gaylord Nelson (D-Wis.), who drafted the measure, said that the widow's tax is unfair because when a man dies, an estate tax is figured on the entire value of a farm or business even though it was jointly held with his wife who contributed to its success for many years. The Internal Revenue Service (IRS) does not recognize her services and will not exempt any portion of the property from her husband's estate tax unless she can prove that she contributed monetarily to the business or farm.

"This tax is grossly unfair for the woman who has spent years working on the family farm or managing the local machine shop and then finds that after her husband dies, her contributions are not considered at all when the IRS figures the estate tax," Nelson said.

Under Nelson's proposal, a woman would get a credit of 2% for each year that she worked in the business. There-fore, a woman who worked for 25 years would be considered to own 50% of the business and the IRS would tax only her husband's half of the business. Nelson said that it would apply equally for a husband whose wife died before he did.

Nelson said that a wife who owns stock in a corporation or an interest in a partnership doesn't have a problem with the widow's tax because the business keeps a record of her contributions. However, about 11 million businesses in the U.S. are unincorporated and their owners tend to be less sophisticated and unfamiliar with the complicated estate-planning techniques that might allow them to avoid this tax.

A recent survey of the county officials of the Wisconsin Farmers' Union revealed that only about half of them had wills.

"This lack of planning plus the dramatic inflation in the value of farm lands during the last 30 years has made farm wives particularly vulnerable to the widow's tax," Nelson said. "This bill would help insure that women who work side-by-side with their husbands are not taxed for their share of the property that they have earned."

This article is reprinted from "Nelson Bill to Eliminate the Widow's Tax," News Release, U.S. Senate Select Committee on Small Business, Fall 1978.

EXAMPLE

51

FARM **Family Living**®

"We want our law to be more like the community property concept, which recognizes that both spouses contribute to estate building,"—JoAnn Vogel

By LAURA LANE

■ You have read a lot about discrimination against women in the application of Federal estate tax laws. But if you haven't looked into laws concerning the property rights of women in your own home state, "you ain't seen nothin' yet."

Many state laws and precedent-setting court cases treat a wife as a second-class citizen.

Some states treat women better than others. For instance, the 1975 amendment to the California community property law cut out most serious inequities there. But after you've said that, you have a hard time finding a runner-up in justice among the other 49 states.

This article will tell you how bad it is in many cases. But if you really want to know about your own situation, you should obtain a copy of 'The Legal Status of Homemakers" for your state, compiled by the National Commission for the Observance of International Women's Year and published by the Federal government. Find out how to order the book for your state later in this article.

Farm women...

YOU HAVE FEWER PROPERTY RIGHTS THAN YOU THINK

The antiquated view which sees a woman as a chattel of her husband is inherited from English common law. State laws treat wives as financially and legally disabled persons, because they do not recognize that the career of homemaking has any economic value. A wife "owes" her husband certain services. So, legally speaking, marriage is not a true partnership.

The author of North Dakota's "Legal Status" book puts it this way: "Until the labors of the homemaker are viewed as contributing equally to the growth of the family resources, a homemaker may always be one man away from economic ruin." Widowed or divorced women are most vulnerable.

"No woman achieves economic security when she marries because of the law; her economic condition reflects her husband's generosity and her own efforts," writes the author of the Missouri book. Statutes governing property rights of married women are like a patchwork quilt—a crazy quilt is more like it. But there are some patterns.

In the 42 "common law" states, generally, property acquired by either spouse during marriage belongs to the one who paid for it. In farming that's usually the husband, unless the wife has an off-farm job or independent wealth. But consider these situations:

What if a farmer in a common law state puts property in joint ownership or in his wife's name? Then he has, legally speaking, made a gift to his wife. The law does not recognize any financial value for the wife's contribution or labor or of homemaking skills—only of her contribution of money.

What if a farm wife's name is on the mortgage? She is equally liable for the debt, even if the title to the farm is in her husband's name and she has no ownership interest.

Individual ownership is determined by whose name is on the record of title. If your husband bought property with your money, but kept it in his name alone, it's his under common law property rules.

To protect her personal property from sale by her husband without her consent, or from seizure by his creditors, a married woman in Arkansas must file a schedule of her separate property with the county recorder. If she does not, she must prove that she bought the property with her separate money.

In Georgia, a couple's house belongs only to the husband, even if the wife earns the wages, supports the husband and pays for the dwelling. He can sell it or burn it down, and she can do nothing about it.

"In Wisconsin, personal property is considered to be solely owned by the husband, while real property can be owned jointly. That is, if the husband 'gives' half to the wife and pays gift tax, or if she can show financial contribution," says dairy wife JoAnn Vogel. Personal property means cars, tractors, cattle, hay, grain—anything but land or buildings, which are real property. "I cannot see how the law can make such a distinction. I don't work all Monday to pay for the real property and stop working Tuesday because we are now working to pay for personal property," she declares.

A farm woman in Iowa literally ran the farm for 18 years during which her elderly husband was physically disabled, but the court held that all the income and acquisitions of the farm during that period were the property of the husband.

Though the law in Pennsylvania permits a woman to keep her own earnings, in order to she must present a petition to the court. But most women do not follow that legal procedure unless their right to retain their earnings is challenged.

"Under Iowa law, both spouses are liable for the reasonable and necessary expenses of the family. This law is most often used against women whose husbands have made purchases and either refuse to pay for them or have no funds. The wife's property has been taken to pay for such 'necessaries' as an organ, gold watch, piano and diamond studs purchased by a husband as a gift to himself," according to the Iowa book. Missouri law permits the husband to retain for himself all that he accumulates.

Can a woman contract with her husband for adequate compensation for homemaking, which is generally considered "free?" Not in all states.

In an Iowa case, the court ruled that "a wife's 20 years of work on a farm, plus her investment of her inheritance into improvements on the house were inadequate to support an agreement that she and her husband would will all the property to the survivor." A husband can even disinherit his wife in some states. In most states, however, the law specifically provides a minimum inheritance for the wife, called a "forced share."

Usually, the inheritance is determined by whether the husband left a will. Under Mississippi law, if a husband leaves no will and there are children, all equally divide the estate after debts are paid. So if there are five children and a widow, she gets a sixth. In Illinois and Ohio, the wife would get a third and

all children would divide the remaining two-thirds.

There's a pattern in community property states, too. But the pattern comes from Spain and France, not England. Community property states are: California, Arizona, Idaho, Louisiana, Nevada, New Mexico, Texas and Washington.

"Briefly, the law recognizes that the husband and wife make up a community and that the labors of both are required to make it function. The earnings and income during marriage are usually community property and belong to both in equal degrees." —Nevada "Legal Status . . ."

But there are qualifications: Louisiana law designates the husband as "head and master of community property with total control." This means everything a farm wife works for, including a home, can be sold without her knowledge or consent. Her earnings belong to her husband. She has no legal means to learn the extent of community property without suing for separation or divorce.

And both spouses need to keep separate property of each distinct from community property, preferably recorded with the county clerk.

How can you protect yourself as a wife?
1. Find out about your legal status by buying "The Legal Status of Homemakers" book for your state. You can order a copy from FARM JOURNAL. Send $1.25 plus 50¢ postage and handling for each copy you want to "Legal Status of Homemakers," FARM JOURNAL, Box 1676, Philadelphia, Pa. 19105. Tell us what state or states you want.
2. Urge state legislatures to change laws which discriminate against women in reality if not in so many words.
3. Work for the Equal Rights Amendment.
4. Insist on knowing the nature and extent of family holdings and debts.
5. Get credit cards in the wife's name as well as the husband's. Arrange for the wife to borrow for some big-ticket item. That way she gets a credit rating of her own.
6. Have His and Her safe deposit boxes.
7. Check with your nearest Social Security office on what a wife's rights are regarding benefits.
8. Keep diaries and other documentation showing the wife's financial and labor contribution to the business.
9. Consider your capabilities. The Montana book on the "Legal Status of Homemakers" suggests: "Even married women who have no immediate financial need to support their families should be asking themselves: If I suddenly had to support myself, for what kind of jobs would I be qualified. Are those jobs the kind I would like to do?" Also, consider how would you get necessary training, skills and credentials.

The role of farm wife and homemaker, valuable as it is, does not offer any guarantee of economic security for women.   ◁

This article is reprinted from Laura Lane, "Farm Women . . . You Have Fewer Property Rights Than You Think," Farm Journal, pp. 35-36, June/July 1978.

Lucey Signs Inheritance Tax Reform Measure

EXAMPLE
52

Dodgeville — Gov. Patrick J. Lucey April 29, signed legislation authorizing a $1.6 million annual inheritance tax break mainly benefiting Wisconsin women who help build their families' farms, homes and businesses.

The legislation (SB 113) "gives overdue recognition to the contributions of Wisconsin women to family enterprises," Lucey said in signing the measure.

Although the bill provides up to a 50 per cent inheritance tax exemption for all surviving joint tenants, women who are joint tenants with their husbands are more likely to benefit because they generally outlive men, Lucey said.

The Revenue Department estimates that each year the new law will benefit about 9,800 widows who are the sole survivors of joint tenancy ownership. Jointly held tenancies involving more than one survivor also would be eligible for a tax break, Lucey added.

The signing ceremony was held at the historic Iowa County Courthouse, built in 1858 and the oldest Wisconsin county courthouse currently in use. Iowa County, Lucey noted, was a center of support for the tax reform legislation, with much of the interest generated by family farmers and farm wives.

"It is appropriate that this historic legislation — designed to save family farms — is signed in Iowa county, which was settled by determined families and family farmers nearly 200 years ago," Lucey added.

"But it is even more significant that the real spark for this legislation was provided by Wisconsin's first woman state senator, Sen. Kathryn Morrison, who worked so hard to achieve this bill's passage."

Morrison, a Platteville Democrat, was joined at the ceremony by Rep. Mary Lou Munts, D-Madison, and Rep. Joanne Duren, D-Cazenovia, also strong supporters of the measure. Farm wives, cooperative leaders, local officials and others also attended.

Recognizes Contributions

The bill, which recognizes the contributions to the estate by both men and women, covers all forms of property, including small businesses, stock certificates and homes. "But, the main benefactors are the farm women who work day and night without pay to build their family enterprises," Lucey said.

In the past, contributions to the estate of time and labor, which women made in lieu of financial contributions, were not fully recognized in determining interest in the estate, Lucey said.

In addition to the 50 per cent allowance, a fixed monetary exemption, established by previous law, will be subtracted from the estate's value for tax purposes.

Example

For example, a woman who helped operate a $200,000 farm or small business with her husband would, upon settlement of her deceased husband's estate, receive a 50 per cent deduction of $100,000 and an automatic $50,000 exemption, leaving $50,000 of taxable property.

That $50,000, however, would be taxed at the same rate accorded for the property's full value tax bracket.

Exemption Varies

The automatic exemption varies, depending on the relation to the deceased.

The new legislation replaces past law which required that the surviving spouse prove contribution "in money or money's worth" to the estate's value in order to qualify for an automatic exemption.

Under the new law, no proof of contribution is needed to be eligible for the exemptions.

"It's ludicrous to penalize women simply because they cannot show their names on credit slips or on mortgage agreements," Lucey said of past practices and law. "The contributions made by women in family farming or women in family business are often those that cannot be given a monetary value."

Increasing Farm Values

But, Lucey also noted that the new law was especially important in light of increasing farm values, which sometimes are so high that the resulting exorbitant inheritance taxes force sale of the family property.

For example, Lucey cited figures from the State Agriculture Department showing that the average value per acre on a Wisconsin farm in 1960 jumped from $133 to $232 in 1970 and to $451 in 1975.

During the same years, the average value of land and buildings per farm (excluding the value of livestock, machinery and equipment) jumped from $21,700 in 1960 to $41,700 in 1970 and $84,700 in 1975.

Other Changes

The measure also makes changes in current tax laws concerning gifts. Under the new provisions, a transfer of real property must be reported as a gift when less than equal financial contribution is made by either spouse.

But, a grace period of almost two years will be provided to allow husbands or wives to decide whether they will treat acquisitions of real property as gifts.

The measure also establishes a study committee attached to the Legislative Council to review remaining problems with the inheritance and gift taxes and to report to the 1977 Legislature.

Four members of the nine-member study committee will be legislators and five will be public members. The public members will be the secretary of revenue or his designee, two will be appointees of the governor, and two appointees of the Legislative Council.

This article is reprinted from "Lucey Signs Inheritance Tax Reform Measure," Wisconsin Farmers Union News, p. 1, May 17, 1976.

EXAMPLE 53

Law Change Avoids Double Taxation

Jointly-held property is often intended as a symbol of the equality and sharing of a marriage. But it can cause economic problems to the very family that it intended to unify.

This was the situation in Wisconsin until Sen. Kathryn Morrison (D-Platteville) spearheaded passage of Chap. 222 in the last legislative session.

Until last July, jointly-held property has been taxed in the same manner by Wisconsin for inheritance tax purposes, and by the Federal government for estate tax purposes.

Property was included in-full in the estate of the first joint tenant–unless the survivor could prove a level of contribution to the property in question. Then it passed to the survivor by the law of tenancy, and was included in-full in the estate of the second. Result was double taxation.

Realizing this inequity for the farmwife in particular, Sen. Morrison sought to have Wisconsin law changed so that at the death of the first spouse, half of the value of the property would be taxed–regardless of whether or not there was a proof of contribution. Then the property would still pass to the surviving tenant, and would be taxed in full at the second death.

But double taxation would be avoided. Chapter 222, Laws of 1975, accomplishes this for estates of decedents dying on or after July 1, 1976.

This change affects all joint tenancies, not just husband and wife tenancies. For example, if there were three joint tenants, and one died, one-third of the value of the property would be used in the computations for inheritance tax purposes.

Property included under the new law is all real property. And tangible property such as an auto, livestock, and farm machinery. And intangible property such as stocks, bonds, and bank accounts.

One exception to the law revolves around intangible property. Checking and savings accounts in banks, savings and loan institutions and credits unions, and U.S. savings bonds will be taxed based on the amount the decedent contributed to the acquisition price. That is if there was no taxable gift when the tenancy was created.

Recent Tax Reform Act by the Federal government also somewhat changes the estate tax status of jointly-held property. But unlike the Wisconsin law, it does not admit that the proof of contribution necessity is discriminatory against wives. It only creates a new method to circumvent it.

For Federal estate tax purposes after Dec. 31, 1976, jointly-held property will also be automatically divided into equal parts at death if it is "qualified property." To "qualify," the tenancy must be set up after Dec. 31 of this year.

Personal property must have been a completed gift for gift tax purposes at the time of creation. Real property must have been treated as a taxable event at the time the joint tenancy is established. Gift tax liability so created will be under the new rates. These are now equal to the estate tax rates.

There are also exceptions to this treatment. Obviously, all tenancies that were set up before Dec. 31 are not included. Also exempt are many joint bank accounts in which either co-tenant can withdraw the entire sum without consent of the other. The exceptions are treated just as all joint property previously was–by using the proof of contribution method.

It may well make good sense for many individuals to consider terminating existing joint tenancies after the first of next year, and re-creating them. By doing so, and if no level of contribution on the part of one spouse can be proven, a gift tax liability would be created. However, the recent law has revised the marital deduction on gifts making it far more favorable for gift amounts under $200,000.

Previously, the marital deduction on gifts was 50% of the amount gifted. Now it will be the full amount up to $100,000. Then there will be no marital deduction between $100,000 and $200,000. After $200,000 the 50% formula again applies. So for gifts in excess of $200,000, there has been no change. But for gifts less than that, there has been a substantial improvement.

If a joint tenancy is severed after Dec. 31 and then re-created, a gift tax liability will be incurred to be offset by this marital deduction. In this manner, a piece of jointly-held property with value up to $200,000 could be severed and re-created without paying a gift tax. And then the property would qualify for the new favorable estate tax treatment at death, such as it will have in Wisconsin for inheritance tax purposes.

If a level of contribution could be proven for the spouse, property valued at more than $200,000 could be so severed and re-created without incurring a tax.

Despite the changes, there are still other good reasons for some people not to own property jointly. If you have a marital trust provision within your will and own a good deal of property jointly, you can over qualify your marital trust. Then you lose some of the savings of that vehicle. Testamentary control is lost for assets so held as they pass outside of any will or trust plan.

Simultaneous death of both spouses can cause problems if a common disaster clause does not affect joint property. In some cases, joint property can cause additional income taxes when depreciable property is involved or in the sale or exchange of individually held property for jointly-held property. That is why, as in all estate planning situations, you should consult with your own advisors.

Example illustrates the potential savings

(Assume wife has contributed 10%.)

Old Law		New Law
$ 0	Amount of joint property qualifying for new treatment	$240,000
$250,000	Joint property not qualifying (intangible under new law; all property under old)	10,000
$250,000	Sub-total	$250,000
$ 25,000	Less exclusion by wife for contribution	1,000
$225,000	Total	$249,000
$ 0	Less: exemption for fractional shares	120,000
50,000	Less: spouse exemption	50,000
$175,000	Amount subject to tax	$79,000
$ 8,125	Inheritance tax	$3,950

This article is reprinted from Betty J. Harris and Basil S. Holder, "Law Change Avoids Double Taxation," **Wisconsin Agriculturalist**, Madison, Wisconsin, December 1976.

ERA and State Property Laws

EXAMPLE 54

Some people are saying . . .

that the Equal Rights Amendment will deprive widows of tax, property, and homestead benefits

TRUE ☐   NOT TRUE ☐

not true . . .

. . . and not only not true but preferential treatment for widows in many states does not exist as the case of Mary Heath, a widow in Cody, Neb. illustrates.

"I worked along-side my husband, Floyd, for 33 years. Together, we'd built up a ranch of 3,400 acres and 120 cows.

"I'd done everything on the ranch, feeding the pigs, milking the cows, driving the tractor. Two years before he died, Floyd was all crippled up so I had to do everything, with the two boys who were still in school. Never did have any help at home either. What was done, I did, although I won't say I had time to be a very good housekeeper.

"Then Floyd died in 1974, and I found out I had to pay $23,000 in inheritance tax for my own ranch. We were already in debt about $40,000 and it's getting worse. I still don't know what's going to happen. If I had died instead of Floyd, he wouldn't have had to pay any tax.

"They told me because I didn't make any monetary contribution to the ranch, I have to pay this inheritance tax. I used to believe what belonged to the husband belonged to the wife, too. I had a few cattle myself and my dad built our house for us, but I never got any credit for that. And I didn't get any credit for my work on the ranch all those years. If I chose to work on the ranch, why should that be worth less than going to town and getting a job?

"And it's not just me. Three of my friends here in Cody had to sell their farms when their husbands died because they just didn't have the money to pay the tax."

The past president of women lawyers says . . .

"The laws of 42 states say that the one who earns a salary is the one who owns the property acquired in a marriage. The homemaker, having no earnings of her own, therefore, has no ownership in that property. If her husband dies without a will, she may be penniless.

"For example, where husband and wife own farm land, even jointly, estate tax laws penalize a widow. Since the law makes the husband sole owner, estate taxes at his death will be measured

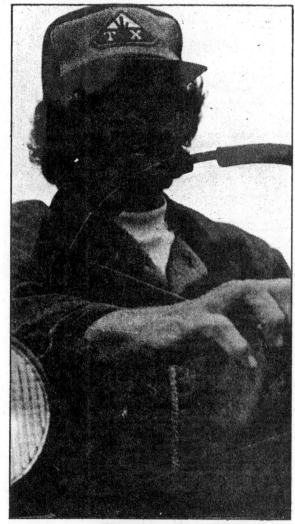

Widow Mary Heath struggles to save her farm as state seeks $23,000 in inheritance tax.

by the whole value and the widow receives only what is left after payment of taxes. She may have to sell all or part of the property to pay the tax.

"On the other hand, if the wife dies first, since no value is placed on her services, the husband does not have to pay any inheritance tax.

"In the eight states which have community property laws, husband and wife each own half of the property acquired during marriage, even though the wife may have no outside earnings. But four of these states still give the husband, and not the wife, the management rights, enabling him to create debts and sell the property without the knowledge or consent of his wife."

Marguerite Rawalt, past president
National Association of Women Lawyers

This article is reprinted from Marguerite Rawalt, "ERA and State Property Laws," Common Cause, p. 5, 1978.

EXAMPLE 55

Why Women Deserve More Opportunity in Farming

By Frances Hill

"Farmer" is a male noun to most Americans. Women have found increased opportunities for meaningful and rewarding careers in many sectors of the economy but not in agriculture.

Women held 17 percent of non-farm administrator and manager positions by 1970 and 40 percent of the nation's professional and technical personnel were women. But only about four percent of all farmers and farm managers were women. The number of women listed in the Census as "farmers and farm managers" declined from a high of almost 308,000 in 1900 to only 63,000 in 1970.

During this period, of course, the number of farms and the number of male "farmers and farm managers" also declined. However the number of male farmers declined by a small percentage from a larger initial number. Women have sought greater economic opportunity the past 15 years, not simply as

> **'Modern farm women take pride in their ability to keep the books, drive tractors, and care for livestock. They resent the suggestion that men farm and women only help'**

wives but as independent economic actors. Why hasn't agriculture provided opportunities for such women?

One common assumption is that women simply do not want to farm. My research among Midwest farm women, married and single, suggests that many women have a keen interest in agriculture. To the surprise of the Extension Service, women have flocked to programs on dairy production and herd improvement once they were invited to attend. What some see as a lack of interest in agriculture may instead be lack of opportunity.

A second reason for the limited number of women in agriculture is the idea that members of the "weaker sex" are too delicate for the physical demands of farming. Current research on physiology and the historical role of women on American farms questions this idea. Whether married or single, American women have always been welcome to "help" with the farm work.

Abigail Adams ran the family's farm while her husband, John tried to run the country.

Frontiersmen settled their wives and children on a farm while they roamed further west in search of opportunity, adventure, and amusement.

Modern farm women take pride in their ability to keep the books, drive tractors, and care for livestock. They resent the suggestion that men "farm" and women only "help." If the Department of Agriculture would begin collecting data on women's as well as men's contributions to farm labor and management, these basic realities of the "family farm" would be more widely recognized.

The hypocrisy of the idea that women are too delicate to farm is suggested by the 141,000 women the Census included in its "farm laborers and farm foremen" category in 1970. This total actually is higher due to the presence of large numbers of undocumented workers in American fields.

Official estimates indicate women currently account for 15 percent of agricultural laborers. In 1910 there were 1.5 million women farm laborers, which was 25 percent of the total farm labor force. This does not include wives, who have always been expected to donate their energy to their family and to the family farm.

Women have worked on farms but that work has been "hidden from history" by a screen of cultural myths about female delicacy and male gallantry. Historical data suggest that chivalry consisted of relieving women of the burden of owning and controlling property, not in freeing them from labor. Discounting the possibility that owning a farm would be more physically taxing than working on one, the reasons that there are few independent women farmers are the same as the reasons there are still few women professors or astronauts or independent businesspersons or bank presidents. Women have been denied the right to control the enterprises on which they have toiled.

A third reason, then, for the limited opportunities open to women in agriculture has been the limited credit available to women. Discrimination against women in granting credit did not become illegal until 1976. Women were always more than welcome to co-sign the mortgage but not to own the property, as farm women have begun to realize when confronting the estate tax laws.

Systematic data on loan application and the rate of approval for single women is not available. Most bankers or Farmers Home Administration directors or Production Credit Association managers will say that they do not discriminate against women. Those few women who have managed to establish their own farming operations agree. However, no one has yet studied women who were rejected for credit or women who wanted to farm but were discouraged in other ways. Most people I interviewed agree there is skepticism, at the very least, about a woman who wants to farm on her own.

Two factors suggest that more women may successfully seek to establish their own farms in the future. First, the agricultural colleges have, during the past three to four years, admitted a significant number of young women to production-related courses. These women will have proved that they are both competent and serious. Second, the struggle by farm women for change in the inheritance tax laws already means more widows are able to keep their farms and farms and that young widows will be able to make careers as independent farmers. Their example may make it easier for single women to enter farming.

This article is reprinted from Francis Hill, "Why Women Deserve More Opportunity in Farming," Catholic Rural Life, pp. 8-10, April 1978.

Section V

Section V

Building Urban and Consumer Food Policies

Inflation—particularly of food and shelter costs—hits everyone, especially the poor and those in lower-middle income brackets. Prices are higher for city dwellers than for suburbanites. This, along with the urban problems of poor food outlets and poor nutrition, contributes to the feeling among many consumers that the food system is beyond their control.

Federal, state and local policy makers are making attempts to solve urban and consumer food problems, but many efforts lack coordination and cooperation with the consumers who are beginning to find that, by working together, they can cut the cost of their food and improve its nutritional quality.

Cities and states have the best opportunities to coordinate efforts with the urban consumer toward building a constructive urban/consumer food policy. City governments can change policy relating to funding, access to land, neighborhood revitalization, sanitation and health codes, administration, and channels of citizen feedback and its implementation. States, in turn, can upgrade the quality of their administration of federal food programs and funding, which too often have not reached their potential to meet the needs of eligible participants. And finally, the federal government programs need to incorporate the ideas behind local initiatives rather than starting new programs that may not take their input into consideration, and thus may not reach the people that they are intended to help.

The most innovative urban and consumer food policy projects are taking place at the local level, pushed by private citizens and grassroots organizations. Chapter 13, *Alternative Marketing and Retailing Opportunities*, outlines new food delivery systems, the revival of farmers' markets, food co-ops, and financial resources for these projects. Chapter 14, *Growing Food in the City*, looks at consumer participation in the food system through gardening, greenhouses, composting, local food processing, and solving land access problems. Chapter 15, *Innovative Food and Nutrition Policies*, covers federal food programs that are executed by states and localities such as the food stamp and school meal programs, as well as creative nutrition-related projects: gleaning or food-salvage efforts, programs combining gardening and nutrition education, and mobile nutrition units.

Chapter 13

Alternative Marketing and Retailing Opportunities

Soaring food prices have caused countless neighborhood and community-based groups to organize around ways to lower the cost of food. Low income families and citizens on fixed incomes are now spending close to 33% of their annual incomes on food. At the same time the retail food industry has initiated a trend of moving chain supermarkets out of the inner-city neighborhoods to suburban communities where profit margins are higher. Finally, the nutritional quality of food available in many urban communities is deteriorating.

People in hundreds of cities and towns across the country are working to build alternative marketing and retailing systems. 94% of the rise in food prices between 1954 and 1974 resulted from costs added by retail food corporations, processors, packagers and long distance transportation. Community groups are attempting to narrow the gaps between farmers markets and other direct marketing opportunities. Other organizations are establishing food buying clubs and cooperative food stores.

In *The Problem of High Food Costs in the Inner Cities*,[1] Steven Haberfeld discusses in detail the complex situation that faces the low-income consumer. The higher cost of food correlates with the higher costs of doing business. First, the smaller stores are the majority of the stores remaining in inner city neighborhoods; and that means no bulk buying, poorer management, extension of customer credit and cashflow shortages. In addition, the exodus of stores has decreased the tax base causing the tax burden to fall on the remaining stores. Secondly, the larger chain markets are leaving to serve suburban customers. Reasons for this exodus are: little money, a lower turnover rate, food stamp sales creating additional administrative costs, inexperienced employees, outdated or inadequate facilities, and poor neighborhood environment. Finally, the supermarket chains do not have the experience of the smaller, locally-based Mom and Pop stores that offer merchandise the inner city customers want: (Ethnic and black groups' preference for exotic fruits, canned and dried goods and meats, for example).

Many cities are looking at a creative approach to solving the problem of rising food costs in urban neighborhoods. Alternative food delivery systems are being proposed and implemented on several levels. Food delivery systems include buying clubs; food cooperatives; farmers markets and co-op warehouses. Many of these local initiatives take advantage of locally grown produce that is often of a higher quality and lower cost; such programs also benefit local farmers.

FARMERS' MARKETS

The most popular marketing alternative initiated by neighborhood groups and city governments is the revival of farmers' markets. There are several social and economic factors that contributed to the decline of the farmers' markets: increased centralization and long distance transportation and refrigeration techniques in the food industry; the urbanization of farmland surrounding American cities; the rapid rise of chain supermarkets and the disintegration of urban neighborhoods; and the rigid enforcement of municipal and federal health regulations. With the recent movement to revitalize inner city neighborhoods, farmers' markets are playing an exciting role in providing fresh produce at affordable costs, and at the same time they are bringing farmers and consumers closer together.

In October 1976, Congress enacted the *Farmer-to-Consumer Direct Marketing Act*; Public Law 94-463. The Act was passed with the hope that direct marketing activity would lower food prices, provide higher returns for farmers, reduce middle man costs, and improve farmer-to-consumer relations. So far, approximately 2 million dollars have been made available through grants to 23 State Cooperation Service Offices. Several cities have initiated or supported innovative farmers market projects. Good examples of programs intended to bring family farm producers and low-income consumers together in an inner city market are those of Savannah, Georgia and Charleston, South Carolina. Both projects are to establish farmers markets and to organize limited-resource farmers from surrounding counties of their respective areas. Unfortunately, the Direct Marketing Act, which has a good two-year track record in assisting the establishment of marketing alternatives, was not reappropriated in October 1978. Plans are to reinstate the program early in the 1979 Congressional session.

The Farmer-to-Consumer Direct Marketing Act had also assisted the existing farmers' market network in cities like New York. For over two years the Greenmarket, a locally run and operated retail farmers' market, has provided produce seasonally from area farmers to five different locations. The program works in cooperation with the city concerning site and sanitation permits. More information on the project is illustrated in **Example 56, Greenmarkets**. The New York State Department of Agriculture and Markets has set up a Farmer-to-Consumer Direct Marketing Center. They work with groups throughout New York State like Greenmarkets in offering workshops, technical assistance and financial resources. Even though the Federal Act has not yet been reinstated, the New York State Department of Agriculture and Markets is committed to seeing farmer-to-consumer direct marketing continue through providing supplementary state funds.

Another exciting effort to revive farmers' markets is underway in Boston. Here local and state governments are working together to lower food prices in a state where over 85% of the food is imported and the cost of food is 10% above the national average (due to the cost of transportation). A newsletter, *The Stalk Exchange*, is spreading information to individuals and organizations as well as farmers from the area about future farmers' market sites in the city. This effort is supported by the Division of Land Use in the State Department of Agriculture; the Massachusetts Federation of Farmers' Markets; the Suffolk County Extension Service, and State Representative Mel King's 1974 *Farm and Gardening Act*. (See **Example 69, The Politics of Food in Massachusetts, Growing Our Own** in Chapter 17.)

In Seattle, a very unique coalition of farmers, buyers from restaurants, retailers, food co-ops and buying clubs have been brought together through the Bulk Commodities Exchange. This non-profit corporation is assisted by the Hunger Action Center, Pike Place Preservation and Development Authority, Metrocenter, and the King County Office of Agriculture. A brochure, **Example 57, Bulk Commodities Exchange**, discusses this market as well as future plans to use Community Development Block Grant funds to develop an integrated food system.

Other cities throughout the country are expanding and/or initiating farmers' markets; examples are Honolulu, Chicago, Washington, D.C., and Hartford, Connecticut. (The Hartford Farmers' Market is discussed in more detail in Chapter 17, *Comprehensive City Food Plans*.)

FOOD CO-OPS

Another alternative consumers have is the food cooperative or buying club. A food co-op usually is a group of neighborhood citizens who gather to buy food in bulk from wholesalers at reduced prices. The food co-op movement grew rapidly in the early 1960s in major cities like Boston, Atlanta, New York, San Francisco, Minneapolis-St. Paul, and Chicago. Many food co-ops have grown to own their own store fronts and expanded to open other stores.

Many food co-ops are located in relatively wealthy or co-op-experienced neighborhoods, but Chicago has the unique example of a network of co-ops involving low-income residents. The Self Help Action Center (SHAC) is an organization that has assisted over 300 co-ops in getting started. SHAC has 35 constituent co-ops with approximately 7,860 household members. The organization estimates that the co-op member saves 30¢ on every food dollar in winter and 50-60¢ in the summer. In addition, the Center provides nutrition education classes, and is starting to build a greenhouse next to their recently purchased headquarters. (The greenhouse project is discussed further in Chapter 14, Growing Food in the City.)

Many people are interested in getting involved in a food co-op. Questions are asked: How to organize? How to manage? How to finance? Food co-ops are learning invaluable lessons from their day to day, month to month, year to year operations. Technical assistance is being sought from individuals, particularly those consumers located in the inner city neighborhoods. In California, for example, existing food co-ops are offering assistance to newly formed co-ops. In New Haven, Connecticut, the New Haven Food Co-op, which occupies an old A&P in a racially and ethnically mixed neighborhood, is looking to offer technical assistance/training workshops to future co-ops throughout New England.

NATIONAL CONSUMER COOPERATIVE BANK ACT

As discussed earlier, consumers are looking for new sources of financing for ventures like food co-ops and other alternative food delivery systems. On August 20, 1978, the *National Consumer Cooperative Bank Act* was passed by Congress. There is a growing cooperative movement consisting of over 1,000 food co-ops with a membership of approximately 1.2 million consumers. Even though there is growing public support for co-ops, legislation for the new finance source had opposition, particularly from the small business groups that see co-ops as competition on the economic front. **Example 58, The Co-op Bank: New Funds for Community Development** includes the history, a summary and the implementation procedures of the future bank. The funding possibilities related to food projects include cooperative farming ventures, direct marketing, consumer education, buying clubs, food supermarkets, urban agriculture and community gardens.

MICHIGAN PUBLIC ACT NO. 331 OF 1975

In January 1975, Michigan enacted Public Act No. 331 which requires the Office of Services to the Aging (OSA) to work with local organizations in developing various types of alternative food delivery systems for senior citizens. Areas being considered are food buying clubs, food cooperatives, community garden projects, direct purchasing of farm produce, and mobile markets. Eight cooperatives are under way with greenhouses planned for the near future. Michigan is one state supporting localities in implementing alternative food distribution systems. **Example 59, Michigan Public Act 331 of 1975,** is reprinted at the end of this chapter.

CONCLUSION

Consumers and farmers are building coalitions to find solutions to the problem of rising food costs as well as attempting to create a better understanding of their respective problems. It is crucial that state and local governments support these grassroots efforts to build viable alternative marketing and retailing systems which provide nutritious food at affordable costs to the American people.

[1]Haberfeld, Steven, "The Problem of High Food Costs in the Inner Cities," **Economic Development Law Project Reporter,** pp. 26-31, September/October 1977.

Resources

ORGANIZATIONS

Agricultural Marketing Project

2606 Westwood Drive
Nashville, Tennessee 37204
(615) 297-4088
Lindsay Jones, John Vlcek, Laurie Heise

Boston Farmers' Markets

Division of Land Use
Massachusetts Department of Food and Agriculture
100 Cambridge Street
Boston, Massachusetts 02202
(617) 727-6633
Elischen Toney

Coop Bank Monitoring Assistance Project

2000 Florida Avenue, N.W.
Washington, D.C. 20009
(202) 387-6030
Lee Webb, Chuck Savitt

Green Markets

24 West 40th Street
New York, New York 10018
(212) 840-7355
Barry Benepe

Hartford Food Systems, Inc.

c/o ConnPIRG
30 High Street (#108)
Hartford, Connecticut 06103
(203) 525-8312
Sally Taylor

North Carolina Agricultural Marketing Project

P.O. Box 12141
Raleigh, North Carolina 27605
(919) 828-1107
Dale Evarts

Pike Place Market Preservation and Development Authority

85 Pike Street
Room 500
Seattle, Washington 98101
(206) 625-4764
Frankie Whitman

BIBLIOGRAPHY

Agricultural Marketing Project (AMP), **Marketing Report on Food Fairs.** AMP, Center for Health Services, Vanderbilt Medical Center, Nashville, Tennessee 37232. 1977. $5.00. On Farmers markets.

Anderson, Dale, "Problems in Delivering Food to Low Income Urban Areas," **Journal of Food Distribution Research.** Vol. 11, No. 2. Food Distribution Research Society, Incorporated. Box 1795, Hyattsville, Maryland 20788. September 1971.

Benepe, Barry, **Greenmarket: The Rebirth of Farmers' Markets in New York City.** Council on the Environment of New York City, 51 Chambers Street, New York, New York 10007.

Bowler, Deborah, **Farmers' Market Organizer's Handbook.** Hunger Action Center, Evergreen College, Olympia, Washington 98505. 1976. $1.00.

Center for Science in the Public Interest (CSPI), **From the Ground Up: Building a Grass Roots Food Policy.** CSPI, 1755 S Street, N.W., Washington, D.C. 20009. 1976. $2.50.

City of Hartford, **A Strategy To Reduce the Cost of Food for Hartford Residents.** Jack Hale, Conn-PIRG, 248 Farmington Avenue, Hartford, Connecticut 06105. 1978. $3.50.

Cotterill, Ronald, David Freshwater and David Houseman, **More Effective Direct Marketing: A Proposal to Establish an Inner-City Farmer-Consumer Warehouse in Detroit, Michigan.** Agricultural Economics Department, Staff Paper #77-101, Michigan State University, East Lansing, Michigan. December 1977.

Council of State Governments (CSG), **Merging Producer and Consumer Interests.** CSG, Iron Works Pike, Lexington, Kentucky 40511. $3.75. Direct Marketing in New York and Pennsylvania.

Department of Community Affairs of the Commonwealth of Massachusetts, **Organizer's Guide for Setting Up an Open Air Farmers' Market.** Food Resource Coordinator, Division of Social and Economic Opportunity, Department of Community Affairs, 10 Fremont Street, Boston, Massachusetts 02108.

Drewry, Virginia, "From Buying Clubs to Regional Networks," **Self-Reliance.** Institute for Local Self-Reliance, 1717 18th Street, N.W., Washington, D.C. 20009.

Economics, Statistics, and Cooperative Service (ESCS), **Market Structure of the Food Industries.** Marketing Research Report No. 971, ESCS, USDA, Washington, D.C. 20250. September 1972.

Evans, Ann, **Food Co-op Bibliography and Guide.** Division of Consumer Affairs, 1021 O Street, Sacramento, California 95818.

Food Co-op Directory. c/o Wild R. Turkey, 106 Girard S.E., Albuquerque, New Mexico 87106.

Food Distribution Research Society, Incorporated, **Quarterly Newsletter.** Food Distribution Research Society, Incorporated, Box 1795, Hyattsville, Maryland 20788.

Goldstein, Jerome, ed., **The New Food Chain: An Organic Link Between Farm and City.** Rodale Press, Incorporated, Book Division, Emmaus, Pennsylvania 18049. Articles on the complementarity of the rural and urban sectors.

Hampshire Community Canning Center, **1976 Annual Report.** Hampshire Community Canning Center, 33 King Street, Northhampton, Massachusetts 01060. March 1977. Description of cannery initially funded by CETA.

Kay, Alan, et al., "The Food Business and the Consumer," **The New Haven Advocate**. Vol. 11, No. 35, New Haven, Connecticut. April 20, 1977. Four articles on negative trends in marketing in New Haven and promising alternatives.

National Consumer Cooperative Bank Act, HR 2777. Available from Conference on Alternative State and Local Policies, 1901 Q Street, N.W., Washington, D.C. 20009.

Smith, Frank, **Food in the City**. Public Resource Center, 1747 Connecticut Avenue, N.W., Washington, D.C. 20009. 1977. $3.00.

Toothman, James S., and Harold S. Ricker, **An Analysis of Small Food Store Supply Systems**. Bulletin 809, Pennsylvania State University Agricultural Experiment Station, University Park, Pennsylvania 16802. June 1976.

U.S. Senate, Subcommittee on Agricultural Production, Marketing and Stabilization of Prices, **Marketing Alternatives for Agriculture: Is There a Better Way?** Superintendent of Documents, U.S. Government Printing Office, Washington, D.C. 20402. November 1976. Examination of policy alternatives to present marketing system.

Vellela, Tony, **Food Co-ops for Small Groups**. Workman Publishing Company, 231 East 1st Street, New York, New York 10022. 1975. $2.95.

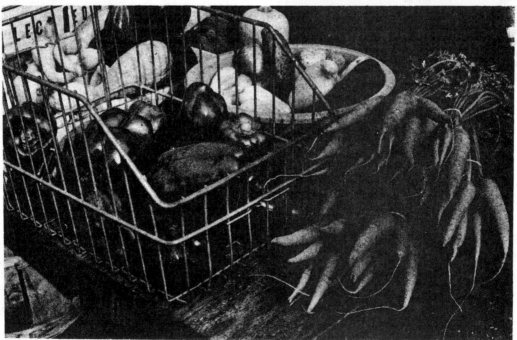

Greenmarket

EXAMPLE 56

The Future of Greenmarket

Greenmarket has already accomplished much of what it set out to do. It has brought food fresh from the farms which most agree is tastier and cheaper than the usual produce. Corn is sweeter and juicier than that available elsewhere. Tomatoes are also juicier, larger and redder. The contact between farmers and residents is warm and friendly, much to the surprise and pleasure of both. An oasis has been created in the city, that brings the rich taste, odor, and feel of the countryside. While only time and future research will tell, early indications are that farmers have also improved their position. It is also hoped that the markets will stimulate the growth of new farms and urban gardens close to and within the city. Vast areas of rubble covering the Bronx and Brooklyn are even now benefiting from an urban gardening program made possible through an appropriation obtained by Congressman Fred Richmond of Brooklyn, Chairman of the Subcommittee on Domestic Marketing, Consumer Relations, and Nutrition.

In addition, the Direct Marketing Act of 1976, also co-sponsored by Congressman Richmond, will provide financial assistance to direct marketing from farmer to consumer in 1977-78. Both sources of funds will be channeled through the Cooperative Extension Service at the land-grant colleges of Cornell and Rutgers in New York and New Jersey. Once tests being currently conducted at Cornell on the level of hazardous heavy metals in urban grown vegetables determine if they are safe to eat, Greenmarket may become the outlet for a new generation of urban farmers. Through Greenmarket, farmers are also beginning to wholesale to restaurants. At least one of the farmers has benefited by his association with Greenmarket by initiating regular sales under contract to the 14 restaurants managed by the International Hilton Company at the World Trade Center.

Greenmarket has the capability of branching out as communities express their interest and willingness to make arrangements for securing sites and local support. We hope to become more a part of the city planning and building process, to help shape and beautify spaces for human activities. Most urban space has been too rigidly defined, over-specialized, and consequently, wastefully used. Farmers markets are only one of the many varied human activities needed to enliven public spaces. These spaces in turn must be planned and designed to bridge homes and civic life, leaving room for a community voice and their actual development and use.

Smaller cities outside New York City have expressed an interest in such markets. Middletown and Poughkeepsie started markets in 1976 and a Greenmarket was opened in Ossining in August 1977. Greenmarket stands ready to assist other communities to set up their own farmers markets.

Hindsight

Greenmarket is still in an experimental stage. Some lessons we have learned, and have yet to follow completely, include the following:

Setting Up: Allow 8 months lead time to find farmers and select sites.

Site Selection: Pick a site on the same day as and as close to existing activity as possible. Have a permanent location, storage, toilets, and signs which can be left up all year around.

Farmers: Check out each applicant as thoroughly as possible through the Cooperative Extension Service and make visits to the farms. Time his entry to coincide with his harvest. Restrict entry to farmers who sell only their own produce or produce purchased directly from known farmers the day before the sale.

Produce: Consistently poor produce should be the basis for exclusion from the market. Leaf produce should be cut the day before the market and kept cool and moist overnight. Farmers should report acreages planted and these should be checked by visits during the growing season.

Manpower: As can be seen from the above, at least one full time and several part-time staff people will be required to administer a program, depending on the number of markets. A person with energy, tact, and organizational ability is necessary to sustain the program. The challenges are varied but worth the effort, not only in the material accomplishments, but in the human contact with farmers and consumers.

This article is reprinted from Barry Benepe, **Greenmarkets**, The Council on the Environment of New York City, 51 Chambers Street, New York 10007, pp. 23-24, 1977.

EXAMPLE 57   Bulk Commodities Exchange

During the 1977 harvest season the Bulk Commodities Exchange brought local farmers together with buyers from restaurants, retailers, food co-ops and buying clubs. The Exchange operated as a non-profit 'pilot project' to evaluate the potential bulk demand for locally grown fruits and vegetables. Project goals included expanding markets for local farms; increase the per unit return to the farmer; decrease the per unit cost to the buyer and create a clearinghouse for high quality local products. The program was initiated to promote agricultural production as it is essential for the nutritional health of local consumers and the economic health of the region. Hunger Action Center, Pike Place Preservation and Development Authority, Metrocenter and the King County Office of Agriculture participated in planning and operation of the Exchange.

HOW THE BCE OPERATED

Commodities were sold on a preorder basis: Bulk buyers placed orders with BCE staff indicating quantity and desired delivery times. Farmers were then contacted directly to fill the order. A final confirmation of varieties, quantity, price and pick-up day was then made with the buyer.

In most cases buyers picked up the orders from a site at the Pike Place Market. During the pilot project delivery was only available in emergency situations. The trial operation was conducted over a nine week period beginning the first week of September through the second week of November.

Nine buying clubs, four retailers, seven restaurants, three service organizations and six other individuals participated. Seventeen growers were also involved.

Large volume items: carrots, potatoes, lettuce, beans, corn and zucchini. Along with fruits and vegetables, honey and eggs were also available.

In 1977 all costs for operating the BCE were assumed by the sponsoring organizations. The costs included staff salaries, promotion, site expenses and minimal transport costs.

PRICE SAVINGS

Total sales for the 18 exchanges was $4,131.00.

The farmer received an average of 18% more than if the commodity had been sold through traditional channels. Buying club members saved 40% over supermarket prices, restaurants saved 37% and retailers 7%.

Purchases by retailers amounted to 57.8% of total sales, buying clubs 20.9%, restaurants 19.4% and all others 1.9%.

PRODUCER EVALUATION

Fifteen of the 17 participating producers responded to an evaluation questionnaire:

60% of the farmers said they sold more produce because of the BCE.

73% plan to grow more next year because of the program.

30% of the farmers currently sell to wholesalers and 53% sell from stalls at the Pike Place Market.

80% are interested in pooling with other farmers to bring in produce for the Exchange.

86% are willing to receive payment through a billing system.

93% like the days and time of the Exchange.

FUTURE PLANS

Long range goals for the Bulk Commodities Exchange involve the development of a non-profit cooperative business, managed by the participating farmers and/or buyers. Based on an analysis by last year's participants, problems limiting participation and volume have been identified. The following recommendations for improvement in the operation have been made:

- Expansion of delivery capabilities
- Establish a permanent site with storage facilities to accommodate more convenient delivery and pick-up times
- Weekly compilation of commodity price sheets to be distributed with producer's name and item variety
- Expand product lines available by providing eastern Washington products not grown in King County
- Earlier starting date and well coordinated advance promotion
- Organization of a participant advisory group to assist in making decisions on the operational structure for 1978

WHAT CONSUMERS SAY

Thirteen of the 21 buyers that participated in the 1977 BCE responded to a questionnaire evaluating the operation:

92% said they received better quality and fresher products through the Exchange.

69% cited better prices and farmer support as reasons for their involvement.

70% found the 7:30 a.m. pick-up time to be inconvenient.

62% said the lack of delivery was a problem. However, 3 of 4 restaurants, 2 of 6 buying clubs and 1 of 3 retailers would be willing to pay for delivery.

A sampling of restaurants and retailers who did not participate indicated that lack of delivery was the major factor preventing their involvement.

WHY A B.C.E.?

As a bulk produce operation marketing directly to buyers, the Bulk Commodities Exchange provided a new wholesale channel for locally grown products. The program was created to increase fruit and vegetable production and improve the quality of commodities available to the local consumer.

Urban competition for land, rising property values, labor problems and taxation have combined to foster a decline in the acreage dedicated to agricultural use in King County. Although average farm sizes have increased along with gross income, the total number of farms has decreased significantly over the last 30 years.

Consumers have experienced an increasing distance between themselves and the producer, making freshness less certain and reducing selection. An increased demand for locally grown foods would not only enhance the viability of local farms, but insure consumers of a more flavorful, fresher and less expensive product.

This article is reprinted from "Bulk Commodities Exchange," Summary Report, c/o Department of Community Development, Seattle, Washington 98104, 1977.

EXAMPLE

58
the Bank in brief...

Existing coops, neighborhood and community groups, statewide community organizations, labor unions and churches all stand to benefit from the Bank. So long as they are structured in a non-profit, cooperative manner, most projects providing consumer goods and services would be eligible for Bank financing. Potential project areas include food, housing, agriculture, health, hardware, energy, art, crafts, auto repairs and insurance.

●

*Legislation calls for $300 million in direct U.S. Treasury funding for the Bank over a five year period—$100 million in the first year and $200 million in the remaining four years. The Bank will be able to borrow up to **ten times** that amount for a total capitalization of $3 billion. The funds will be used for **market rate** loans to consumer cooperatives with a special provision that the Bank make an effort to allocate at least 35% of its assets to low-income coops. No more than 30% may be used for housing cooperatives and up to 10% may be used for producer coops.*

●

*An Office of Self-Help Development and Technical Assistance will be established to provide up to $75 million in equity grants and interest subsidies to low-income cooperatives who would otherwise be unable to use the Bank. The Office will also provide technical assistance to **all** cooperatives, including education and training, feasibility studies and market research.*

action-by-action summary of the Act

the COOP BANK:
New Funds for Community Development

Conference / Alternative State and Local Policies

2000 Florida Ave., N.W.
Washington, D.C. 20009

THE COOP BANK ACT

Long struggling consumer cooperatives in America's rural and urban areas are about to get real financial and technical assistance from the federal government. After years of lobbying by progressive organizations, a National Consumer Cooperative Bank has been created which will provide long-term loans, interest subsidies and technical assistance to a wide range of consumer groups.

Section-by-Section Summary

Section 101. Creation and Charter of Bank.—The National Consumer Cooperative Bank is chartered as a mixed ownership government corporation to encourage the development of consumer cooperatives.

(1) By providing specialized credit and technical assistance:

(2) By broad-based control of the Bank by its voting stockholders;

(3) By encouraging broad-based ownership and active member participation of eligible cooperatives;

(4) By improving the quality and availability of goods and services to consumers; and

(5) By encouraging ownership of its equity securities by cooperatives with the objective of retirement of government seed capital as early as possible.

Section 102. General Corporate Powers.—The Bank is authorized to make and service loans, credit commitments, guarantees, and furnish financially related services and technical assistance to eligible cooperatives. The Bank is authorized to establish one or more branch offices and, in order to obtain local input into Bank policies, one or more advisory committees in connection with such branch offices.

Section 103. Board of Directors.—The original 13 member Board will be appointed by the President, with the advice and consent of the Senate, 7 members being selected from officers of agencies and departments of the U.S. government, and 6 members selected from the general public who have extensive experience in the several classes of cooperatives expected to be eligible for assistance under the bill. For the public members, the President shall consider nominees submitted by associations of cooperatives. The terms of directors are generally for three years, but the Board may stagger the terms of stockholder elected directors. The President may remove appointed directors, with or without cause, and may fill vacancies until the next annual meeting at which time the vacancy is to be filled for the remainder of the term, by the President or by stockholder election. When borrower capital equals at least $3 million, three members appointed by the President from the general public shall resign. When borrower capital equals at least $10 million, three additional Presidential appointees from *the public sector shall resign. The first three of these vacancies are to be filled by election of stockholder directors representing housing, low-income cooperatives and consumer goods or consumer services. Thereafter at elections by stockholders to fill vacancies on the Board, other classes of cooperatives shall be represented.

Section 104. Capitalization.—The capital of the Bank is to be provided by the purchase of $100 million of class A preferred stock by the Secretary of the Treasury for the year ending September 30, 1979, and for the next 4 fiscal years an amount not exceeding $200 million; by the purchase of class B stock by borrowers at a rate required by the Bank, which shall not be less than 1 percent nor more than 10 percent of the face value of the loan; and by the purchase of class C stock by investors who are eligible to borrow or are controlled by eligible borrowers. Class A stock has absolute priority, but only class B and class C stock are voting stocks. No holder of voting stock is entitled to more than one vote, regardless of the number of shares held except as provided in the bylaws of the Bank.

Section 105. Eligibility.—Any organization chartered or operated on a cooperative, not-for-profit basis for furnishing or producing goods, services, or facilities, primarily for the benefits of its members who are ultimate consumers of such goods, services, or facilities, will be eligible for the services of the Bank if it pays dividends within the limits approved by the Bank; allocates its net savings to members or patrons; makes membership available without discrimination and provides for voting control on a one vote-per-person basis. Mutual savings banks, mutual savings and loan associations and credit unions, are ineligible, except that credit unions serving low-income persons will be eligible for technical assistance under title II. Other self-help organizations which produce, market or furnish goods, services or facilities on behalf of their members as primary producers may receive assistance so long as the dollar volume of loans to them does not exceed 10 percent of the gross assets of the Bank at any one time. Such organizations would include those which purchase supplies for its artisan or handicraft members or market articles made by their members.

Section 106. Annual Meetings.—Annual meetings of stockholders of the Bank are required and must be open to the public.

Section 107. Borrowing Authority.—The Bank is authorized to obtain funds through the sale of bonds and other obligations, but the amount of such obligations outstanding at any time

Condensed from the Report of the Committee on Bank, Housing and Urban Affairs, United States Senate, April 1978 shall not exceed five times the paid-in capital and surplus.

Section 108. Lending Powers. — The Bank may make or guarantee loans for as long as 40 years with variable interest rates, make commitments, purchase or discount obligations of members of eligible organizations after determining that the borrower has sound organizational structure and future income prospects to permit full repayment of the loan. The criteria for loan making or guarantee must include an assessment of the impact of the loan on existing small business enterprises in the area. At the end of five years, the loans for residential housing purposes shall not exceed 30 per cent of the gross assets of the Bank and the Board is required to use its best efforts to see that at least 35 per cent of loans outstanding at the end of each fiscal year are to (1) cooperatives at least a majority of the members of which are low-income persons, and to (2) other cooperatives which use the proceeds of such loans to finance a facility, activity, or service that will be used by predominantly low-income persons.

Section 112. Authorization. — In addition to other specific authorized appropriations, there is authorized to be appropriated $2 million for the fiscal year ending September 30, 1979, and for the next 2 fiscal years such sums as may be necessary. Any sums so appropriated will remain available until expended. The funds so provided will not be used to retire any indebtedness of the Bank.

Section 113. Appeals. — Applicants for assistance are given the right of appeal to the Board of Directors from a decision denying in whole or in part their requests.

Section 114. Conflict-of-Interest. — The Board is required to adopt conflict-of-interest rules at least as stringent as the Federal Executive conflict-of-interest rules.

Section 115. Examination and Audit. — Until all class A stock is retired the operations of the Bank shall be audited annually under the direction of a Federal agency designated by the President (including the General Accounting Office). When two-thirds of the stock of the Bank is held by others than the Secretary of the Treasury, the President is directed to establish an Office of Supervision and Audit to examine and audit the Bank and assure that the objectives of title I are being carried out and make annual reports to Congress.

OFFICE OF SELF-HELP AND TECHNICAL ASSISTANCE

Section 201. Establishment. — There is established within the Bank Office of Self-Help Development and Technical Assistance, headed by a dDirector appointed by the President and confirmed by the Senate, who shall not be a member of the Board. The Director will promulgate rules, policies and procedures governing the operations of the Office, which shall be subject to review by the Board. There is authorized to be appropriated to the Office for fiscal year ending September 30, 1979, $10 million and for the next 2 fiscal years, an aggregate amount of not to exceed $65 million.

Section 203. Capital investments and Interest Supplements. — The Office may make advances out of the account to the capital structure of a cooperative serving low-income persons if it is determined that such advances can be paid with interest out of members equity within 30 years. Also authorized are interest supplements on loans to low-income cooperatives which the Office determines cannot pay a market rate interest because it sells goods or services to or provides facilities for the use of low-income persons.

Section 204. Organizational Assistance. — Information and services concerning the organization and re-organization and financing and management of cooperatives may be made available by the Office directly or through other agencies and it may accept grants or transfers of funds for such purposes.

Section 205. Investigations and Revenues. — The Office is authorized to undertake investigations of new types of services and surveys of areas where use of cooperatives will contribute to the purposes of the act.

Section 206. Financial Analysis and Market Surveys. — At the request of any eligible cooperative, the Office may provide a financial analysis or market survey for the organization.

Section 207. Director and Management Training Assistance. — The Office may make available a program of training directors and staff of eligible cooperatives. Membership studies, membership education, general public information programs and management consultation are also authorized.

Section 208. Government Assistance Programs. — The Office is directed to work with all agencies of the U.S. Government offering programs for which consumer cooperatives may be eligible and to pass information concerning such programs to eligible cooperatives.

Section 209. Authorization. — There is authorized to be appropriated to the Office $2 million for the fiscal year ending September 30, 1979, and for the next 2 fiscal years such sums as may be necessary for the administration of title II. Such sums are to remain available until expended.

Section 210. Fees for Services. — The Office may charge fees for its services, but may furnish services available without charge depending on the nature of the service or on ability to pay.

Since **The Conference** was founded in June 1975, it has provided a major meeting place and forum for the ideas of progressive elected officials, community organizers, political activists, and technically trained experts interested in alternative policies and programs at the state and local level.

In addition to holding an annual national meeting, the organization holds frequent regional issue conferences and publishes numerous books and pamphlets which focus on the increasingly complex problems facing state and local government today.

Write for publication list and a complimentary copy of **The Conference** newsletter, *Ways & Means.*

Conference on Alternative State and Local Policies

2000 Florida Avenue, N.W.
Washington, D.C. 20009
(202) 387-6030

Legislative History

Senator Thomas McIntyre (D.-N.H.) first introduced the National Consumer Cooperative Bank Bill in November 1975, and a companion bill was introduced in the House by Representative Ferdinand St. Germain (D.-R.I.) in June, 1976. Because of the adjournment of the 94th Congress, the Bill was re-introduced in February 1977, and despite White House opposition, was passed by the House in July 1977. The margin of victory was one vote!

Opposition to the Coop Bank came from established business interests, including the U.S. Chamber of Commerce and the large food chains. Supporting the Bill was a wide coalition of consumer and cooperative groups, such as the Cooperative League of the United States, the Consumer Federation of America, the NAACP and the United Auto Workers.

After intensive lobbying by these and other groups, and after the Senate recommended that funding for the Bank be reduced from $500 million to $300 million, the White House came out in support of the Bill.

Final passage of the legislation became certain during the 95th Congress when the Senate voted down an amendment sponsored by Senators Tower and Proxmire which would have substituted a two-year pilot study to analyze the financial needs of cooperatives. Other crippling amendments were similarly beaten back. Finally, in July 1978, the Senate voted overwhelmingly to approve the Bank. A House-Senate Conference Committee adopted the Senate version of the Bill, and increased the Bank's borrowing capacity to ten times the initial government appropriation, as had been proposed in the original House Bill. The President signed the Bill into law on August 20, 1978.

Implementing the Bank

The rules and regulations, the make-up of the Board of Directors and the level of appropriations will be decided before the Bank makes its first loans. Decisions made at this stage will critically affect the future of the Bank and will determine, for example, how responsive the Bank is to low-income communities and whether the lending policies will be more flexible than those of existing lending institutions.

Rules and Regulations

An Interagency Task Force has been established to draft proposed rules and regulations for the Bank. Made up of interested agencies, and under the direction of the Treasury Department, the Task Force has divided its work into five subcommittees:

1/ **Internal Procedures,** Chair—HUD. *Board procedures, Bank Officer selection, stock holder voting power, conflict of interest rules and reports to Congress.*

2/ **Priorities,** Chair—Office of Consumer Affairs, White House. *Policy guidelines, and for apportioning loans, guarantees, interest subsidies and technical assistance among eligible cooperatives.*

3/ **Finance and Lending Policies,** Chair—Treasury. *Fees and interest rates to be charged to participating Coops, Coop Bank borrowing policies and questions concerning stock.*

4/ **Self-Help Development Fund,** Chair—ACTION. *All questions relating to the Self-Help Development Fund.*

5/ **Technical Assistance,** Chair—Commerce. *All questions relating to technical assistance, including fee setting and the establishment of branch offices.*

Board of Directors

Nomination of the first thirteen members of the Board of Directors will be by the President. Seven will be federal agency representatives and six will be cooperative representatives. The Senate is expected to act upon these nominations by March 1979. The Board will then promulgate the dfraft rules and regulations, will hire staff and officers, and begin operating by early summer, 1979. The President will also nominate a Director of the Office of Self-Help Development and Technical Assistance subject to Senate confirmation.

Appropriations

Funds authorized by the legislation must still be appropriated. Supplemental funding for fiscal year 1979 is being requested so that the Bank can begin operating with the next year. The legislation authorizes up to $100 million for the Self-Help Development Fund, and an additional $2 million for the technical assistance program and for the administration of the Development Fund. These appropriations requests will be acted on by Congress in early 1979.

This article is reprinted from **The Co-op Bank: New Funds for Community Development,** Conference on Alternative State and Local Policies, November 1978.

EXAMPLE 59

Michigan Public Act 331 of 1975

AN ACT to amend section 3 of Act No. 146 of the Public Acts of 1975, entitled "An act to create an office of services to the aging, a commission on services to the aging, and an interagency council on services to the aging; to authorize the designation of area agencies on services to the aging; to prescribe the powers and duties of the office, the commission, the council and the area agencies; and to repeal certain acts and parts of acts," being section 400.543 of the Compiled Laws of 1970; and to add section 3a.

The People of the State of Michigan enact:

Section 1. Section 3 of Act No. 146 of the Public Acts of 1975, being section 400.543 of the Compiled Laws of 1970, is amended and section 3a is added to read as follows:

Sec. 3. The office of services to the aging shall:

(a) Function as the single state agency within the state to supervise the administration of the older Americans act of 1965, as amended, being 22 U.S.C. sections 3001 to 3067 (1970).

(b) Cooperate with agencies of the federal government and receive the federal funds for any purposes authorized by the legislature.

(c) Make necessary contracts incidental to the performance of its duties and the execution of its policies. The contracts may be with state agencies, local public agencies, private agencies, organizations, associations, and individuals to enhance the availability and accessibility of services to older individuals.

(d) Provide technical assistance to state and local agencies for the purposes of program development, administration, and evaluation.

(e) Collect, analyze, and disseminate data concerning services which affect older persons. Coordinate educational and public information programs for the purpose of developing appropriate attitudes regarding the problems and opportunities of aging and older persons; encourage professional groups to recognize and deal with the problems; make information about the programs available to organizations dealing with aging problems and to the general public; encourage the development of community programs to improve the status of aging and older persons.

(f) Evaluate the effect of state statutes on the life-styles of older persons and recommend to the governor and legislature appropriate changes when indicated by the evaluation.

(g) Evaluate in cooperation with appropriate state departments and agencies, the effectiveness of public and private services which affect older persons in the state funded by federal, state, local, and private resources, including but not limited to the provision of educational, physical, economic, legal, social, emotional, housing, and recreational services, and other activities for the purpose of providing protection and insuring self-sufficiency and social independence.

(h) Cooperate with local political subdivisions and private programs for the purpose of reviewing and evaluating services which affect older persons funded by public and private resources.

(i) Make recommendations to the governor and the legislature on budget and grant requests for public funds to be allocated for educational, physical, legal, economic, social, emotional, housing, and recreational services and other activities for the purpose of providing protection and insuring self-sufficiency and social independence of aging individuals.

(j) Encourage, promote, and aid in the establishment of services for aging and older persons by designing surveys that can be used locally to determine needs of older people, recommending the creation of services and facilities as appear to be needed, serving as a clearinghouse for the collection and distribution of information on aging and older persons, and assisting organizations and the community in such other ways as the director deems appropriate.

(k) Participate in the development of the annual plan of services that is required to be submitted to the department of health, education and welfare under the provisions of title 20 of the social security act, and provide recommendations to the governor on the components of the plan which relate to services to aging and older persons.

(l) Develop annually, in cooperation with the commission on services to the aging and the state interagency council on aging, a report regarding the problems of older persons, the effectiveness of existing public policies and recommendations for future state and local action. The first report shall be submitted to the governor and the legislature not later than April 1, 1976 and by January 31 of each year thereafter.

(m) Supervise the establishment of demonstration programs for services to aging and older persons in selected communities in the state. Particular emphasis shall be given to services designed to foster continued participation of older persons in family and community life and to prevent insofar as possible unnecessary and extreme dependency and the need for long-term institutional care. The program shall be established to demonstrate and test their effectiveness and to stimulate continued support for programs and to create new services, using federal, state, local, or private funds and resources.

(n) Establish and evaluate opportunities for older individuals to provide volunteer services.

(o) Receive on behalf of the state any grant or gift and accept the same so that the title shall pass to the state. All grants and gifts shall be deposited with the state treasurer and used for the purposes set forth in the grant of the gift if the purposes are within the powers conferred on the office and the use is approved by the legislature. If the use is not so approved, the grant or gift shall revert to the donor or the donor's administrator or assigns.

(p) Monitor the progress of area agencies on aging and other agencies receiving funds from the office in meeting specified objectives.

(q) Establish food delivery systems for older persons in selected areas which the office shall determine pursuant to section 3a.

Sec. 3a. (1) The office shall train and assign 2 existing personnel who shall institute food delivery systems and inform older persons in those selected areas of the existence of the systems in order to enlist their participation. The personnel shall also train older persons to operate the food delivery systems. The sole responsibility of these personnel shall be to carry out this section.

(2). The office shall develop means to reduce the cost of food to older persons and increase the nutritional adequacy of food purchased and consumed in the following manner:

(a) Various means should be employed to accomplish the objective such as the provision of technical assistance to local clubs, groups, or organizations of older persons for the development of buying clubs, food cooperatives, or shopping assistance programs; provision of education in purchase and preparation of foods; encouraging retail grocers to package raw food in meal size proportions; or other means as deemed appropriate and feasible by the office.

(b) The activities and programs should be designed to enlist the continuing participation and support of older persons.

(c) Ongoing assistance shall be provided until such time as the individual projects become self-sufficient.

(d) The efforts shall be coordinated with or developed in conjunction with those of other state or local public or private agencies such as the cooperative extension services, public health agencies, senior nutrition projects, the department of social services, the retail grocers association, the department of agriculture, and others deemed appropriate by the office.

(e) The office shall provide a report to the governor and the legislature on the effect of the programs by April 1, 1976.

(3) The office shall only provide trained personnel, technical assistance, and coordination with other state agencies and shall not provide funds for any food delivery system other than congregate or home delivered nutrition services which are funded from federal and state appropriations.

This act is ordered to take immediate effect.

This article is reprinted from **Michigan Public Act 331 of 1975**, c/o Office of Services to the Aging, Lansing, Michigan 48909, 1975.

Chapter 14

Growing Food in the City

Growing one's own food is one solution consumers have found to fight rising food prices. In hundreds of cities across the nation, people are creating urban garden projects on formerly abandoned lots and demolition sites. A Gallup Poll estimates that over half of all Americans are now involved in growing their food, while millions of others would like to if there were access to land, resources and technical assistance.

In many ways the urban agriculture movement has been the first step in bringing communities together. Besides helping city residents save money on food and the positive effects of people getting back in touch with the food system, many neighborhood groups and city officials are discovering that there are a variety of economic development and employment opportunities related to urban agriculture.

Growing food in the city is an integral part of the larger movement supporting the development of appropriate technologies. "The main goal of appropriate technology is to enhance the self-reliance of people on a local level," says the National Center for Appropriate Technology (NCAT). Urban agriculture includes garden and composting projects, greenhouses, canneries and community access to land. Hundreds of such projects are being initiated by neighborhood and community groups across the country. The common theme of their efforts is to build a stronger sense of community and to encourage local economic development in our nation's cities.

URBAN GARDENING

Just as farmers' markets are the most popular vehicle consumers have found to creative marketing alternatives, urban gardening is the most vital component of the urban agriculture movement. There are thousands of gardens operated by community and neighborhood groups in our cities. Support has come from city and state governments, federal programs, and private and non-profit organizations. The benefits are immediate, with an average family of four saving $250 annually on their grocery bill.

There are several important problems groups must face as they attempt to garden in the city. These include: lack of general and horticultural technical assistance, pest control, vandalism, insurance, land access, poor or no soil, and organizational skills. There is a tremendous amount of "people power" that supports these gardens. City and state governments can often act to help city residents overcome these problems.

The success of the urban gardening movement varies throughout the country. USDA has sponsored an Urban Gardening Demonstration Program initiated by Congressman Richmond (NY) in 16 cities. Unfortunately, the program has often failed to meet community needs because of its structure. Funding and operations are through the State Cooperative Extension Service, which has led to a lack of community control. Federal guidelines have restricted technical assistance and financial resources to the people working for Cooperative Extension rather than the community. So far, 1.5 million dollars have been appropriated in the first two years to the 16 cities such as New York, Boston, Chicago, Philadelphia, Los Angeles, Detroit and Houston. Much of these funds has been tied up in administrative and salary costs, leaving very little support for the community groups.

Despite the obstacles, there are many exciting urban gardening programs throughout the country. Four of the most innovative programs are summarized as follows:

- **New York City:** The gardening movement has an unusual number of groups and programs that range from the Cornell Urban Gardening Program (a Cooperative Extension Agency which includes an excellent nutrition program as well as technical assistance); the Green Guerillas (a volunteer organization that spearheaded the gardening movement in the city); Council on the Environment (a non-profit organization that provides technical assistance, workshops, and a "Grow Truck" that lends tools to the five boroughs); the New York Horticultural Society (a non-profit organization providing technical assistance, workshops, CETA workers, seeds and plants); and finally, numerous other technical assistance groups and neighborhood organizations that help organize these garden projects in the five boroughs.

- **Boston:** Presently, there are over 10,000 urban gardens with an estimated $350 in annual food costs savings to a family of four. The Boston Urban Gardeners (BUG) is a coalition of technical assistance people and community organizations that work to strengthen the gardening program of Boston. The core staff issues *BUG* (a newsletter) and provides training and funding ideas. The Cooperative Extension Program funding is just getting underway.

- **Seattle:** In 1971, the P. Patch began in Seattle on private land. The program is named after Rainci Picardo (owner of the original land), and stands for *P*icardo, *P*ublic and *P*roduces. Seattle urban gardens have been fortunate because the City government has supported its program by setting up an Agricultural Task Force, providing increasing funds (operation and CETA positions) over the years, providing coordinators, and expanding the program to include over 3,000 gardeners and 950 plots. This urban gardening program along with the Marketing Project has helped to create an integrated and comprehensive City Plan for Seattle. (See Chapter 16, Comprehensive City Food Plans)

- **California:** Community gardening is sponsored throughout the State's cities by the state itself. Funding is provided by local, state and federal sources. The creation of the Office of Appropriate Technology (OAT) by the state government offers technical assistance, and an informational newsletter on small grants and resources, etc. Unfortunately, their funds and programs have recently been cut back by the impact of Proposition 13.

From the success of gardening in New York, the state legislature passed an act to amend the executive law in support of gardening. **Example 60, New York Article 38, Community Gardens**, illustrates the different areas of state cooperation in furthering community gardening. It was signed by the governor in 1978.

LAND

When neighborhood groups attempt to organize a community garden, access to land is often the most serious problem. Many cities are faced with the reality that the increased abandonment of buildings is leading to demolition rubble lots and lost tax revenues. New York City has over 10,000 lots possessed through urban renewal, purchase, condemnation and in-rem foreclosure. Cities can look at positive short and long range planning schemes for the rubble lots. "Greenbelts" created through gardens, greenhouses and parks, by private and public development, are one solution. In addition, planning to help prevent land speculation and stimulate public ownership is needed.

One short range solution to make land accessible to community gardeners is through Operation Green Thumb; a program which leases lots for $1 a year. Operation Green Thumb is a New York City project through the Department of General Services, and was initiated by the New York Horticulture Society. Gardeners can have an option to renew the lease on a yearly basis. Assistance by the Department of Sanitation for initial lot clean-up is available to gardeners. Previous to this program, many gardeners occupied lots illegally because of extensive paper work and/or lack of a lot possession procedure.

The Trust for Public Land is a non-profit organization which has for the past five years assisted city residents and neighborhood groups on land and open space related issues.[1] In 1975, the National Urban Land Program was initiated to work with urban gardens and parks throughout the country. The program has focused on developing a new profession of non-profit land acquisition, pioneering new technologies of land preservation, and funding. The Trust has made a serious commitment to get minorities and inner-city residents involved in the urban-based conservation movement.

The Trust works out of a basic philosophy of community development which starts from the "bottom up," using neighborhoods as building blocks. Not only do they work closely with grassroots organizations, but also with city governments such as Oakland City Council government and New York City's Housing and Preservation Department. In Newark, Trust negotiated for special auction prices for non-housing projects with the City and State. In addition, Trust staff worked closely with state officials to draft an *Open Space Bond Issue* (1977). The legislation allows the state to channel funds directly to neighborhood renewal: **Example 61, Land Trusts: Putting Empty Lots to Use**, explains Trust's approach and concepts further.

YEAR-ROUND GARDENING

Community gardens allow urban residents to grow more of their own food, but many gardeners have short growing seasons. Through year-round gardening, people can greatly supplement their food supply. Greenhouses have been in operation for years, but there are tremendous energy costs in heating them. Solar energy offers one solution to these high costs. In addition, neighborhood groups can use solar cold frames and greenhouse windows. Through help with grants from private foundations, NCAT (National Center for Appropriate Technology) and local CETA programs, El Sol Brillante Community Garden on the Lower East Side of New York has constructed passive solar cold frames to encourage year-round gardening.

Greenhouses also have the potential to use rooftop spaces, but upstart construction costs, lack of mobility, inadequate roof structures, and city codes limit the number of rooftop greenhouses constructed. Cities can help encourage year-round growing projects such as greenhouses, solar coldframes, and greenhouse windows. Change in policy recommendations in funding for construction and CETA/VISTA programs (to assist greenhouse projects) is critical. In addition, antiquated city codes for ground and rooftop level construction need to be changed.

One demonstration project that has initiated ten more greenhouse projects with a coalition of neighborhood groups, is the CAM (Christian Action Ministry) Greenhouse in Chicago. **Example 62, A Multility Grows in Garfield Park** and **Example 63, Ten Neighborhood Solar Greenhouse Projects** shows how a coalition of neighborhood groups with the assistance of the Neighborhood Technology Center have been able to receive funding for an extensive program through the Chicago Department of Human Services, VISTA, CETA and private foundations.

COMPOSTING

Another recent development in cities across the country is the interest in recycling urban waste. Materials such as sludge, animal manures, vegetable trimmings, leaves, tree waste (wood chips), and industrial wastes such as hulls, husks, and pulps can all be composted into fertilizer. Composting is another example of appropriate technology that many city dwellers are starting to implement. Soil is a *valuable* commodity in growing food and many cities virtually have little and/or unhealthy soil. People are learning that they can "make their own soil" through the natural process of composting.

Composting projects are being initiated in most community gardens. Cities are looking at composting for solutions to waste problems and soil reclamation. Massachusetts is considering setting up a Compost Authority to help local efforts in the state. In the Bronx (a wasteland of rubble lots and abandoned buildings) a unique project, the Bronx Frontier Composting Operation, is underway. This project is part of a program called "The Greening of the Bronx" that includes community gardens, open space development (parks, trees, etc.) and composting. Support for this project comes from private foundations and city, state and federal grants.

FOOD PROCESSING

Another solution to seasonal gardening is food processing, such as canneries. Consumers can put food away through canning and freezing when food supply is in abundance. Many canneries have been successful in operating throughout communities. They offer a link between farmers and consumers, as well as being a nutritional education center. In **Example 64, Community Food and Nutrition Center**, a Northampton Cannery and its goals are discussed. Their experience has been that the cannery alone is not economically viable unless incorporated with other food projects such as direct marketing, food co-ops, and gardening projects. Other cities are looking at integrated programs to include processing centers. Pike Place Market in Seattle is considering incorporating a cannery with their farmers' market.

CONCLUSION

Growing one's own food has many benefits for the urban consumer. The benefits range from cutting food costs and putting people in touch with the food system to creating jobs and potential for economic development, stimulating community self-reliance, and assisting in the rebuilding of many neighborhoods.

State and local governments can encourage the urban agriculture movement through making funds more readily available, providing technical assistance, improving antiquated codes on fire prevention, sanitation and construction, and providing access to land. Sanitation, Housing, Parks and Recreation Community Development departments and CETA offices can become supportive to the needs of the "urban farmer."

[1]Karin Abarbanel, "The National Urban Land Program," **Foundation News.** Volume 18, Number 6, pp. 11-16, November/December 1977.

Resources

ORGANIZATIONS

Council on the Environment

50 Chambers Street
New York, New York 10007
(212) 566-0990
Liz Christy, Director

National Center for Appropriate Technology

P.O. Box 3838
Butte, Montana 59701
(406) 723-6533

Trust for Public Land

82 Second Street
San Francisco, California 94106
(415) 495-4015
Steve Costa

254 W. 31 Street
New York, New York 10001
(212) 563-5959
Peter Stein

BIBLIOGRAPHY

Abarbanel, Karen, "The National Urban Land Program: Greening America's Cities," **Foundation News.** Council on Foundations, Incorporated, 888 Seventh Avenue, New York, New York 10019. November/December 1977. Review of Trust for Public Land's Programs.

Boston Urban Gardeners Newsletter. Boston Urban Gardeners, c/o Horticultural Hall, 300 Massachusetts Avenue, Boston, Massachusetts 02115. $1.00 membership fee.

Bureau of Outdoor Recreation, **Profiles of California Garden Projects.** Bureau of Outdoor Recreation, Box 36062, 450 Golden Gate Avenue, San Francisco, California 94102.

Community Environmental Council (CEC), **Agriculture in the City.** CEC, 109 East de la Guerra, Santa Barbara, California 93101. 1976.

Dalrymple, Dana, **A Global Review of Greenhouse Food Production.** Economic Research Service, USDA, Washington, D.C. 20250. 1973. History, economics and recent trends in greenhouse agriculture.

DeClue, Denise, "A Multility Grows in Garfield Park," **Reader, Chicago's Free Weekly.** Vol. 6, No. 49, p. 120-124. September 9, 1977.

Drake, Susan York and Roberta Lawrence, **Recreational Community Gardening.** U.S. Department of the Interior, Bureau of Outdoor Recreation, Washington, D.C. 1976.

Friend, Gil, "Getting the Lead Out," **Self-Reliance.** Institute for Local Self-Reliance, 1717 18th Street, N.W., Washington, D.C. 20009.

Friend, Gil, "Poisoned Cities and Urban Gardens," **Elements.** Institute for Local Self-Reliance, 1717 18th Street, N.W., Washington, D.C. 20009. January 1976.

Friend, Gil and David Morris, **Energy, Agriculture and Neighborhood Food Systems.** Institute for Local Self-Reliance, 1717 18th Street, N.W., Washington, D.C. 20009.

Gardens for All, **Community Garden Procedural Manual.** Gardens for All, P.O. Box 164, Charlotte, Vermont 15445.

Gardens for All, **Guide to Community Garden Organization.** Gardens for All, P.O. Box 164, Charlotte, Vermont 15445. 1977.

Hunger Action Center, **Community Garden Handbook.** Hunger Action Center, Evergreen State College, Olympia, Washington. 1976.

Institute for Local Self-Reliance, **Community Self-Reliance Series.** Institute for Local Self-Reliance, 1717 18th Street, N.W., Washington, D.C. 20009. 1975. The institute published a series of papers on urban agricultural techniques; sprouting composting, waste utilziation, etc.

Integrative Design Associates, **Appropriate Technology and Agriculture in the United States.** Superintendent of Documents, U.S. Government Printing Office, Washington, D.C. 20402. 1977.

Lerza, Catherine, "Urban Gardens Take Off," **The Elements.** No. 18. Public Resource Center, 1747 Connecticut Avenue, N.W., Washington, D.C. 20009. April 1976. Benefits of urban gardening; includes short list of urban agricultural projects.

Menninger, Rosemary, **California Green.** Office of Appropriate Technology, State of California, 1530 10th Street, Sacramento, California 95814.

Menninger, Rosemary, **Community Gardens in California.** Office of Appropriate Technology, State of California, 1530 10th Street, Sacramento, California 95814. 1977.

Moorhead, John, "City Rooftops Sprout Vegetables," **Christian Science Monitor.** July 19, 1977. Short review of successful urban gardens around the U.S.

National Association for Gardening, **Spotlight on Community Gardening.** National Association for Gardening—Gardens for All, P.O. Box 164, Charlotte, Vermont 15445. Newsletter, $14.00/year.

Neighborhood Works. Center for Neighborhood Technology, 570 West Randolph Street, Chicago, Illinois 60606. Bimonthly newsletter.

Office of Appropriate Technology (OAT), **Grants Newsletter.** OAT, State of California, 1530 10th Street, Sacramento, California 95814.

Olkowski, Helga and Bill, **The City People's Book of Raising Food.** Rodale Press, Incorporated, Book Division, Emmaus, Pennsylvania 18049. 1975.

Smith, Miranda, "How Does Your Garden Grow," **Self-Reliance**. No. 5. Institute for Local Self-Reliance, 1717 18th Street, N.W., Washington, D.C. 20009. January 1977. Issues of urban gardening.

Smith, Miranda, and Miriam Klein, **How to Organize a Community Garden; An Annotated Bibliography.** The National Center for Appropriate Technology, P.O. Box 3838, Butte, Montana 59701.

EXAMPLE 60

New York Article 38, Community Gardens

SENATE-ASSEMBLY

March 30, 1978

AN ACT to amend the executive law and the general municipal law, in relation to community gardens and repealing section ninety-six of the general municipal law relating thereto

The People of the State of New York, represented in Senate and Assembly, do enact as follows:

Section 1. Legislative findings. The legislature hereby finds that the publicly owned vacant lands in and around population centers are of great value to the community when properly used. Permanent garden sites are a community asset both as attractive open space and as a source of locally produced food.

Gardening serves as a productive use of vacant lands which otherwise untended often become unsightly and unsafe dumping grounds. Open space given to use as community gardens reduces vandalism, engenders a sense of community involvement and increases surrounding property values. In addition, neighborhood gardening offers environmental, educational, recreational and nutritional benefits to the community.

The legislature further finds that many more people in the state would garden if provided access to land and assisted with necessary technical information. The resulting food production would be a substantial cost savings to low-income families and nutritional benefit to all participants.

It is hereby declared to be the policy of the state to encourage community gardening efforts by providing access to land and offering technical and material assistance to those groups seeking to rehabilitate or better utilize vacant lands by gardening.

§ 2. The executive law is hereby amended by adding a new article thirty-eight to read as follows:

ARTICLE 38
COMMUNITY GARDENS

Section 848. Definitions.
848-a. Use of vacant public land for community gardens.
848-b. Inventory of state owned land.
848-c. Produce not to be sold.
848-d. Cooperative extension and county extension associations; community gardens.

§ 848. Definitions. As used in this section unless another meaning is clearly indicated by the context:

1. "Community garden" shall mean lands, including public lands, upon which citizens of the state have the opportunity to garden on lands which they do not individually own.

2. "Cooperative extension" shall mean a unit of the New York state college of agriculture and life science and the New York state college of human ecology at Cornell University.

3. "County extension association" shall mean the agencies established under subdivision eight of section two hundred twenty-four of the county law.

4. "Community organization" shall mean, without limiting the generality of its application, such incorporated groups or unincorporated associations, including neighborhood or block associations, church groups, clubs, garden clubs, youth or scouting organizations, senior citizen groups, and other organizations desiring to participate in community gardening activities.

5. "Garden" shall mean a piece of land appropriate for cultivation of horticultural products including, but not limited to, herbs, fruits, flowers or vegetables.

6. "Municipal corporation" shall mean any county, town, village, city, school district or other special district.

7. "State agency" shall mean any agency, department, board, public benefit corporation, public authority or commission.

8. "Office" shall mean the office of general services.

9. "Use" shall mean to avail oneself of, or to employ without conveyance of title, gardens on vacant lands by any individual, group or organization.

10. "Vacant public land" shall mean land to which a state agency or municipal corporation has title to a leasehold interest in, an easement on, or other rights to, and that is not presently used, is unoccupied or idle; including open space within the perimeter of a public facility.

§ 848-a. Use of vacant public land for community gardens. 1. State agencies with vacant public lands shall permit use of such lands by individuals or community organizations for community gardening, except upon a finding by the chief executive officer of such state agency that;

(a) community garden use would conflict with the primary use of the property by the state or municipal corporation;

(b) construction upon the land or other agency use of the site is imminent and would be incompatible with community garden use; or

(c) existence of use restrictions in the state constitution, or any statute or local law or ordinance which explicitly prohibits such use of the vacant public land.

2. Use of vacant public land may be conditioned on the possession of liability insurance and written acceptance of liability for injury or damage resulting from use of vacant public land for community gardening.

3. A state agency may assist the development of a community garden by contributing, or providing at cost, from resources under the control of such agency, upon agreement with the user of such land as approved pursuant to the state finance law: initial site preparation, including top soil and grading; water systems; perimeter fencing; storage bins or sheds, and other necessary appurtenances or equipment.

4. State agencies or municipal corporations that receive an application for use of vacant public lands for community gardening shall render a decision upon the application within forty-five days.

5. Users of vacant public land may be evicted from such land on thirty days notice by the state agency or municipal corporation holding title to a leasehold interest in, an easement on, or other rights to said land; except that during a growing season the users of the land will be allowed to harvest their crops, unless an emergency requires immediate action. Notice shall be effected by posting on the premises and notification by certified mail to the sponsoring community organization.

§ 848-b. Inventory of state owned land. The commissioner of general services shall make available to the cooperative extension at Cornell University an inventory of state agency lands listed by county and by agency. This list shall be prepared and submitted to cooperative extension not more than thirty days after the effective date of this article.

§ 848-c. Produce not to be sold. The produce of community gardens located on public lands shall be used and consumed only by those gardening and members of their households; provided, however, that such produce may be given to others, or bartered for other produce or things of value, so long as no money consideration is asked or received.

§ 848-d. Cooperative extension and county extension associations; community gardens. In addition to, and without limitation upon, the powers and duties of Cornell University for cooperative extension and of county extension associations under section two hundred twenty-four of the county law, the cooperative extension, in support of county extension associations, shall:

1. Upon request, identify vacant lands within a given geographic location and provide information regarding jurisdiction and the relative suitability of such land for community garden purposes;

2. Establish a clearinghouse to provide information and referrals to gardeners on topics including, but not limited to, garden planning, supplies and equipment, organic methods of cultivation and pest controls, and the safe application of appropriate chemicals;

3. Encourage the participation of schools, community action groups, government agencies, and non-profit organizations to further participation in community gardens;

4. Support and encourage contact and coordination between community garden programs already in existence and those programs in the initial stages of development;

5. Publicize the existence of this section and solicit information for clearinghouse purposes; and

6. Seek and provide such assistance, for the purposes identified in this section.

§ 3. Section ninety-six of the general municipal law is hereby **repealed** and a new section ninety-six is added to read as follows:

§ 96. Municipal community garden activities. 1. A municipality is authorized to

EXPLANATION—Matter in *italics* is new; matter in brackets [ ] is old law to be omitted.

This article is reprinted from "New York Article 38, Community Gardens," Section 848 a-d, New York State, Albany, New York, March 30, 1978.

Land Trusts: Putting Empty Lots to Use

EXAMPLE 61

OAKLAND—Take a single step into the lot-sized garden plot in Oakland's "Jingletown" neighborhood of modest bungalow homes, and the urban farmers emerge in numbers to check you out.

Frank Nunes, John Santos, George McDowell and their neighbors in the heavily Portuguese and Mexican American neighborhood have a lot of sweat invested in their East 9th Street plot. They depend on it for generous harvests of horse beans, onions, snow peas, cabbage, radishes, beets, chili peppers —and incredible quantities of garlic. "In pretty much every food I eat I use garlic," Nunes announces.

Jingletowners have another reason to prize and defend their garden plot: As members of the Fruitvale Land Trust, the land, until 1976 a weedstrewn lot held by an absentee owner, is legally theirs. The owner has asked $5,000 for the plot, but agents for the San Francisco–based Trust for Public Land (TPL) persuaded him to sell for just $500, writing off the remainder on his taxes. The plot joins dozens of others that TPL has obtained and then conveyed to neighborhood-controlled land trusts.

TPL has taken the tools of non-profit land acquisition, previously used only to obtain and protect jewels of open-space land in exurbia or wilderness areas, and begun to apply them in the new "urban wilderness" of troubled inner-city areas hit hard by housing abandonments and unsightly trash-strewn empty land.

There's an element of Robin Hoodism to TPL's own approach. The organization, formed in 1973, devotes much of its energy to scouting out and then acquiring at strategic moments valuable pieces of natural landscape from private owners, either as gifts or well below market prices. It then resells the parcels it has assembled to local, state or federal governments for prices averaging 30 percent below fair market value. From those operations, which have secured for permanent public enjoyment 20,000 acres in exquisite tracts of land from the Florida Keys to California's North Coast, TPL earns a modest "increment" (the non-profit world's euphemism for profit). That money helps finance its pioneering inner-city endeavors.

Perhaps more than any other public-interest group, TPL fuses rural and urban natural resource and human values—the legacy of founder Huey Johnson, now California's secretary of natural resources. TPL's success could be the harbinger of an important common front between environmentalists and the forces fighting inner-city decay.

TPL began its national urban land program in Oakland in 1975. Through low-cost purchases or gifts from businesses and government, it has acquired 38 parcels of Oakland land, with a market value of $150,000, for about $10,000. The parcels are owned by eight neighborhood land trusts. TPL then started some San Francisco operations and courageously tackled two of the East's toughest areas, Newark and the South Bronx.

TPL may add a few more cities, but many other groups will have to emulate its techniques if the benefits are to reach any "critical mass." TPL President Joel Kuperberg, at the group's San Francisco headquarters, told me he'd be happy to see another half dozen TPLs spring up around the country, perhaps sponsored by city foundations.

Already, TPL has developed clear, innovative concepts ready for transfer to more cities by:

• Introducing inner-city people—some of whom may never have been property owners—to the value of land stewardship. "We emphasize that land is the basis of life," says Steven Costa, who directs TPL's city projects. There's immense value, he notes, when people have the successful experience of "taking over a piece of land covered with rubble, and in a short time acquiring that property and recycling what was a liability into an assest for their neighborhood."

• Stressing self-sufficiency and neighborhood control. Owning land in common, says Kuperberg, makes a neighborhood far more self-sufficient and less dependent on government. The result is true neighborhood "empowerment." Speculators have less influence; if property values start to escalate through middle-class return, the neighborhood shares in the windfall.

• Combating empty-lot eyesores and saving city park funds. Land trusts fill in for hard-pressed city governments in developing small neighborhood parks and then maintaining them permanently. They move much faster than goverments can—in Oakland only 60 days from acquisition of a lot to budding of the first vegetables. Costs are far lower, and often corporations or foundations contribute materials or funds to get the job done.

• Encouraging neighborhood plans. City planners often produce park plans that miss community residents' needs. Not so when a neighborhood land trust does the planning. In Newark, Hispanic neighborhoods planned fairly bare open areas with tables and barbeque pits, replicating the sense of Puerto Rican plazas—an idea that probably never would have occurred to a city planner.

This article is reprinted from Neal R. Pierce, "Land Trusts: Putting Empty Lots to Use," The Washington Post, p. A-17, Tuesday, August 8, 1978.

EXAMPLE
62

A Multility Grows in Garfield Park

Three years ago, academics from a Northwestern University think tank began to plant radical ideas in this down-and-out west-side neighborhood. Now its residents are harvesting a bumper crop of new solutions to age-old inner city problems.

By Denise DeClue

The cukes are ready now, way up on the roof of the Christian Action Ministry building at 3932 West Madison Street in Garfield Park. The peppers are coming along and the Chinese cabbage is full and leafy green. Melon vines are spreading across the growing boxes and blossoming right on schedule.

Senior citizens are creaking up the stairs, mixing nutrients in huge drums, digging and planting in the vermiculite-perlite mixture in which the vegetables grow. They can tell you all about hydroponic gardening and the value of growing vegetables in an inert base and controlling the nutrient feed. They've taken to rooftop gardening just like the fat green cucumbers, and they're selling the produce for 50 cents a pound at churches and senior centers all over the neighborhood.

Most of the large chain grocery stores moved out of the Garfield Park community years ago, and fresh fruits and vegetables are scarce there in summer, even scarcer in winter. This winter, though, things will be different. This January, the CAM greenhouse will be growing strong. The way Clay Collier, director of CAM's Health Action Program, sees it, after one more practice crop the 880-square-foot greenhouse will be producing four crops a year—about 6,500 pounds of vegetables per crop.

And the greenhouse will also serve as a solar collector, absorbing heat from the sun and shooting it into the former savings and loan building's heating system; at night, excess heat from the building will keep the veggies warm.

That's the plan, anyway, and if all goes as scheduled, next year the CAM greenhouse will produce some 26,000 pounds of fresh cabbages, peppers, greens, scallions, cantaloupes, tomatoes, cucumbers, melons, and other vitamin-rich fruits and vegetables; and the greenhouse will pay for itself; and it will prove that rooftop gardens can be therapeutic, energy saving, and economically profitable as well. And in ten years. . . . Flat rooftops all over Garfield Park will be covered with domes, and vegetables and fruits will be harvested by families and food coops, and statistics like the infant mortality rate in Garfield Park—which is now one of the highest in the nation—won't be so grim.

The CAM greenhouse may seem at first glance like a good deed in the ghetto, a nifty scheme for self reliance. But the men who conceived and built it see it as much more: to them, it's an experimental neighborhood technology "tool," a "multility," a radical approach to solving iatrogenic health care problems.

Our city neighborhoods, said Hallett, are terribly vulnerable to the impact of extended technologies. Their incomes are tied to jobs that are tied to technologies that are controlled from remote and generally invisible centers of power. People in city neighborhoods increasingly seem to be the victims, rather than the beneficiaries, of technological change.

People in city neighborhoods should be able to have control over their basic needs. They should be able, for instance, to grow their own food. "A variety of age groups, working together, making things happen, watching things grow, with a new sense of security is perhaps not as strange as it may seem," Hallett said. "Fifty percent of U.S. families garden now, and fifty percent of those who don't say they would like to, if they had the opportunity.

"What we need on the west side are 'multilities,' not utilities. We need the opposite of Commonwealth Edison. We need a tool which will not only provide for the nutritional needs of inner-city people, but will cut energy costs, put people to work, beautify the city.

"What we need at CAM," said Hallett, "is food instead of foodstamps. What we need is a greenhouse on the roof."

So Hallett and Bernstein discussed the idea with the CAM health task force, and plans were made. They found that a prefabricated greenhouse could be bought, mounted on platforms, and strapped to the roof, rather than staked down on the ground. A lightweight inert growing base could be used, so tons of dirt wouldn't have to be hauled up onto the roof. A well-run greenhouse, they discovered, could produce about ten pounds of food per square foot—four times a year. And if that produce were sold at 50 cents a pound, the greenhouse could pay for itself in four crops.

So the CAM greenhouse was constructed and senior citizens were recruited to work in it, and now kids from neighborhood day-care centers come by on unannounced field trips so they can watch, and maybe get a taste of a rooftop cucumber.

The seedlings are just sprouting for the second CAM crop and Stan Hallett and Scott Bernstein and community organizer Jesse Auerbach are already moving on to phase two of the greenhouse plan. They are organizing a Center for Neighborhood Technology to help community organizations set up projects demonstrating new advances in urban neighborhood technology: rooftop and vacant lot gardens; park and lagoon farming; energy alternatives like solar heating; housing rehabilitation and waste management.

This article is reprinted from Denise DeClue, Excerpts from "A Multility Grows in Garfield Park," **Reader, Chicago Free Weekly**, Vol. 6, No. 49, pp. 1, 20-24, Friday, September 9, 1977.

EXAMPLE 63
Ten Neighborhood Solar Greenhouse Projects

NEIGHBORHOOD-BASED ORGANIZATION	MAJOR PURPOSES	NEIGHBORHOOD & GROUPS SERVED	PLANNED USE OF GREENHOUSE
Christian Action Ministry	Wide range of social programs	E. & W. Garfield Park, S. Austin, N. Lawndale; Mostly black; low income	Job creation, healthful produce, reduce food costs for seniors and other constituents
Chrysalis Learning Community	Alternative high school	Uptown, Ravenswood; Appalachian, Native American, Latino, low-income	New curriculum in science, health, shop and job training, reduce operating costs in food and energy
18th Street Development Corporation	Housing rehab and rehab employment training	Pilsen; low-income Latino	New marketable skills, job creation and training, heat savings, crop income
Operation Brotherhood	Hot meals service, food distribution & activity center for senior citizens	N. & S. Lawndale, other West Side; Low-income, mostly black, and residents at s.c. housing throughout Chicago	Food for sale in current operating food distribution system, job creation and training, heat savings at program center
Jane Addams Center Hull House	Settlement house with range of social & educational programs	Lakeview; Multi-ethnic & wide income/class range	New educational focus, youth employment, satisfying program to bring seniors and teens together
Self-Help Action Center	Linking family farmer producer cooperatives with city consumer co-operatives	West Englewood, Auburn-Gresham, most other S. Side communities; Multi-ethnic and low-income	Food for distribution in ongoing program; energy savings at headquarters; program cost reduction; youth and senior job creation
South Shore Neighborhood Institute & South Shore Commission	Community development bank & block club based community organization	South Shore; Mostly mixed (lower & upper middle) income black, balance middle income white	Crop income; neighborhood tech. demonstration; cut rehab energy costs; job creation
Voice of the People	Rehab and tenant management of multi-family buildings	Uptown; Appalachian, Native American, Black; Low-income	Crop income; cutting energy costs; developing marketable skills
1st Presbyterian Church	Socially minded church, programs in food distribution & outdoor gardening	Woodlawn, Hyde Park; Black & White, mixed income	Crop income; expansion of existing greenhouses for community use; work opportunity
North River Commission	Commercial revitalization, housing management; neighborhood development	Albany Park and other North River area communities; multi-ethnic and mixed income	Crop income; rehab existing greenhouses for community use; work opportunity

This article is reprinted from "Ten Neighborhood Solar Greenhouse Projects," Center for Neighborhood Technology, 570 West Randolph Street, Chicago, Illinois

Community Food and Nutrition Center

EXAMPLE 64

For over a year now, Community Self-Reliance, Inc., and Women in Agriculture, Inc.,have been exploring the idea of constructing or renovating a building in Northampton to house a complex of activities centered around decentralized food self-sufficiency. This would consist of a variety of enterprises linked by their relationship to food production, processing, storage, distribution and consumption. By clustering these activities under the same roof, it could: (1) create a solid focus for public education about our local agricultural system, food policy and nutrition; (2) provide a site where residents, particularly the elderly and those without cars, would walk to purchase fresh, locally grown food; (3) share the expense of building acquisition, renovation, operation and maintenance so that revenue-producing operations activities could subsidize those that "break even" or lose money; (4) establish a Food Center Model having nationwide implications for direct marketing, rural development, urban revitalization, adaptive re-use of old buildings, and public/private sector cooperation.

Increased use of the Community Canning Center has made its present location inadequate for accommodating the demand for its use during the peak growing season. Although there is new equipment waiting to be installed, there is not enough space to accommodate it. Also, there are three projects that operated out of Community Self-Reliance this past year, creating a need for more office space in order to function most effectively. We are presently housed in an "expansion room" which has been donated free of charge for our use by the Hampshire County Commissioners. However, this is under temporary agreement, and if any urgent use for the room should arise, the Canning Center would be required to move upon request. Since Community Canning Centers traditionally do not generate enough income to be self-sufficient, a new location that demanded rental or mortgage payments would be out of the question. However, if income-generating operations were located in the same building, this problem could be solved by subsidizing the Canning Center's space requirement.

The Old Post Office Building in the center of town has become available for bidding from the private sector. The Architectural Conservation Trust of Boston, a non-profit organization dedicated to adaptive re-use of historical buildings, is presently conducting a feasibility study of locating a Community Food and Nutrition Center in this building. The Nacul Center of Amherst has also cooperated by providing advice on architectural renovations based on the possibilities of using alternative energy in the building.

Depending on further deliberation and study, a tentative list of occupants could include the Community Canning Center, the Agricultural Resource Library, a store front food co-op, a plant store, a bakery, storage space for root crops or bulk items in the basement, and a farmers' market. There could also be office space for public and private agencies dealing in food-related activities such as an emergency food program, agricultural services, and services to the elderly, as well as classroom/meeting space for educational activities. An interesting feature of the Old Post Office Bulding is a flat roof, which could possibly be used for a year-round solar greenhouse.

The feasibility of the idea of a Community Food and Nutrition Center rests on the commitment and hard work of those involved. Administrative structure, principles of operation, and financial considerations would need to be worked out among all concerned. However, if these groups could be brought together under one roof, there is a possibility that they could flourish rather than just survive, establishing credibility and visibility as a group that has not been possible as single operations. But most importantly, it would provide access to food, nutrition, education, and public services related to these issues and integrate these into the community at large.

PROJECTED GOALS

In the next year, the staff and board members of Community Self-Reliance look ahead to extending and expanding projects and ideas of this year, as well as generating new ones.

Low Income Outreach/Education

In keeping with our belief that food self-reliance and stimulation of our local agricultural economy can be affected by comprehensive consumer education, we have sought funding from the Department of Health, Education and Welfare to expand our current educational outreach program, Project Greenbean. If funding is awarded, more households will be added to the project, and visual aids such as slide shows will be produced to augment the hands-on approach. In an effort to affect awareness of the general public, as well as the target population of low-income, minority and the elderly, video tapes will be produced for airing on local cable and education TV networks, and a film on the local farming economy will be made available to community groups. A vigorous publicity campaign around the issues of locally-grown produce, food preservation (especially at the Canning Center) and nutritional awareness is also proposed. If funding is not made available by HEW, other funding will be sought for these priorities.

Public School Program

As a result of our outreach efforts with elementary school children and the strong, positive feedback we received, we have been encouraged to seek funding for the development of an educational program for use in public schools.

Direct Marketing

The Seed-to-Table direct marketing research work group is interested in obtaining funds to implement its suggestions for a direct marketing model in this county. Projected goals include the establishment of more farmers' markets in the area and the possibility of a food storage/distribution warehouse central to the Greater Northampton-Amherst area.

Self-Help Canning

Central to the whole concept of food self-reliance is a means by which food grown here in the summer growing season can be preserved for use in the winter months. Therefore, it is essential that the Canning Center continue functioning. Funds need to be secured for staff salaries and for the installation of new equipment which is currently in storage but needed to meet the increasing demand for use of the Center. A skeletal proposal has been written toward this end and specific funding is currently being sought.

Commercial Canning

Commercial canning has been considered as one means of making the Canning Center financially self-sufficient. The possibilities and limitations of commercial canning are discussed in a previous section of this report. Although traditional approaches to this idea do not appear viable, processing for special needs groups (i.e., elderly, diabetics, etc.) should be investigated.

New Space

Finally, a need of all the projects is that of more space. The Canning Center itself could accommodate nearly twice as many canners if there were room to install its new equipment. With the addition of new projects and the expansion of existing ones, it is clear that our current space is inadequate. Staff members, in conjunction with Women in Agriculture, are in the process of trying to secure a centrally located building for use as a Community Food and Nutrition Center which would house a farmers' market, a food co-op, and other food and agricultural related offices along with the Canning Center. Details on this aspect of our program have already been described. Now, monies for a feasibility study need to be secured as does funding for renovation of the building and for moving expenses.

Beyond the projects we can foresee, it is hoped that the members of the Coordinating Council and the community will suggest ideas and other new projects.

This article is reprinted from "Community Food and Nutrition Center," **Community Self-Reliance, Inc.,** 1977 Annual Report, Northampton, Massachusetts, pp. 25-27, 1977.

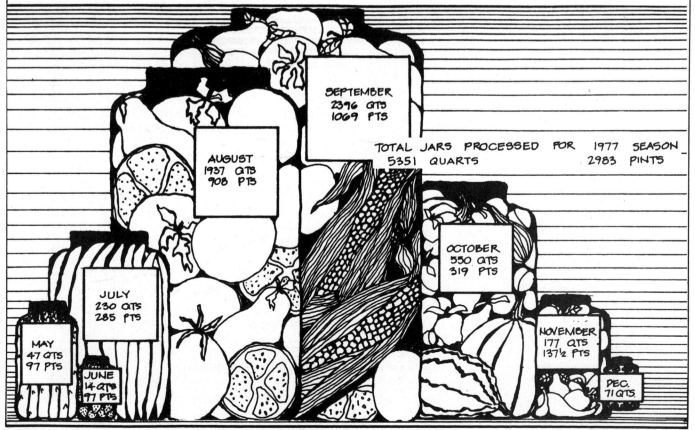

SEPTEMBER
2396 QTS
1069 PTS

TOTAL JARS PROCESSED FOR 1977 SEASON
5351 QUARTS   2983 PINTS

AUGUST
1937 QTS
908 PTS

OCTOBER
550 QTS
319 PTS

JULY
230 QTS
285 PTS

NOVEMBER
177 QTS
137½ PTS

MAY
47 QTS
97 PTS

JUNE
14 QTS
97 PTS

DEC.
71 QTS

Chapter 15

Innovative Food and Nutrition Policies

Many exciting projects dealing with food and nutrition issues are being initiated throughout the country at the state and local level. These projects include nutritional feeding programs; "gleaning" and food salvage efforts; nutrition education programs and campaigns to repeal food sales taxes.

Even though many of the federal feeding programs such as W.I.C., Food Stamps and the School Breakfast and Lunch Programs are considered national projects, the reality of the impact and effectiveness of these programs is determined at the state and local level. It is at the local level that innovations are being initiated by individuals and organizations active on food and nutrition issues.

There are several key organizations which assist community groups across the country who are working on issues such as hunger and malnutrition, nutrition research, food tax repeals and the feeding programs. These include: Community Nutrition Insitute (CNI), monitoring and advocacy on food and nutrition issues; the Children's Foundation, advocacy for child nutrition programs; the Center for Science in the Public Interest (CSPI), publications and information on nutrition, food quality and community and citizen action strategies on food related issues, and the Food Research and Action Center (FRAC), a public interest law firm and advocacy organization for federal food programs. Their addresses are listed in the bibliography following this narrative.

FOOD AND NUTRITION PROGRAMS

There are numerous food and nutrition programs available to low-income consumers. They range from School Lunch and Breakfast Programs to the Food Stamp Program and W.I.C. (Reducing Malnutrition Among Women, Infants and Children). These programs are sponsored by the federal government and implemented at the state level. The School Breakfast Program is an example of an excellent initiative that few states—only about 20%—have taken advantage of to date.

States can make changes in existing legislation to increase the quality of the various school food programs. One illustration of changes needed is that there are 70,000 participating schools in the School Lunch Program, while only 21,000 of these schools take advantage of the School Breakfast Program. There are an estimated 9 million children who could receive free school breakfasts—or meals at greatly reduced costs—but are now unable to benefit. This is the type of problem localities can act on through remodeling state legislation. FRAC has prepared an extremely useful resource publication; *A Guide to State School/Food Legislation* for local and state action. **Example 65, A Bill: To Improve School Fo** illustrates how groups can prepare model legislation to change and breakfast programs so that they are more effective.

The Food Stamp Program is the most controversial of all the federal feeding programs. It is attacked for fraud, waste, and as being a hand-out program. In reality, the number of frauds is low (24 out of every 1,000), and the majority of the participants are on welfare or unemployed. What is needed is sound and innovative administration of the Food Stamp Program at the local level. There are numerous campaigns underway to change and improve the Food Stamp Program by local groups. The Center for Science in the Public Interest suggests in its defense of the Food Stamp Program: "Make food stamps a multi-faceted political topic: relief for the victims of our economic ups and downs, a boost to the working poor; a way to bring federal money to the local level; redistribution of wealth, and a forward looking investment in the health and strength of our people."[1]

Most food stamps are currently sold at banks or post offices. Criticisms raised about this arrangement are the short hours during which these agencies are open and an environment that many low-income people do not feel comfortable in. What is needed are new state regulations permitting community groups to operate stamp sales offices. In Massachusetts, Representatives Doris Bunte and Mel King supported such a proposal. The state (through the federal Food Stamp Program) pays a certain fee to the vendor for each sale and this usually covers the costs of the operation. Not only do participants have a more pleasant environment to buy their food stamps in, but this approach provides significant economic support for local businesses through increased sales at neighborhood grocery stores.[2]

Banning junk food vending machines (which sell candy, soda pop, potato chips, etc.) in public schools is another local campaign taken on by concerned citizens. Twenty-five states have adopted regulations banning junk food in school vending machines. School boards in communities such as Washington, D.C.; Dallas, Texas; Bloomington, Indiana; and Burlington, Wisconsin have taken steps to eliminate junk food sales at public schools.

REPEALING FOOD TAXES

"Did you know that if your state's food tax were repealed you'd be able to buy 2.5 weeks of groceries with the money you would save in a year? That's almost like walking into a grocery store and walking out with 2.5 weeks of free groceries!

"Henry Ford makes 1,000 times more money than you do, yet he doesn't eat much more. You are both paying the same tax rate on food, yet it hurts you and your pocketbook much more than it hurts Henry Ford's."[3]

These are statements Michigan consumers heard during efforts to repeal their state food tax. Sales tax on food is the most regressive of all taxes. People must eat. Americans pay over one billion dollars in sales taxes on food each year. Since the poor have lower annual incomes, they spend a larger proportion of their money on both food and food taxes than do middle and upper income Americans. In **Example 66, Repealing State Food Taxes**, Diane Fuchs explains which states have repealed or are attempting to repeal food taxes.

There are many creative approaches to food tax repeal campaigns across the United States. The Missouri Tax Reform Group published a fact sheet which looked like a grocery receipt to catch the attention of consumers. In Washington, the Hunger Action Center out of Seattle sponsored a massive campaign to repeal the food tax. Through coalition building, lobbying, brochures and telephoning, they were able to educate and convince citizens to vote to repeal the food tax. **Example 67, Food Taxes Are Hard to Swallow**, from a brochure issued by the Hunger Action Center, illustrates the valuable information which was passed along to the consumer during this campaign.

INNOVATIVE PROJECTS

- **Gleaning:** There is an exciting network of organizations that are involved in "gleaning projects." This process involves gathering excess food that grocery stores or farmers have to dispose of and distributing it to needy families. Gleaning can be considered a component of the alternative food delivery system and it also fulfills human nutritional needs and helps to eliminate the tremendous waste that is found in our modern system of food production and distribution. Grassroots organizations are working closely with city officials, local health and sanitation departments, food program agencies and major chain stores to develop "gleaning projects." There are some incentives for the large chain grocery stores to cooperate in gleaning efforts. One such incentive is a federal tax law (Public Law 94-455) which states that "a corporation may deduct, as a charitable contribution, its cost plus one-half of its normal gross profit, on items of inventory contributed to certain qualified public charity organizations for use in (tax) exempt purposes for the care of the ill, needy or infants."

  A group that has been instrumental in creating a network of "food banks" of gleaners is Second Harvest Food Banks. This program grew out of a local Food Bank program that is divided into two projects; a salvage bank to distribute bulk food to feeding agencies and a "food box" program to supply three-day food boxes for emergency situations. **Example 68, St. Mary's Food Bank Salvage Program**, is a fact sheet that describes this gleaning program. Second Harvest Food Banks provides technical assistance, fact sheets, workshops and a newsletter; *Thought for Food.*

- **Nutrition Education and Gardening:** Another innovative approach that localities are implementing is nutrition education linked to community gardening—particularly for low-income people living in inner city neighborhoods. Gardening programs such as Chicago's, and New York City's Urban Gardening Program are trying to include nutritional education in their projects. As Ruth Lowenberg, Nutritional Coordinator of the Cornell Urban Gardening Program, writes: "these nutritional programs capitalize on the enthusiasm generated from growing one's own food to motivate participants to think in more general terms about how food habits affect health." Workshops through day care centers, community centers, schools, libraries and garden projects are given, and recipe books on nutritional preparation of foods are provided.

  Another nutrition education project that works in conjunction with a gardening program has been initiated by a grassroots organization; the Bronx Frontier Development Corporation in New York. They have a "Chuck Wagon" that is a mobile van unit complete with audio-visual equipment, display shelves, stage and kitchen. Through gr___ from private foundations they were able to purchase an old b___ carry on outreach work on how to grow and prepare ___ recipes and how to strengthen the consumer's dolla___

Wagon" is sponsored by Bronx Frontier in cooperation with the Bronx Division of the New York Public Library, the Parks and Recreation Commission for the City of New York and the Cornell Extension NYC Gardening Program—all of which are public agencies operating at the local level.

• **Operation Brotherhood:** Operation Brotherhood is an integrated food and nutrition operation meeting the needs of senior citizens in Chicago's west side. It is a seven-day-a-week non-profit organization housed in three warehouses that carries on activities ranging from a feeding program to a health care center and a food co-op, to gardening, transportation, and arts and crafts. One of the most exciting components of their program is a mobile grocery store. Through the Chicago Department on the Aging, Operation Brotherhood received funds to serve 1,000 elderly persons who are "shut-in" at seven high-rise aging homes in neighborhoods with no grocery stores. Plans to expand their greenhouse and buy another warehouse for a Farmers' Market are underway. **Example 69, Operation Brotherhood,** describes this unique organization in detail.

CONCLUSION

Food is a basic issue around which people representing diverse constituencies and interests can organize. It is at the local level that individuals concerned about food, "hunger" and nutrition issues are joining organizations and forming coalitions to develop the new approaches and public policies needed to deal with many critical problems. The issues they are addressing range from making the federal food programs more effective to ensuring that high quality food is made available to low-income families and the elderly, and from banning sales of "junk food" in public schools to repealing food taxes at the state level.

[1]Center for Science in the Public Interest (CSPI), **From the Ground Up: Building a Grass Roots Food Policy,** p. 79, 1976.

[2]Perry, Stewart E., **Building a Model Block Community: The Roxbury Action Program,** Center for Community Economic Development, Cambridge, Massachusetts, p. 72, 1978.

[3]Center for Science in the Public Interest (CSPI), **From the Ground Up: Building a Grass Roots Food Policy,** p. 32, 1976.

PEANUTS / by Charles M. Schulz

Resources

ORGANIZATIONS

Center for Science in the Public Interest

1755 S Street, N.W.
Washington, D.C. 20009
(202) 332-4250
Michael Jacobson, Director

The Children's Foundation

1420 New York Avenue, N.W.
Washington, D.C. 20005
(202) 347-3300
Barbara Bode, President

Community Nutrition Institute

1146 19th Street, N.W.
Washington, D.C. 20006
(202) 833-1730
Rod Leonard, Director

Food Research and Action Center

2011 Eye Street, N.W.
Washington, D.C. 20006
(202) 452-8250
Nancy Amidei, Director

BIBLIOGRAPHY

Center for Science in the Public Interest (CSPI), "Special Food Day Issue," **Action Faction**. Vol. 1, No. 4, CSPI, 1012 14th Street, N.W. #901, Washington, D.C. 20005. April 1977. What the consumer can do to improve food quality.

The Community Food and Nutrition Program, **Organizing a Nutrition Coalition in the Community**. Community Food and Nutrition Program, 1910 K Street, N.W., Washington, D.C. 20006. 1977.

Connor, M., **The Urban Farmer and Gardening for Health and Nutrition**. Institute for Local Self-Reliance, 1717 18th Street, N.W., Washington, D.C. 20009. $3.00 plus 50¢ postage.

Council for Agricultural Science and Technology Task Force (CAST), **Dietary Goals for the United States: A Commentary**. Report no. 71, CAST, Agronomy Building, Iowa State University, Ames, Iowa 50011. November 30, 1977.

Food Research and Action Center (FRAC), **FRAC's Guide to State School Food Legislation**. FRAC, 2011 I Street, N.W., Washington, D.C. 20006. March 1978. Practical guide to drafting, lobbying and monitoring desired state food legislation. FRAC publishes many such practical guides to influencing state nutrition programs, summer food programs, county food stamp programs, and child-care food programs.

Food Research and Action Center (FRAC), **Guide to State School Food Programs**. FRAC, 2011 I Street, N.W., Washington, D.C. 20006. 1978.

Food Research and Action Center (FRAC), **FRAC's Guide to the Food Stamp Program**, FRAC, 2011 Eye Street, N.W., Washington, D.C. 20006, January 1978, $1.00.

National Agricultural Library, **Food Science and Technology: A Bibliography of Recommended Materials**. Richard Wallace, Editor. National Agricultural Library, USDA, Beltsville, Maryland 20705. February 1978. List of sources on almost every facet of food science and nutrition.

U.S. Senate, Select Committee on Nutrition and Human Needs, Hearings on **National Meals-On-Wheels Program**. 95th Congress, first session. Superintendent of Documents, U.S. Government Printing Office, Washington, D.C. 20402. April 4, 1977.

Wieloszynski, Roberta B., **Toward a Rational Policy on Nutrition and Food in America**. Consumer Affairs Office, Syracuse, New York. Recommendations at the local, state and federal level for improving the American diet.

World Hunger Education Service, **Who's Involved With Hunger: Organization Guide**. WHES, 2000 P Street, N.W., Washington, D.C. 20036. 1979. $2.50.

GRIN & BEAR IT / by Lichty & Wagner

"I don't think a farmers' strike will affect our operation, men ... we haven't used any farm products in our bread for some time."

EXAMPLE 65

A Bill: To Improve School Food Service

Section 1. Legislative Intent

(a)   The Legislature finds that: 1] the proper nutrition of children is a matter of the highest state priority, and 2] there is a demonstrated relationship between the intake of food and good nutrition and the capacity of children to develop and learn, and 3] the teaching of the principles of good nutrition in schools is urgently needed to assist children at all income levels in developing the proper eating habits essential for life long good health.

(b)   It is the policy of the state of _____ that no child shall go hungry at school and that schools have an obligation to provide for the nutritional needs and the nutrition education of all pupils during the school day.

(c)   The Legislature further recognizes the need to establish a plan for permanent funding to provide qualifying local agencies with continuous financial support for the operation of school nutrition programs.

Section 2. Definitions

As used in this act:

(a)   "Board" means the governing body of a local school district.

(b)   "Department" means the State Department of Education.

(c)   "Especially needy school" means any school in which twenty percent (20%) or more of the children in attendance are eligible for free or reduced priced meals.

(d)   "Free lunch or breakfast" means a lunch or breakfast for which neither the pupil or any member of the pupil's household reimburses or compensates the school district.

(e)   "Household" means a person or a group of persons who are living together as one economic unit.

(f)   "Parent" means a parent, guardian, custodian, or other person upon whom a pupil is dependent for care.

(g)   "Pupil" means a person attending a school other than a person enrolled in an adult education program.

(h)   "Reduced price lunch or breakfast" means a lunch or breakfast which meets all of the following criteria: the price is less than the full cost of the meal; the price does not exceed the maximum allowable rate established by the National School Lunch Act, 42 U.S.C. 1758, and the Child Nutrition Act of 1966, 42 U.S.C. 1773, and the price is in cash and no other form of reimbursement or compensation is required.

(i)   "School" means any public school, private school, parochial school, kindergarten, child care center, local or state agency or institution which qualifies for federal aid under the National School Lunch Program or the School Breakfast Program prescribed respectively by Chapter 13 (commencing with Section 1751) and Chapter 13A (commencing with Section 1771) of Title 42 of the United States Code.

(j)   "State Board" means the State Board of Education.

Section 3. School Feeding Programs

(a)   By no later than [date]   ,each board shall establish and operate a School Lunch Program under which a lunch shall be made available to all pupils enrolled in the schools of the district. The lunch shall meet standards prescribed by the department. The Board may charge a fee for each lunch, except that the Board shall provide free and reduced price lunches to pupils eligible under the rules promulgated pursuant to Section 4 (b) (2). The fee charged shall not exceed the actual average daily cost of the lunch less the amount of food and financial assistance received by the Board for each lunch served.

(b)   By no later than [date]   , each Board shall establish and operate a School Breakfast Program under which a breakfast shall be made available to all pupils enrolled in all schools of the district. The breakfast shall meet standards prescribed by the Department. The board may charge a fee for each breakfast, except that the board shall provide free and reduced-price breakfasts to pupils eligible under the rules promulgated pursuant to Section 4(b) (2). The fee charged shall not exceed the actual average daily cost of the breakfast less the amount of food and financial assistance received by the board for each breakfast served.

(c)   Beginning [date]   , each board shall establish and operate a Supplemental Milk Program under which milk shall be made available to all pupils who are enrolled in the schools of the district. The board may charge a fee for the milk, except that the board shall provide free milk to pupils eligible under the rules promulgated pursuant to Section 4 (b) (2). The fee charged for milk shall not exceed the cost of the milk and accessories less the amount of financial assistance received by the board.

Section 4. Duties of the State Board of Education

(a)   Within 90 days after the effective date of this Act, the State Board shall promulgate rules in accordance with this Act and in conformity with United States Department of Agriculture regulations to implement and administer the School Lunch, Breakfast and Supplemental Milk Programs required by Section 3. Such rules shall be promulgated in accordance with the State Administrative Procedure Act.

(b)   The rules shall:

(1)   Establish minimum nutrition requirements for School Lunch, and Supplemental Milk Programs. The requirements, at a minimum, shall meet standards prescribed by the United States Department of Agriculture for lunches, breakfasts, and supplemental milk in accordance with 42 U.S.C. §1758, 1773 and 1772 respectively, and each meal

shall supply at least one third (1/3) of the daily dietary allowance established by the National Research Council of the National Academy of Sciences.

(2) Establish standards of income eligibility for free and reduced price lunches and breakfasts and free supplemental milk based upon income guidelines which are determined by household size. The standards of income eligibility shall be the maximum allowable household income limits for free and reduced priced meals and free milk that are prescribed by the United States Department of Agriculture, pursuant to 42 U.S.C. §§1758, 1773 and 1772 respectively.

(3) Prescribe uniform methods for determination, and obtain a determination of pupil eligibility for free and reduced price lunches and breakfasts and free supplemental milk. The methods shall ensure the confidentiality of the information contained in the application for free and reduced price lunches and breakfasts and free supplemental milk. Such methods shall also ensure that all parents and pupils are made aware of the existence of the free and reduced price meals.

(4) Prescribe guidelines to assure that a pupil or household eligible to receive free or reduced price lunches or breakfasts or free supplemental milk is not discriminated against or overtly identified.

(5) Prescribe methods for parent, pupil and school board participation in the planning and evaluation of school meals and other foods sold or dispensed on school premises.

(6) Ensure that the food preference of pupils shall be accommodated, to the maximum extent feasible, including the provision of meals that fulfill the ethnic food preferences of children attending each school.

(7) Prescribe nutritional standards for foods other than those included in subdivision (a) that are permitted to be sold or dispensed on school premises Such standards shall require that all such food sold or dispensed on school premises are high in nutritional content and will contribute to the sound nutritional habits of students.*

(8) Prescribe a uniform reporting system for the collection, compilation, and analysis of data relative to the administration of this Section and Section 3.

(9) Establish rules which, to the maximum extent feasible, encourage on-site preparation of meals, the employment of local people and the use of small and minority-owned businesses. If a school board has inadequate or no food preparation facilities, establish rules pursuant to which it may contract with another school board, a public agency or a private non-profit agency within the State for the preparation and delivery of meals.

(10) Establish procedures pursuant to which all valid claims for reimbursement of any kind are paid within 30 days of submission.

(11) Prescribe other necessary standards and procedures to efficiently and effectively administer this Section and Section 3.

Section 5. Compliance

Each board shall submit to the Department, in the manner prescribed by the Department, a plan for compliance with Section 3. The plan shall be submitted within 90 days after receiving directives for plan content from the Department.

Section 6. Non-discrimination

Each board shall ensure that a pupil eligible to receive a free or reduced price lunch or breakfast or free supplemental milk shall not be discriminated against nor shall there be any overt identification of an eligible pupil by the use of special tokens or tickets; the announcement, posting, or publication of names; physical separation; choice of meal; or by any other means.

Section 7. Reimbursement

(a) The Department shall pay a school district for each free breakfast and each free lunch served by a school which participates in the National School Breakfast or Lunch Program and complies with this section and Section 3. The payment shall be calculated by subtracting the sum of the federal reimbursement rate for a free lunch or breakfast including the value of

commodities received from the actual average cost of such meal, but not to exceed _____ cents per meal.

(b) The Department shall pay a school district for each reduced price lunch and breakfast served by a school which participates in the National School Breakfast or Lunch Program and complies with this section and Section 3. The payment shall be calculated by subtracting the sum of the federal reimbursement rate for a reduced price breakfast or lunch including the value of commodities received plus the fee charged from the actual average cost of such meal, but not to exceed _____ cents per meal.

(c) The payments required by subsections (a) and (b) shall be in addition to disbursements made by the Department from funds credited to the State's matching share required by Section 5 of Public Law 94-105, 42 U.S.C. §1756.

(d) The Department shall make every effort to ensure that any especially needy school, as defined in Section 2(c) of this Act, receives the higher rate of reimbursement to which it is entitled pursuant to 42 U.S.C. §1773 for each free and reduced price breakfast served.

(e) The Department may disapprove any claim for reimbursement for meals served if it finds that balanced, nutritious meals are not being served in accordance with the standards prescribed pursuant to Section 4(b)(1) of this Act.

Section 8. Food Service Equipment Assistance

The Department shall prescribe a method for determining, and shall determine, the actual, reasonable and necessary initial equipment and capital outlay costs incurred by a school district after the effective date of this Act for the specific purpose of complying with Section 3 and shall report to the legislature with recommendations for full reimbursement of all such costs not otherwise reimbursed or scheduled to be reimbursed with federal or state funding or permissible pupil payments. The legislature shall appropriate

*   P.L. 95-166 which was enacted November 10, 1977, allows the Secretary of Agriculture to issue regulations in this area but he has yet to do so.

and the Department shall allocate, as part of the annual Department appropriations, the approved amount due the school district under this Subsection.

Section 9. Compliance

(a)   The Commissioner of Education shall supervise the implementation of this Article and shall investigate acts of alleged non-compliance. In the event that the Commissioner finds that a school board has failed to comply with the provisions of this Article, the Commissioner shall certify such non-compliance to the Attorney General. The Attorney General shall conduct such investigation as may be necessary to establish non-compliance. The Attorney General may then seek injunctive relief in any court of law of competent jurisdiction.

(b)   Any pupil, parent or school board aggrieved by the actions or inactions of any person or institution in complying with the provisions of this Act, shall have the right to bring suit in any court of competent jurisdiction to enforce their respective rights under this Act. Nothing contained in Section 9 (a) shall be construed to limit, supersede or in any way affect this right.

Section 10. Nutrition Information, Education, and Training

The Department shall formulate the basic elements of a nutrition education program. Such program shall coordinate classroom instruction with the food service program and shall be of sufficient variety and flexibility to meet the needs of pupils in the total educational spectrum. The Department shall encourage effective dissemination of scientifically valid nutrition information and provide training in food management skills and the fundamentals of nutrition for food service personnel.

Section 11. Outreach

The Department shall make known the existence of the School Lunch Program, 42 U.S.C. §§ 1751 et seq.; the School Breakfast Program, 42 U.S.C. §1773; and the Special Milk Program, 42 U.S.C. §1772 to all schools and institutions in the State which are eligible to participate in these programs and assist them in entering the programs if they wish to do so.

Section 12. Annual Report

The Department shall make an annual report to the Legislature relating to the implementation and administration of this Act and shall send a copy of the report to each school board.

TECHNICAL ANALYSIS OF SCHOOL FOOD LEGISLATIVE PROVISIONS

You have many options in drafting a school food bill. A number of legislative provisions are listed below to help you, with an indication of which states have included them.

STATE	Mandatory Breakfast	Mandatory Lunch	Phase-In Time	Emphasize Especially Needy	Additional State Subsidy Provided	Non-food Assistance	Nutrition Requirement	Nutrition Education	Student/Parent Involvement	Non-discrimination Provision	Local Board Accountability to State	State Accountability to Legislature	Enforcement Provision	Emergency Exemption	Federal Law Change Exemption	Vended Food Provision
South Carolina	X															
New Jersey		X	X				X									
New York	X*		X	X	X		X								X	
California	one or the other	X	X	X	X	X	X				X		X			
Ohio	X	X	X	X										X		
Michigan	X	X	X	X	X	X	X		X	X	X	X		X	X	X
Massachusetts	X*	X	X	X	X		X	X								
Illinois		X	X	X	X		X									

* Only in cities of a specified size

CONTACT PERSONS ON STATE LEGISLATION

CALIFORNIA *

Food Law Center
California Rural Legal Assistance
115 Sansome Street, Suite 900
San Francisco, CA 94104
(415) 421-3405
Att'n. Rob Teets

California Nutrition Action Committee
1419 Broadway
Oakland, CA 94612
(415) 834-2896
Att'n: Vicki Katayama

The Children's Rights Group
693 Mission Street, 2nd Fl.
San Francisco, CA 94104
(415) 495-6420
Att'n: Edward J. Polk, Bob Spence

CONNECTICUT *

Project FEAD
112 Main Street
P.O. Box 322
Danielson, CT 06239
(203) 774-0455
Att'n: E. Cooney

FLORIDA *

Florida Legal Services
236 Pensacola Street
Tallahassee, FL 32301
(904) 222-2151
Att'n: Robert F. Williams

ILLINOIS *

American Friends Service Committee
Chicago Regional Office
407 South Dearborn Street
Chicago IL 60605
(312) 427-2533
Att'n: J. Gottsegan

Food Action and Community Training
343 South Dearborn Street
Chicago, IL 60604
(312) 341-1070
Att'n: Nelson A. Soltman

LOUISIANA *

Louisiana Hunger Coalition
226 Carondelet St., No. 205
New Orleans, LA 70130
(504) 529-7551
Att'n: Jeanne Keller

MAINE *

Pine Tree Legal Services
154 State Street
Augusta, ME 04330
(207) 623-2971
Att'n: Marshall Cohen, Neal Shankman

MARYLAND *

Maryland Legal Aid Bureau
341 North Calvert Street
Baltimore, MD 21401
(301) 539-5340
Att'n: J. Lyko

Maryland Food Committee, Inc.
105 West Monument Street
Baltimore, MD 21201
(301) 837-5667
Att'n: Betsy Dunklin

MASSACHUSETTS *

Emergency Food Service
36 Concord Street
Framingham, MA 01701
(617) 872-4853
(617) 879-4870
Att'n: Cliff Walton

Massachusetts Advocacy Center
2 Park Square
Boston, MA 02116
(617) 357-8431
Att'n: Tom Mela

MICHIGAN *

School Breakfast/Lunch Committee
Episcopal Diocese of Michigan
4800 Woodward Avenue
Detroit, MI 48201
(313) 832-4400

Michigan Legal Services Food
  Litigation Project
220 Bagley Avenue, 900 Michigan Bldg.
Detroit, MI 48226
(313) 964-4130
Att'n: Nida Donar

Governor's Office of Nutrition
352 Hollister Building
Lansing, MI 48926
(517) 373-9230
Att'n: Laura Hess

NEW JERSEY *

National Child Nutrition Project
46 Bayard Street
New Brunswick, NJ 08901
(201) 846-1161
Att'n: Barbara Zang

NEW YORK *

Community Action for Legal Services
  Food Law Project
335 Broadway
New York, NY 10013
(212) 966-6600
Att'n: Alice McInerney

New York City School Breakfast Committee
711 Amsterdam Avenue
New York, NY 10025
(212) 850-6804
Att'n: K. Goldman

District Council 37, AFSCME – AFL – CIO
  Local 372 Employees
140 Park Place
New York, NY 10007
(212) 766-1199
Att'n: Charles Hughes

Community Services Society
103 E. 22nd Street
New York, NY 10010
(212) 254-8900
Att'n: F. Barrett

OHIO *

Ohio State Legal Services
155 No. High Street, 3rd Floor
Columbus, OH 43215
(614) 221-2668
Att'n: Bob Mullinax; Bob Mapes

Hunger Task Force of Columbus and
  Central Ohio
65 South Fourth Street
Columbus, OH 43215
(614) 464-1956
Att'n: Marion Wearly

SOUTH CAROLINA *

Piedmont Legal Services
Suite 200
Library Street Office Building
180 Library Street
Spartanburg, SC 29301
(803) 582-0369
Att'n: Allen Holmes

TEXAS *

Texas Impact
2702 Greenlawn Parkway
Austin, Texas 78757
(512) 459-7569
Att'n: Carl Siegenthaler
          100 E. 27th Street
          Austin, TX 78705

VIRGINIA

The Virginia Commission on Children and Youth
9th Street Office Building
Richmond, VA 23216
(804) 786-4834
Att'n: R. Pumphrey

WASHINGTON

Hunger Action Center
1063 Capitol Way No. 206-207
Olympia, WA 98501
(206) 352-7980
Att'n: Mary Lynne McDonald

          THE LEGISLATIVE COMMITTEES OF THE
U.S. CONGRESS ARE:

Committee on Education and Labor
U.S. House of Representatives
Washington, D.C. 20515
(202) 225-4527
Carl Perkins (D-Ky.), Chairperson

Committee on Agriculture, Nutrition and Forestry
U.S. Senate
Washington, D.C. 20510
(202) 224-2035
Herman Talmadge (D-Ga.), Chairperson

KEY	
*	Proposed School Food Legislation
**	Introduced in Leglislature but not enacted
***	Enacted Leglislation

This article is reprinted from Alice Scott, Paula Roberts, and Jeff Kirsch, "A Bill: To Improve School Food Service," FRAC's Guide to State School Food Legislation, Food Research Action Center (FRAC), Cover and pp. 12-15, March 1978.

EXAMPLE
66 Repealing State Food Taxes

The sales tax on food is the most regressive tax of all. It takes the most from those who have the least. It is a tax on a necessity which must be paid by everyone, regardless of income.

Twenty-three states currently tax food with rates ranging from 2% in Oklahoma to 5% in Mississippi.

The tax is regressive because high-income families spend less of their income on food and on the tax than do low-income families. For instance, a family of four with an income above $25,000 spends about 8.9% of its income on food, or an average of 2.7% on the food tax. A family with an income under $8,000 spends almost a quarter of its income on food, or 7.4% for the tax.

A number of states that tax food have dealt in part with the regressivity of the tax by enacting income tax credits. Colorado, Idaho, and Nebraska compensate in this way. In addition, Hawaii, New Mexico and Vermont provide credits on their income tax to generally compensate for sales taxes, including those on food.

Another 23 states and the District of Columbia simply exempt food from the general sales tax.

Eliminating the tax, however, also removes a hefty source of state revenues. As a result, fears of increases in other taxes led voters in Colorado and Missouri to reject ballot measures in 1976; and voters in Arkansas defeated a similar ballot initiative, sponsored by ACORN, this past November.

These revenues could be made up in other ways, however. For instance, the general sales tax could be extended to non-necessity items, such as services purchased mainly by businesses and those in upper-income brackets. Other additional revenue sources might be generated by:

- More efficient sales tax administration, including the pre-collection of the tax from the wholesaler rather than retailer.

- More effective tax administration, generally including membership in the Multistate Tax Commission.

- An increase in the upper levels of the state income tax or enactment of one where none exists.

- Placement of a tax on intangible personal property.

- An increase in corporate taxes.

In their upcoming sessions, the legislatures in Utah and Mississippi will be considering bills to exempt food from the sales tax.

This article is reprinted from Diane Fuchs, "Repealing State Food Taxes," **Ways and Means**, Conference on Alternative State and Local Policies, December 1978.

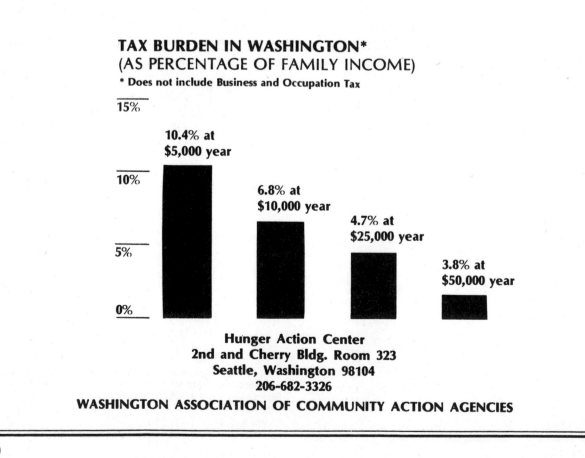

TAX BURDEN IN WASHINGTON*
(AS PERCENTAGE OF FAMILY INCOME)
* Does not include Business and Occupation Tax

15%

10.4% at $5,000 year

10%

6.8% at $10,000 year

4.7% at $25,000 year

5%

3.8% at $50,000 year

0%

Hunger Action Center
2nd and Cherry Bldg. Room 323
Seattle, Washington 98104
206-682-3326

WASHINGTON ASSOCIATION OF COMMUNITY ACTION AGENCIES

Food Taxes Are Hard to Swallow

EXAMPLE 67

How Much Could Low Income Families Save If The Sales Tax On Food Were Removed?

Senior citizens on fixed incomes and low income families will save the cost of two to three weeks of groceries.

Budget	Food at home	Food as % of total	$ Saved
Lower Budget $10,365	$2,677	26%	$142.00
Middle Budget $14,618	$3,293	21%	$174.00
Higher Budget $22,100	$4,006	18%	$212.00

The poor will still pay a heavy burden in property taxes (usually paid indirectly through the landlord as part of the rent), taxes on utilities and sales tax on purchases other than food and medicine.

The repeal of the sales tax on food will take some of the regressive bite out of the sales tax.

If the sales tax is removed and replaced by, for example, a 1% flat income tax, low income families will still save.

	1% Flat Income	Present Food Sales Tax	$ Saved
Lower Budget $10,365	$103.65	$142.00	+$38.35
Middle Budget $15,618	$156.18	$174.00	+$17.82
Higher Budget $22,100	$221.00	$212.00	-$9.00

The Sales Tax On Groceries Is Unfair!!

Low-income family budget $5,000

40% of a low-income budget is used for food.

2.2% of a low-income budget is eaten away by the sales tax on food.

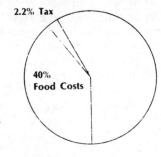

Moderate-low income budget $10,365

26% of a moderate income budget is used for food.

1.4% is swallowed-up by the sales tax on food.

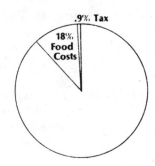

Higher-income budget $22,100

18% of a higher budget is used for food.

0.9% goes for the sales tax on food.

Repeal The Sales Tax On Food!!

This article is reprinted from "Food Taxes Are Hard To Swallow," Hunger Action Center, 2nd and Cherry Building, Room 323, Seattle, Washington 98104, 1976.

EXAMPLE 68

Fact Sheet of St. Mary's Food Bank Salvage Program

Origin . . . . . .   Established in December 1967.

Purpose . . . . .   To reduce food costs of charities by providing surplus or salvage food as available. We act as a food clearing house.

Policy . . . . . .   **WE ARE AN EXCHANGE AGENT FOR FOOD FOR CHARITIES!!**
We take salvageable food products such as: outdated products, day-old bakery goods, dented canned goods, broken packaging, shrinkage ice cream, bruised meat products, seconds in produce, mistakes in manufacturing, etc. These things can and do help the hungry of this area!

As an exchange agent, we are cautious to protect brand-name items and distribute them to charitable organizations who will see that they are consumed immediately. Each of the Participating Agencies do "on premises feeding" and have signed disclaimers freeing both St. Mary's and the Donors from responsibility. Participating Agencies cooperate in food pick ups. We are non-denominational in our pass-outs — and sell nothing.

Funding. . . . .   We are funded only by individual contributions of the people of this community with the exception of three P.S.E. employees.

Budget. . . . . .   The Food Bank is staffed by volunteer help. There are no salaries and consequently no administrative cost. Our yearly budget has yet to exceed $15,000.00.

Participation .   By 237 local charities, social workers and churches – from a starting group of 30 in 1967.

Results . . . . . .   From 250,000 lbs. of food in 1968 to 1,800,000 lbs. in 1975. An average of over 35 agencies draw daily from our stock.

Projection . . . .   1977 should exceed 1975 & 76 — future growth will depend entirely on additional co-operation from the local community. It is impossible to *increase* our services without additional support, as the transportation costs, building expenses, (cost of running 5 large walk-in freezing units) and building rent use up the total present operating budget.

Success? . . . .   The accountant suggests that each $1.00 spent returns $17.00 in local charity making the Food Bank a very very practical program. In a way we are a working (physical) charity and a "positive protest" against bureaucratically oriented waste. Our eligibility rules and surroundings are simple and there is little red-tape.

YOUR HELP WOULD BE APPRECIATED AND GO DIRECTLY TO THE POOR! To some extent we hope to keep Phoenix from becoming a problem area because of hunger. Please do not throw away or destroy food, the need is great.

Early 1976 Report. . . . . . .   Volume 1,527,173 lbs.
Daily average - 35 charities per day - (up5) No increase in volume but much better quality.

Operational Manager, Ed Mulvey
For further information call **254-9762.**

This article is reprinted from "Fact Sheet of St. Mary's Food Bank Salvage Program," St. Mary's Food Bank, 724 South First Avenue, Phoenix, Arizona 85003.

Operation Brotherhood

EXAMPLE
69

A MULTI-PURPOSE CENTER FOR THE ELDERLY/HANDICAPPED

The purpose of Operation Brotherhood at 3745-53 West Ogden Avenue is to provide needed services to the elderly on Chicago's Westside and to assist them in having healthful, meaningful and more creative lives. In order to accomplish this, various programs are conducted at the Center.

Operation Brotherhood is based on the philosophy that the elderly have much to contribute to their communities. Unfortunately, due to the limited family contacts, seniors are institutionalized. Most times this institutionalization is unwarranted. Through our homemaker service, we attempt to maintain those elderly persons in their home with the following services:

HOMEMAKER SERVICE

- **Chore Housekeeping**—Three days per week, four hours per day, a trained home helper aide comes into the elderly client's home to assist in light housekeeping, meal preparation, laundry, shopping and other light duties to maintain that person in their home. At this time this service is extended to 250 clients per month.

- **Home Delivered Meals**—On the average, 100 individuals per day receive a hot meal through this service. When meals are prepared for our daily afternoon luncheon, these meals are packaged and delivered by our volunteer drivers, to the pre-identified elderly. This service is extended to seniors who due to some physical or mental disability are unable to prepare their meals and have no other resources to obtain adequate nutrition. This service is provided five (5) days per week and provisions through food packages from our food co-op are supplied for the weekend. There is a minimal charge of 50¢ per day unless the client is assessed as having no resources to pay this charge.

- **Mobile Grocery Store**—In January of 1977, the mobile grocery store became an extension of our homemaker service. The truck makes two (2) stops per day at senior buidings to those who are shut-in. Employees of Operation Brotherhood take orders, fill these orders and deliver them to the senior's door.

Other elderly people who are shut-in, but not necessarily in senior buildings merely call in their grocery orders to us and a staff person in the co-op prepares the order to be delivered by one of the drivers. The store is manned by ten (10) persons; a driver, six (6) distribution assistants, and three (3) cashiers. This program services approximately 1,100 individuals per month.

- **Medical, Grocery Shopping and Transportation**—To complement the Health aspect of the homebound elderly, our volunteer drivers take our clients to the clinic or hospital appointments. We also provide a volunteer driver to transport groups of ambulatory elderly to a grocery store or shopping centers to buy their own items. These people are unable to take public transportation because of some physical or mental disability, cannot afford to employ a cab and have no other family resources to accommodate their transportation needs. Through this service we transport approximately 250 individuals per month through group grocery shopping.

NUTRITION AND RECREATIONAL PROGRAM

The facilities of Operation Brotherhood are open to the elderly seven (7) days per week. We are providing nutrition and recreation activities on all these days.

- **Daily Nutrition Site**—Each day a noon meal is prepared for our participants. The meal is served hot to these persons and our menu is based on what is provided by the Mayors Office for Senior Citizens Nutrition Program. Each Wednesday there is a fellowship luncheon for 150 elderly men and women. Participation on the other six (6) days ranges from 50 to 75 persons. Although a donation is not required, some of the participants donate 50¢ per day for the meals.

- **Arts and Crafts Activities**—On Mondays through Fridays we have instructional classes in arts and crafts. Some of the classes offered are ceramics, crocheting, knitting and sewing. These classes convene once a week and the participants are free to work at the Center on any projects after the classes are dismissed. We have enrollment of 25 persons in these four programs and some persons are allowed to sit in at request and permission from the instructor of the class.

- **Social Activities and Physical Fitness**—A number of special activities are conducted at Operation Brotherhood. On our Wednesday fellowship, birthdays are celebrated of the participants whose birthday falls during that week. Special activities such as our Men's Club, Sing-along, Women's Tea Party, Rummage Sale and numerous other activities are within our thrust for social development and entertainment for our elderly participants. We also have Body Dynamics sessions for all participants at our Wednesday activity day.

• **Fellowship Hour**—Each Wednesday we have the fellowship hour for spiritual development and uplifting. During this hour, there are singers and speakers to challenge and stimulate the spiritual activities of the participants.

• **Transportation**—Our volunteer drivers assist in transporting the participants to the Center for meals if for some reason they are unable to come on their own accord. However, quite a number of our participants do come unassisted. When our schedule permits we also transport the seniors here for recreational classes.

SELF-HELP FOOD CO-OP

The food cooperative remains open six (6) days per week not only for the convenience of the elderly, but also for the residents of the surrounding neighborhood. The co-op is a member of the Self Help Action Association and is one of the fourteen (14) food co-ops located in the Chicago area. The elderly benefit from the co-op because those who cannot shop for themselves receive deliveries of fresh produce to their residence at cost according to their daily or weekly needs. The fresh produce includes fruits, vegetables, eggs, poultry, meat and dairy products.

CLOTHING CENTER

The center also houses a clothing center. New and used clothing, household appliances and furnishings are donated to the center and sold to the community residents and elderly persons at a minimal cost.

INFORMATION AND REFERRAL

Through the assistance of our staff social worker and cooperating community resources, our staff receives a quarterly update on the services and programs being sponsored for the elderly. Staff also is notified when any program changes or the criteria is revised. Through presentations, staff relay this information to elderly participants whether through individual contact or group discussion. On numerous occasions, we invite speakers in to speak to our group during the luncheon hours.

FRIENDLY VISITATION

The Retired Senior Volunteer Program and the Chicago Junior Chamber of Commerce assist us in visiting with our shut-in elderly persons. They visit approximately twice a week and deliver goods and food from our center if need be. Also paid staff visit in their off hours the elderly/handicapped shutins, sick and blind. These visits are made to support the senior in his struggle for recup-eration and to give reassurance that someone is concerned about his welfare. This program is extended to about twenty (20) persons per week.

EMERGENCY ASSISTANCE PROGRAM

Operation Brotherhood services on the average of 75 persons per month who have encountered some financial setback or displacement from their homes. The reason for their displacement is usually fire, eviction, or breakdown of essential equipment (i.e., heaters, gas, electricity, or the condemnation of a building). We provide emergency food packages and clothing for any person or family regardless of age. For the elderly the service is a bit more involved. Our service will provide emergency food, clothing, and assistance in locating temporary or permanent shelter. Our social worker will assess their needs and indicate and contact other resources for help. In addition, minimal cash advances have been allocated to eligible individuals not to exceed $75.00 per situation.

SPECIAL PROGRAMS

• **Solar Garden**—Through our cooperation with the Neighborhood Center of Technology we have on our premises a greenhouse under the concept of hydroponic gardening. The overall goal of this program is to eventually raise the food through this solar energy plan and serve the products in our nutrition site year round.

• **Mini-Farm**—We employ senior citizens on a part time basis to work in a one-acre mini-farm cultivating, tilling, planting and growing vegetables seasonally that are prepared and served in our nutrition program.

This article is reprinted from "Operation Brotherhood," 3745-53 West Ogden Avenue, Chicago, Illinois.

Section VI

Section VI

Implementing State and Local Food Plans

One of the most exciting and promising developments in the last five years has been the increasing number of state and local governments and non-profit organizations which have drafted comprehensive agricultural and food plans. In the preceding fifteen chapters, many diverse issues have been addressed, and concrete policy alternatives and innovative solutions to these problems have been described.

State and city "food plans" are efforts to take an integrated and creative approach to future policy recommendations at the local level. They are attempts to find ways for state and local governments to work towards meeting a wide range of important goals, all of which are interrelated. These goals include strengthening the family farm; protecting farm land; conserving energy and natural resources; assisting low-income farmers and farm workers; and meeting the needs of consumers.

Increasingly, people are realizing that a wholistic approach to developing and implementing innovative farm, land and food policies is necessary. At the state level, what use is it to extend credit and develop new marketing outlets for family farmers if speculation and development pressures continue to force these same farmers to sell their land? States which have been leaders in alleviating these problems are Vermont, Massachusetts, Maine and California.

Cities—notably Hartford and Seattle—are also taking an integrated approach to food related issues and problems. They are not only trying to find ways to lower the cost of food to middle- and low-income people, but at the same time are attempting to bring consumers and farmers closer together through support of farmers markets and encouraging the revitalization of neglected inner city neighborhoods through community gardens, parks and community or cooperative grocery stores. In addition, these cities are beginning to explore a variety of related projects which will encourage both employment opportunities and local, community economic development potential.

Two important points should be raised about this approach. First, consumers, farmers and community leaders should be involved in the Task Forces and Commissions which are making policy recommendations. Unless strong citizen participation is included, this approach runs the danger of becoming an elitist process in which professional planners and "experts" determine the policies and strategies which are needed. As important as these efforts are, they must be accountable to the people whose lives their decisions and recommendations will affect.

Secondly, comprehensive and integrated agricultural and food plans are only valuable if they are then translated into action. In some cases this may require drafting legislation or implementing new programs. In most cases, however, what is needed is slight changes in or amendments to existing laws and redirecting the priorities of already established agencies and programs.

The final two chapters of *New Directions in Farm, Land and Food Policies* describe the efforts of cities and states to develop and implement comprehensive agricultural and food plans.

Chapter 16

State Agriculture and Food Plans

A number of Governor's Commissions, State Task Forces and non-profit organizations have drafted state-wide agriculture and food plans in the 1970s. State plans are attempts to integrate the diverse—and often conflicting—goals of supporting the family farm, meeting consumer needs, protecting farm land and other natural resources, assisting low-income farmers and inner-city residents, and revitalizing local, rural and urban economies. How can public policies be made to respond to the many issues and problems which have been described throughout this reader? One strategy is to draft a comprehensive and long-range vision, or overall plan, which pulls these otherwise fragmented proposals and policy initiatives together.

At the state level, farm organizations, citizen and community activists and concerned public officials are taking a growing interest in adopting a wholistic approach to recommending policy directives which meet these goals. In **Example 70, We Need New Food and Farmland Policies,** Chaitanya York clearly outlines "workable alternatives" to the current system of agricultural production and distribution. The common theme behind these state policy alternatives is the goal of rebuilding a more permanent "sustainable" agriculture which is economically viable, socially and environmentally responsible and democratically controlled.

State governments, farmers and citizens have realized that national agricultural policy has been unable, and often unwilling, to address the critical problems people are facing at the state and local level. New York Secretary of Agriculture Robert Barber states that "it is high time that we recognize that the objectives of our state food policies are necessarily different than the objectives of the food policy established by our national leaders."[1] In **Example 71, A State Food Policy,** the Center for Science in the Public Interest (CSPI) briefly outlines thirteen suggested policy goals for state action. These include support for the family farm; access to a nutritionally adequate diet at affordable costs; encouragement of direct farmer-to-consumer marketing systems; anti-trust action in monopolized food industries; repeals of state sales taxes on food and increased citizen participation in agriculturally-related agencies and policy formation.

NEW ENGLAND

The New England states have pioneered efforts to draft state agriculture and food plans. Many of these states are attempting to find solutions to the enormous problems which have been caused by their disintegrating agricultural economies. The New England states estimate that their dependency on "imported" food has reached 80% to 90%. This dependency leads to higher food prices due to increased transportation costs and at the same time has aggravated the situation of local farmers who are left without viable local and regional markets. These states have also been prompted into action by the rapid loss of farm land to development pressures and land speculation.

As the once vital and diversified agricultural economies of the New England states have collapsed, farm-related jobs and industries also decline. The end results are depressed local economies and increasing stress on life in New England's small towns and rural communities.

Massachusetts and Vermont were the first states to draft state food plans. The Governor's Commission on Food in Massachusetts released a final report, *In Search of a Food Policy*, in June of 1974. The state issued a shorter and updated version, *A Policy for Food and Agriculture in Massachusetts*, in 1976. In that same year the Vermont Legislature passed a bill (H. 476) which created the Agricultural Development Commission, whose purpose was to develop a comprehensive agricultural policy for the state. The Vermont Commission on Food issued a lengthy report and a summary of their findings, *Proposals for Vermont's Agriculture and Food Future*.

In 1977 the Commission on Maine's Future published a report which included a chapter on the state's agriculture, reprinted as **Example 72, The Agricultural Resource**. Although the chapter is extremely brief in its analysis and its recommendations, public concern about the seriousness of the problems facing the state's agriculture resulted in the creation of the Food and Farmland Study Commission by the Maine Legislature.

New Jersey also established a Task Force to recommend the new directions and policy initiatives needed to support the state's agriculture. **Example 73, Highlights of the Report**, summarizes the recommendation made in the final *Report of the Blueprint Commission on the Future of New Jersey Agriculture*. The summary includes a discussion of land policy and protection of farmland; marketing, natural resources, taxation, management, research and education, farm labor and the role of the New Jersey Rural Advisory Council. Finally, New Hampshire issued a brief report in 1978, *And When We Went There, the Cupboard was . . . Who Will Feed New Hampshire Residents?*, which begins to take a comprehensive look at the state's agricultural and food situation.

THE NORTHEAST TASK FORCE ON FOOD AND FARM POLICY

The next step beyond drafting state agriculture and food plans is translating their recommendations into action. The Northeast Task Force on Food and Farm Policy was created to provide a vehicle for bringing together state legislators and public officials, farmers, consumers, and academics and others interested in developing progressive agricultural and food policies in nine Northeastern states. The Task Force serves as a "clearinghouse" of contacts and information on new bills and legislative proposals, distributes a newsletter and organizes frequent meetings and "working" conferences.

Original supporters of the Northeast Task Force included Massachusetts Governor Dukakis, Massachusetts Commissioner of Agriculture Winthrop, Pennsylvania Secretary of Agriculture McHale, Massachusetts Representative Mel King, New York Assemblyman Maurice Hinchey, and Speaker Stanley Steingut, of the New York Assembly. Assemblyman Hinchey was also instrumental in initiating the New York Assembly Task Force on Food, Farm, and Nutrition Policy. The Task Force serves as a catalyst for legislation on food-related issues in the state. **Example 74, 1978 Legislative Status Update**, summarizes the 25 bills which were dealt with by the New York Task Force under the chairmanship of Assemblyman Hinchey. These bills range from restrictions on corporate farming to improvement of the state's direct marketing efforts, and support for the WIC supplemental feeding program to legislation which encourages school districts to purchase farm products grown in New York State.

THE CALIFORNIA SMALL FARM VIABILITY PROJECT

The most recent effort to draft a comprehensive state plan proposing the policies and programs needed to support family farmers and rural communities is that of the California Small Farm Viability Project. The Project's *Final Report*, which was issued in 1978 after two years of research, meetings and ongoing public participation, is one of the most detailed and comprehensive of any state food plans written to date.

The Project was sponsored by the California Department of Employment Development with the cooperation of the Governor's Office of Planning and Research, the State Department of Food and Agriculture and the Department of Housing and Community Development. Six task forces were established to deal with the areas of marketing, finance, training, technology, natural resources, and community services. The Task Force drew upon the experiences of many kinds of people involved in food, agricultural and rural issues in California. Task force members included state legislators, public officials from state and local agencies, small farmers, farm worker representatives, professors, and representatives of community-based organizations.

Each of the six task forces issued a set of concrete and detailed policy recommendations which were then compiled into a final report. The project is now coordinating efforts to translate these recommendations into both executive and legislative action.

In conclusion, state plans are important mechanisms for developing integrated and progressive agricultural and food policies at the state level. They can also be useful in stimulating public awareness and concern over the most critical farm, land and food issues facing state and local governments. The strength of this approach depends both on the degree to which farmers and consumers participate in the process and on whether the recommendations are then translated into more creative and responsive legislation and programs at the state and local level.

[1] Lerza, Cathy, "State Food Plans," The Elements, June 1976.

Resources

ORGANIZATIONS

California Food Policy Project

1535 Mission Street
San Francisco, California 94103
(415) 863-7480
Don Rothenberg, Director;
Linda Akulian, Associate Director

California Small Farm Viability Project

c/o Department of Employment Development
& Rural Affairs
800 Capitol Mall, MIC 77
Sacramento, California 95814
(916) 322-4440

Conference on Alternative State and Local Policies

The Agriculture Project
2000 Florida Avenue, N.W.
Washington, D.C. 20009
(202) 387-6030
Henry Hyde, Maggie Kennedy

IMPACT

State Affiliates (12 in 1978)
110 Maryland Avenue, N.E.
Washington, D.C. 20002
(202) 544-8636
Bob Odean, National Director

Maine Consortium for Food Self-Reliance

c/o Richards Land/CHES
Freeport, Maine 04032
(207) 865-4338
Bill Seretta, Coordinator

Maine Food and Farmland Study Commission

State Planning Office
184 State Street
Augusta, Maine 04333
(207) 289-3261
Chaitanya York, David Vail; Commission Members

Massachusetts Food and Agriculture Coalition

Box 709
Boston, Massachusetts 02123
(617) 261-8280
Michael Scully, Coordinator and Legislative
Aide to Representative Mel King

National Family Farm Coalition

918 F Street, N.W.
Washington, D.C. 20004
Catherine Lerza and Robin Rosenbluth, Coordinators

New Jersey Food Policy Project

c/o World Hunger Year/New Jersey
27-06 High Street
Fairlawn, New Jersey 07410
(201) 791-8585
Bill Wildey and Bob Halsch, Coordinators

New York State Assembly Task Force on Food, Farm & Nutrition Policy

Room 404—Legislative Building
Albany, New York 12248
(518) 472-2330
Assemblyman Maurice Hinchey, Chairman

New York State Coalition for Local Self-Reliance

P.O. Box 6222
Syracuse, New York 13217
David Brown, President

New York State Food Coalition

23 Elk Street
Albany, NY 12207
(518) 463-1896

Northeast Task Force on Food and Farm Policy

1111 Twin Towers
99 Washington Avenue
Albany, New York 12248
(518) 455-5206
Mabel Gil, Coordinator;
Assemblyman Maurice Hinchey, Chair

Rural America State Affiliates Program

1346 Connecticut Avenue, N.W.
Washington, D.C. 20036
(202) 659-2800
Kris Wisniewski

BIBLIOGRAPHY

Burrill, George and James Nolfi, "Regional Food Strategies: New Ways of Bringing Farmer and Consumer Closer Together As Food Policy Becomes a State Issue," **Organic Gardening and Farming**. January 1976.

California Public Policy Center, **Working Papers on Economic Democracy: Towards a New Rural California.** California Public Policy Center, 304 South Broadway, Room 224, Los Angeles, California 90013.

California Small Farm Viability Project, **Final Report.** State CETA Office, Rural Affairs, Department of Employment Development, 800 Capitol Mall, Sacramento, California 95814. 1977. Six Task Force Reports available.

Center for Science in the Public Interest (CSPI), **From the Ground Up: Building a Grass Roots Food Policy.** CSPI, 1755 S Street, N.W., Washington, D.C. 20009. 1976. $2.50.

Commonwealth of Massachusetts, **A Policy for Food and Agriculture in Massachusetts.** Executive Office of Environmental Affairs, Department of Food and Agriculture, 100 Cambridge Street, Boston, Massachusetts 02202. 1976. To be revised in 1978.

Gorham, Lucy, **Revitalizing Maine's Agriculture.** Maine Audubon Society, Gilsland Farm, 118 U.S. 1, Falmouth, Maine 04105. 1975.

Governor's Commission on Maine's Future, **Final Report.** Maine State Planning Office, 184 State Street, Augusta, Maine 04333. 1977.

Guyer, Cynthia, "State and Local Governments Lead the Way," in "The Family Farm: Can It Be Saved?" **E/SA Forum.** United Methodist Church, 110 Maryland Avenue, N.E., Washington, D.C. 20002. October 1978.

Guyer, Cynthia and Lee Webb, "Agricultural Group Seeks Out Non-Federal Answers," **Catholic Rural Life.** 4625 N.W. Beaver Drive, Des Moines, Iowa 50322. September 1978.

Lerza, Catherine, "State Food Plans," **The Elements.** Public Resource Center, 1747 Connecticut Avenue, N.W., Washington, D.C. 20009. June 1976.

Maine Land Advocate, "Through the Looking Glass: Commission on Maine's Future," **Maine Land Advocate.** Sam Ely Community Services Corporation, P.O. Box 2762, Augusta, Maine 04330. September 1977.

Marshall, Ray and Thompson, **Status and Prospects of Small Farmers in the South.** Southern Regional Council, 75 Marietta Street, N.W., Atlanta, Georgia 30303. 1976. $5.00.

Massachusetts Governor's Commission of Food, **In Search of a Food Policy.** Department of Food and Agriculture, 100 Cambridge Street, Boston, Massachusetts 02202. 1974. To be revised in 1978.

New Hampshire Cooperative Extension Service, "And When We Went There, The Cupboard Was . . . Who Will Feed New Hampshire Residents?" Cooperative Extension Service, University of New Hampshire, Durham, New Hampshire 03824. 1978.

New Jersey Commission on the Future of Agriculture, **Report.** Secretary of Agriculture, Box 1888, Trenton, New Jersey 08625. 1973, reprinted 1977.

New York State Assembly Task Force on Food, Farm and Nutrition Policy (Food Policy Task Force), **1978 Legislative Status Update.** Food Policy Task Force, c/o Assemblyman Hinchey, The Capitol, Albany, New York 12248.

Northeast Task Force on Food and Farm Policy, **Averting Northeast Food Shortages in the 80's: Components of a Revived Agriculture.** 1977 Conference Proceedings. Northeast Task Force on Food and Farm Policy, 1111 Twin Towers, 99 Washington Avenue, Albany, New York 12248. July 1977.

Northeast Task Force on Food and Farm Policy, **Newsletter.** NTFFFP, 1111 Twin Towers, 99 Washington Avenue, Albany, New York 12248.

Southern Regional Council, Task Force on Rural Development, **Increasing the Options.** Southern Regional Council, 75 Marietta Street, N.W., Atlanta, Georgia 30303. 1977.

Southern Rural Policy Congress (SRPC), **Program Profile.** SRPC, 915 South Hull Street, Montgomery, Alabama 36104. 1978.

United States Department of Agriculture (USDA), "Northeast Agriculture: A Tale of Yankee Ingenuity," **Farm Index.** Vol. XVI, no. 10, USDA, Washington, D.C. 20250. October 1977. Overview of northeast agriculture, emphasizing the small farm and the dairy industry.

Vermont Agricultural Development Commission, **Agricultural Policy Statement.** Vermont Department of Agriculture, Montpelier Vermont 05602. 1977.

Vermont Governor's Commission on Food, **Proposals for Vermont's Agriculture and Food Future, A Summary.** Department of Agriculture, Montpelier, Vermont 05602. 1976.

Vermont Institute of Community Involvement, **A Research Report on the Potential for Food Self-Sufficiency in Vermont.** Center for Studies in Food Self-Sufficiency (Nolfi and Burrill), 90 Main Street, Burlington, Vermont 05401. 1976. $2.50.

York, Chaitanya, "We Need New Food and Farmland Policies: Workable Alternatives," **Maine Organic Farmer and Gardener.** 110 Water Street, Hallowell, Maine 04347. September 1978.

EXAMPLE 70

We Need New Food and Farmland Policies

The following is a transcript of a speech Chaitanya York gave to the Council of State Governments on August 1, 1978 in Atlantic City, New Jersey. Other speakers were Lou Meyer, Director, Task Force for a Food Policy in the Northeast, and Maurice Henchey, Assemblyman, N. Y. State Assembly.

My colleagues have done an excellent job of examining the unworkability of our present centralized and energy-inefficient agricultural system. I share their concern and propose that you create a food policy that redirects the patterns of our food system — production, distribution, and consumption — at both the national and regional level. I'm asking you to study the small family farm and greater regional self-sufficiency as viable economic and social alternatives to our present system.

How does the problem look in Maine? Seventy-five percent of the food we consume is produced out-of-state, usually on the opposite coast. (Fifty years ago only 30% of our food was grown elsewhere.) Our dependence on the present industrialized food system may prove disastrous in our future. We are at the end of both oil pipelines and trucking routes. Present agricultural practices have contributed to the loss of nearly a third of this nation's topsoil. The quality of our food is questionable and prices continue to fluctuate. Every time we lose six farms we also lose one small business. Our present food system supports neither the family farm nor regional culture.

In completing agricultural study for the U.S. Environmental Protection Agency, Joe Belden discussed an interesting California socioeconomic study which came out of Senate Study Committee work initiated in the forties with an update in 1960. Two towns were involved — Arvin, with 137 farms averaging 297 acres, and Dinuba, with 635 farms averaging 45 acres and the results were startling.

Although Dinuba had 30% less land it was more affluent and supported more church, social, and civic groups. Dinuba had higher incomes, better sales, public works, more schools, and better homes. When the town was revisited in 1960 it continued to have a markedly higher level of education. The farms in Arvin were large and owned by absentee landlords, with a population of primarily land-less, poor, agricultural laborers. In Dinuba more than half the population were farmers and merchants, while in Arvin these people amounted to only 1/5 of the population.

In 1970 the director of FmHA used this study in discussing the value of family farms before a congressional hearing. "The whole dialog of social virtues and social values of family in this country," he said "has died." We are examining that dialog with you today. Phillip Rump, an economist, in speaking before the same Congress, observed that "large farms are far less efficient than family operations when their total effect on the community is evaluated."

I'm in agreement with Mr. Rump and I want to examine some areas in rural development such as marketing and research, look at successes and failures and propose areas of support. I'm drawing on my general experience with small farmers as well as specific work with the State of Maine Food and Farmland Study Commission and the Task Force for a Food Policy in the Northeast.

Marketing

Our present marketing system, over a quarter of a century in development, has destroyed the local infrastructure, and small farmers find it difficult to compete with the power of importers. "Direct" marketing is an exciting local alternative. Direct marketing, "straight from producer to consumer without middlemen," provides the most fair income to farmers and the least cost to consumers, and usually requires cooperation among farmers. The food is local and fresh, and the supply — ideally — is dependable. Two traditional examples are farmers' markets and roadside stands.

Three years ago in Maine we had three farmers' markets. Today we have twenty-four. Coastal Enterprises, a community action group in Bath, has not only established a producers' co-op but is storing root vegetables cooperatively to provide that much-needed "consistency of supply" to local institutions. Sunrise County Farmers' Market, a producers' group working through a Community Action Program in Washington County, is selling year-round through a storefront, supplying a government "Meals for Me." program for the elderly, and negotiating with wholesalers. A federation of farmers' markets is now being discussed. This all constitutes a beginning — inspiring direction for the future.

Support is crucial. Greater diversity in

both marketing and production must be developed. Basic study of our present distribution system, potential institutional markets, small farm management and technology are essential.

Our Department of Agriculture, under the capable direction of Commissioner Williams, has been supporting the development of direct marketing as well as inviting cooperative participation of experienced organizers and farmers in this process. Department work to date, completed with the assistance and support of small farm groups, has included a revised market report, a farmers' market brochure, a Maine proposal through the U.S. Producer-to-Consumer Direct Marketing Act, and a "Buy Local" campaign.

Maine's No. 2 financial producer is agriculture, and yet the department receives less than 1% of the total budget. Every agriculture department in the Northeast should have a specific direct marketing attack plan, and development funds will be required.

Legislation is a key tool in supporting direct marketing alternatives. State bills similar to Maine's Direct Marketing Act of 1978, which calls for Department of Agriculture promotion, research, and technical assistance, or the 1978 Massachusetts Act requiring state institutions to "buy local" are necessary. Important pieces of national legislation include the revised Producer-to-Consumer Act, which permits funding direct to local projects, and The Family Farm Development Act of 1978, a vital comprehensive bill supporting numerous aspects of family farm development besides direct marketing such as research, financing, and land use.

Land Use

Cumberland County, our most urban district, lost 70% of its cropland to either development or abandonment between 1949 and 1974. Aroostook County, Maine's potato country, loses 10-15 tons of topsoil per acre per year plus accompanying loss of fertility — both due to existing practices. FmHA continues to fund construction on cropland, and some state laws — particularly those relating to septic systems — make ideal farming soils the best for development. So let's look at what works and choose appropriately.

Small and particularly part-time farmers are major contributors to the preservation of farmland in Maine and must be supported. Successful expansion in local production and marketing will preserve farmland through economic feasibility.

We need to appreciate the synergistic relationships of city and country in order to truly support the prosperity of both communities in the whole. Attractive cities which meet the needs of those who live in them will house people who might otherwise have wasted time and energy commuting from country homes freshly planted in farmland. Farmers not competing with development prices created in part by urban refugees can more successfully supply urban communities of increasing stability.

Study groups like the State of Maine Food and Farmland Study Commission at the state level and The Threshold of Maine, an R.C. & D. at the local level, can be helpful. Be sure to make them democratic with broad representation from the "whole" community and communicate results through the community at all levels. No single piece of legislation is going to solve a state's problems, and all legislation Maine's Farmland and Open Space Law, Vermont's purchase of development rights or British Columbia's zoning mandate — should be studied to create the best regional policy.

Finally, there's a need to support wise farmland management such as crop rotation and green manuring, possibly even by mandation where only this will protect water/soil quality. Why couldn't FmHA make loans contingent upon continued sound soil management practices? It's all in seeing and dealing creatively with the problems.

Finances

The rising cost of land is a problem, particularly for young people entering farming, and inheritance taxes often require daughters and sons of farmers to sell part of the farm in order to save it and pay the tax. Loans are difficult to obtain and require the largest payments initially during the "entrance into farming" period when young farmers are least capable of repaying. How can we set up a more equitable situation here?

A state loan guarantee with deferred or reduced payments until 5 years after start-up, as provided by Minnesota's Family Farm Security Act of 1976, is one way to preserve the family farm. Inheritance tax reform would definitely be helpful, as would an overhaul of FmHA, S.B.A., and Federal Land Bank policy so that they are more responsive to the needs of small farmers. And we need bankers educated in agriculture so that they are sensitive to the reality of the people with whom they're dealing.

Education

We need to educate the general public concerning the state of our agriculture and give them the opportunity to support the most viable alternative out of their own discovery. Courses for farmers in small farm management and appropriate technology are essential. Cooperative Extension responds to farmers, and if extension agents are to better serve small farmers they need more training in these methods, particularly biological farming and appropriate technology. Ideally we'll create competent advisors making regular farm visits and working more closely with farmers.

Small and part-time farmers' Advisory Boards to the land grant colleges, such as the one at the University of Maine, are important communication vehicles for these farmers to have input to University research and education. The Maine group has been instrumental in initiating research in biological methods as well as developing an E-TV series in small and part-time farming.

In general there's a need for increased practical education at all levels — kindergarten through college, e.g. gardening courses, farm visits, apprenticeship programs, vo-ag, greenhouse management. It is a matter of expanding beyond what we've started.

Research
There appears to be a monopoly of research contracts at land grant schools with most work directed towards large-scale operations and monocultures. It seems only equitable to create research more responsive to the needs of smaller scale, diversified agriculture. Biological agriculture, besides being more environmentally sound, is now proving to be a viable economic alternative, and research will improve methods for all farmers. Claude Aubert, a French agronomist and advisor, has observed, "If

there were as much research about biological methods as there is for chemical, all problems would be solved. But the discovery of natural ways holds no promise of profits or rewards or fees for the discoverer. All it promises is benefits for all society."

Small and part-time advisory boards, as I've already mentioned, are excellent vehicles for identifying research needs. Federal funding for grass roots research and demonstration projects outside the universities such as that provided by C.S.A. through the National Center for Appropriate Technology, and D.O.E. through the AT (Appropriate Technology) Small Grants Program is a step in the right direction. The International Institute for Biological Husbandry, a private group in Switzerland, receives ⅓ of its funding from the Swiss government. I'd like to see a similar practice here.

Areas requiring research are numerous — root storage, crop strains, rock powders, etc. Some of it has been completed and it's simply a matter of inventorying the data on file — old, new, North American, European — and making it available.

We must cooperate and go beyond our own self-righteousness (mine included) and entrenched beliefs to really study the present agricultural system and discover what works and what doesn't — what best serves our society — what is most democratic. Look at the total picture — at our historic modes of production, distribution, marketing, and processing. The question is one of our willingness — of **personal** commitment to create a permanent "sustainable" agriculture — economically viable, environmentally sound, morally justifiable, and most importantly, democratically controlled.

This article is reprinted from Chaitanya York, "We Need New Food and Farmland Policies," **Maine Organic Farmer and Gardener**, pp. 15-16, September 1978.

A State Food Policy

EXAMPLE
71

1. Every American should have a guaranteed income adequate to insure access to a nutritionally adequate diet. Until this is a reality, all state (or city) agencies, including the legislature, executive, and departments of health, welfare, and education, should make a major effort to see that all federal food assistance programs---including food stamps, school lunch, school breakfast, food for day care centers, and meals for the elderly---are fully and fairly implemented. This means that all the poor and near poor should be informed of their eligibility, and that administrative procedures should be made as efficient and humane as possible, so that all those in need may be served.

2. High prices, low quality, and reduced variety are due in part to monopoly and oligopoly in the food industry. Antitrust actions should be taken by the State Attorney General to end existing monopolies in the food industry. State (or city) officials should lobby for Federal actions to the same end.

3. In recent years, states have seen many thousands of acres of prime agricultural land lost to urbanization, resort development, highways, energy siting, and other uses. The state (or county) should assess its current and future patterns of land use and ownership, and develop a strong program to protect its agricultural land, utilizing agricultural districts, acquisition or transfer of development rights, use-value assessment of agricultural land, and other means at its disposal.

4. The family farmer should be protected by the enactment and strong enforcement of state laws restricting involvement in farming by corporations other than "family farm" or other relatively small and closely-held corporations.

5. Nourishing food should be easily accessible, whether in a country grocery store, a city supermarket, a fast-food restaurant, or a vending machine.

6. The state should undertake a major nutrition education effort, making full use of schools, TV, radio, and other media, to encourage the public (a) to eat a balanced diet based to a large extent on whole grains, vegetables, nuts, low-fat dairy products, poultry, grass-fed beef, seafood and fruit; and (b) to reduce their intake of fat, sugar, and cholesterol.

7. Consumer interests should be equitably represented on state market order boards that help determine production levels, quality standards, and prices of certain foods.

8. Individual, school, and community gardens yield learning, recreation, community spirit, and high-quality, low-cost foods. The state should encourage its citizens to garden, and should assist municipalities and groups in setting up community garden projects by coordinating information and resources and making vacant public land available for gardens.

9. Agricultural research and extension, through the state's land grant college, should orient its efforts to assist small-scale farmers, and to breed more nutritious and less energy-intensive crops and livestock.

10. Direct farmer-to-consumer marketing, as well as other "alternative" marketing structures, can provide great benefits for both consumers and small farmers. The state's Department of Agriculture should develop specific programs to encourage and assist farmers to market through farmers markets, "U-Pick" operations, roadside markets, and other direct marketing enterprises, and to assist municipalities wishing to organize farmers' markets. The state (or city) should also identify, promote, and provide technical assistance to consumer food buying clubs and cooperatives, and help facilitate their purchase of farm goods directly from producers. The state should develop a revolving credit fund to help establish food production, distribution, and retailing cooperatives.

11. The potential for conflicts of interest in state agencies that regulate food should be minimized by (a) forbidding employees to join a regulated industry after leaving the agency until substantial time has elapsed; and (b) balancing former industry people in government agencies with persons who have worked with pro-consumer groups.

12. State sales taxes on food clearly impose a special burden on those least able to afford an adequate diet. If the state has a sales tax on food items, it should be repealed, and replaced by more equitable revenue sources.

13. The State Department of Agriculture should issue guidelines defining "organically grown" food to prevent consumer fraud and to facilitate an ecologically sound way of farming. The Department should encourage all farmers to be judicious and frugal in their use of fertilizers, pesticides, and fuel.

This article is reprinted from "A State Food Policy," **From The Ground Up: Building A Grassroots Food Policy,** Center for Science in the Public Interest, pp. 16-18, 1977.

EXAMPLE 72   The Agricultural Resource

Although agriculture has declined severely in economic importance over the last century, it is the ninth largest industry in Maine, with a gross product of almost 300 million dollars. Maine still has thirty-one percent of all the farmland in New England.

This reduction in farming is very disturbing to the commission as it looks ahead and sees the probable increase in difficulty of importing adequate fresh produce from states upon which Maine has become increasingly dependent. It is reasonable to assume that in the future, states such as California and Florida will have sufficient population growth as to demand their farm products be retained within their boundaries. Maine, already in a disadvantageous position in regard to transportation costs and increasing energy costs, is going to find it expensive, if not prohibitive, to continue to rely on other regions of the U.S. for staple foods.

Economic conditions are having a serious impact on agricultural land. In the southern, more populated areas of the state, the incentive to convert farmland to non-farm uses is high. Population growth pressures and changing housing patterns have encouraged development outside urban areas — often on the most productive farmlands. Prime agricultural lands have not only the best soils for growing, but also the best characteristics for building houses, roads, shopping centers, and parking lots. Once converted, agricultural land cannnot be reclaimed for agricultural production.

In northern Maine, mismanagement and poor farming techniques have led to serious soil erosion and the depletion of necessary soil nutrients. Erosion and depletion of soils is occurring so rapidly that within twenty-five to fifty years it may no longer be possible to grow potatoes in much of Aroostook County. At a time when food production is of critical concern the world over, the state must take an active role in encouraging and promoting as much economic use of Maine's natural soil base as is consistent with long-range, sustainable activity.

Commission Policy Recommendation

V.   **It be the policy goal of the State of Maine to preserve and reclaim agricultural land and to encourage the production, marketing, and diversification of agricultural products.**

Possible Means Of Implementation

1. Investigate the feasibility of the development of greenhouse gardening of vegetables and other fresh produce utilizing the waste heat of utilities and industries.

2. Encourage controls to prevent soil loss and develop legislation to enforce these controls when voluntary cooperation fails.

3. Modify tax assessment of farmlands to reflect current use value and also modify, to the extent necessary, estate and inheritance taxes to ensure orderly transfer of farmland and the continuity of farming.

4. Develop and promote a packaged quality of Maine potatoes higher in quality and uniformity of size than is required currently by U.S. Grade A.

5. Encourage, through the Congressional delegation, incentive programs to be administered by the State Department of Agriculture to effect the reclamation of agricultural land.

6. Because sound soil management is vital to the protection of agricultural land, the Department of Agriculture, in cooperation with the University of Maine, should continually assess the rate of soil erosion on agricultural lands and develop reasonable requirements to prevent further erosion and to refurbish the soil base.

7. Promote the use of non-petrochemical fertilizers for agricultural use, utilizing to the greatest extent possible resources within Maine. Research should be geared toward establishing small industries to produce and market natural fertilizers.

8. Make sales tax treatment of farm equipment identical to the tax treatment of industrial production equipment.

Citizen Comments

"We must have tax relief for those who are using land or would like to develop agricultural or forestry use for their lands. . ."

"Develop a new variety of potato to meet consumer needs or processing needs. The finances will take care of themselves. . ."

"I feel great stress should be placed on reviving agriculture in this state as it has the resources available to do so. Tax incentives or whatever are necessary to encourage more people to go into it. Adult evening discussion courses should be offered on the various campuses."

"Stop blacktopping farm land."

"Drastic steps to stop erosion, immediate steps to improve soil, and a 25-year-plan objective. . ."

"Reclaim old farms. Encourage people to rebuild soil and grow food. Educate in schools, elementary level and up. . ."

"Important that soil depletion be reversed and that organic, non-petrochemical fertilizers be used. . ."

This article is reprinted from "The Agricultural Resource," Final Report: Commission on Maine's Future, pp. 31-34, December 1, 1977.

Highlights of the Report

EXAMPLE

73

THE NEW JERSEY AGRICULTURAL SITUATION

Agriculture in New Jersey operates in the most densely populated area in the nation, hence has both problems and opportunities. Farmland declined rapidly from 1954 to 1968, and has substantially slowed down since then, due, in part, to the Farmland Assessment Act.

There are presently about 1.1 million acres in farms in the state, which is over 600,000 acres less than in 1950.

Due largely to forces external to itself, agriculture in New Jersey is operating under the influence of an impermanence syndrome which leads to short-term decision making, less investment in agricultural enterprises, and slower technological adaptation. This can be corrected by creating a permanent land preserve for agricultural production and by making it feasible for farmers to farm this land and make a profit. This report addresses itself to both of these objectives.

I. A LAND POLICY FOR PERMANENT AGRICULTURE

1. There is a converging of the interests of the environmentalists and those interested in agricultural production. Both recognize that land use management is of prime importance as a means of achieving their goals.

2. As a source of food and fiber and environmental open space, agriculture exists for the public benefit and, as an industry, in turn, is affected by the public interest. New Jersey needs its agriculture:
   a. To provide productive, tax-paying, privately maintained, open space with its environmental benefits, including rural aesthetics and enhanced air and water quality.
   b. To provide consumers with a ready access to wholesome, locally grown food products and protect the consumer buying power for food.
   c. To encourage the productive use of land and natural resources which contribute significantly to the income and employment of many citizens of the state and the New Jersey economy in general.
   d. To allow for the recycling of sewage wastes on land as a partial alternative to existing methods and as technical problems are resolved.

   e. To establish a land reserve for future generations and prohibit premature development.

3. Present land use policy for the state, including the Farmland Assessment Act, exhibits foresight and noble goals, but at best offers only partial solutions. A more comprehensive program is needed.

4. **The Commission recommends** the adoption of an agricultural open space plan administered jointly by the state and local municipalities with the following features:
   a. Under the plan, each municipality in the state would be required to designate an Agricultural Open Space Preserve within its boundaries composed of at least 70 percent of its prime farmland. The preserve would become part of the local master plan and should reflect the local community needs for open space and other agricultural benefits.
   b. Landowners whose properties are located in a preserved area would be able to sell the development easement to their land to the state administering agency or to others.
   c. The rate of compensation for development easements would be the difference between the market value for the land and its farm value.
   d. At the option of the landowner, the easements could be held for later sale and the compensation for delayed sales would reflect the increased development value of the easement had the preserved area not been established.
   e. The program would be financed by a tax on all real estate transfers in the state. The rate would be at 4 mills, or 4/10 of 1 percent of the transfer value at the time of the sale. In nearly all instances, the tax would be paid from realized capital gains on the real property transferred.
   f. The responsibility for administration of the program would be vested in a Board of Directors composed of persons appointed by the Governor and approved by the Senate and selected ex officio members of state government. The professional staff would be attached to the Department of Agriculture.

II. EDUCATION

Educational programs must be in tune with the social and economic needs and demands related to agriculture, renewable natural resources, and environmental protection.

The Commission recommends development of an overall plan for career orientation and exploration in the primary and junior high school grades, widespread agricultural and natural resource education in the high schools and technical education for natural resources and agricultural occupations in New Jersey at the junior college grades or technical level. It recommends a comprehensive technical institute; continuing education for commercial farmers, others employed in agribusiness, and seasonal workers; and periodic reevaluation and strengthening of curricula offered for professional education in agriculturally-related fields at Rutgers University.

III. FARM LABOR

A major effort has been made over the past 15 years to improve conditions for farmworkers in spite of difficult, competitive problems facing agriculture.

The Commission recommends state and federal legislation to bring agriculture under a labor-management relations act designed for agriculture; support for the Child Labor Law Study Commission in its preliminary report proposing legislation to increase employment of youth in agriculture and other occupations; establishment of a farm and rural safety and health committee, which may also serve in an informal advisory capacity to the Federal Occupational Safety and Health Act; training and retraining of farm workers; a pilot program for a multi-state skilled farmworkers corporation; and establishment of a Council on Farm Labor within the Department of Labor and Industry.

IV. FARMLAND ASSESSMENT

The Farmland Assessment Act has served agriculture well and in the way it was intended. Unquestionably, it makes it possible for production farming to continue in our urbanizing state.

The Commission recommends strong support be given to the current farmland assessment program, that the Division of Taxation further clarify the term "actively devoted" in the Act to insure proper application, and enactment of S-620 to increase program eligibility requirements.

V. FEDERAL ESTATE AND STATE INHERITANCE TAXES

The transfer of valuable farm property from a decedent to his heirs inevitably causes a liquidity and family crisis. The market value of the property may have little relationship to the agricultural income which must provide for the Federal estate and State inheritance taxes.

The Commission recommends federal legislation to increase the taxable estate exemption and to tax qualified land for estate purposes on the basis of its agricultural value, state legislation to increase the taxable estate exemption, and that qualified farmland should be taxed on its agricultural value for inheritance taxes, but, as a condition for such treatment, farmland must remain in agricultural use for ten years or be subject to a penalty payment.

VI. MANAGEMENT

The business of farming grows ever more risky, costly, complicated, and regulated, and the farmer must serve in many roles in his operation.

The Commission recommends that farmers must continue to be committed to upgrading their management capabilities and learn to effectively use the tools, skills, and equipments of farm business management and that a farm management advisory committee should be established under the aegis of the Cooperative Extension Service to strengthen all facets of farm management application.

VII. MARKETING

Effective marketing of New Jersey farm products requires a special effort if the producer is to obtain a profitable return.

The Commission recommends further development of direct farmer-to-consumer marketing channels, establishment of a New Jersey agricultural export committee to stimulate overseas trade, a feasibility study for a central agricultural distribution center, more adequate state labeling laws for commodities, and the appointment of an advisory committee for the creation of an organization to coordinate the existing production and marketing programs and to further develop a total systematic approach to producing and selling our agricultural products.

VIII. NATURAL RESOURCES

Natural resource conservation, soil surveys, conservation cost sharing, agricultural water resources, and multiple uses of agricultural lands are discussed.

The Commission recommends prompt completion of the Cooperative Soil Survey so that the lack of basic data does not delay the agricultural land preservation program; further direct state funding for the State Soil Conservation Committee and its district units; a three-year pilot program for cost-sharing with private landowners for priority conservation practices; water resource studies, demonstrations and pilot projects, including evaluation of "waste" waters for agricultural production purposes and potential ground water replenishment; development of more nonfood functions on farmland; information about the benefits flowing from private open lands; and possible leasing of private lands for specialized recreational activities.

IX. ORGANIZATIONS

New Jersey agriculture is represented by many organizations, all of which were developed for particular purposes. The effectiveness and future role of all existing organizations should be evaluated.

The Commission recommends that each agricultural organization should establish a special evaluation committee to review its goals, functions, and effectiveness; that agricultural interests reaffirm to the state government the importance of maintaining the State Board of Agriculture, Department of Agriculture, and Board of Managers, Rutgers College of Agriculture and Environmental Science (Cook College); and that a unified policy and voice for the farm community of the state be developed wherever possible through the cooperation and/or consolidation of the numerous farm organizations in New Jersey.

X. RECYCLING WASTE

It is imperative that the vast quantities of biodegradable agricultural and municipal wastes being generated in New Jersey be utilized and recycled whenever possible.

The Commission recommends that an Agricultural Waste Council be formally established by law in the Department of Agriculture. It would promote research, develop feasibility studies and desirable legislation in regard to recycling wastes.

XI. RESEARCH

Research is a basic service to New Jersey agriculture. It improves production and marketing technologies and it develops new ones. The New Jersey Agricultural Experiment Station emphasizes its work in improving the physical quality of the environment, expanding the socio-economic and cultural opportunities of people to improve their environment, improving agricultural and forest production, and generating and disseminating knowledge needed to develop new and improved food products and processes, protect consumer health, improve the nutrition and physical well-being of the people, and to assure a secure supply of wholesome foods to consumers in the state.

The Commission recommends that the Agricultural Experiment Station should continue its present research program, strengthen it with adequate financial support, periodically update its research priorities, coordinate its research with industrial concerns to assure full coverage of problem areas, and avoid unnecessary duplication.

XII. RURAL ADVISORY COUNCIL

An emerging comprehensive rural development program and a population expanding into rural agricultural areas calls for a broadened public program to deal with these complex unsettling changes.

The Commission recommends that the Rural Advisory Council in the New Jersey Department of Agriculture serve in an advisory capacity to an expanded agricultural and rural development program which would include an agricultural plan for the state; improvement of economic and social conditions of agriculture and rural areas; programs to minimize the impact of urbanization on agriculture; studies and recommendations on agricultural and rural issues; and consultation with other state agencies on issues peculiar to agricultural and rural areas.

XIII. TAXATION

New Jersey agriculture suffers from the heavy burden of local property taxes. Farmland tax per acre is the highest in the nation, and the property tax represents nearly 34 percent of the farmer's net income, as opposed to less than 10 percent for nonfarm incomes which range up to $15,000. The Farmland Assessment Act has helped, but municipalities can make charges against farmland for public facilities, such as sanitary sewer lines, on the basis of acreage owned or front footage.

The Commission recommends that legislation be enacted to require local municipalities or special purpose utility authorities to make all charges against the property for the construction or installation of public facilities on the basis of current assessments rather than a front-footage charge. It also endorses the sales tax exemptions applying to qualified farmers.

This article is reprinted from "Highlights of the Report," Report of the Blueprint Commission on the Future of New Jersey Agriculture, New Jersey Department of Agriculture, Trenton, New Jersey, pp. 5-7, April 1973.

EXAMPLE 74

1978 Legislative Status Update

The Assembly Task Force on Food, Farm and Nutrition Policy under the chairmanship of Assemblyman Maurice Hinchey dealt with legislation which affects your family's food supply and the land on which commodities are produced. Below is a partial list of legislation towards which Assemblyman Hinchey devoted efforts.

Assembly Bill Number/Sponsor	Brief Description	Final Status
4167 Kidder	Defines agricultural value for the purposes of agricultural value assessments	Passed Assembly and Senate. Recalled from Governor for additional amendments
7800 Hinchey, Amatucci	Creates within the Department of Agriculture & Markets a Commodities Clearinghouse program to provide a direct marketing information network between producers and consumers	In Assembly Ways & Means Committee
7853-B Bianchi, Kidder	Alters the appointment procedure for members of the Agricultural Districting Advisory Committees and establishes coordination efforts between the Department of Agriculture & Markets and the Agriculture Resources Commission with respect to rules and regulations for appointments and terms of office	Passed Assembly and Senate but recalled from Governor for additional amendments
7945-A Steingut, Hinchey	Requires foods in cans, jars, bottles or packages to be labeled with a statement of number of grams of sugar added in 100 grams of such food and in specific servings	In the Assembly Agriculture Committee
9078 Hinchey	Creates a temporary commission to study institutional consumption of New York State produced foods	In Assembly Ways and Means Committee
9079-A Hinchey	Allows commodities which are grown locally to be purchased by school districts thus providing our children with fresh, quality commodities while supporting our local producers	Passed Assembly
9080-A Hinchey	Empowers the Department of Agriculture and Markets to analyze, acquire and disseminate information relative to state programs which affect farmers	Passed Assembly
9902 Hinchey	Consolidates and renumbers the Agriculture & Markets Law for legibility	In Assembly Agriculture Committee for revision
10155 Hinchey, Amatucci	Empowers the Department of Agriculture & Markets to establish an information network between producers and consumers to facilitate direct marketing	Chapter 189 of the Laws of 1978
12099 Hinchey	Requires that the examination for license as a physician include comprehensive questioning to evaluate knowledge of nutrition on the part of the candidate	In Assembly Higher Education Committee
12100 Hinchey, Serrano	Requires that each full time student be allowed a minimum of 30 minutes for a lunch period daily	In Assembly Education Committee

12101 Hinchey	Establishes a uniform dating system for ultra-pasteurized cream products	Passed Assembly
12117 Hinchey	Places restrictions on corporate holdings in farms and farm lands	In Assembly Agriculture Committee
12151-A Koppell, Hinchey	Establishes a mechanism whereby Cooperative Extension Service acts as a clearinghouse for persons interested in community gardening	Chapter 632 of the Laws of 1978
12199-C Hinchey, Rappleyea	Extends for another 10 years the tax exemption for farmers who build new structures on their farms so that they will have more working capital for the production of farm commodities	Chapter 743 of the Laws of 1978
12220 Hinchey, Graber, D. Walsh	Provides for the accelerated identification and inventory of soil resources in designated areas	In Assembly Ways and Means Committee
12221 Hinchey, Walsh	Establishes a voluntary program for the improvement of direct marketing of New York State products at roadside markets	Passed the Assembly
12222 Hinchey, Bianchi	Establishes a voluntary program for farmland preservation	In Assembly Ways and Means Committee
12240-A Hinchey	Changes the procedure for notification of agricultural value assessment to a mail notification	Chapter 663 of the Laws of 1978
12317 Hinchey, Landes, Nadler, Ferris	Reduces the incorporation fee for food cooperatives to $10 annually	Passed the Assembly
12404-A Hinchey, Serrano, Steingut	Establishes a nutritional services act designed to improve the quality of school feeding programs in New York State schools	Passed the Assembly
12405-A and 13105 Hinchey, Serrano Steingut	Establishes the Women, Infant and Children (WIC) Supplemental Feeding Program in New York State law while improving the operation of the program and advancing it funding for the 1979 fiscal year in anticipation of increased federal funding	Passed the Assembly
12406-C Hinchey, Steingut	Allows eligible senior citizens and SSI beneficiaries the option of using food stamps in selected restaurants which offer meals at reduced prices	Passed the Assembly, but returned for amendments
12407-B Hinchey, Serrano, Steingut	Establishes guidelines for implementing the Nutrition Education and Training Program (P.L. 95-166) in which Congress appropriated approximately $4 million to New York State for educating teachers, students and food service personnel	Passed Assembly but returned for amendments
12975 Hinchey	Provides for the assessment of farm land to be completed with appraisal data collection forms which are geared toward agricultural properties	In Assembly Real Property Tax Committee

This article is reprinted from "1978 Legislative Status Update," **New York State Assembly Task Force on Food, Farm and Nutritional Policy,** November 1978.

Chapter 17

Comprehensive City Food Plans

City governments have recently adopted a new concept in dealing with urban and consumer food related issues by developing city food plans. The preceding section, *Building Urban and Consumer Food Policies*, surveyed a variety of new programs and policy alternatives which local governments and community-based organizations are implementing in cities and towns across the country. By drafting city food plans, local governments are taking an integrated approach to solving urban food problems.

In taking a comprehensive approach, city governments are working with community organizations to encourage local economic development and neighborhood revitalization; to lower the cost of food for low-income families and the elderly; to increase public access to land for gardens and community parks, and to ensure optimum use of available federal, state and local funds.

State and local governments can help support these new initiatives to develop integrated city food plans. In Boston, there is state support for access to land, composting projects, the community garden movement, and farmers' markets in the city. In **Example 75, The Politics of Food in Massachusetts, Growing Our Own,** Rory O'Connor describes the support and policies which are needed to create an integrated food system.

The article also discusses the need to build urban-rural food coalitions. In Boston, an ad-hoc group of individuals representing both urban and rural communities hold regular meetings to discuss new ideas, programs and policies and advocate for the state and local legislation and funds needed to support these innovations. Groups such as Boston's can help to encourage a closer relationship between grassroots organizations and public officials at the state or the local level.

Two cities have taken the lead in drafting comprehensive city food plans; Seattle, Washington, and Hartford, Connecticut. In both cases the city governments have helped to facilitate the creation and implementation of these programs.

SEATTLE

Examples of Seattle's participation in the overall urban agriculture movement have already been mentioned several times in preceding chapters through descriptions of the Pike Place Market, The Bulk Commodities Exchange and the P-Patch Program.

The city government of Seattle has been very involved in the evaluation of neighborhoods as the arenas for an integrated urban agricultural food system. Seattle's Department of Community Development saw the potential of projects like the Pike Place Market and Bulk Commodities Exchange growing into programs such as community greenhouses, educational workshops and a food processing center. What was needed was an overall plan that included feedback, input and recommendations from citizens. Community Block Grant Funds were seen as the most likely source of funding to get these demonstration projects underway.

The Department's staff took the initiative to draft working papers; to set up an Urban Agricultural Technical Advisory Committee; to receive recommendations, and finally, to submit policy recommendations. **Example 76, A Background Paper on Urban Agriculture**, and the **1979 Capital Improvement Policy Plan**, contain excerpts related to why a city should be, and how it can be involved in urban agriculture. These policy recommendations were developed by the Seattle Department of Community Development, reviewed by citizens and then approved by the Mayor and the City Council.

This process in turn has laid the groundwork for Block Grant funding for the recently incorporated Neighborhood Technology Coalition. This coalition includes 15 community groups, a core staff, technical assistance groups, and the involvement of city agencies through "in kind" staff time. The Coalition will be able to make small grants to projects related to housing, energy, food, waste, and water issues.

HARTFORD

The city of Hartford requested a draft of a Food Plan for the city. Funding to commission the draft came through the "New Venture Development Program," a program initiated through Community Development Block Grant. The draft was then reviewed by various city agencies, community organizations and activists working with food related projects. *A Strategy To Reduce the Cost of Food for Hartford Residents* (research by Cathy Lerza) basically articulates the need for an alternative food system at a city level. Components of this food system include community gardens, food distribution, farmers' markets, canning, food buying clubs and cooperatives, and economic development opportunities. In **Example 77, Farms, Urban Food**, Cathy Lerza discusses the establishment of an urban food system in Hartford.

A unique feature of Hartford's five year plan is the education component. The Hartford Board of Education has set aside funds to create a Hartford Regional Vocational Agricultural Center. The Center will serve two Hartford school districts as well as nearby county districts. It will emphasize agriculture, horticulture, natural resource conservation, and small enterprise business management as these pertain to urban and suburban student populations and community needs. This invaluable education/training project will assist the various components of the food system in becoming more self-reliant.

Hartford's Food Plan has now become a reality with the incorporation of the Hartford Food System in the Summer of 1979. The organization's Board includes representatives of community organizations, technical assistance groups and city officials. Besides the Educational Center, a Farmers' Market is in full operation with organizers working with city residents as well as farmers from surrounding counties. Garden projects have been operating with assistance from the Knox Parks Foundation. CETA positions and VISTA workers are also playing an important role in getting these various and interrelated projects underway.

Resources

ORGANIZATIONS

Conference on Alternative State and Local Policies
The Agriculture Project
2000 Florida Avenue, N.W.
Washington, D.C. 20009
(202) 387-6030
Henry Hyde, Director; Maggie Kennedy

Department of Community Development/Seattle

400 Zester Building
Seattle, Washington 98104
(206) 625-4492
Daryl Grothaus, Director; Susan Appel

Hartford Food Systems, Inc.

c/o ConnPIRG
30 High Street (#108)
Hartford, Connecticut 06103
(203) 525-8312
Jack Hale, Mark Winne, Sally Taylor

Public Advocates, Inc.

1535 Mission Street
San Francisco, California 94103
(415) 431-7430
Angela Blackwell

BIBLIOGRAPHY

Center for Science in the Public Interest (CSPI), **From the Ground Up: Building a Grassroots Food Policy.** CSPI, 1755 S Street, N.W., Washington, D.C. 20009. 1976. $2.50.

Community Environmental Council, **Agriculture in the City—El Mirasol Educational Farm.** Community Environmental Council, 109 East De La Guerra Street, Santa Barbara, California 93101. 1976. $2.50.

Friend, Gil and David Morris, **Energy, Agriculture and Neighborhood Food Systems.** Institute for Local Self-Reliance, 1717 18th Street, N.W. Washington, D.C. 20009.

Hartford, City of, and Catherine Lerza, **A Strategy to Reduce the Cost of Food for Hartford Residents.** Hartford Food Systems, Inc., c/o Conn PIRG, 248 Farmington Avenue, Hartford, Connecticut 06105. 1978. $3.50.

Lerza, Catherine, "State Food Plans," **The Elements.** Public Resource Center, 1747 Connecticut Avenue, N.W., Washington, D.C. 20009. June 1976.

Lerza, Catherine and Michael Jacobson, **Food for People, Not for Profit.** Ballantine Books, New York, New York. 1975.

Neighborhood Works. Center for Neighborhood Technology, 570 West Randolph Street, Chicago, Illinois 60606. Bimonthly newsletter.

O'Connor, Rory, "The Politics of Food in Massachusetts, Growing Our Own," **Real Paper.** Pages 20-24. 929 Massachusetts Avenue, Cambridge, Massachusetts 02139. July 22, 1978.

Seattle Office of Policy Planning, **1979 Capital Improvement Policy Plan.** Seattle Office of Policy Planning, Department of Community Development, 400 Zester Building, Seattle, Washington 98104. 1979.

Smith, Frank, **Food in the City.** Public Resource Center, 1747 Connecticut Avenue, N.W., 20009. 1977. $3.00.

The Politics of Food in Massachusetts, Growing Our Own

EXAMPLE
75

Standing six-foot-four and wearing his customary jumpsuit, State Representative Mel King (D–South End, Roxbury) looks big, black, bald, bearded and *bad*. Meeting him for the first time, you might mistake him for Isaac Hayes. One thing you would never guess, however, is that Boston's King has quietly become the most outspoken legislative advocate of agricultural development in Massachusetts.

Although many of his constituents have never even seen a Massachusetts farm, Mel King now devotes a large portion of his time pondering and acting upon such arcane topics as soil toxicity, "heavy metals," sludge farming and composting techniques. The first bill he ever filed called for the funding of community gardens, and during the course of his three-term tenure on Beacon Hill King has become involved, visible and vocal on such issues as farmland assessment, state purchase of development rights, a state composting authority and methods of spurring the Commonwealth's food production and processing industries.

"My constituents need to eat good food that doesn't take too much of their income," explains King. "Growing more food, both in Massachusetts and the whole region, is clearly part of the solution to that problem."

Such direct, deceptively clear thinking is the hallmark of a budding coalition of politicians, community activists, professional dreamers and just plain folks that has come together in the past five years to reexamine this state's food and land-use policies. As persistent and hardy as the city weeds that crop up in the "rubble gardens" they've sponsored, this emergent urban/rural alliance has already met with some success and has loudly begun to demand more.

Their victories so far have been small. The 1974 Farm and Gardening Act provided minimal ($42,000 this year) funding for urban community gardens; another bill allowed farmland to be assessed at its value to the farmer rather than at the speculative market rate; yet another appropriated $5 million to purchase development rights of endangered active farmland; and a number of farmers' markets opened this month in the heart of Boston aimed at providing fresh-from-the-farm produce at less-than-retail prices to inner-city inhabitants.

The ultimate goals of this emerging group, however, are much more encompassing. In the short run, they comprise central composting facilities, to provide much-needed topsoil for urban gardening on vacant, abandoned city lots; establishing an affiliated canning and nutrition education center; beginning garden supply-and-service businesses for roto-tilling, compost bins, greenhouses and the like; and creating community land trusts to ensure the permanence of such creations.

In the long run, as their dreams slowly begin to take shape, the members of this unlikely coalition will be forced to look beyond their own neighborhoods and cities. What they see on the state and regional level frightens and appalls them. Massachusetts and the Northeast as a whole are woefully dependent on outside sources for the very staff of life. In an emergency, we could probably last a week on the amount of food the region has on hand at any given time. It's bad enough that we can barely heat our homes in the winter, but must Massachusetts be at the end of the food pipeline as well?

Currently, more than 85 percent of all food consumed in the Commonwealth is produced and processed out-of-state. Moreover, the situation is bound to get worse before it gets better. The number of working farms in the state has decreased from 35,000 to 6000 since World War II, and some experts say the Massachusetts farmer may almost be extinct by 1985.

"Obviously we in Massachusetts are never going to become totally self-sufficient in food," notes Mel King bluntly. "But merely growing 10 percent *more* of our own food could turn into a substantial industry."

A quick look at the figures proves King's point. Since the estimated annual food budget for Massachusetts is more than $2 billion, if in-state food production and processing were just boosted from the current 15 percent to a paltry 25 percent, an instant $200-million-a-year industry could conceivably be generated. As King puts it, "We could increase astronomically the cash flow within the state and region, and at the same time, instead of growing garbage, the city lots could begin growing food."

"Self-sufficiency," notes a recent edition of the *Massachusetts Farm Bulletin*, "is a term swollen with current appeal." So swollen, say the editors, that the recent passage of the Development Rights Law by the state legislature was a sure thing, despite the fact that the body is ruled by urban representatives ("And rightly so," argues the *Bulletin*, "for 93 percent of us are non-farmers").

So popular has the code phrase "self-sufficiency" become, so well does it fit in with our Puritan heritage, that to speak against it is considered heresy in almost all circles, conservative or progressive. But, as King asserts, Massachusetts will never be able to grow all its own food. For one thing, the modern American diet is too varied for that. Climate and soil dictate that at least 25 percent of our present diet must come from out-of-state, and our addiction to a meat-heavy diet ensures that the figure will remain even higher than that. Unless we change our diets substantially to conform with whatever we *are* able to produce, we in the Northeast are destined to maintain some level of dependence on outside sources for food requirements.

Even so, there are steps that can be taken right now to alleviate the present situation. Ironically, the passage of development purchase rights legislation, such as this year's Chapter 780 (the aforementioned Development Rights Law), may not be the answer. Although it *is* important to preserve currently active farmland, since we now have less than a fifth of an acre of growing land in production for every person in the Commonwealth, studies show that only one-quarter of our best farmland is now being farmed. It is remarkable, then, that on this land Massachusetts farmers manage to grow all the cranberries, strawberries and sweet corn consumed here, as well as half our milk, a third of our eggs and 80 percent of our apples.

About half of the best farmland in the state now lies fallow or under forest cover. And despite alarm about urban encroachment on active farmland by real estate speculators and developers, only about 12 percent of our growing lands have been taken for residential purposes. Purchasing development rights, creating community land trusts, and similar measures are necessary, but may really be only holding actions. They will probably not increase food production in the near future. For Massachusetts to grow a larger percentage of its own food, two things are necessary: increased state planning and direct funding on all levels, and a further twist in the economic equation that will convince both growers and consumers that they can exchange good, fresh food at mutually beneficial prices.

"The system that we live under will inevitably drive people to build pockets of self-sufficiency," observes King, with neither rancor nor rhetoric. "Prices are going to push people into it. Besides, we can't sit back and wait for a crisis to develop. It should be obvious that we need a better balance between import and home production. Not total self-sufficiency, but why not the entirely reasonable possibility of increasing production by another 10 percent? I don't think it's such a dream, you know. It's really quite realistic."

King and his adherents on the community, city and state levels believe that it is only bread-and-butter issues, like unemployment and inflation, that will force Massachusetts residents to become actively involved in the problems of food production, processing and distribution. "These are really life-support issues we're discussing," he says. "People always worry about the fuel disappearing, but what about the *land itself?* Unless the situation turns around soon, it'll already be too late."

Although all but the politicians refuse to come right out and say it, most members of the new coalition of urban/agrarian reformers see the importation of most of Massachusetts' food as a fundamentally

political problem. Again, Mel King probably says it best. Besides, he's the only one willing to say it for attribution. The rest — community organizers, activists who've temporarily slipped through the cracks in the bureaucratic maze, "small-is-beautiful" theoreticians, et al. — are still too scared of frightening their devotees with overt political statements.

"For a long time people in this country and particularly this region have felt powerless," says King. "So powerless that they're just now becoming aware that they can do something about food other than go to a supermarket and buy it. But that's changing. People are putting a lot less faith in Big Brother and his specialists to come across with the goods. They're realizing that the political reality is that we all have to begin dealing with this problem, that we have to start taking some degree of control over our lives again."

AN URBAN-RURAL FOOD COALITION?

But in order to begin instituting such a fundamental change, the urban agrarians quickly realized they would have to transcend their own narrow local interests and start thinking in much broader terms. From individual, back-yard plots of land to community gardens to citywide organizations like BUG, the natural progress of the movement has been rapid and clear. Recently, the new coalition has begun pushing its way out of the confines of the cities and involving other parts of the state in its messianic greening process. The brand-new farmers' markets are probably the best examples of the urban gardeners' realization that their coalition would have to be expanded to include the rural growers too.

"It's not hard to envision an even newer, more powerful coalition between urban and rural interests," commented one organizer. "Right now the city people have somewhat of a political base but not much land. The farmers have land but absolutely no political base. A merger could solve a lot of problems for both parties."

Once the political/cultural movement begun by the urban gardeners started reaching out to the rest of the state, it was only a matter of time before the planned inclusion of the rest of New England, and the Northeast region as a whole. Although the regional phase of the new coalition is in its infancy, there are already signs that it is beginning to have some impact.

Three New England states — Massachusetts, Vermont and Connecticut — have already made official studies of their food policies, and others are in the planning stage. As the 1976 Vermont report put it, "We need not postulate food, feed grain and petroleum scarcities or national catastro-

phes to make a policy of agriculture development sensible. Present-day continuously rising cost of energy, transportation and food, in fact of all that we import, consume and use, provides sufficient justification to develop Vermont's agricultural potential."

The introduction to the Massachusetts Policy for Food and Agriculture, penned by the Honorable Michael Stanley Dukakis, is even more blunt. "Alarmed by the persistent rise in local food prices at the retail level and the rapid decline of farming and farmland in Massachusetts, and haunted by the realization that the State has no guiding policy on these matters . . . [we] have undertaken to identify the root causes of these problems and to recommend remedial programs for state government to follow." The report that follows specifically recommends policies to increase production and processing of local products and holds as its primary goal "making Massachusetts more nearly self-sufficient."

Besides policy studies by several states, there are also a number of organizations that have begun to emphasize the need for regional food and land-use planning. One such group is the Northeast Task Force for Food and Farm Policy, which is headquartered in Albany, New York, and promotes conferences throughout the region.

Other organizations that might contribute to the developing dialogue on regional food production include the New England Regional Council, the Coalition of Northeastern Governors, the Northeast Association of State Departments of Agriculture, and a recently constituted group sponsored by the latter two organizations known as the Northeast Agricultural Leadership Assembly (NALA). NALA was begun as a regional effort to help the individual Northeast states improve their agricultural and rural economies. Leaders in these areas from everywhere in the region (including Delaware, New Jersey, New York, Vermont, Maine, Pennsylvania, Connecticut, Rhode Island, New Hampshire, Washington, D.C., and Massachusetts) plan to discuss the food and farming needs of the region at the Assembly with key legislators, congressional delegates and other state and federal officials. Their announced aim is "to hammer out a set of meaningful and realistic policy recommendations."

Over the course of the next few months, according to NALA Coordinator Pat Lewis Sackrey, eight different Assembly Subject Committees will be meeting to prepare background information and suggested policies. Then, September 16 through 19, the results will be presented for consideration at a NALA Conference in Cherry Hill, New Jersey. Although clearly only a beginning, the Cherry Hill NALA conference should serve as a harbinger of change for enlightened state officials.

With programs, policies and planning beginning to occur simultaneously on the city, state and regional level, it comes as no surprise that the first glimmers of the nascent urban/agrarian revolution are on the national horizon as well. Already two different planning groups have begun to address the issues of reorganizing national food production and distribution, as well as the need to protect the vanishing family farm and preserve locally active farmland.

The first such group was the National Conference on Alternative State and Local Public Policies, a Washington-based citizens' lobby that recently prepared an excellent informational packet on the methods and means employed in many different states in an attempt to force legislators to grapple with both new and traditional problems in agriculture. As noted in the introduction to the report, written by editor Lee Webb, "Using a combination of new technical innovations and old populist models, concerned legislators, farm and consumer organizations have flooded state legislatures with bills to protect the family farm and agriculture. These bills are aimed at putting the states in the forefront of a national campaign to save the family farm and threatened agricultural land."

Why should the states be front and center on a question of federal policy? For two reasons: the state legislatures, being smaller and closer to the farmer and consumer, are more receptive to new approaches and ideas; and agribusiness and corporate farming have the political leverage to squelch any threatening initiatives at the national level.

There is no single national agenda for restructuring farm economies. Nor should there be. Each state (or at least each region) has unique problems and considerations. The Great Plains States, for example, already have a family-owned farm economy that is fairly prosperous, and the major fear in that region is of prosperity itself.

States with rapidly expanding urban areas, however, are reacting to the urban sprawl and land development that is destroying prime farm acreage every day. Concerned states, cities and even suburbs are already experimenting with such devices as land-use plans, zoning restrictions and tax incentives.

Here in the Northeast, there are difficulties that are specific and unique to the region as well. Since farming is at best marginal throughout most of the region, the immediate concern must be to prevent the total disappearance of farming and agriculture generally. In a state where there were more than 2 million acres of farmland thirty years ago, there now remain only 700,000, and that figure is shrinking fast.

As a result of the Northeast's specific problems, the focus of the current effort must be to foster strong assistance from the state governments to revive the flagging farm economy. Given the gravity of our situation, it should come as no surprise that the most comprehensive strategies for dealing with the disappearing American farm have been developed in Vermont and Massachusetts.

A survey recently prepared by the National Conference on Alternative State and Local Public Policies has focused discussion of possible legislative action on proposals to limit or prohibit corporate farming, assist new farmers with financing, find new markets for farm products, protect agricultural land from development and lower taxes on farmers.

The other group that has addressed itself directly to the development of regionally based national food policy is the pioneering economic think tank known as the Exploratory Project for Economic Alternatives (EPEA). Early last year, EPEA issued a sweeping report called *Toward a National Food Policy*. Headed by the prominent, unconventional economist Gar Alperovitz, EPEA proposed a drastic restructuring of the entire American food production system that would subsidize farmers to keep prices down and radically curb the growth of agribiz.

Upon releasing the report, project director Alperovitz said, "If we are ever going to make progress in reducing unemployment, it is necessary to make a direct attack on inflation, and food inflation is one of the major sources of the problem."

The EPEA report drew heavily upon precedents from both the United States and other advanced industrial nations in outlining a step-by-step, decade-long shift in food policy geared to the unstable world market. The program, parts of which echo plans proposed but never implemented during the Truman administration, calls for managing both supplies and prices on behalf of consumers, while simultaneously protecting family farm income with direct government payments. At the same time the report also addresses the structural problems of the food industry, including monopoly influences over production, processing and distribution, excessive scale and energy use, and the mutual dependence of the United States and the Third World on food trade.

Briefly, the EPEA's comprehensive food policy consists of the following: 1). *Low-cost food*. The government's already existing supply management system should be expanded to keep prices low for middle-income and low-income families. This could be done by matching production with domestic demand; by creating emergency reserves, such as currently exist with wheat and some other commodities; by extending governmental control over agricultural trade; and by breaking up monopoly control.

2). *A stable family-farm income*. This could come about by federal guarantees of market-income supplements to small and medium-sized family farmers.

3). *Resource conservation and improved nutrition*. If farming were to become more labor-intensive and organic production intensified, this could become a possibility.

4). *World food self-sufficiency*. The US international food policy should be redirected toward aiding Third World food production and discouraging corporations from pursuing cash-crop projects abroad.

Given the coming era of increasing food inflation, resource and energy shortages and massive pollution, it seems clear that the United States can no longer continue its narrowly based policy of supporting agribusiness at the expense of the family farmers, and by extension, of the rest of us. The present system has led to unstable, overinflated prices for overprocessed and sometimes carcinogenic food; the disappearance of millions of family-farms and the near-total decline of rural life, at least in the Northeast; waste of precious energy and pollution through the overuse of agricultural chemicals and inorganic production aids; and the creation of a dependence in other countries on food aid and exports from the United States.

The EPEA food policy study makes so much sense that it is sure to be ignored on the federal level. In addition, its "catch" is that it would be largely financed by a steeply progressive income tax, which its authors say would be "more equitable and less inflationary" than paying for cost increases with higher food prices. But it must have some allure even for the federal bureaucrats. After all, our agricultural system has substituted machines and fuel for labor and land for too long. But as the EPEA report wryly notes, "Unfortunately, today we have a surplus of labor and a shortage of energy."

Perhaps we should learn our lesson from the everyday experiences of the coalition of urban and rural forces still being born in this country. Although they still feel compelled to adopt a tactic of hiding the political ramifications of their actions, the many community activists beginning to coalesce around the simple act of planting a seed are already quite aware and articulate about what they're doing. "Growing food is without a doubt the most political action you can take these days," said one. "But it's certainly not the old politics of rhetoric, terminology, semantics. Nor is there a "left" or a "right" any longer. Only the inescapable conclusion that people must come before profits." ∎

This article is reprinted from Rory O'Connor, "The Politics of Food in Massachusetts, Growing Our Own," **The Real Paper**, pp. 20-23, July 22, 1978.

Background Paper on Urban Agriculture

EXAMPLE
76

Why the City Should Be Involved in Urban Agriculture

During the last ten years, the demand has increased on local municipalities to provide more basic social services in health and food areas. The various federally funded food programs (food stamps, child nutrition, elderly feeding programs, etc.) are nationally recognized as being inadequate. They create dependence. They strip dignity. Important as it is to provide immediate tangible assistance to the millions of needy adults and children in this country, the programs have not substantially reduced the incidence of malnutrition. One of the main reasons is that even with the increases in funding for these programs and the increases in participation, inflation (especially its effect on the price of food) has virtually eliminated any advantages the food program offered to the poor person. The cost of food has increased at a faster rate than the benefit allotment of either welfare assistance or food stamps. Other reasons have to do with administrative problems, the basic design of the programs, and the lack of adequate funding (e.g., long waiting lists for participation in the Women-Infant-Children program exist in nearly every city in Washington).

Urban agriculture programs will not eliminate hunger or poverty. They are not a substitute for jobs and a decent income. They cannot fulfill the need that nutritious breakfasts to school children fulfill—helping children do well in school and grow up healthy and strong. They won't eliminate the fear of the elderly person to go grocery shopping. They won't eliminate the increasing demands for services on the city.

Urban agriculture programs *can*, however, move Seattle toward helping individuals and neighborhoods meet their food needs through their own efforts.

The dietary goals set by the U.S. Senate Committee point out the enormous need for education on food and nutrition. Urban agriculture programs have demonstrated their effectiveness in serving as educational forums. The City of Cleveland has had a school-home garden program since 1904. It is a tested example of how nutrition education can be easily and effectively incorporated into ongoing programs. The Seattle P-patch program, started in 1974, involves 3,000 gardeners, many with little or no gardening experience. The gardening program has given them the opportunity to learn about nutrition, the soil, and political issues related to food; and to examine their own personal food habits.

Month after month, thousands of Seattle residents request emergency food assistance. Urban agriculture programs can help by preserving food raised in gardens or greenhouses, or purchased at low cost in large quantities (through co-ops). Food buying clubs and co-ops can help all through the year by saving the individual 10-30%

on their purchases. Second, on an organizational level, community groups can utilize urban agriculture programs to build up a supply of food for emergency use. Extra food can be preserved and purchased (utilizing some of the income generated by the programs themselves) to help neighbors who are confronted with an emergency.

One of the most serious problems facing Seattle neighborhoods today is displacement. The pressures of the housing market force many lower income persons out of their neighborhoods. The lure of financial gain encourages many to sell and leave a neighborhood. Urban agriculture cannot address the economic factors of this problem. However, by helping to improve the quality of the neighborhood through tangible programs which provide short-term payoffs, urban agriculture might give some homeowners more reasons to stay in their neighborhoods. By itself, urban agriculture is not going to convince people to forfeit windfall profits. With other incentives and with the variety of neighborhood improvement programs the City is presently engaged in, urban agriculture programs can be a strong encouragement for people to stay and invest their lives there.

Conclusion

Urban agriculture can offer effective tools to help the city meet its stated objectives. It can directly help low-income people reduce their monthly food costs. Through land use, community development and income generation strategies, it can help strengthen Seattle's neighborhoods. As a way of investing limited resources, it can have a multiplier effect: urban agriculture programs can serve many functions such as energy conservation and food production; waste utilization and soil development. Most importantly, they can provide an immediate, tangible product for the people involved. It is an area which deserves the attention and creative energies of the City.

Seattle 1979 Capital Improvement Policy Plan

Community Development

The City also intends to experiment with urban agriculture programs to determine if these programs can have a significant impact on the lives of low-income people and the conditions of their neighborhoods.

Mann-Minor, Atlantic, Columbia

Objectives:
Increase the real and disposable incomes of existing low-income residents of the target neighborhoods. Increase the capacity of residents and neighborhood groups to meet the community development needs in their neighborhoods.

Strategies:
Provide increased and improved open space and recreation facilities where these are inadequate or where part of a specific improvement plan; encourage the use of open space for food production, where appropriate.

1979 Funding Policies:
Target Area Planning: A proposal will be considered from the Department of Community Development to continue funding the development of neighborhood improvement strategies in the target areas. This planning effort should include identification of structures needing rehabilitation, public improvements, neighborhood marketing strategies, human service needs, employment opportunities for low-income residents, energy conservation and food production strategies, etc.

- Vacant Lots: Proposals will be considered for innovative and productive methods of eliminating and controlling blight and more effectively using vacant lots within the three target neighborhoods.

- Proposals must demonstrate the benefits to the community environment, such as added food production, employment of low-income residents, or safety improvements.

- Priority will be given to proposals which include the production of food for low-income people.

Pike Place Market

Objectives:
Strengthen the Market as an outlet for locally grown food, and expand its food-related uses to better serve regional food producers and City residents.

1979 Funding Policies:
A proposal will be considered to provide some staff capacity to assist in the expansion of the Market Area as a center for food distribution activity in the region. The proposal must describe the specific responsibilities of this staff, and the expected results from the work.

Public Housing Neighborhoods

Objectives:
Increase the real and disposable incomes of public housing residents.

Strategies:
Develop programs to create jbos for public housing residents, and programs to reduce food costs.

1979 Funding Policies:
Proposals will be considered for funding demonstration urban agriculture programs.

Other Neighborhood Improvement Efforts in CDAs

Objectives:
Reduce expenditures by low-income residents for basic needs such as energy and food.

Strategies:
Provide technical assistance to neighborhoods to undertake self-help projects.

1979 Funding Policies:
Technical Assistance: Proposals will be considered for the provision of specific technical assistance to neighborhoods to carry out self-help projects.

Community Facilities: Proposals will be considered for small scale improvements to existing publicly owned facilities which improve the quantity or quality of service delivery. (See Community and Municipal Facilities Policy 6.1.)

Economic Development

Objectives:
Better utilize vacant and underutilized non-residential land and structures.

Strategies:
In addition to providing job opportunities as a means to increase incomes, encourage projects, programs and services which result in a lowering of costs to low-income City residents of basic goods and services (shelter, food, health care).

1979 Funding Policies:
Physical Improvements: Proposals will be considered for neighborhood improvement projects in Target Areas which employ low-skilled unemployed community residents, and which will improve the livability of the neighborhood.

Housing

A third goal, not explicitly stated in the Policy Plan but related to the above, has been to find practical ways to reduce the operating and maintenance costs associated with living in housing.

1979 Funding Policies:
New Projects and Programs: Proposal must include a means to develop standards for energy use reduction and to determine the feasibility of alternative energy sources or energy substitution.

Proposals will be accepted for cost effective ways to promote residential energy conservation as new directions for our weatherization, rehab, and repair programs (furnace maintenance or feasible fuel substitution programs) or as limited alternative energy source demonstration (solar greenhouse, for example).

This article is reprinted from "Background Paper on Urban Agriculture" and "1979 Capital Improvement Policy Plan," Seattle Department of Community Development, Seattle, Washington, 1978.

EXAMPLE 77 Farms: Urban Food

SUMMARY OF COSTS AND BENEFITS OF FIVE APPROACHES TO FOOD COST REDUCTION
(Per Household)

	Community Gardens	Solar Greenhouses	Buying Clubs	Canning Center	Farmers' Market
Annual Savings	$195	$195	$265	$25	$150
Annual Subsidy	20	15	15	25	5
Capital Requirements	minimal	1,000	40	70	minimal

The city of Hartford, Connecticut, is considering establishment of an urban food system whereby unemployed youngsters will be put to work on CETA funds to grow food for the city's lower-income population.

This scheme, discussed in a report for the city by Catherine Lerza of the Public Resource Center, argues that a combination of increased community gardens, canning centers, farmers markets, rooftop greenhouses and buying clubs can substantially reduce the cost of food for the city's inhabitants, and at the same time involve a relatively small capital cost.

Hartford, like other communities in New England, imports 85 percent of its food, much of it by truck, which is doubly expensive. As a result, food costs are six to ten percent higher than the national average. Rising food costs, of course, hit everyone, but in Hartford, where a disproportionate part of the population consists of lower-income people, food costs are a major problem. (A low-income family in the city spends 30 percent of its money on food, compared to 21 percent for an upper-income family.)

Not only are food costs going up, but availability of food for residents of inner city areas is a difficulty. Unlike upper-middle-class people, inhabitants of the inner city cannot shop around for bargains simply because the food chains, which now control 57 percent of the food at retail, are pulling out of the inner city. They cite ancient stores, high insurance costs and security risks as reasons for the pullout.

Lerza's report urges establishment of a new public food system comprised of the following major parts:

- Community Gardens. There now are 16 different community gardens within the city of Hartford with a combined total of 500 plots. The proposal would sharply increase the number of gardens by utilizing available public lands in towns adjacent to Hartford. To fertilize the plots, Hartford's wastes could be turned into compost.

    Further, the city should seriously look into raising rabbits and poultry on sites adjacent to Hartford.

    Unemployed youth could be hired with Labor Department funds to grow food for their own families and for those who need emergency food relief.

    Lerza believes that it may well be possible to ex-

tend the growing season in a city such as Hartford through introduction of solar greenhouses, with cold frames as complements. Greenhouses last for 20 years and are not expensive: $5 per square foot when free-standing; $2.50 when attached to an existing building.

- Food Distribution. Here the proposal urges a wide scale adoption of buying clubs, co-op stores, and co-op warehouses. A key to the plan is to develop anew a relationship with the small farmers in the Hartford area, luring them away from the big regional produce terminals outside the city, and getting them back into the city where they can sell through farmers' markets. Market days should be planned around arrival of welfare checks, and the markets should be certified to take food stamps.

    Cost reductions achieved through the foregoing distribution setup can be enhanced through introduction of small community canneries. Estimates are that canning can result in food cost savings from $25 to $75 per household each year.

Lerza writes that the proposed food system "is based on maximizing household self-sufficiency in food production, processing and distribution. The system substitutes the labor of Hartford residents for the labor of Western farmworkers, cross-country truckers and local warehousers and supermarket checkers. The proposed food system is not a job-creation strategy. It is, in fact, exactly the opposite, a proposal to channel some of the surplus labor of under-employed Hartford residents into the provision of certain services to themselves.

"Viewed from a national perspective, the effort of the proposed food system is to take dollars and jobs out of the economy. Viewed from a local perspective, however, the proposed food system should increase the demand for regional produce. Three elements of the proposed food system—the buying clubs, the farmers' market and the food-processing center—could have a significant impact on local commercial agriculture, if large numbers of Hartford residents eventually participate in these programs."

All of this means preserving farmland. A bill before the Connecticut state legislature would subsidize farmers to hold prime agricultural land away from real estate development, while pledging its continued use to farming. The Hartford Board of Education, for its part, plans to establish a vocational agricultural high school, initially serving ninth to 12th grades. Eventually, the new school will accept students from the adult population, and attempt to recruit out-of-school teenage youth.

Education aside, one of the most difficult problems in agriculture is the large amount of money needed by new farmers to start up operations. The Hartford report makes this proposal:

"Truck farming, as most forms of small business operations, requires a large initial capital investment. There are several debt financing programs under the Federal Farm Credit System which make mortgages to farmers to purchase land and farm equipment. However, all of their programs require 10 to 20 percent equity participation by the farmer. Increasingly, the total amount of equity required prohibits new and young farmers from entering the market. A means needs to be devised to enable young and new farmers to generate equity through their own work. One possible public resource for this purpose is the Federal Public Service Employment Program, funded under Title VI of the *Comprehensive Employment Training Act of 1974*. The Public Service Employment Program is administered locally by the Hartford Comprehensive Man-

power Program. Public Service Employment funds, for example, could be used to pay the wages of new and young farmers working on a public 'incubator' farm. The revenue generated by the sale of farm produce could be used to make capital grants to 'graduates' of the farm."

Stable markets are essential. Lerza suggests the basis for such a market may be found in the Board of Education, which now purchases $1.8 million of food annually for its school lunch program. In addition, the Community Renewal Team of Greater Hartford spends $360,000 each year for nutrition programs that serve the elderly and youngsters. Both these programs might divert some of the funds used for food purchases from contractors to buying from the new network of city-sponsored co-ops, community gardens, canneries, and from nearby small farmers.

For copies of this report, write Jack Hale, CONN-Pirg, 248 Farmington Avenue, Hartford, Connecticut 06105. The cost is $3.50.

This article is reprinted from Cathy Lerza, "Farms, Urban Food," **The Elements**, pp. 1-3, May 1978.

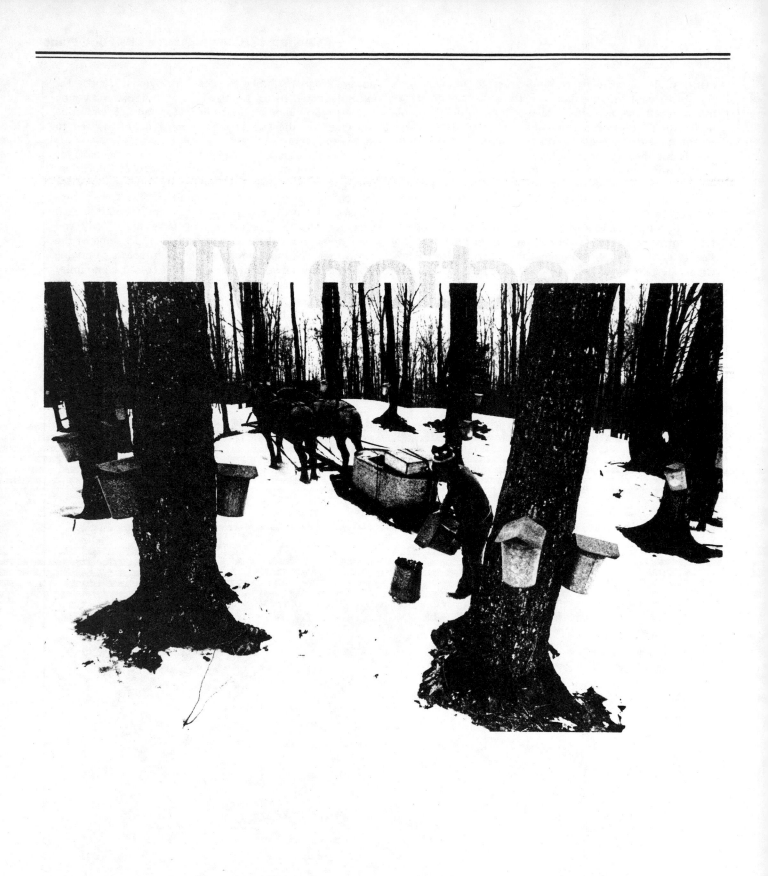

Section VII

Section VII

Resources and Contacts

This section was written to provide the means by which community groups, individuals, activists and public officials can obtain current and ongoing information, technical assistance, analysis of legislation, and other helpful resources dealing with agriculture, land and food issues and policies. The first part, Published Resources, contains useful books, articles, pamphlets, and newsletters, while the Organizational Resources section lists public interest groups, governmental and educational institutions, and other organizations which can be helpful contacts.

PUBLISHED RESOURCES

- General Bibliography
- Newsletters
- How to Find Other Useful Publications on Local, State and Federal Policies
- How to Obtain Information About Political Campaigns and Techniques

ORGANIZATIONAL RESOURCES

- Key Organizations to Contact
- National Farmers Union: State Offices
- State Land Grant Colleges
- State Departments of Agriculture
- State Legislative Agriculture Committees
- Federal Agricultural Committees and Organizations
- National Associations of State and Local Officials
- Agencies of the U.S. Department of Agriculture

General Bibliography

Barnes, Peter, Editor, **The People's Land: A Reader on Land Reform in the United States**. Rodale Press, Emmaus, Pennsylvania 18049. 1975.

Barnes, Peter and Larry Casalino, **Who Owns the Land**. National Land for People, 2348 North Cornelia, Fresno, California 93711. $.75 each.

Belden, Joe and Gregg Forte, **Toward a National Food Policy**. Exploratory Project on Economic Alternatives, 2000 P Street, N.W., Washington, D.C. 20036. 1976. $5.00.

Center for Science in the Public Interest, **From the Ground Up: Building a Grassroots Food Policy**. CSPI, 1757 S Street, N.W., Washington, D.C. 20009. $2.50. 1976.

Cochrane, Willard, and Mary Ryan, **American Farm Policy**. University of Minnesota Press, Minneapolis. 1976. Discussion of goals and shortcomings of official U.S. farm policy.

Earthwork, **Directory of Films on Food and Land—1976**. Earthwork, 3410 19th Street, San Francisco, California 94110. Catalogues over 300 films and distributors. $2.75.

General Accounting Office (GAO), **The Changing Character and Structure of American Agriculture: An Overview**. #CED-78-178, GAO, Washington, D.C. 20548. September 26, 1978.

Gussow, Joan Dye, **The Feeding Web: Issues In Nutritional Ecology**. Bull Publishing Co., P.O. Box 208, Palo Alto, California 94302. 1978.

Guyer, Cynthia, "State and Local Governments Lead the Way," in "The Family Farm: Can It Be Saved?," **E/SA Forum**. United Methodist Church, 110 Maryland Avenue, N.E., Washington, D.C. 20002. October 1978.

Guyer, Cynthia and Lee Webb, "Agricultural Group Seeks Out Non-Federal Answers," **Catholic Rural Life**, 4625 N.W. Beaver Drive, Des Moines, Iowa 50322. September 1978.

Hightower, Jim, **Eat Your Heart Out: How Food Profiteers Victimize the Consumer**. Crown Publishers, Incorporated, New York. 1975.

Hightower, Jim and Susan De Marco, **Hard Times, Hard Tomatoes: The Failure of the Land Grant Complex**. Schenkman Publishing Company, Cambridge, Massachusetts. 1973.

Institute for Southern Studies, "Our Promised Land," **Southern Exposure**. P.O. Box 230, Chapel Hill, North Carolina 27514. $3.50. Fall 1974.

Interfaith Center on Corporate Responsibility (ICCR), **Manual on Agribusiness Corporations**. ICCR, 475 Riverside Drive, Room 566, New York, New York 10027. 1978. $5.00.

Interreligious Task Force on U.S. Food Policy (Taskforce), **Family Farming and the Common Good**. Hunger Bulletin Number 7, Taskforce, 110 Maryland Avenue, N.E., Washington, D.C. 20002. February 1977. 10 or more; 10¢, 100 or more; 7¢.

Kotz, Nick, **Let Them Eat Promises**. Doubleday & Company, Incorporated, Garden City, New York. 1971. Chronicle of discovery of hunger in U.S. by Senator Kennedy and the ensuing unfulfilled promises.

Krebs, Al, **1978-1979 Directory of Major Food Corporations**. Earthwork, 3410 19th Street, San Francisco, California 94110. $6.00.

Lappe, Frances, Joseph Collins and Cary Fowler, **Food First: Beyond the Myth of Scarcity**. Houghton Mifflin Company, Boston. 1977.

Lerza, Catherine, "Farmers on the March," **The Progressive**. June 1978.

Lerza, Catherine and Michael Jacobson, **Food for People, Not for Profit: A Sourcebook on the Food Crisis**. Ballantine Books, New York. 1975.

Merrill, Richard, Editor, **Radical Agriculture**. Harper & Row, New York. 1976.

Morgan, Dan, **Merchants of Grain**. Viking Press, New York. 1979.

National Family Farm Coalition and National Consumer League, **Who's Squeezing the Consumer?** NFFC, 918 F Street, N.W., Washington, D.C. 20004. A consumer's guide to farm policy.

National Conference of State Legislatures (NCSL), **State Legislatures**. Vol. 3, No. 4, NCSL, 1405 Curtis Street, 23rd Floor, Denver, Colorado 80202. September/October 1977. Good section on rural America.

National Rural Center (NRC), **A Directory of Rural Organizations**. NRC, 1828 L Street, N.W., Washington, D.C. 20036.

Perelman, Michael, **Farming for Profit in a Hungry World**. Allanheld, Oseum & Company, 19 Brunswick Road, Montclair, New York 07042. 1978.

Policy Studies Organization, **Policy Studies Journal**. Vol. 6, No. 4, Policy Studies Organization, 361 Lincoln Hall, University of Illinois, Urbana, Illinois 61801. Excellent articles on the political economy of U.S. agriculture.

Prestbo, Editor, **This Abundant Land**. Dow Jones Books, Princeton, New Jersey. 1975. Articles on social, political and economic trends of U.S. agriculture.

Ray, Victor, **The Corporate Invasion of American Agriculture**. National Farmers Union, 12025 East 45th Avenue, Denver, Colorado 80239. 1968.

Rodefeld, Richard D., et al., **Change in Rural America: Causes, Consequences and Alternatives**. C.V. Moseby Company, St. Louis, Missouri. 1978.

Rodefeld, Richard and Kevin Goss, **Corporate Farming in the United States: A Guide to Current Literature, 1967-1977**. Department of Agricultural Economics and Rural Sociology, Penn State University, University Park, Pennsylvania 16802. 1977.

Rosapepe, James C., **Food and Agricultural Policy: Emerging Roles for State Governments**. Prepared for the Center for Policy Research and Analysis, National Governors' Conference. August 2, 1977. Rosapepe, Fuchs and Associates, 918 F Street, N.W., Suite 410, Washington, D.C. 20004.

Rural America, **Strategies for Rural Action: 1977 Conference Working Papers**. Rural America, 1346 Connecticut Avenue, N.W., Washington, D.C. 20036. Listing of and prices for 14 papers.

Rural America, **Toward a Platform for Rural America— 1978**. Rural America, 1346 Connecticut Avenue, N.W., Washington, D.C. 20036.

Smith, Charles, **Bibliography: Land Reform in America**. Earthwork, 3410 19th Street, San Francisco, California 94110. $1.00. Over 1,000 references, most comprehensive bibliography on land issues available.

Smith, Charles, **Bibliography: 160 Acre Anti-Monopoly Water Laws**. National Land for People, 2348 North Cornelia, Fresno, California 93711.

United Methodist Church, "The Family Farm: Can It Be Saved?," **Engage/Social Action**, United Methodist Church, 110 Maryland Avenue, N.E., Washington, D.C. 20002. October 1978. Entire issue.

United Presbyterian Church, **Who Will Farm?** Church and Society Program Area, United Presbyterian Church, USA, 1244 Interchurch Center, 475 Riverside Drive, New York, New York 10027. 1978. $1.00.

U.S. Department of Agriculture, **Handbook of Agricultural Charts**. Number 524. Office of Communication, USDA, Washington, D.C. 20250. November 1977.

U.S. Department of Agriculture, **List of Available Publications**. Office of Communication, USDA, Washington, D.C. 20250. 1977.

U.S. Department of Agriculture, **Status of the Family Farm: Second Annual Report to the Congress**. AER-434. Economics, Statistics and Cooperatives Service, USDA, Washington, D.C. 20250. September 1979.

U.S. Department of Agriculture, **Structure Issues of American Agriculture**. AER-438. Economics, Statistics, and Cooperative Service, USDA, Washington, D.C. 20250. 1979.

U.S. General Accounting Office (GAO), **Food: Reports, Legislation and Information Sources: A Guide**. Number CED-78-37. The Comptroller General, GAO, 4th and G Streets, N.W., Washington, D.C. 20548. May 1978.

U.S. Senate, Committee on Agriculture and Forestry, **Farm and Food Policy**. Superintendent of Documents, U.S. Government Printing Office, Washington, D.C. 20402. September 15, 1976. Discussion of objectives and current issues of U.S. agriculture policy. Also outlines major organizations involved in farm policy and provides brief history of U.S. agriculture policy.

Wellford, Harrison, **Sowing the Wind**. Grossman Publishers, New York. 1972. Food technology and food safety.

WIN. Vol. 8, No. 12, WIN, Box 547, Rifton, New York 12471. July 1972. Issue on "The Death of the American Farmer."

Newsletters

Ag World

1186 W. Summer Street
St. Paul, Minnesota 55113

Bimonthly; $15/year.

AgBiz Tiller

c/o Agribusiness Accountability Publications
3410 19th Street
San Francisco, California 94110

Intermittently, $12/12 issues.

Catholic Rural Life

4625 N.W. Beaver Drive
Des Moines, Iowa 50322

Monthly; $10/year
($7.50/year for low-income).

Center for Rural Affairs Newsletter

P.O. Box 405
Walthill, Nebraska 68076

Monthly; free.

CNI Weekly

1146 19th Street, N.W.
Washington, D.C. 20036

Weekly; $35/year.

Des Moines Register

Circulation Dept.
P.O. Box 957
Des Moines, Iowa 50304

Daily; write for subscription details.

Family Farm Monitor

National Family Farm Coalition
918 F Street, N.W.
Washington, D.C. 20004

Periodically; write for more information.

Food Advocate

Hunger Action Center
2524 16th Avenue South
Seattle, Washington 98144

Bimonthly; free.

Food Critic

Lorne Nystrom, M.P.
House of Commons
Ottawa, Ontario K1A 0A6
CANADA

Monthly; free.

Food Monitor

350 Broadway (#209)
New York, New York 10012

11 Issues; $15/year. Low-income rates are available.

Food Policy Notes

Interreligious Taskforce on U.S. Food Policy
110 Maryland Avenue, N.E.
Washington, D.C. 20002

Semi-monthly; $5/year. Updates federal legislation, programs and Congressional activities on both domestic and international food policy.

Forty Acres and a Mule

564 Lee Street, S.W.
Atlanta, Georgia 30310

Bi-monthly; $2/year.

Land, People, Food

National Land for People
2348 North Cornelia
Fresno, California 93711

$10/year includes membership to NLP. $5/year for low-income membership and subscription. Covers family farm issues, farmworkers, water and irrigation issues, land ownership, corporate farming.

Maine Organic Farmer and Gardener

P.O. Box 187
Hollowell, Maine 04347

Bimonthly; $6/year.

NFO Reporter

National Farmers Organization
475 L'Enfant Plaza, S.W.
Washington, D.C. 20024

Monthly; $2 /year for non-members. Monitors federal legislation, programs and Congressional activities.

The National Farmworker

NAFO
1332 New York Avenue, N.W.
Washington, D.C. 20020

Monthly; $15/year. Free to NAFO members.

The New Farm

33 East Minor Street
Emmaus, Pennsylvania 18049

Monthly; $10/year.

New Land Review

Center for Rural Affairs
P.O. Box 405
Walthill, Nebraska 68607

Quarterly; $.50/issue, suggested price. Covers farm related issues and policies in Nebraska—of particular interest to people and organizations in the Great Plains region.

Newsletter of the Northeast Task Force on Farm and Food Policy

1111 Twin Towers
99 Washington Avenue
Albany, New York 12248

Free. Updates policy innovations and legislative activities for over 10 states in the Northeast region.

Nutrition Action

Center for Science in the Public Interest
1755 S Street, N.W.
Washington, D.C. 20009

Monthly; $10/year. Articles on nutrition, food policy, family farms.

Ozarka

Ozark Institute
Box 549
Eureka Springs, Arkansas 72632

Quarterly; $15/year.

Ruralamerica

1346 Connecticut Avenue, N.W.
Washington, D.C. 20036

Monthly; $10/year includes membership. An excellent newsletter with articles on a variety of rural issues, programs, policies and events.

Small Farmers' Journal

P.O. Box 197
Junction City, Oregon 97448

Quarterly; $10/year.

Thought for Food

1001 N. Central Avenue
Phoenix, Arizona 85004

Quarterly; write for subscription information.

Tilth

13217 Mattson Road
Arlington, Washington 98223

Quarterly; $5/year. Journal of alternative agriculture for the Pacific Northwest.

U.S. Farm News

U.S. Farmers Association
Box 496
Hampton, Iowa 50441

11 issues; $3/year.

Washington Memorandum

Catholic Rural Life Conference
4625 N.W. Beaver Drive
Des Moines, Iowa 50322

Monthly; $4/year.

Washington Newsletter

National Farmers Union
1012 14th Street, N.W.
Washington, D.C. 20005

Weekly, $10/year. Monitors federal legislation, programs and Congressional activities.

How to Find Other Useful Publications on Local, State and Federal Policies

The Almanac of American Politics: 1976. The Senators, the Representatives, the Governors — Their Records, States, and Districts. Michael Barone and others. Dutton. New York. 1975. Well organized and concise. First issued for 1972 elections.

The Book of the States. Available from the Council of State Governments, P.O. Box 11910, Iron Works Pike, Lexington, Kentucky 40578. The Book of States is the recognized authority on state government. Published since 1935, the Book is the only single volume reference work providing a convenient, dependable source of information on state government. Coverage includes hundreds of pages of articles and precise tables on the financing of state governments, their structure, and programs.

Congressional Directory. Government Printing Office, Washington, D.C. 20402. 1977. Cloth, indexed $12.95; cloth $8.50; paper $6.50. Lists members of Congress, aides, committees, federal departments and agencies, courts, embassies and other useful contacts in Washington, D.C.

The County Yearbook. National Association of Counties, 1735 New York Avenue, N.W., Washington, D.C. 20006. $21.00 prepaid. Yearbook of articles and data relevant to counties.

Dateline Washington. National Conference of State Legislatures, 444 North Capitol Street, N.W., Washington, D.C. 20001. $25.00 per year. An eight page bi-weekly newspaper covering congressional activities and national policy decisions that affect the states.

Directory of Organizations and Individuals Professionally Engaged in Governmental Research and Related Activities. Governmental Research Association. New York. Annual. Includes local and state agencies, independently organized research agencies, taxpayers' associations, citizens' and voters' leagues, college and university government research divisions, legislative reference agencies, and tax supported agencies, by state and city.

Directory of Staff Assistants to the Governors. National Governors' Association, Hall of the States, 444 North Capitol Street, Washington, D.C. 20001. Lists staff of governors.

Directory '77. National Association of Regional Councils, 1700 K Street, N.W., Washington, D.C. 20006. Lists regional councils and associations.

The Federal Register: What It Is and How to Use It. Available from the Government Printing Office, Washington, D.C. 20402. Stock Number 002-003-00934-5. $2.50.

Help: A Directory of Services for Nonprofit Organizations. The Youth Project, 149 Ninth Street, San Francisco, California 94103. 1977. $3.50. Includes sections on fundraising, media, professional consultants, community organization and the use of volunteers.

Index Digest of State Constitutions. Second edition. Columbia University. Legislative Drafting Research Fund. 1959. Statement and analysis of all provisions of the 50 state constitutions, allowing for review and comparison. Entries listed alphabetically under 200 major titles or subject. Updated by supplements in pocket. Actual texts of state constitutions found in **Constitutions of the United States, National and State, 1962.**

Legislative Research Checklist. Available from the Council of State Governments, P.O. Box 11910, Iron Works Pike, Lexington, Kentucky 40578. Lists reports by legislative research agencies, other study committees and commissions in the states, and independent organizations that have published material appropriate for review by state agencies. Includes information as to availability of materials listed and addresses where they may be obtained. Annual subscription $10.00.

Newly Elected State Officials and Legislators. Available from the Council of State Governments, P.O. Box 11910, Iron Works Pike, Lexington, Kentucky 40578. Updates rosters of elected officials and legislators for states which held elections in November 1977 (Kentucky, New Jersey, and Virginia). 12 pages. 1977. $1.50.

1978 Suggested State Legislation. Available from the Council of State Governments, P.O. Box 11910, Iron Works Pike, Lexington, Kentucky 40578. Since 1941, the Council of State Governments has published annual volumes of draft state laws on subjects likely to be considered in upcoming state legislative sessions. The drafts are prepared to aid state legislators who already may be contemplating legislation on the topics. Draft acts are selected by a committee of more than 150 persons representing all states. Previous volumes of Suggested State Legislation are still available (please inquire). 238 pages. 1977. $7.50.

State Elective Officials and Legislatures. Available from the Council of State Governments, P.O. Box 11910, Iron Works Pike, Lexington, Kentucky 40578. Names, addresses, and political affiliations of the nation's almost 7,600 state legislators are given in this biennial volume, published as soon after the general elections as possible. In addition, names of statewide elected oficials are given. A valuable source of information about the officials of each state and territory. Companion volume to **State Administrative Officials (Classified by Functions)**. 170 pages. 1977. $10.00.

State Legislative Leadership, Committees and Staff. 1979 Edition. Available from Council of State Governments, P.O. Box 11910, Iron Works Pike, Lexington, Kentucky 40578. Names, addresses, and telephone numbers of the men and women who staff the nation's legislatures. Provides the chairs of legislative standing committees. Codes indicate which offices perform various legislative duties such as research, management, fiscal affairs, bill drafting, and auditing. 206 pages. 1979. $13.00.

U.S. Government Manual. Available from the Government Printing Office, Washington, D.C. 20402. Stock Number 022-003-00924-8. $6.50. Lists and describes all federal departments and agencies.

Working for Consumers — A Directory of State and Local Organizations. Consumer Federation of America, 1012 14th Street, N.W., Suite 901, Washington, D.C. 20005.

Working in the System: A Comprehensive Manual for Citizen Access to Federal Agencies. James R. Michael, ed., Basic Books, New York. 1974. $14.95. Written by Ralph Nader's Center for Study of Responsive Law.

How to Obtain Information About Political Campaigns and Techniques

Compiled by Mona Hochberg

This bibliography was first compiled for a series of campaign workshops that were held this spring. The idea was to sort out the numerous manuals and books that are available; a task that most busy candidates do not have time to do.

Absent from the list are philosophical statements of what a candidate and his/her respective ideology has to offer. Sam Brown's and Tom Hayden's books will suffice here for liberal candidates running strong issue campaigns. The National Conservative Political Action Committee's manual, and other publications I have noted, include conservative stands as well as detailed practical information. There is no reason to read only those books whose politics you feel you would agree with; valuable tips can be gotten from the "other side"— and, of course, it is always important to see where your opponent is getting information from.

Any progressive candidate needs to find out the specific filing date for his office and state. After that, it is all the issues, the media, your staff, your stamina . . . and some help from the following books.

Books

Brown, Sam, *Storefront Organizing: A Mornin' Glories Manual*, Pyramid Books, 1972.

This is based on Brown's experiences fund-raising and organizing with the peace movement and the McCarthy campaign. It is not a what-to-do manual as much as recollections of what other politicians have done, along with a logical theory approach to campaigning.

Myer, D.C., *The Winning Candidate: How to Defeat Your Political Opponent*, James Heineman, Inc., 1966.

Good chapters on involving others in your issue campaigns and on organizing political rallies. Read this book for its suggestions on speech writing and on playing up the candidate's strengths.

Mulchaky, Kevin and Katz, Richard, *America Votes*, Prentice-Hall, 1976.

A short, very readable and recent book with useful charts about voting behavior, parties and state election patterns.

Nichols, David, *Financing Elections: The Politics of an American Ruling Class*, New Viewpoints, 1974.

Though this will not tell you *where* to get money for your campaign, it thoroughly documents how the rich and mighty give money for campaigns.

Seligman, King, Kim and Smith, *Patterns of Recruitment: A State Chooses Its Lawmakers*, Rand McNally, 1974.

This book concerns the politics of Oregon, but is useful for anyone in a state race who would need to gather and interpret state voting patterns. Good information on what to do during the filing, primary and election periods.

Simpson, Dick, *Winning Elections: A Handbook in Participatory Politics*, Swallow Press.

Detailed strategies for candidates and an excellent annotated bibliography make this an excellent beginners book.

Simpson, Dick and Beam, George, *Strategies for Change: How to Make the American Political Dream Work*, Swallow Press.

A thorough citizen action book for "Winning issue campaigns without violence."

Schwartzbaum, Edward, *Campaign Craftsmanship*, Universe Books, 1973.

A good comprehensive book written especially for local candidates in their first election who want to use "professional" techniques.

Wilson, James, *Political Organizations*, Basic Books, 1973.

A huge book concentrating on the effects of parties, unions, business, and civil rights organizations on campaigns. No direct, practical how-to's, but a book someone important in a campaign organization should read to better understand how to deal with large special interest groups.

Manuals

The following manuals written by organizations and individuals can be ordered from the addresses listed. The prices for these books run from 35c to $4. Exact prices can be obtained from the organizations.

American Association of University Women. *Tool Catalog: Techniques and Strategies for Successful Action Programs*, 2401 Virginia Ave. NW, Washington, DC.

This is a huge book, incredibly useful, which does not concentrate on campaigns specifically, but is loaded with information on action projects, and the techniques of dealing with institutions, holding demonstrations, researching, and publicity planning. The AAUW also has two smaller publications, *An Action Bag* and *Power Quotient Bag*. Both have charts, lists of questions and activities, and posters.

Carr, Billie, *Don't Default to the Bastards: Organize! A Common Sense Handbook for Left-Wing Democrats*, 2418 Travis, Suite 3, Houston, TX 77006.

Instruction on how to run a successful liberal precinct club. Carr's belief is that liberals get their strength running as Democrats in grass-roots elections and then working their way up. A wonderfully serious yet humorous manual, Carr's deep convictions are always clear. It is a great guide on how to run a tough, aggressive campaign.

Democratic National Committee: *The Democratic Campaign Manual, 1976*, 1625 Massachusetts Ave., NW, Washington, DC 20036.

This is a good survey book with a bibliography and an exceptional section on communications covering everything from television to direct mailings. Special section on dealing with minority voters.

Hayden, Tom, *Make the Future Ours*, 204 Santa Monica Blvd., Santa Monica, CA 90401.

From Hayden's bid for the Senate, a manual explaining why we must go from "protest to political power". The book is useful for those running an issue campaign, looking for analyses of the problems the country faces today. Hayden covers energy, the environment, communications, the economy and equality for minority groups.

League of Women Voters: *Making an Issue of It: The Campaign Manual*, 1730 M St. NW, Washington, DC 20036.

Geared towards getting legislation passed, there are short but practical paragraphs on building coalitions and committees, lobbying, testifying and overcoming the opposition. The League also has a yearly campaign guide, written by their education fund, discussing the issues and how to rally community strength around them.

National Conservative Political Action Committee: *In Order To Win: A State Legislative Campaign Manual*, 1911 N. Fort Meyer Dr., Suite 706, Arlington, VA 22209.

Information is mostly from professional political consultants, on "how to run a professional campaign on limited resources of people and money." The book does succeed in being all-inclusive in 50 pages, covering campaign structure and personnel, finances, communications and getting the votes. This is a decent survey specifically designed to assist state legislature races and lower level political offices.

Republican National Committee, 310 First St. S.E., Washington, DC 20003.

The GOP publishes booklets on a variety of subjects. There are the usual topics, thoroughly handled, of fundraising, organization, media, and advertising. Then there is a book comprised of the do's and many more don't's for candidates' wives and a manual on opposition research, "a composite of ideas on how to develop a complete picture of your opponent, assess his strengths and exploit his weaknesses." If you don't know the fine points of investigating your opponent's tax returns, military and scholastic records, then you need this manual.

The Woman Activist, 2310 Barbour Rd., Falls Church, VA 22043.

This organization has small but substantial booklets geared towards women running for local office. Printed in '73 and '74, they are full of optimism for the coming years' possibilities. Good bibliography and easy reference charts and timetables for organization of duties. There is a 1976 guide to precinct politics. It is excellent for both sexes and this grass-roots book has some interesting ideas for volunteers and voters.

Key Organizations to Contact

We have attempted here to compile a comprehensive list of important organizations that work on farm, land and food-related issues throughout the country. However, we realize that we have probably overlooked many equally active groups. We would appreciate hearing about any which have been left off the list, for our future use.

Agricultural Marketing Project

2606 Westwood Drive
Nashville, Tennessee 37204
(615) 297-4088
Lindsay Jones, John Vlcek, Laurie Heise

AMP organizes farmers' markets, or "food fairs," in 19 southern cities. Issues excellent pamphlets on food and agricultural issues for both consumers and farmers. Field offices in Tuscaloosa, Alabama and North Carolina.

Agricultural Teams

Farm to Market Project
312 N. Walnut Street (#106)
Youngstown, Ohio 44505
(216) 746-8551
Ron Daniels, Project Coordinator

Project on direct marketing alternatives for low-income and minority farmers.

American Agriculture Movement

Main Office
Springfield, Colorado 81073
(303) 533-6223 or 523-6666

Washington Office
308 2nd Street, S.E.
Washington, D.C. 20003
(202) 544-5750

AAM is the new farm organization which grew out of the 1978 "farm strike" and the movement to enact 100% parity at the federal level.

American Agri-Women

Estate Tax Issues Committee
Springfield, Nebraska 68059
Doris Royal, Coordinator

Working committee on estate and inheritance tax problems faced by farm women.

American Friends Service Committee

1501 Cherry Street
Philadelphia, Pennsylvania 19102
(215) 241-7133
Domingo Gonzalez, National Representative for Farm Laborers and Rural Affairs

Technical assistance for farmworkers and laborers.

American Land Forum, Inc.

1025 Vermont Avenue, N.W.
Washington, D.C. 20005
(202) 347-4516
Charles Little

Provides a national forum for government and academic experts to resolve the major issues concerning the use and conservation of American land resources. Publishes a quarterly ALF report.

Black Land Services

Penn Community Center
P.O. Box 126
Frogmore, South Carolina 29920
(803) 838-2669
Joseph McDomick, Director

Concentrates on the legal problems facing black land owners in the "sea island" region of the Southeast. Excellent paralegal booklet available; Got Land Problems?

Blobaum and Associates

Main Office
1340 42nd Street, Suite A
West Des Moines, Iowa 50265
(515) 225-6035
Roger Blobaum

Washington Office
1346 Connecticut Avenue, N.W.
Washington, D.C. 20036
(202) 659-4367

Consultant on agricultural and food issues/policies.

Boston Area Farmers' Markets

Division of Land Use
Massachusetts Department of Food and Agriculture
100 Cambridge Street
Boston, Massachusetts 02202
(617) 727-6633
Elischen Toney

Provides technical assistance and issues a newsletter to community groups working on farmers' markets and urban agriculture projects.

Boston Urban Gardeners
The Garden Building
250 Boylston Street (#312)
Boston, Massachusetts 02116
(617) 267-4825
Charlotte Kahn, Judy Wagner

Coalition of neighborhood community organizations and urban agriculture activists that provides technical assistance, organizes workshops, and publishes a newsletter, BUG.

Bread for the World

207 East 16th Street
New York, New York 10003
(212) 260-7000
Arthur Simon, Director

Religious lobby devoted to anti-hunger work.

California Agrarian Action Project

P.O. Box 464
Davis, California 95616
(916) 756-8518
Paul Barnett, Don Villarejo and Katherine Bertolucci

Ongoing work on the impact of agricultural research at the University of California; special emphasis on the problems of California farm workers. Publications, slide show and newsletter available.

California Food Policy Coalition

c/o Food Policy Advocate
1300 N Street
Sacramento, California 95814
(916) 442-3676
Anna Hackenbracht

Coalition of consumer activists, public interest research groups and church/hunger organizations working on a broad range of agricultural and food policy issues in California.

California Food Policy Project

1535 Mission Street
San Francisco, California 94103
(415) 863-7480
Don Rothenberg, Director;
Linda Akulian, Associate Director

Includes persons from labor, the food industry, agriculture and agricultural cooperatives, consumer activists, and State government policy makers interested in the California food system.

California Office of Appropriate Technology

1530 10th Street
Sacramento, California 95814
(916) 445-1803
Gil Friend and Rosemary Menninger

Issues *Grants News* and provides technical assistance, contacts and small grants to groups working on a variety of appropriate technology projects in California. A State Agency.

California Rural Legal Assistance

115 Sansome Street (9th Floor)
San Francisco, California 94104
(415) 421-3405
Al Meyerhoff

CRLA is handling a lawsuit against the University of California concerning the impact of publicly funded agricultural mechanization research on California farmworkers. Also works on the pesticide issue in California.

California Small Farm Viability Project

c/o Department of Employment Development
& Rural Affairs
800 Capitol Mall, MIC 77
Sacramento, California 95814
(916) 322-4440
Bill Myers, Director

Issued an excellent report in 1977; *The Family Farm in California*, with recommendations for new approaches and public policies for the state to adopt in order to support small and family farmers.

Center for Community Change (CCC)

1000 Wisconsin Avenue, N.W.
Washington, D.C. 20007
(202) 338-6310
Pablo Eisenberg, Director
Norm Deweaver, Rural Development

CCC monitors federal policies and programs affecting rural communities, farmworkers and small farmers. Provides information and technical assistance to rural community-based groups. Has helped to initiate a Rural Coalition; a network of groups which will together advocate for increased attention, funds and programs for rural communities—especially the rural poor.

Center for Rural Affairs

P.O. Box 405
Walthill, Nebraska 68067
(402) 846-5428
Marty Strange, Don Ralston; Co-Directors

Focusing on Nebraska, CRA's staff works on projects and research which supports family and small farmers; monitors federal, state and local policies; issues excellent publications on issues such as rural credit and irrigation issues. Publishes two newsletters; *New Land Review* and the *Center for Rural Affairs Newsletter*.

Small Farm Advocacy Project
Gene Severens, Attorney;
Chuck Hassebrook, Field Organizer

CRA's project on legal assistance to small and family farmers.

Center for Rural Communities

Cooperative Extension Service
Stockbridge Hall
University of Massachusetts
Amherst, Massachusetts 01002
(413) 545-2715
Pat Sackrey

The Center is sponsoring a variety of innovative projects which support small and family farmers and encourage rural community economic development in Massachusetts.

Center for Science in the Public Interest (CSPI)

1755 S Street, N.W.
Washington, D.C. 20009
(202) 332-9110
Michael Jacobson, Director

Publications and information on nutrition, food quality, and community/citizen action strategies on food related issues. Publications listing available.

Central Coast Counties Development Corporation (CCCDC)

7000 Soquel Drive
Aptos, California 95003
(408) 688-9000
Miguel Barragan

CCCDC works with farmworker cooperatives and organizations in a multi-county area; providing technical assistance, training and financial advice.

Children's Foundation

1420 New York Avenue, N.W. (Suite 800)
Washington, D.C. 20005
(202) 347-3300
Barbara Bode, President

Advocacy for child nutrition programs, including school lunch and breakfast, food stamps, WIC, and others. Has regional offices in Atlanta, Georgia; Santa Fe, New Mexico; and Reno, Nevada.

Clearinghouse for Enforcement of the Reclamation Law

c/o Rural America, Inc.
1346 Connecticut Avenue, N.W.
Washington, D.C. 20036
(202) 659-2800
Peggy Borgers, Coordinator

The Clearinghouse was established to coordinate information and activity on the 160-Acre Limitation/1906 Reclamation Law.

Clergy and Laity Concerned

Politics of Food Program
198 Broadway
New York, New York 10003
(212) 964-6730
Jack Nelson, Director

National interfaith organization which works on peace and justice issues. "The Politics of Food" is one of its four program priorities.

Community Nutrition Insitute (CNI)

1146 19th Street, N.W.
Washington, D.C. 20006
(202) 833-1730
Ellen Haas, Rob Stein

Monitors legislation and acts as an advocate on food and nutrition issues. Publishes excellent weekly newsletter; *CNI Weekly Report.*

Conference on Alternative State and Local Policies

2000 Florida Avenue, N.W.
Washington, D.C. 20009
(202) 387-6030
Lee Webb, Executive Director

The Agriculture Project:
Henry Hyde, Coordinator

The Coop Bank Monitoring Assistance Project:
Chuck Savitt, Coordinator

Focus is on state and local policy innovations. Publications, technical assistance, workshops and a "Clearinghouse on Alternative Legislation."

Connecticut Conservation Association

Northrop Street
Bridgewater, Connecticut 06572
Robert Kunz, Director

Spearheaded effort to enact Connecticut's Farmland Preservation Bill (passed 1978). Issues reports on the need to protect agricultural land in the state.

Connecticut's Office of Legislative Research

Legislative Office Building
18-20 Trinity Street
Hartford, Connecticut 06115
Lawrence Furbish, Research Analyst

Produced a series of excellent memos on many of the state and local bills and programs to protect farmland from development.

Conservation Foundation

1717 Massachusetts Avenue, N.W.
Washington, D.C. 20036
(202) 797-4300
Robert Healy

Publishes *Conservation Foundation Letter*, $1/issue. Book to be published in 1979 on preservation of agricultural land.

Consumer Federation of America (CFA)

1012 14th Street, N.W.
Suite 901
Washington, D.C. 20005
(202) 737-3732
Stephen Brobeck, Director

The largest consumer group in the U.S.A. Research and advocacy on consumer issues, including an ongoing focus on U.S. food and agricultural policies. Publishes a newsletter.

Cooperativa Central

Technical Assistance Project
53 Russell Road
Salinas, California 93906
(408) 449-3996
Gabino Marquez, Director

Technical assistance to farmworker agricultural cooperatives.

Cooperative League of the U.S.A. (CLUSA)

1828 L Street, N.W.
Washington, D.C. 20036
(202) 672-0550

National federation of customer owned businesses. Advocates for producer and consumer cooperatives, direct marketing and support for family and small farms. Publications list available.

Council on Environmental Quality

722 Jackson Place, N.W.
Washington, D.C. 20006
(202) 395-5832
Charles Warren, Director

Oversees compliance with NEPA (National Environmental Policy Act) as related to farmland, and is working closely with many agencies on farmland protection policies.

Council on the Environment

50 Chambers Street
New York, New York 10007
(212) 566-0990
Liz Christy, Director

City-wide organization providing technical assistance, workshops, seeds, plants and publications to community groups working on urban agriculture projects.

Domestic Working Group on Hunger & Poverty

c/o National Council of Churches
475 Riverside Drive
New York, New York 10027
(212) 870-2307
Mary Ellen Lloyd, Director

An ecumenical task force concerned with U.S. food and agricultural policy. Organizes regional and state-wide conferences to bring people together around these issues at the local level.

Earthwork/Center for Rural Studies

3410 19th Street
San Francisco, California 94110
(415) 626-1266
Dahlia Rudavsky, Kathleen Connell, Kathy Cecil

Clearinghouse of information on farm and land related issues (library, publications, films, etc.). List of publications is available.

Emergency Land Fund (ELF)
and
National Association of Landowners (NAL)

564 Lee Street, S.W.
Atlanta, Georgia 30310
(404) 758-5506
Joseph Brooks, Director

ELF does excellent work on the legal problems facing black farmers and landowners. NAL is a membership organization of black farmers in the Southeast.

Environmental Action

1346 Connecticut Avenue, N.W.
Washington, D.C. 20036
(202) 833-1845
Victoria Leonard, Coordinator

Advocacy on environmental issues. Publishes *Environmental Action* magazine and conducts "Dirty Dozen" campaign against anti-environmental members of Congress.

Environmental Defense Fund

1525 18th Street, N.W.
Washington, D.C. 20036

(202) 833-1484
Maureen Hinkle, pesticides coordinator

Initiates lawsuits on problems threatening people and the environment, such as pesticides and food additives.

Environmental Policy Center (EPC)

317 Pennsylvania Avenue, S.E.
Washington, D.C. 20003
(202) 547-6500
Louise Dunlap, Director
Jack Doyle, Energy and Agriculture Issues

Excellent work on the impact of energy-related developments (strip-mining, power-line siting, etc.) on agricultural land and rural communities. EPC is an extremely effective lobbying group at the federal level.

Environmental Protection Agency

401 M Street, S.W.
Washington, D.C. 20024
(202) 755-0442

On-going monitoring and lobbying on agricultural land preservation issues.

Exploratory Project on Economic Alternatives (EPEA)

2000 P Street, N.W.
Washington, D.C. 20036
(202) 833-3208
Gar Alperowitz, Jeff Faux

Ongoing research and publications on national food policy alternatives. Published *Towards a National Food Policy* by Joe Belden and Greg Forte.

Farm Labor Organizing Committee

714½ St. Clare
Toledo, Ohio 43609
(419) 243-3456
Baldemar Velasquez, Chairperson

Organizing farm workers throughout Ohio. Coordinating a major, national boycott against Del Monte and Campbells in 1979.

Farralones Institute

Center for Sustainable Agriculture
15290 Coleman Road
Occidental, California 95465
(707) 874-3060
David Katz

Alternative training center to be established in 1978/1979. Emphasis on self-sufficiency and appropriate technology skills.

Federation of Southern Cooperatives

Rural Training Center
P.O. Box 95
Epes, Alabama 35460
(205) 652-9676
John Zippert, Charles Prejean

Federation provides technical assistance to farmer cooperatives and rural, community-based organizations throughout the Southeast. Operates a Training Center in Alabama and an office in Atlanta.

Food, Agriculture and Rural Affairs Information Services

c/o Earthwork
3410 19th Street
San Francisco, California 94110
(415) 626-1267

A clippings service designed to make valuable press and media resources available to individuals and groups, plus a computerized cross-referenced index designed to provide an on-going compilation of key word descriptions of all clips. Free brochure on request with a self-addressed, stamped legal size envelope.

Food Policy Center

538 7th Street, S.E.
Washington, D.C. 20003
(202) 547-7070
Marty Rogol, Director

Research, information and lobbying on hunger, food and farm related issues—both domestic and international. Involved with the White House Commission on World Hunger.

Food Research and Action Center (FRAC)

2011 Eye Street, N.W.
Washington, D.C. 20006
(202) 452-8250
Nancy Amidei, Director

A public interest law firm and advocacy organization for federal feeding programs as they affect states and localities.

Graham Training Center

c/o Rural Advancement Fund
P.O. Box 95, Route 3
Wadesboro, North Carolina 29170
(704) 851-9346
Cary Fowler

Established in 1973 to provide innovative training opportunities to small farmers, sharecroppers and rural community organizations in the areas of agriculture and co-operative/community development.

Greenmarkets

24 West 40th Street
New York, New York 10018
(212) 840-7355
Barry Benepe, Director

Technical assistance, contacts and resources on farmers' markets and direct marketing alternatives.

Hartford Food Systems, Inc.

c/o ConnPIRG
30 High Street (#108)
Hartford, Connecticut 06103
(203) 525-8312
Sally Taylor, FarmMarket Director

The non-profit organization which was set up to initiate and then operate the various components of the integrated system which was developed from the *Hartford Food Plan* under the City's initiative (1976/1977).

Hunger Action Center

2524 16th Avenue, South
Seattle, Washington 98144
(206) 324-5731

Issues publications dealing with agriculture and food-related topics.

IMPACT

110 Maryland Avenue, N.E.
Washington, D.C. 20002
(202) 544-8636
Bob Odean, National Director

Affiliated with the Interreligious Task Force on U.S. food policy, IMPACT issues the action-oriented news bulletins. Twelve (12) state-wide IMPACT offices were established in 1978.

Institute for Food and Development Policy

2588 Mission Street
San Francisco, California 94110
(415) 648-6090
Frances Moore Lappé, Joseph Collins

Researches international food and agricultural issues, with emphasis on potential for food self-sufficiency in all countries. Lappé and Collins co-authored the excellent book, *Food First.*

Interfaith Center on Corporate Responsibility (ICCR)

475 Riverside Drive, Room 566
New York, New York 10027
(212) 870-2316
Bob Morris, Director, Agribusiness Project;
Leah Margulies, Coordinator,
Agribusiness Campaigns

Coordinates church-related investments re: corporate accountability in the food and agricultural industries. Research and publications on agribusiness.

Interfaith Committee on Corporate Responsibility

3410 19th Street
San Francisco, California 94110
(415) 863-8060
Robin Jurs

Research on corporations in the food industry, focus on Del Monte and the impact of food corporations on local economies.

International Independence Institute (III)

National Community Land Trust Center
639 Massachusetts Avenue, Suite 316
Cambridge, Massachusetts 02139
(617) 661-4661
Robert Swann, Director

Excellent resource for information and technical assistance on land trusts and land banking concepts. III's book, *The Community Land Trust: A Guide to a New Model for Land Tenure in America,* is the best available publication on the land trust concept.

Interreligious Task Force on U.S. Food Policy

110 Maryland Avenue, N.E.
Washington, D.C. 20002
(202) 543-2800
George Chauncey, Director; Buff Main

Washington based staff working for the American religious community (the Task Force is interdenominational) on support for the family farm, nutrition policy, estate tax reform and international development assistance programs. Monitors federal programs and policies.

Domestic Food Policy Task Force
245 Second Street, N.E.
Washington, D.C. 20002
(202) LI7-4343
Don Reeves, Director

Monitors, testifies and lobbies on domestic agricultural and rural development legislation.

Iowa Department of Justice

Farm Division
Hoover State Office Building
Des Moines, Iowa 50319
(515) 421-3405
Neil Hamilton

Will enforce both the Iowa Family Farm Act, which limits corporate ownership of farm land, and the Iowa Non-Resident Alien Ownership Act, which restricts Iowa landowners from selling their farm land to foreign agricultural interests. Promoting legislation to make state loan guarantees available to the beginning farmer.

Kansas Legislative Research Department

Statehouse (545-N)
Topeka, Kansas 66612
(913) 296-3181
Raney Gillaland

Maine Consortium for Food Self-Reliance

c/o Richards Land/CHES
Freeport, Maine 04032
(207) 865-4338
Bill Seretta, Coordinator

A consortium of six active groups who are focusing on agricultural and food related issues and policies in the state of Maine.

Maine Food and Farmland Study Commission

State Planning Office
184 State Street
Augusta, Maine 04333
(207) 289-3261
Chaitanya York, David Vail; Commission Members

State Commission taking a comprehensive and integrated approach to future policy recommendations relating to agricultural and food issues in Maine.

Maine Organic Farmers and Gardeners Association (MOFGA)

Box 187, 110 Water Street
Hallowell, Maine 04347
(207) 622-3118
Chaitanya York, Director

A dynamic, growing, membership-based organization providing information on organic agriculture, producer and consumer cooperatives and many other issues. Publishes an excellent newsletter, *The Maine Organic Farmer and Gardener.*

Massachusetts Food and Agriculture Coalition

Box 709
Boston, Massachusetts 02123
(617) 261-8280
Michael Scully, Coordinator and Legislative Aide to Representative Mel King

Informal alliance of individuals and organizations working within the state to build a broad-based multi-issue statewide coalition.

Missouri Small Farm Project

Cooperative Extension
228 Mumford Hall
University of Missouri
Columbia, Missouri 65201
(314) 822-2728
Edward Wiggins, Jerry West

Uses successful small farmers as paraprofessionals in an extension program which provides production, marketing and management skills to limited-resource farmers. A publication summarizing the Program is available.

Migrant Legal Action Program

806 15th Street, N.W.
Washington, D.C. 20005
(202) 347-5100
Rafael Gomez, Director

A Legal Services Corporation-funded support center, focusing on farm labor cases, for legal aid offices.

Montana Land Reliance

P.O. Box 335
Helena, Montana 59601
(406) 443-7027
Barbara Rushmore

Attempts to keep agricultural lands in productive use by acquiring land and leasing it to farmers and ranchers, by taking donations of development rights through conservation easements to assure continued agricultural use, and by providing public education about agriculture land preservation.

National Agricultural Lands Study

722 Jackson Place, N.W.
Washington, D.C. 20006
(202) 395-5832
Bob Gray, Director

Inter-agency task force co-chaired by the Secretary of Agriculture and the Chairperson of CEQ. It will examine the problem of agricultural land loss as well as the various state, local and federal policies which relate to this problem.

National Association of Conservation Districts

1025 Vermont Avenue, N.W.
Washington, D.C. 20005
(202) 347-5995
Neil Sampson, Director

Organization of conservation districts and related state associations. Publishes a newsletter, the *Tuesday Letter,* ($10/year).

National Association of County Officials (NACO)

1735 New York Avenue, N.W.
Washington, D.C. 20006
(202) 785-9577
Bob Weaver

Concentrates on the issue of protecting agricultural land from development for NACO. Recently initiated the Agricultural Lands Project, a clearinghouse for land preservation.

National Association of Farmworker Organizations (NAFO)

1332 New York Avenue, N.W.
Washington, D.C. 20020
(202) 347-2407
Tom Jones, Director; Susan Hoechstetter, Food and Rural Development Advocacy of the Hunger and Nutrition Division

Advocacy and monitoring on farmworker issues. Serves as an information clearinghouse and source of training for farmworker organizations. NAFO is a membership organization—its members being local farmworker groups and unions throughout the country.

National Catholic Rural Life Conference

4625 N.W. Beaver Drive
Des Moines, Iowa 50322
(515) 270-2634
Bill Schaeffer, Director

Educational materials, workshops, training sessions, research and Rural Ministry Project. Focus on food policy, rural development and social change.

National Center for Appropriate Technology (NCAT)

P.O. Box 3838
Butte, Montana 59701
(406) 723-6533

Washington Office
815 15th Street, N.W.
Washington, D.C. 20005
(202) 347-9193
Scott Sklar, Washington Director

Sponsored by CSA, NCAT offers technical assistance and small grants to primarily low-income groups working on appropriate technology projects, i.e., in food production, solar technology, methane generation.

National Conference of State Legislatures

444 North Capitol Street
Washington, D.C. 20001
(202) 624-5400

Bob Davies

On-going interest in farmland preservation issues.

AERED

2403 San Mateo Boulevard, N.E.
Albuquerque, New Mexico 87110
(505) 268-2421
Ray Lopez, Director

La Raza's project; Assistance Group for Rural Economic Development provides technical assistance and training to individuals and community-based organizations in the Southwest.

National Council of La Raza

1725 Eye Street, N.W.
Washington, D.C. 20006
(202) 659-1251
Raul Yzaguirre, President

National Extension Evaluation Project

United States Department of Agriculture (USDA)
Room 6435—South Building
Washington, D.C. 20250
(202) 447-4478
Fred Wood, Director; Susan DeMarco

A USDA in-house evaluation of the Extension Service. The **Final Report** which was originally slated to be out in April 1979 will be issued in Spring 1980.

National Family Farm Coalition

918 F Street, N.W.
Washington, D.C. 20004
(202) 638-6848
Catherine Lerza, Robin Rosenbluth,
Jay Sherman

Membership, lobby group set up to coordinate information and public education on the **Family Farm Development Act**, introduced to Congress in 1978.

National Family Farm Education Project

918 F Street, N.W.
Washington, D.C. 20004
(202) 638-4254
Catherine Lerza, Robin Rosenbluth,
Co-coordinators

Provides information, resources, research on the role of the family farms in the U.S. food system. Conducts Agricultural Roundtables in Washington to bring citizens' groups together to talk about agriculture policy. Publishes **Family Farm Monitor**, available free, and Factsheets on Agriculture.

National Farmers Organization (NFO)

720 Davis Avenue
Corning, Iowa 50841

(515) 322-3131
DeVon R. Woodland, President

National headquarters. Non-partisan organization of farmers; major thrust is collective bargaining for sale of farm commodities.

NFO—Washington Office

475 L'Enfant Plaza, S.W.
Washington, D.C. 20024
(202) 484-7075
Charles Frazier, Director

Legislative office; monitors federal legislation and programs affecting NFO members/farmers.

National Farmers Union (NFU)

12125 East 45th Avenue
Denver, Colorado 80239
(303) 371-1760
George Stone, President

National headquarters. Organization of family farmers; conducts ongoing education and legislative programs and activities.

NFU—Washington Office

1012 14th Street, N.W.
Washington, D.C. 20005
(202) 628-9774
Robert Lewis, National Secretary
Reuben L. Johnson, Director of Legislative Services
Robert Mullins, Ruth Kobell, Legislative Staff

Legislative office, monitors federal legislation and programs affecting NFU members/farmers.

*See list of state NFU offices included in this section.

National Governors' Association

444 NO. Capital Street
Washington, D.C. 20001
(202) 624-5338
Susan Seladones

National Land for People

2348 North Cornelia
Fresno, California 93711
(209) 233-4727
George Ballis, Director

Research, litigation and public education on issues involving land and water rights. Excellent work on the 160 Acre Limitation/Reclamation Law. Concerned with both family farmers and farmworkers. List of publications and media presentations is available.

National Rural Center (NRC)

1828 L Street, N.W.
Washington, D.C. 20036

(202) 331-0258
John Cornman, President
Heather Tischbein, Small Farm Policy Project

Research, information and projects on a broad range of rural issues and policies; focusing on low-income rural communities. Information clearinghouse monitors federal rural policy legislation and programs. Regional offices in Atlanta and Austin. Publishes the excellent *Directory of Rural Organizations* and other extremely useful publications.

National Rural Development and Finance Corporation (NRD&FC)

1300 19th Street, N.W. (Suite 360)
Washington, D.C. 20036
(202) 466-6950
Alfredo Navarro, Director
Barbara Rose

Non-profit corporation established in 1978 to address the problems of the rural poor using the techniques of community-based economic development. NRD & FC's goal is to develop an effective mechanism of providing development assistance, capital and other resources increasing economic opportunities for low-income, rural people.

National Rural Fellows

250 West 57th Street (#316)
New York, New York 10019
(212) 541-5711
Starry Krueger, Director

Mid-career fellowship in rural development for men and women who have demonstrated leadership potential. The formal program includes two summer academic sessions and a nine-month field placement.

Natural Resources Defense Council

Main Office
122 East 42nd Street
New York, New York 10017
John Adams, Director

Washington Office

1725 I Street, N.W. (#600)
Washington, D.C. 20006
(202) 223-8210
Tom Barlow, Soil Conservation Specialist

Litigation and research on a variety of environmental issues.

Neighborhood Technology Coalition

909 Fourth Avenue
Seattle, Washington 98104
(206) 447-3625
Lucy Gorham, Coordinator

City-wide coalition of community and technical assistance groups working on small-scale housing, energy, food, waste and water projects.

Network

806 Rhode Island Avenue, N.E.
Washington, D.C. 20018
(202) 526-4070
Carol Coston, Director; Nancy Sylvester

Catholic lobbying group for progressive national legislation on food and agriculturally-related issues.

New England Small Farm Institute

Jepson House, Jackson Street
Belchertown, Massachusetts 01007
(413) 323-4531
Judy Gillan, Coordinator

Proposed regional Training Center for small farm skills. Affiliated with both Women in Agriculture and the Center for Rural Communities in Massachusetts.

New Jersey Food Policy Coalition

c/o World Hunger Year/New Jersey
27-06 High Street
Fairlawn, New Jersey 07410
(201) 791-8585
Bill Wildey, Bob Halsch, Coordinators

A project of World Hunger Year/N.J., the Coalition organized a state-wide conference in June 1979 and is seeking funding to carry on various projects and organizing efforts in the future.

New York State Assembly Task Force on Food, Farm & Nutrition Policy

Room 404—Legislative Building
Albany, New York 12248
(518) 472-2330
Assemblyman Maurice Hinchey, Chairman

Assemblyman Hinchey established the Task Force to encourage more activity on agricultural and food issues within the New York State Legislature.

New York State Coalition for Local Self-Reliance

P.O. Box 6222
Syracuse, New York 13217
David Brown, President

Food policy and local integrated food economy program

New York State Food Coalition

23 Elk Street
Albany, New York 12207
(518) 463-1896

Initiated in the Fall of 1979, this statewide coalition works through regional coordinators in hopes of influencing New York's agricultural and food policies and relevant state agencies.

Northeast Task Force on Food & Farm Policy

1111 Twin Towers
99 Washington Avenue
Albany, New York 12248
(518) 455-5203

Network of state and local officials, activists, and others interested in food and agricultural policy for the Northeastern U.S. Publishes newsletter, sponsors conferences and meetings.

North Carolina Agricultural Marketing Project

P.O. Box 12141
Raleigh, North Carolina 27605
(919) 828-1107
Dale Evarts

Box 264
Faison, North Carolina 28341
(919) 267-3911
Barbara Wallace

Market organizing for small fruit and vegetable growers, bulk and retail. Education on local farm, food and land issues.

North Dakota Department of Agriculture

Capitol Building
Bismarck, North Dakota 58505
(701) 224-2232

One of the most innovative state Departments of Agriculture in the U.S. Staff members are enormously responsive to North Dakota family farm issues.

Office of Congressperson James Jefford

429 Cannon House Office Building
Washington, D.C. 20515
(202) 225-4115
Roger Allbee, Legislative Staff

Covering the bill Jefford (D-VT) authored and introduced to Congress in 1978 and 1979 on the preservation of farmland. On-going interest in the agricultural land loss.

Oregon Food Action Coalition

1414 Kincaid
Eugene, Oregon 97401
(503) 344-0009 or (503) 235-9672
Peg Kehrer, Coordinator

Ozark Institute

Box 549
Eureka Springs, Arkansas 72632
(501) 253-9601
Edd Jeffords, Director

Established to conduct research and information programs of benefit to individuals, organizations, and communities in the rural Ozark Mountains of Arkansas and Missouri.

Pike Place Market Preservation and Development Authority

85 Pike Street
Room 500
Seattle, Washington 98101
(206) 625-4764
Frankie Whitman, Coordinator

Provides technical assistance to various local projects such as a new farmer's equipment co-op and direct marketing efforts in Seattle and the surrounding area.

Public Advocates, Inc.

1535 Mission Street
San Francisco, California 94103
(415) 431-7430
Angela Blackwell

Represents a state-wide coalition of inner-city organizations working on the problem of inner-city food distribution, that petitioned Gov. Brown to take immediate action to alleviate the inner-city food crisis.

Public Interest Opinion Research

918 F Street, N.W. (Suite 410)
Washington, D.C. 20004
(202) 783-2303
James C. Rosapepe

A survey research firm that conducts all types of market surveys for non-profit groups, coops, and alternative businesses, among others.

Resources for the Future

1755 Massachusetts Avenue, N.W.
Washington, D.C. 20036
(202) 462-4400
Pierre Crosson

Ongoing research on land use and the preservation of agricultural land.

Rosapepe, Fuchs and Associates

918 F Street, N.W. (Suite 410)
Washington, D.C. 20004
(202) 783-2303
James C. Rosapepe

A public policy consulting firm that does policy analysis and lobbying for government agencies and progressive groups.

Rural Advancement Fund/ National Sharecroppers Fund

2128 Commonwealth Avenue
Charlotte, North Carolina 28205
(704) 334-3051
Kathryn Waller, Director

RAF/NSF has worked for over 30 years to provide technical assistance and training to small farmers and tenant farmers in the Southeast. Operates the Graham Training Center and Demonstration Farm in Wadesboro, North Carolina.

Rural America

1346 Connecticut Avenue, N.W.
Washington, D.C. 20036
(202) 659-2800
David Raphael, Director
Peggy Borgers, Food and Agriculture Policy

National membership organization advocating on behalf of rural people. Monitors federal legislation and programs, conducts policy oriented research, organizes annual conferences and offers technical assistance on rural issues/policies. Publishes an excellent monthly newsletter, *Rural America.*

Rural American Women

1522 K Street, N.W.
Washington, D.C. 20005
(202) 785-4700
Jane Threatt, Director

Membership and advocacy organization concerned with problems of rural women. Publishes a regular newsletter, *Rural American Women.*

Rural Coalition

1035 30th Street, N.W.
Washington, D.C. 20007
(202) 338-7200
Barbara Rose, Director

Comprised of 50 regional and national public interest organizations concerned with the need for a comprehensive, progressive national policy on rural development.

Rural Education Center

c/o Stoneyfield Farm
Wilton, New Hampshire 03086
(603) 654-6077
Samuel Kaymen

A rural-skills and small farm training center. Specializes in biological method of agriculture.

Seattle Department of Community Development

400 Zester Building
Seattle, Washington 98104
(206) 625-4492
Daryl Grothaus, Director; Susan Appel

Developing and supporting programs for neighborhood groups aiming to reduce food costs through alternative food projects. Leveraging federal community development funding for these local efforts.

Second Harvest Food Banks

1001 N. Central Avenue
Phoenix, Arizona 85004
(602) 252-1777
Bob McCarty, Jon Van Hengel

National food salvage/gleaning network which provides ongoing technical assistance, workshops and issues a newsletter.

Small Farm Energy Project

P.O. Box 736
Hartington, Nebraska 68739
(402) 254-6893
Dennis Demmel, Ron Krupka

Demonstration and research program helping small farmers install and use alternative energy systems. A model for what the county extension service could be doing in this field. The Project issues a newsletter.

Soil Conservation Service/USDA

Environmental Services Division
P.O. Box 2890
Washington, D.C. 20003
(202) 447-3839
Norman Berg, Associate Administrator;
Darwyn Briggs, Research Staff

The division within the Department of Agriculture playing the most active role in the issue of farmland preservation. Reports, statistics, policy recommendations.

Soil Conservation Society of America

7515 Northeast Ankeny Road
Ankeny, Iowa 50021
Max Schnepf

Ongoing concern about land use related issues. Publishes the *Journal of Soil and Water Conservation*, ($15/year).

Southern Cooperative Development Fund (SCDF)

1601 Surrey Street
Lafayette, Louisiana 70501
(318) 232-9206
Reverend McKnight, Director

A strong organization providing technical and financial assistance to a great number of rural community economic development projects throughout the Southeast. SCDF's *Annual Report* is available.

Southern Rural Policy Congress

79 Commerce Street (Room 508)
Montgomery, Alabama 36104
(205) 265-0251
Bill Harrison, Director

Articulate vanguard of organizations working to advance and improve the quality of life for the poor in the rural South.

Texas Farmworkers Union

P.O. Box 876
San Juan, Texas 78589
(512) 787-5984
Antonio Orendain, Director

TFWU is organizing farmworkers state-wide. Publishes a regular newsletter which updates the Union's activities (bi-lingual).

Texas Intensified Farm Planning Program

A & M University Cooperative Extension Program
Drawer B
Texas A & M University
Prairie View, Texas 77445
(713) 857-2023
Hoover Carden, Dempsey Seastrunk

An extremely effective extension program using paraprofessionals in local communities to assist low-income farmers and rural residents.

Trust for Public Land

82 Second Street
San Francisco, California 94105
(415) 495-4014
Steve Costa

254 W. 31 Street
New York, New York 10001
(212) 563-5959
Peter Stein

Provides information, training, technical assistance and financing for community ownership of land, assisting in a variety of open space projects, including community gardens and parks.

Tuskegee Institute

Cooperative Extension
Tuskegee, Alabama 36088
(205) 727-8011
Philip Brown, Director

Tuskegee's extension program works specifically with low-income, minority farmers in Alabama. Publications are available.

Small Farm Demonstration Project
Tuskegee, Alabama 36088
Booker T. Whatley, Director

Professor Whatley is developing a "model farm" which will test crop varieties, production methods and consider marketing outlets—all geared towards the small, limited-resource farmer in the Southeast.

United Farmworkers of America AFL-CIO

Box 67
Keene, California 93531
(805) 822-5571
Cesar Chavez, President
Dolores Huerta, Vice-President

Headquarters of the first, most successful farmworkers' union. The UFW has concentrated its organizing and legislative efforts in California, but is a national union which intends to expand into other states where farmworkers remain unrepresented and unprotected.

Urban Land Institute

1200 18th Street, N.W.
Washington, D.C. 20036
(202) 331-8500
Ronald Rumbaugh, Executive Vice-President

Publishes *Environmental Comment*, $25/yr., monthly. Runs articles in agricultural land preservation. See especially the entire issues; May 1975 and January 1978.

U.S. Farmers Association

Box 496
Hampton, Iowa 50441
Fred Stover, President;
Merle Hansen, Vice-President

The smallest and most progressive of the national farm organizations. State chapters. Publishes *U.S. Farm News.*

Women's Family Farm Project

United Methodist Church
475 Riverside Drive
New York, New York 10027
(212) 678-6161
Ruth Gilbert, Coordinator

Works with rural women throughout the country on a variety of issues of concern such as estate and inheritance tax problems, protection of farmland, and inadequate social services to rural communities.

Women in Agriculture

33 King Street
Northampton, Massachusetts 01060
(413) 545-0648
Pat Sackrey, Christina Platt, Judy Gillan

Organization and network of individuals in Massachusetts who are actively involved in many critical rural and agricultural issues.

Women Involved in Farm Economics (WIFE)

Box 484
Osceola, Nebraska 68651
Betty Majors, National President

Box 316
Roundup, Montana 59072
Gay Holliday, National Officer

Clearinghouse for information on farm and rural issues as they relate to women.

World Hunger Year

350 Broadway (#209)
New York, New York 10013
(212) 226-2714

WHY publishes *Food Monitor*. "Sister" organization to the Food Policy Center in Washington, D.C. In charge of public education and outreach.

National Farmers Union: State Offices

Arkansas Farmers Union
C.D. (Bill) McCarty, President
Box 4309 Asher Station
(5320 W. 12th Street)
Little Rock, Arkansas 72214
(501) 661-9680

Illinois Farmers Union
Harold Dodd, President
P.O. Box 2356
(407 Iles Park Place)
Springfield, Illinois 62705
(217) 528-7339

Indiana Farmers Union
Harold Wright, President
1331 North Delaware Street
Indianapolis, Indiana 46202
(317) 634-6485

Iowa Farmers Union
Lowell Gose, President
6538 University Avenue
Des Moines, Iowa 50311
(515) 279-0257 or 274-2519
Home: Route 2, Box 236
        Jefferson, Iowa 50129
        (515) 386-2558
Curt Sorteberg, Assistant to President

Kansas Farmers Union
Dale Lyon, President
P.O. Box 1064
(1st & Buckeye)
McPherson, Kansas 67460
(316) 241-6630
Home: Route 1
        Athol, Kansas 66932
        (913) 695-2358

Michigan Farmers Union
Donna Cootware, President
P.O. Box 30
Ralph, Michigan 49877
(906) 246-3444

Minnesota Farmers Union
Cy Carpenter, President
1717 University Avenue
St. Paul, Minnesota 55104
(612) 646-4861

Montana Farmers Union
Terry Murphy, President
P.O. Box 2447
(750-6th Street, S.W.)
Great Falls, Montana 59403
(406) 452-6406

Nebraska Farmers Union
Neil Oxton, President
P.O. Box 2667
(1305 Plum Street)
Lincoln, Nebraska 68502
(402) 432-8815

New Mexico Farmers Union
Paul Hudson
Chairman of Advisory Board
P.O. Box G
1100 Mitchell Street
Clovis, New Mexico 88101
(505) 762-7816
Home: Route 2
        Melrose, New Mexico 88124
        (505) 458-4335
John B. Casada, Exec. Secretary,
New Mexico Farmers Union

North Dakota Farmers Union
Stanley M. Moore, President
P.O. Box 651
(1415-12th Avenue, S.E.)
Jamestown, North Dakota 58401
(701) 252-2340

Ohio Farmers Union
Virgil Thompson, President
P.O. Box 363
(1011 North Defiance Street)
Ottawa, Ohio 45875
(419) 523-5300
Home: 305 W. Townline
        Payne, Ohio 45880
        (419) 263-2006
Charlie Nash, Executive Director

Oklahoma Farmers Union
George W. Stone, President
P.O. Box 24000
(1141 West Sheridan)
Oklahoma City, Oklahoma 73124

Oregon-Washington Farmers Union
Dwyte Wilson, Exec. Vice President
10453-4th Plain Boulevard, N.W.
Vancouver, Washington 98662
(206) 256-8940

Pennsylvania Farmers Union
Victor K. Ray
State Project Director
National Farmers Union
(Denver address below)

Leonard Zemaitis, Administrative Assistant
Locust Court (Suite 608)
212 Locust Street
Harrisburg, Pennsylvania 17101
(717) 232-9648

Forney Longenecker
Chairman, Advisory Committee
820 Woodcrest Avenue
Lititz, Pennsylvania 17543
(717) 626-8274

Rocky Mountain Farmers Union
John Stencel, President
P.O. Box 39628
(4605 Paris Street)
Denver, Colorado 80239
(303) 371-9090

South Dakota Farmers Union
Ben Radcliffe, President
P.O. Box 1388
(14th and Dakota Avenue, South)
Huron, South Dakota 57350
(605) 352-6761

Texas Farmers Union
Jay Naman, President
800 Lake Air Drive
Waco, Texas 76710
(817) 772-7220

Utah-Idaho Farmers Union
Roy L. Holman, President
564 East 3rd South
Salt Lake City, Utah 84102
(801) 363-3063

Wisconsin Farmers Union
Leland E. Mulder, President
117 West Spring Street
Chippewa Falls, Wisconsin 54729
(715) 723-5561

Correspondence should go to both the office and home addresses.

For more information, write:

Washington, D.C. Office
Robert G. Lewis
1012-14th St., NW
Washington, DC 20005
(202) 628-9774

Denver Office
George Stone, President
P.O. Box 39251
12025 East 45th Avenue
Denver, Colorado 80239
(303) 371-1760

State Land Grant Colleges

```
*Land Grant Institution
•1890 Black Land Grant College
```

Alabama
•* Alabama A & M University
   Normal, Alabama 35762
 * Auburn University
   Auburn, Alabama 36830

Alaska
 * University of Alaska
   Fairbanks, Alaska 99701

Arizona
 * University of Arizona
   Tucson, Arizona 85721

Arkansas
 * University of Arkansas
   Fayetteville, Arkansas 72701
•* University of Arkansas, Pine Bluff
   Pine Bluff, Arkansas 71601

California
 * University of California (entire system)
   University of California, Berkeley
   Berkeley, California 94720
   University of California, Davis
   Davis, California 95616
   University of California, Irvine
   Irvine, California 92717
   University of California, Los Angeles
   Los Angeles, California 90024
   University of California, Riverside
   Riverside, California 92521
   University of California, San Diego
   La Jolla, California 92093
   University of California, Santa Barbara
   Santa Barbara, California 93107

Colorado
 * Colorado State University
   Fort Collins, Colorado 80523

Connecticut
 * Connecticut Agricultural Experiment Station
   New Haven, Connecticut 06504
 * University of Connecticut
   Storrs, Connecticut 06268

Delaware
•* Delaware State College
   Dover, Delaware 19901
 * University of Delaware
   Newark, Delaware 19711

District of Columbia
 * University of the District of Columbia
   Washington, D.C. 20005

Florida
•* Florida A & M University
   Tallahassee, Florida 32307
 * University of Florida
   Gainesville, Florida 32611

Georgia
•* Fort Valley State College
   Fort Valley, Georgia 31030
 * University of Georgia
   Athens, Georgia 30602

Guam
 * University of Guam
   Agana, Guam 96910

Hawaii
 * University of Hawaii
   Honolulu, Hawaii 96822

Idaho
 * University of Idaho
   Moscow, Idaho 83843

Illinois
 * University of Illinois
   Urbana, Illinois 61801

Indiana
 * Purdue University
   West Lafayette, Indiana 47907

Iowa
 * Iowa State University
   Ames, Iowa 50011

Kansas
 * Kansas State University
   Manhattan, Kansas 66502

Kentucky
•* Kentucky State University
   Frankfort, Kentucky 40601
 * University of Kentucky
   Lexington, Kentucky 40506

Louisiana
 * Louisiana State University
   Baton Rouge, Louisiana 70803
•* Southern University
   Baton Rouge, Louisiana 70813

Maine
 * University of Maine
   Bangor, Maine 04401

Maryland
 * University of Maryland, College Park
   College Park, Maryland 20742
•* University of Maryland, Eastern Shore
   Princess Anne, Maryland 21853

Massachusetts
 * Massachusetts Institute of Technology
   Cambridge, Massachusetts 02139

* University of Massachusetts, Amherst
Amherst, Massachusetts 01003

Michigan
* Michigan State University
East Lansing, Michigan 48823

Minnesota
* University of Minnesota
Minneapolis, Minnesota 55455

Mississippi
•* Alcorn State University
Lorman, Mississippi 39096
* Mississippi State University
Mississippi State, Mississippi 39762

Missouri
•* Lincoln University
Jefferson City, Missouri 65101
* University of Missouri
Columbia, Missouri 65201

Montana
* Montana State University
Bozeman, Montana 59715

Nebraska
* University of Nebraska
Lincoln, Nebraska 68583

Nevada
* University of Nevada, Reno
Reno, Nevada 89557

New Hampshire
* University of New Hampshire
Durham, New Hampshire 03824

New Jersey
* Rutgers University
New Brunswick, New Jersey 08903

New Mexico
* New Mexico State University
Las Cruces, New Mexico 88003

New York
* Cornell University
Ithaca, New York 14853

North Carolina
•* North Carolina A & T State University
Greensboro, North Carolina 27411
* North Carolina State University
Raleigh, North Carolina 27607

North Dakota
* North Dakota State University
Fargo, North Dakota 58102

Ohio
* Ohio State University
Columbus, Ohio 43210

Oklahoma
•* Langston University
Langston, Oklahoma 73050
* Oklahoma State University
Stillwater, Oklahoma 74074

Oregon
* Oregon State University
Corvallis, Oregon 97331

Pennsylvania
* Pennsylvania State University
University Park, Pennsylvania 16802

Puerto Rico
* University of Puerto Rico
San Juan, Puerto Rico 00936

Rhode Island
* University of Rhode Island
Kingston, Rhode Island 02881

South Carolina
* Clemson University, P.O. 992
Clemson, South Carolina 29631
•* South Carolina State College
Orangeburg, South Carolina 29117

South Dakota
* South Dakota State University
Brookings, South Dakota 57006

Tennessee
•* Tennessee State University
Nashville, Tennessee 37203
* University of Tennessee
Knoxville, Tennessee 37916

Texas
•* Prairie View A & M University
Prairie View, Texas 77445
* Texas A & M University System
College Station, Texas 77843

Utah
* Utah State University
U.M.C. 14
Logan, Utah 84332

Vermont
* University of Vermont
Burlington, Vermont 05401

Virgin Islands
* College of the Virgin Islands
St. Thomas, Virgin Islands 00801

Virginia
* Virginia Polytechnic Institute and State University
Blacksburg, Virginia 24061
•* Virginia State College
Petersburg, Virginia 23803

Washington

* Washington State University
  Pullman, Washington 99164

West Virginia

* West Virginia University
  Morgantown, West Virginia 26506

Wisconsin

* University of Wisconsin
  Madison, Wisconsin 53706

Wyoming

* University of Wyoming
  Laramie, Wyoming 82070

For more information, write:

National Association of State Universities
and Land-Grant Colleges
One Dupont Circle, N.W.
Washington, D.C. 20036

State Departments of Agriculture

National Association of State Departments of Agriculture
1616 H Street, N.W.
Washington, D.C. 20006

Alabama
McMillan Lane, Commissioner
Department of Agriculture and Industries
Richard Beard Building
1445 Federal Drive
P.O. Box 3336
Montgomery, Alabama 36109
(205) 832-6693

Alaska
Domonic L. Carney, Director
Division of Agriculture
Department of Natural Resources
P.O. Box 1088
Palmer, Alaska 99645
(907) 745-3236

Arizona
James R. Carter, Director
Arizona Commission of Agriculture and Horticulture
1638 West Adams—Room 421
Phoenix, Arizona 85007
(602) 255-4373

Arkansas
Robert W. Anderson, Director
Arkansas State Plant Board
P.O. Box 1069
Little Rock, Arkansas 72203
(501) 371-1021

California
Richard Rominger, Director
Department of Food and Agriculture
1220 N Street—Agriculture Building
Sacramento, California 95814
(916) 445-7126

Colorado
Morgan Smith, Commissioner
Department of Agriculture
424 State Service Building
1525 Sherman Street
Denver, Colorado 80203
(303) 892-2811

Connecticut
Leonard E. Krogh, Commissioner
Department of Agriculture
165 Capitol Avenue
Hartford, Connecticut 06115
(203) 566-4667

Delaware
Alden S. Hopkins, Jr., Secretary
Department of Agriculture
P.O. Drawer "D"
Dover, Delaware 19901
(302) 678-4811

Florida
Doyle Conner, Commissioner
Department of Agriculture and Consumer Services
The Capitol
Tallahassee, Florida 32301
(904) 488-3022

Georgia
Thomas T. Irvin, Commissioner
Department of Agriculture
Agriculture Building, Room 204
Capitol Square
Atlanta, Georgia 30334
(404) 656-3600

Hawaii
John Farias, Jr., Chairman
Board of Agriculture
P.O. Box 22159
Honolulu, Hawaii 96822
(808) 548-7101

Idaho
Max Hanson, Commissioner
Idaho Department of Agriculture
2270 Old Penitentiary Road
Boise, Idaho 83701
(208) 384-3240

Illinois
John R. Block, Director
Department of Agriculture
State Fairgrounds
Springfield, Illinois 62706
(217) 782-2274

Indiana
Terry Strueh, Assistant to the Dean
Purdue University
Agricultural Administration Building
West Lafayette, Indiana 47907
(317) 749-6092

Iowa
Robert H. Lounsberry, Secretary
Department of Agriculture
Wallace Building
Des Moines, Iowa 50319
(515) 281-5322

Kansas
W.W. "Bill" Duitsman, Secretary
State Board of Agriculture
P.O. Box 678
Topeka, Kansas 66601
(913) 296-3558

Kentucky
Alben W. Barkely, Commissioner
Department of Agriculture
712 Capital Plaza Tower
Frankfort, Kentucky 40601
(502) 564-4696

Louisiana
Robert Odom, Commissioner
Department of Agriculture
P.O. Box 4456, Capitol Station
Baton Rouge, Louisiana 70804
(504) 342-7011

Maine
Stewart N. Smith, Commissioner
Department of Agriculture
State Office Building
Augusta, Maine 04333
(207) 289-3871

Maryland
Wayne A. Crawley, Jr., Secretary
Maryland Department of Agriculture
Parole Plaza Office Building
Annapolis, Maryland 21401
(301) 269-2166

Massachusetts
Frederic Winthrop, Jr., Commissioner
Department of Food and Agriculture
100 Cambridge Street
Boston, Massachusetts 02202
(617) 727-3000

Michigan
Dean M. Pridgeon, Director
Department of Agriculture
Box 30017
Lansing, Michigan 48913
(517) 373-1050

Minnesota
Mark W. Seetin, Commissioner
Department of Agriculture
420 State Office Building
St. Paul, Minnesota 55155
(612) 296-2856

Mississippi
Jim Buck Ross, Commissioner
Department of Agriculture and Commerce
P.O. Box 1609
Jackson, Mississippi 39205
(601) 354-6563

Missouri
Jack Runyan, Director
Department of Agriculture
P.O. Box 630
Jefferson City, Missouri 65101
(314) 751-3359

Montana
W. Gordon McOmber, Director
Department of Agriculture
Scott Hart Building
Capitol Complex
Helena, Montana 59601
(406) 449-3144

Nebraska
E. Mickey Stewart, Director
Department of Agriculture

P.O. Box 94947
Lincoln, Nebraska 68509
(402) 471-2341

Nevada
Thomas W. Ballow, Executive Director
Department of Agriculture
350 Capitol Hill Avenue
P.O. Box 11100
Reno, Nevada 89510
(702) 784-6401

New Hampshire
Howard C. Townsend, Commissioner
Department of Agriculture
Park Plaza
85 Manchester Street
Concord, New Hampshire 03301
(603) 271-3551

New Jersey
Phillip Alampi, Secretary
Department of Agriculture
P.O. Box 1888
Trenton, New Jersey 08625
(609) 292-3976

New Mexico
Dr. William P. Stephens, Director
Department of Agriculture
P.O. Box 3189
Las Cruces, New Mexico 88003
(505) 646-3007

New York
J. Roger Barber, Commissioner
Department of Agriculture and Markets
State Campus Building 8
Albany, New York 12235
(518) 457-4188

North Carolina
James A. Graham, Commissioner
Department of Agriculture
P.O. Box 27647
Raleigh, North Carolina 58505
(919) 733-7125

North Dakota
Myron Just, Commissioner
Department of Agriculture
601 Capitol Building
Bismarck, North Dakota 58501
(701) 224-2231

Ohio
John Stackhouse, Director
Department of Agriculture
65 South Front Street Room 606
Columbus, Ohio 43215
(614) 466-2732

Oklahoma
Jack D. Craig, Commissioner
State Department of Agriculture
122 State Capitol Building
Oklahoma City, Oklahoma 73105
(405) 521-3868

Oregon
Leonard Kunzman, Director
Department of Agriculture
Salem, Oregon 97310
(503) 378-4665

Pennsylvania
Penrose Hallowell, Secretary
Department of Agriculture
2301 North Cameron Street
Harrisburg, Pennsylvania 17120
(717) 787-4737

Rhode Island
W. Edward Wood, Director
Department of Environmental Management
Division of Agriculture
83 Park Street
Providence, Rhode Island 02963
(401) 277-2771

South Carolina
G. Bryan Patrick, Jr., Commissioner
Department of Agriculture
Wade Hampton Office Building
P.O. Box 11280
Columbia, South Carolina 29211
(803) 758-2426 Ext. 24

South Dakota
Honorable Clint R. Roberts, Secretary
Department of Agriculture
State Office Building
Pierre, South Dakota 57501
(605) 773-3375

Tennessee
Jere Griggs, Commissioner
Tennessee Department of Agriculture
P.O. Box 40627
Melrose Station
Nashville, Tennessee 37204
(615) 832-6155

Texas
Reagan V. Brown, Commissioner
Department of Agriculture
P.O. Drawer 12847
Capitol Station
Austin, Texas 78711
(512) 475-2760

Utah
Dr. Kenneth Creer, Commissioner
Department of Agriculture
147 North 200 West
Salt Lake City, Utah 84103
(801) 533-5421

Vermont
William H. Darrow, Jr., Commissioner
Department of Agriculture
State Office Building 116 State Street
Montpelier, Vermont 05602
(802) 828-2413

Virginia
S. Mason Carbaugh, Commissioner
Department of Agriculture and Commerce
P.O. Box 1163
Richmond, Virginia 23209
(804) 786-3501

Washington
Bob J. Mickelson, Director
Department of Agriculture
406 General Administration Building
AX-41
Olympia, Washington 98504
(206) 753-5050

West Virginia
Gus R. Douglas, Commissioner
Department of Agriculture
State Capitol
Charleston, West Virginia 25305
(304) 348-2201

Wisconsin
Gary Rohde, Secretary
Wisconsin Department of Agriculture,
    Trade and Consumer Protection
P.O. Box 8911
Madison, Wisconsin 53708
(608) 266-7100

Wyoming
Larry J. Bourret, Commissioner
Department of Agriculture
2219 Carey Avenue
Cheyenne, Wyoming 82002
(307) 777-7321

Guam
Antonio S. Quitugua, Director
Department of Agriculture
Government of Guam-USA
Agana, Guam 96910
734-2840

American Samoa
Pemerika L. Tauiliili, Director
Department of Agriculture
American Samoa
P.O. Box 366
Pago Pago, American Samoa 96799
633-5276

Puerto Rico
Heriberto Martinez Torres, Secretary
Department of Agriculture
Stop #19
P.O. Box 10163
San Juan, Puerto Rico 00908
(809) 722-0291

U.S. Virgin Islands
Rudolph Shulterbrandt
Department of Agriculture
Kingshill-St. Croix
U.S. Virgin Islands 00850
(809) 772-0990

State Legislative Agriculture Committees

This list is a guide to the committees of each state legislature that are most likely to deal with legislation relating to agriculture, land, and food policy. Requests for copies of legislation can be addressed to the chairman of the appropriate committee.

Alabama
Chairman, House Committee on Agriculture or
Chairman, Senate Committee on Agriculture
State Capitol
Montgomery, Alabama 36130
(205) 832-6011

Alaska
Chairman, House Committee on Resources or
Chairman, Senate Committee on Resources
State Capitol
Juneau, Alaska 99811
(907) 465-2111

Arizona
Chairman, House Committee on Agriculture or
Chairman, Senate Committee on Agriculture
State Capitol
Phoenix, Arizona 85007
(602) 271-4900

Arkansas
Chairman, House Committee on Economic and Industrial
Resources and Development or
Chairman, Senate Committee on Economic and Industrial
Resources and Development
State Capitol
Little Rock, Arkansas 72201
(501) 371-3000

California
Chairman, House Committee on Agriculture or
Chairman, Senate Committee on Agriculture
State Capitol
Sacramento, California 95814
(916) 445-4711

Colorado
Chairman, House Committee on Agriculture or
Chairman, Senate Committee on Agriculture
State Capitol
Denver, Colorado 80203
(303) 892-9911

Connecticut
Chairman, House Committee on the Environment or
Chairman, Senate Committee on the Environment
State Capitol
Hartford, Connecticut 06115
(203) 566-2211

Delaware
Chairman, House Committee on Agriculture or
Chairman, Senate Committee on Agriculture
Legislative Hall
Dover, Delaware 19901
(302) 678-4000

Florida
Chairman, House Committee on Agriculture or
Chairman, Senate Committee on Agriculture
State Capitol
Tallahassee, Florida 32304
(904) 488-1234

Georgia
Chairman, House Committee on Agriculture or
Chairman, Senate Committee on Agriculture
State Capitol
Atlanta, Georgia 30334
(404) 656-2000

Hawaii
Chairman, Senate Committee on the Environment or
Chairman, House Committee on Agriculture
State Capitol Building
Honolulu, Hawaii 96813
(808) 548-2211

Idaho
Chairman, House Committee on Agriculture or
Chairman, Senate Committee on Agriculture
State Capitol
Boise, Idaho 83720
(208) 384-2411

Illinois
Chairman, House Committee on Agriculture or
Chairman, Senate Committee on Agriculture
State House
Springfield, Illinois 62706
(217) 782-2000

Indiana
Chairman, House Committee on Agriculture or
Chairman, Senate Committee on Agriculture
State House
Indianapolis, Indiana 46204
(317) 633-4000

Iowa
Chairman, House Committee on Agriculture or
Chairman, Senate Committee on Agriculture
State Capitol
Des Moines, Iowa 50319
(515) 281-5011

Kansas
Chairman, House Committee on Agriculture or
Chairman, Senate Committee on Agriculture
State House
Topeka, Kansas 66612
(913) 296-0111

Kentucky
Chairman, House Committee on Agriculture or
Chairman, Senate Committee on Agriculture
State Capitol
Frankfort, Kentucky 40601
(502) 564-3130

Louisiana
Chairman, House Committee on Agriculture or
Chairman, Senate Committee on Agriculture
State Capitol
Baton Rouge, Louisiana 70804
(504) 389-6601

Maine
Chairman, House Committee on Agriculture or
Chairman, Senate Committee on Agriculture
State House
Augusta, Maine 04330
(207) 289-1110

Maryland
Chairman, House Committee on Environment or
Chairman, Senate Committee on Economic Affairs
State House
Annapolis, Maryland 21401
(301) 267-0100

Massachusetts
Chairman, House Committee on Agriculture or
Chairman, Senate Committee on Agriculture
State House
Boston, Massachusetts 02133
(617) 727-7030

Michigan
Chairman, House Committee on Agriculture or
Chairman, Senate Committee on Agriculture
State Capitol
Lansing, Michigan 48901
(517) 373-1837

Minnesota
Chairman, House Committee on Agriculture or
Chairman, Senate Committee on Agriculture
State Capitol
St. Paul, Minnesota 55155
(612) 296-6013

Mississippi
Chairman, House Committee on Agriculture or
Chairman, Senate Committee on Agriculture
New Capitol
Jackson, Mississippi 39205
(601) 354-7011

Missouri
Chairman, House Committee on Agriculture or
Chairman, Senate Committee on Agriculture
State Capitol
Jefferson City, Missouri 65101
(314) 751-2151

Montana
Chairman, House Committee on Agriculture or
Chairman, Senate Committee on Agriculture
State Capitol
Helena, Montana 59601
(406) 449-2511

Nebraska
Chairman, Committee on Agriculture
State Capitol
Lincoln, Nebraska 68509
(402) 471-2311

Nevada
Chairman, House Committee on Agriculture or
Chairman, Senate Committee on Agriculture
Legislative Building
Carson City, Nevada 89701
(702) 885-5000

New Hampshire
Chairman, House Committee on Agriculture,
Chairman, Senate Committee on Resources, or
Chairman, Senate Committee on Environment
State House
Concord, New Hampshire 03301
(603) 271-1110

New Jersey
Chairman, House Committee on Agriculture or
Chairman, Senate Committee on Agriculture
State House
Trenton, New Jersey 08625
(609) 292-2121

New Mexico
Chairman, Senate Committee on Conservation or
Chairman, House Committee on Agriculture
State Capitol
Santa Fe, New Mexico 87503
(505) 827-4011

New York
Chairman, House Committee on Agriculture or
Chairman, Senate Committee on Agriculture
State Capitol
Albany, New York 12224
(518) 474-2121

North Carolina
Chairman, House Committee on Agriculture or
Chairman, Senate Committee on Agriculture
State Legislature Building
Raleigh, North Carolina 27611
(919) 733-1110

North Dakota
Chairman, House Committee on Agriculture or
Chairman, Senate Committee on Agriculture
State Capitol
Bismarck, North Dakota 58505
(701) 224-2000

Ohio
Chairman, House Committee on Agriculture or
Chairman, Senate Committee on Agriculture
State House
Columbus, Ohio 43215
(614) 466-2000

Oklahoma
Chairman, House Committee on Agriculture or
Chairman, Senate Committee on Agriculture
State Capitol
Oklahoma City, Oklahoma 73105
(405) 521-2011

Oregon
Chairman, House Committee on Agriculture or
Chairman, Senate Committee on Agriculture
State Capitol
Salem, Oregon 97310
(503) 378-3131

Pennsylvania
Chairman, House Committee on Agriculture or
Chairman, Senate Committee on Agriculture
Main Capitol Building
Harrisburg, Pennsylvania 17120

Rhode Island
Chairman, House Committee on Special Legislation or
Chairman, Senate Committee on Special Legislation
State House
Providence, Rhode Island 02903
(401) 277-2000

South Carolina
Chairman, House Committee on Agriculture or
Chairman, Senate Committee on Agriculture
State House
Columbia, South Carolina 29211
(803) 758-0221

South Dakota
Chairman, House Committee on Agriculture or
Chairman, Senate Committee on Agriculture
State Capitol
Pierre, South Dakota 57501
(605) 224-3011

Tennessee
Chairman, Senate Committee on Environment or
Chairman, House Committee on Agriculture
State Capitol
Nashville, Tennessee 37219
(615) 741-3011

Texas
Chairman, House Committee on Agriculture or
Chairman, Senate Committee on Natural Resources
State Capitol
Austin, Texas 78701
(512) 475-2323

Utah
Chairman, House Committee on Agriculture or
Chairman, Senate Committee on Agriculture
State Capitol
Salt Lake City, Utah 84114
(801) 533-4000

Vermont
Chairman, House Committee on Agriculture or
Chairman, Senate Committee on Agriculture
State House
Montpelier, Vermont 05602
(802) 828-1110

Virginia
Chairman, House Committee on Agriculture or
Chairman, Senate Committee on Agriculture
State Capitol
Richmond, Virginia 23219
(804) 786-0000

Washington
Chairman, House Committee on Agriculture or
Chairman, Senate Committee on Agriculture
Legislative Building
Olympia, Washington 98504
(206) 753-5000

West Virginia
Chairman, House Committee on Agriculture or
Chairman, Senate Committee on Agriculture
State Capitol
Charleston, West Virginia 25305
(304) 348-3456

Wisconsin
Chairman, House Committee on Agriculture or
Chairman, Senate Committee on Agriculture
State Capitol
Madison, Wisconsin 53702
(608) 266-2211

Wyoming
Chairman, House Committee on Agriculture or
Chairman, Senate Committee on Agriculture
State Capitol
Cheyenne, Wyoming 82002
(307) 777-7011

Federal Agricultural Committees and Organizations

Congressional Agriculture Committees:

U.S. House of Representatives
House Agriculture Committee
1301 Longworth Building
Washington, D.C. 20515
(202) 225-0417
Jim Swiderski, Staff

U.S. Senate
Senate Agriculture Committee
322 Russell Building
Washington, D.C. 20510
(202) 224-2035

Congressional Rural Caucus

309 House Annex 1
Washington, D.C. 20515
(202) 225-5080

Family Farm Task Force

c/o Sen. Donald Stewart
U.S. Senate
Washington, D.C. 20510
(202) 224-5744
Kevin Putt, Legislative Staff
(202) 547-4343

Food Policy Center

538 7th Street, S.E.
Washington, D.C. 20003
(202) 547-7070
Marty Rogol, Director

Interreligious Task Force on U.S. Food Policy

Domestic Policy Task Force
245 Second Street, N.E.
Washington, D.C. 20002
(202) 547-4343
Don Reeves, Director

National Family Farm Coalition

918 F Street, N.W.
Washington, D.C. 20004
(202) 638-6848
Catherine Lerza, Robin Rosenbluth

National Farmers Union

1012 14th Street, N.W.
Washington, D.C. 20005
(202) 628-9774
Ruth Kobell, Robert Mullins; Legislative Staff

National Rural Center

1828 L Street, N.W.
Washington, D.C. 20036
(202) 331-0258
John Cornman, President

Rural America

1346 Connecticut Avenue, N.W.
Washington, D.C. 20036
(202) 659-2800
Peggy Borgers, Legislative Staff

National Associations of State and Local Officials

Council of State Governments
P.O. Box 11910, Iron Works Pike
Lexington, Kentucky 40511
(606) 252-2291
William J. Page

Joint Center for Political Studies
Suite 926, Woodward Building
1426 H Street, N.W.
Washington, D.C. 20005
(202) 638-4477

National Association of Counties
1735 New York Avenue, N.W.
Washington, D.C. 20006
(202) 785-9577
Bob Weaver

National Association of State Departments of Agriculture
1616 H Street, N.W.
Washington, D.C. 20006
(202) 628-1566
J.B. Grant, Executive Secretary

National Association of State Universities and Land Grant Colleges
One Dupont Circle, Suite 710
Washington, D.C. 20036
(202) 293-7120
Ralph Huitt, Director

National Conference of State Legislatures
1405 Curtis Street, 23rd Floor
Denver, Colorado 80202
(303) 623-6600

National Governors' Association
444 North Capitol Street, N.W.
Washington, D.C. 20001
(202) 624-5300

Small Towns Institute
P.O. Box 517
Ellensburg, Washington 98926
(509) 963-3221

United States Conference of Mayors
1620 I Street, N.W.
Washington, D.C. 20006
(202) 293-7330

Agencies of the U.S. Department of Agriculture

U.S. Department of Agriculture
Washington, D.C. 20250

The U.S. Department of Agriculture (USDA) has local offices at the regional, state and county level. These include the following agencies:

Agricultural Stabilization and Conservation Service (ASCS)

Ten special rural development/conservation projects in 10 states have been funded at $1.3 million to help small farmers solve conservation and water quality problems. ASCS conducts the USDA cost sharing programs with farmers that install needed soil, water, woodland and wildlife conserving practices, and the Federal Crop Insurance Program which provides farmers with all-risk insurance that repays crop production costs lost because of bad weather, insects, disease and other unavoidable natural causes.

Farmers Home Administration (FmHA)

The FmHA provides loans, grants and technical advice to small farm operators including: ownership, operating and emergency farm loans; financing single and multiple rural homes for people unable to satisfy financial needs elsewhere.

Cooperatives: Economics, Statistics, and Cooperative Services (ESCS)

ESCS provides organization and management help to cooperatives in connection with financing provided by the Farmers Home Administration and other organizations.

County Agents: Cooperative Extension Service (CES)

Extension Service is the educational arm in the field for the Department of Agriculture and Land Grant universities and colleges; including the 1890 colleges. There is a county Extension office in nearly every county in the nation and it is usually located in the county seat town—listed under county government in the telephone directory. County agents have materials on production, marketing, nutrition, rural and community development and 4-H youth programs.

Food and Nutrition Service (FNS)

The FNS conducts the Food Stamp Program for low-income households. Some small farm families qualify for food assistance programs administered by USDA in cooperation with appropriate state and local agencies.

Forest Service (FS)

Together, the Forest Service and State Forestry agencies give technical advice to small private non-industrial forestry landowners to help bring their woodlots under improved management. Increased production of fuelwood, pulpwood, and sawtimber can provide supplemental income. Help is available to contact buyers of these forest products. After tree harvest, assistance is given with tree planting and other management activities to maintain production and improve the property.

Soil Conservation Service (SCS)

Through local Conservation Districts, farm families request technical assistance to develop conservation plans and apply needed practices for the protection and proper use of soil resources, water and wildlife. Increasing production of pastures, range lands and crops may provide increased income.

Briefly, that is a summary of services and programs of USDA agencies with local offices. Programs of these agencies and others operating programs out of USDA headquarters in Washington, D.C. are listed in further detail as follows:

Agricultural Stabilization and Conservation Service (ASCS)

Administers programs to maintain production of wheat, feed grains, substitute crops or soybeans, at a level sufficient to satisfy market demand and meet food and feed assistance commitments through purchases and loan and price guarantees • Administers a cotton program to assure adequate, but not excessive, supplies through purchases and loan and price guarantees • Administers acreage allotments and marketing quotas when applicable under law to certain major crops, to help keep supplies in line with demand • Administers loans, purchases and payments specified by law, and manages commodity inventories • Administers the National Wool Act and the Dairy Program • Administers programs to help obtain adequate farm and commercial storage drying equipment for farm products • Administers cost sharing programs with farmers to install needed soil, water, woodland and wildlife conserving practices and pollution prevention and abatement practices of enduring community-wide benefits under the Agricultural Conservation Program (ACP) • Conducts monitoring activities during periods of anticipated shortages of fuel, fertilizer, pesticides and other key farm production items • Assists and cooperates with the Foreign Agricultural Service in making government-held food stocks available for foreign assistance program • The Commodity Credit Corporation, administered by ASCS, with its $25 billion borrowing authority (effective October 1, 1978), finances the commodity stabilization program, domestic and export programs, including commodity disposal, foreign assistance, storage activities and related programs and operations of the Department • Administers the Federal Crop Insurance Program which provides farmers with all-risk insurance that repays crop production costs lost because of bad weather, insects, disease and other unavoidable natural causes.

Agricultural Marketing Service (AMS)

Helps the marketing system move food and other farm products from producer to consumer • Establishes standards for grades. For instance, the Federal Grain Inspection Service operates acceptance services to make sure contract specifications are agreed to by individual firms.

Animal and Plant Health Inspection Service (APHIS)

Helps safeguard the health and quality of the nation's animals and plants • Protects consumers by maintaining a strong system of Federal-State inspection of meat and poultry products to assure wholesomeness and truthful labeling • Maintains close surveillance of all animal and plant imports, cargoes, and passengers' baggage for foreign pests or disease • Cooperates with the states and the agricultural industry to eradicate and control animal diseases of national importance • Cooperates with the states and industry to control or eradicate native or alien pests and diseases of plants which pose an interstate menace • Administers the Federal Meat Inspection Act and the Poultry Products Inspection Act.

Forest Service (FS)

Directs multiple-use management programs on forest and rangelands of the 187 million acre National Forest System, an area covering one-twelfth of America's land. Located in 44 states and Puerto Rico, the 155 National Forests in the System contain the major resources of timber, forage, watersheds, wildlife habitats, outdoor recreation, minerals and natural beauty • Carries on cooperative programs on about 400 million acres on non-Federal commercial forest lands with state foresters, other state, public and private organizations, private owners of forested lands (small woodland owners and wood processors) • Concerns itself with marketing and utilization of forest products, prevention and suppression of wildfires, land use planning, urban forestry, river basin surveys, control of forest insects and diseases, flood prevention, watershed protection, and forest management incentives to small forest owners (such as the production and distribution of seedling and planting stock). Other cooperative programs stimulate the proper management of state, county, municipal and community forests.

Economics, Statistics and Cooperatives Service (ESCS)

Analyzes factors affecting farm production and their relationship to the environment, prices and incomes, and the outlook for various commodities • Studies production efficiency; marketing costs and potentials; rural development and natural resources; agricultural trade, production and Government policies • Estimates crop and livestock production and prices paid and received by farmers. Keeps statistical methods used by USDA accurate and responsive to changing needs • Conducts economic research to help farmers market their products and purchase supplies cooperatively. It also helps all rural people to obtain other business through cooperatives • Assists farmers and other rural people by conducting educational work to help them improve the effectiveness of their cooperatives.

Farmers Home Administration (FmHA)

Provides loans, grants and technical advice to farm and other rural and small town people and their communities unable to satisfy financial needs elsewhere for rural development and related purposes • Administers loans and grants through county FmHA offices for many types of agricultural, housing, community facility and business and industry purposes. This assistance includes but is not limited to: ownership, operating and emergency farm loans; financing modest but adequate single and multiple rural homes; financing water, sewer, health, fire-fighting, educational and similar facilities; and guaranteeing payment of business and industry loans made by conventional lenders.

Food and Nutrition Service (FNS)

Administers USDA programs to provide food assistance to all Americans who need such help, in cooperation with appropriate state and local agencies • Administers the Food Stamp Program that enables low-income households to buy more food of greater variety to improve their diets.

The Packers and Stockyards Administration (PSA)

Administers the Packers and Stockyard Act which helps to maintain free and open competition in the marketing of livestock, poultry and meat production • Prohibits unfair, deceptive, discriminatory and monopolistic marketing practices which would deprive the farmer of a fair price for his product, and deprive the market of a reasonable profit for market services.

Science and Education Administration (SEA)

Carries out research on crops, livestock, soil and water conservation, energy conservation, agricultural engineering, control of insects and other pests, human nutrition and consumer and food economics • Develops new and expanded uses for farm commodities, and conducts and administers a research program using the physical and biological sciences to solve problems of market quality, transportation and facilities • Handles Federal grant payments for research at the agricultural experiment stations and eligible schools of forestry • Assists state experiment stations, land-grant colleges, and USDA agencies in planning and coordinating scientific research programs • Through Extension, is the field educational arm of the Department of Agriculture and land-grant universities and colleges. Federal, state and local governments cooperatively share in financial support. Extension is administered by the land-grant university through a director in the 50 states, District of Columbia, Puerto Rico, Virgin Islands and Guam. The county agricultural agent is the contact. The office is usually located in the county seat • Helps people apply new research findings and technological developments to the everyday problems of living and making a living. Major areas include efficient production and marketing of agricultural products; improved family living, including nutrition, 4-H development and community and rural development.

Rural Electrification Administration (REA)

Finances electric and telephone facilities in the rural areas of 46 states. Most REA borrowers are cooperatives.

Soil Conservation Service (SCS)

Develops and carries out a national soil and water conservation program through 2,949 conservation districts (Public Law 46, 74th Congress, 1935) • Helps develop and carry out watershed protection and flood prevention projects in 11 major watersheds in cooperation with other agencies (Flood Control Act, Public Law 534, 78th Congress, 1944) • Administers the Great Plains conservation program (Public Law 1021; 84th Congress, 1956; amended by Public Law 793, 86th Congress, 1960; extended and amended by Public Law 118, 91st Congress, 1969) • Helps local sponsors develop and carry out multicounty resource conservation and development projects (Food and Agriculture Act, Public Law 703, 87th Congress, 1962) • Helps develop USDA's conservation cost-sharing programs. Is responsible for assisting in the preparation of long-term conservation plans of operation and for most of the permanent conservation practices provided by these programs. Provides technical assistance to participating farmers and ranchers and prepares designs and specifications for work undertaken • Appraises potential for outdoor recreation developments. Helps establish income-producing recreation areas on privately owned land in public water-based recreation and fish and wildlife areas in watershed protection and resource conservation and development projects • Gives technical assistance to land users participating in the conservation credit program of the Farmers Home Administration • Assists land users to develop conservation plans and apply conservation treatment for the reclamation, conservation, and development of eligible coal mined lands and water.

Source: United States Department of Agriculture, Washington, D.C. 20250.

Index to Article Examples

1. "Summary of Family Farm Security Act," **Senate Agriculture Hearings on: Young Farmers Homestead Act (S. 2589)**, pp. 93-95, June 10-11, 1976, U.S. Senate Agriculture Committee.

2. "Land Bank Lease Becomes Family's Farm," **The Commonwealth**, June 14, 1978.

3. **Where Have All the Bankers Gone?**, The Center for Rural Affairs, pp. 4-7, 26-30, March 1977.

4. "Finance Task Force: Final Report," **The Family Farm in California: The Small Farm Viability Project**, pp. 61-62.

5. "County Goes Into Vegetable Business," **Montgomery Journal**, Montgomery, Alabama, July 7, 1977.

6. **Direct Marketing**, Department of Agriculture, Marketing Services Division, 2301 N. Cameron Street, Harrisburg, Pennsylvania 17120, December 1977.

7. "Where You Can Buy Fresh Pennsylvania Fruits and Vegetables," Bureau of Markets, Pennsylvania Department of Agriculture, 2301 Cameron Street, Harrisburg, Pennsylvania 17120, November 16, 1976.

8. "Map of King and Pierce County," Puget Sound Farm Markets Association, 85 Pike Street, Room 500, Seattle, Washington 98101.

9. Roger Blobaum, "Corporate Farm Invasion Far Exceeds 'Official' Statistics," **NFO Reporter**, January 1977.

10. "Brief Digest of Salient Points of State Corporate Farm News," **Corporate Farming and the Family Farm**, CSG Research Brief, pp. 16-19.

11. Jack Anderson, "Foreign Speculation on American Farms," **United Feature Syndicate**, 1978.

12. "Foreign Investors Flock to U.S. Farmlands," **Business Week**, p. 79, March 27, 1978.

13. "Limited Impact of State Laws on Foreign Investment in U.S. Farmland," **Foreign Ownership in U.S. Famland—Much Concern, Little Data**, U.S. Comptroller General, pp. 2-5, 10-12.

14. "Donations: to University of California for Agricultural Research," **California Agriculture**, pp. 19-20, January 1978.

15. Jim Hightower and Susan DeMarco, "Introduction: The Obvious Failure," **Hard Tomatoes, Hard Times**, Schenkman Press, Cambridge, 1973.

16. Robert Lindsey, "And Now California Develops a Square Tomato," **New York Times**, March 8, 1977.

17. "California Agrarian Action Project," **The Workbook**, Southwest Research and Information Center, P.O. Box 4524, Albuquerque, New Mexico 87106, Vol. 3, no. 2, pp. 53, March 1978.

18. **No Hands Touch the Land**, California Agrarian Action Project, Parts 1-4, pp. 1-4, July 1977.

19. Jerry West, "Summary and Recommendations," **Missouri Small Farm Program: An Evaluation with a Control Group**, University of Missouri-Columbia, College of Agricultural Economics, Columbia, Missouri 65201, p. 25, October 1975.

20. Karl Ostrom, "The Nation's First Rural Studies Program Launched," **Catholic Rural Life**, pp. 21-23, January 1978.

21. "Training Task Force: Final Report," **The Family Farm in California**, pp. 1-2 (Abstract Appendix A), 113-114 and 153-154, November 1977.

22. **The B.C. Land Commission—Keeping the Options Open**, B.C. Land Commission, 4333 Ledger Avenue, Burnaby, British Columbia U5G1H1, pp. 8, 12, 14.

23. Alexandra D. Dawson, "Notes on the Law: A New Way to Save Our Farmland," Metropolitan Area Planning Council, Boston, Massachusetts, p. 4.

24. "Suffolk's Farmland Preservation Program," New York Cooperative Extension, 246 Giffing Avenue, Riverhead, New York 11901.

25. "Transferable Development Rights," **State Legislatures**, NCSL Communications Department, 1405 Curtis Street, 23rd Floor, Denver, Colorado 80202, p. 24, April/May 1977.

26. "The Farmland Assessment Law: A Proposal for Reform," Montgomery County Council, Maryland.

27. "Use-Value Assessment and Land Conservation," **California Agriculture**, University of California, Division of Agricultural Sciences, pp. 12-14, March 1977.

28. Byron L. Dorgan, "The Progressive Land Tax: A Tax Incentive for the Family Farm," North Dakota Tax Commission, April 1978.

29. Richard Barrows, "Wisconsin's Farmland Preservation Program," Cooperative Extension Programs, Wisconsin Department of Agriculture Trade and Consumer Protection, November 1977.

30. Paul Shinoff, "Industrialization of Farms Threatens U.S. Topsoil," **Washington Post**, January 5, 1978.

31. "Something for Nothing," **Farm Bulletin**, Issue 19, pp. 1,3,4, March 22-April 12, 1977.

32. Norma Jane Skjold, "Nitrates: An Insoluble Problem?" **New Land Review**, The Center for Rural Affairs, pp. 10-11, Fall 1977.

33. "A Miracle of Cooperative Planning," **Nature Is; Man Becomes**, City of Northglenn, Colorado 80234.

34. "The Family Farm Water Act," Initiative 59 (1977), Legislative Research Council, Olympia, Washington

35. "How Corporations Violate Family Farm Water Rights," **Catholic Rural Life**, pp. 11-13, May 1977.

36. Marty Strange, "Energy: New Directions for Farm Research," **New Land Review**, The Center for Rural Affairs, pp. 6-7, Fall 1977.

37. Paul Shinoff, "Big Farms Adopt Organic Methods to Control Pests," **Washington Post**, January 9, 1978.

38. "Seeds of Life or Destruction," Agriculture Marketing Project, Nashville, Tennessee, 1977.

39. Dennis Demmel, "Farmers Think Small, Earn Big Profits," **New Land Review**, The Center for Rural Affairs, p. 5, Summer 1976.

40. Manning Marable, "Black Agriculture in the Seventies," **In These Times**, p. 16, January 21-25, 1978.

41. C. Scott Garber, "A Blight Hits Black Farmers," **The Nation**, pp. 269-272, March 11, 1978.

42. "How Co-ops Help Migrant Workers Get Farm Land," **National Catholic Rural Life**, pp. 17-20, March 1976.

43. **AGRED: The Assistance Group for Rural Economic Development**, The National Council of La Raza, pp. 2-5, 1978.

44. "Improve Your Farming," **A Directory of Services Available to the Small Farmer of Illinois**, Illinois State Economic Opportunity Office, 1978.

45. Karen Spelman, "Alabama Landowners Protest FmHA Nomination," **Rural America**, May 1977.

46. Donald Sullivan, "Aid for Migrants Urged by Cahill," **New York Times**, November 8, 1970.

47. "Agricultural Labor Relations—Initiative Statute," California Legislature, Sacramento, California, pp. 52-55.

48. Cesar Chavez, "Square Tomatoes and Idle Workers: The Farm Workers' Next Battle," **The Nation**, pp. 330-332, December 1977.

49. Byron Dorgan, "The American Estate Tax—A Death Penalty," **State Government**, North Dakota, pp. 6-9, Spring 1976.

50. "Nelson Bill to Eliminate the Widow's Tax," News Release, U.S. Senate Select Committee on Small Business, Fall 1978.

51. Laura Lane, "Farm Women . . . You Have Fewer Property Rights Than You Think," **Farm Journal**, pp. 35-36, June/July, 1978.

52. "Lucey Signs Inheritance Tax Reform Measure," **Wisconsin: Farmers Union News**, pp. 1, May 17, 1976.

53. Betty J. Harris and Basil S. Holder, "Law Change Avoids Double Taxation," **Wisconsin Agriculturalist**, Madison, Wisconsin, December 1976.

54. Marguerite Rawalt, "ERA and State Property Laws," **Common Cause**, p. 5, 1978.

55. Francis Hill, "Why Women Deserve More Opportunity in Farming," **Catholic Rural Life**, pp. 8-10, April 1978.

56. Barry Benape, "Greenmarkets," The Council on the Environment of New York City, 51 Chambers Street, New York 10007, pp. 23-24, 1977.

57. "Bulk Commodities Exchange," Summary Report, c/o Department of Community Development, Seattle, Washington 98104, 1977.

58. **The Co-op Bank: New Funds for Community Development**, Conference on Alternative State and Local Policies, November 1978.

59. **Michigan Public Act 331 of 1975**, c/o Office of Services to the Aging, Lansing, Michigan 48909, 1975.

60. "New York Article 38, Community Gardens," Section 848 a-d, New York State, Albany, New York, March 30, 1978.

61. Neal R. Pierce, "Land Trusts: Putting Empty Lots to Use," **The Washington Post**, p. A-17, Tuesday, August 8, 1978.

62. Denise DeClue, Excerpts from "A Multility Grows in Garfield Park," **Reader, Chicago Free Weekly**, Vol. 6, No. 49, pp. 1, 20-24, Friday, September 9, 1977.

63. "Ten Neighborhood Solar Greenhouse Projects," Center for Neighborhood Technology, 570 West Randolph Street, Chicago, Illinois

64. "Community Food and Nutrition Center," **Community Self-Reliance, Incorporated**, 1977 Annual Report, Northampton, Massachusetts, pp. 25-27, 1977.

65. Alice Scott, Paula Roberts, and Jeff Kirsch, "A Bill: To Improve School Food Service," **FRAC's Guide to State School Food Legislation**, Food Research Action Center (FRAC), Cover and pp. 12-15, March 1978.

66. Diane Fuchs, "Repealing State Food Taxes," **Ways and Means**, Conference on Alternative State and Local Policies, December 1978.

67. "Food Taxes Are Hard to Swallow," Hunger Action Center, 2nd and Cherry Building, Room 323, Seattle, Washington 98104, 1976.

68. "Fact Sheet on St. Mary's Food Bank Salvage Program," St. Mary's Food Bank, 724 South First Avenue, Phoenix, Arizona 85003.

69. "Operation Brotherhood," 3745-53 West Ogden Avenue, Chicago, Illinois

70. Chaitanya York, "We Need New Food and Farmland Policies," **Maine Organic Farmer and Gardener**, pp. 15-16, September 1978.

71. "A State Food Policy," **From The Ground Up: Building a Grassroots Food Policy**, Center for Science in the Public Interest, pp. 16-18, 1977.

72. "The Agricultural Resource," **Final Report: Commission on Maine's Future**, pp. 31-34, December 1, 1977.

73. "Highlights of the Report," **Report of the Blueprint Commission on the Future of New Jersey Agriculture**, New Jersey Department of Agriculture, Trenton, New Jersey, pp. 5-7, April 1973.

74. "1978 Legislative Status Update," **New York State Assembly Task Force on Food, Farm and Nutritional Policy**, November 1978.

75. Rory O'Connor, "The Politics of Food in Massachusetts, Growing Our Own," **The Real Paper**, pp. 20-23, July 22, 1978.

76. "Background Paper on Urban Agriculture" and "1979 Capital Improvement Policy Plan," Seattle Department of Community Development, Seattle, Washington, 1978.

77. Cathy Lerza, "Farms, Urban Food," **The Elements**, pp. 1-3, May 1978.

PUBLICATIONS

☐ **Corporate Flight: The Causes and Consequences of Economic Dislocation**

A groundbreaking study providing new documentation and analysis of the extent of plant closings in this country and the rising levels of joblessness and economic dislocation caused by unrestrained capital movement. The authors assess the extent of capital mobility and the social costs of unregulated private investment decisions.
By Barry Bluestone and Bennett Harrison; co-published with the Progressive Alliance. (Oct. 1980) 32 pp.
$3.95; $7.95 Institutions

☐ **Plant Closings: Resources for Public Officials and Community Leaders**
(1979) 85 pp.
$4.95; $6.95 Institutions

☐ **Plant Closings Briefing Book: Issues, Politics, and Legislation**
(1980) 70 pp.
$4.95; $9.95 Institutions

☐ **Industrial Exodus**
Ed Kelly (1977) 30 pp.
$2.95; $5.95 Institutions

☐ **The Cities' Wealth**
(1976) 85 pp.
$3.95 $7.95 Institutions

☐ **Tax Abatements: Resources for Public Officials and Community Leaders**
(1979) 80 pp.
$4.95 $9.95 Institutions

☐ **Economic Democracy: The Challenge of the 1980s**
Martin Carnoy and Derek Shearer (1980) 430 pp.
$9.95 $19.95 Institutions

☐ **Developing the Public Economy: Models From Massachusetts**
Edited by Pat McGuigan and Bob Schaeffer. (1979) 208 pp.
$9.95 $19.95 Institutions

☐ **The Battle of Cleveland: Public Interest Challenges Corporate Power**

Thorough examination of the corporate/public interest conflict in Cleveland with emphasis on the election of Mayor Kucinich, and why he lost in his re-election bid.
Edited by Dan Marschall with the assistance of The Ohio Public Interest Campaign (1979) 180 pp.
$7.95 $15.95 Institutions

☐ **Public Employee Pension Funds: New Strategies for Investment**
(1979) 180 pp.
$9.95 $19.95 Institutions

☐ **State and Local Tax Revolt: New Directions for the '80s:**

A comprehensive guide to state and local tax issues and what can be done to make these taxes more equitable. 29 chapters written and edited by nationally known progressive tax experts.
Edited by Dean Tipps and Lee Webb (June 1980) 380 pp.
$9.95 $19.95 Institutions

☐ **The Public Balance Sheet: A New Tool for Evaluating Economic Choices**
David Smith (1979) 22 pp.
$2.95 $5.95 Institutions

☐ **New Initiatives in Energy Legislation: A State-by-State Guide 1979-1980**
(1980) 110 pp.
$3.95 $7.95 Institutions

☐ **The Shifting Property Tax Burden: The Untold Cause of the Tax Revolt**
Robert Kuttner (1980) 80 pp.
$3.95 $7.95 Institutions

☐ **Manual on Pay Equity: Raising Wages for Women's Work**

Thorough review of the "equal pay for work of comparable value" movement: legislative initiatives, litigation, news of organizing campaigns, comparable worth studies, collective bargaining update and the latest research. Includes proceedings from the October 1979 Washington Conference on Pay Equity, extensive resource listing, and guides to action.
Edited by Joy Ann Grune in cooperation with the Committee on Pay Equity (1980) 230 pp.
$9.95

☐ **Moderate Rent Control: The Experience of U.S. Cities**
John Gilderbloom (May 1980) 60 pp.
$3.95 $7.95 Institutions

☐ **Women in the Economy: A Legislative Agenda**
(1979) 133 pp.
$4.95 $9.95 Institutions

☐ **New Directions in Farm, Land and Food Policies: A Time for State and Local Action**
(2nd edition, Aug. 1980) 320 pp.
$9.95 $19.95 Institutions

☐ Subscribe now to **Ways and Means,** the bi-monthly magazine of The Conference featuring in-depth reporting on progressive state and local legislation, political trends and events, and news of useful publicaitions and reports.
One year, $10, Institutions $20.

ORDER FORM